HANDBOOK
OF ACADEMIC
EVALUATION

Assessing Institutional Effectiveness,
Student Progress,
and Professional Performance
for Decision Making
in Higher Education

PAUL L. DRESSEL

HANDBOOK
OF ACADEMIC
EVALUATION

Jossey-Bass Publishers
San Francisco · Washington · London · 1976

HANDBOOK OF ACADEMIC EVALUATION
Assessing Institutional Effectiveness, Student Progress, and
Professional Performance for Decision Making in Higher Education
by Paul L. Dressel

Copyright © 1976 by: Jossey-Bass, Inc., Publishers
                      615 Montgomery Street
                      San Francisco, California 94111
                              &
                      Jossey-Bass Limited
                      44 Hatton Garden
                      London EC1N 8ER

Library of Congress Catalogue Card Number LC 75-44881

International Standard Book Number ISBN 0-87589-276-0

Manufactured in the United States of America

JACKET DESIGN BY WILLI BAUM

FIRST EDITION
     First printing: April 1976
     Second printing: December 1976

Code 7604

The Jossey-Bass Series
in Higher Education

Preface

The *Handbook of Academic Evaluation* is the result of many years of involvement in evaluation and research in higher education. As such, it inevitably represents some of my convictions—and no doubt prejudices—about the nature and role of evaluation in higher education. My first conviction is that evaluation is inevitable and ever present. Every educational or social program is initiated and continues or is discarded because of some form of evaluation by some individuals or groups. In fact, all phases of higher education—programs, course offerings, instructional procedures, administrative policies—are the results of evaluations and value commitments, although these are not always clear or consistent. My concern here is to urge that the evaluations be systematic and that the value implications be explicit. The issue is not whether evaluations are made. How, when, by whom, and why are the questions to be resolved.

My second conviction is that formal evaluation, no matter how well conducted, will never be the sole basis of major decisions for two reasons. First of all, since some of the factors

involved in a decision are highly subjective, affect and politics
are as much involved as evidence. Evaluation, when carefully
done, may temper these but can never eliminate them. In the
second place, evaluation itself deals with complex relationships
between processes and outcomes and is therefore often ambiguous. Assumptions, interpretations, and especially the imputa-
tion of causal relationships among inputs, processes, and outcomes are all subject to critical reviews.

My third conviction is that institutions of higher education
have a special obligation to students and society: to exemplify
use of the best possible model in deciding how to use resources
to achieve desired ends. If rational, though value-based, processes and decisions cannot be found in the university, there is
little hope either for the university or for a better society.

My fourth conviction is that the central goal of education
is to inculcate in students the ability to make wise judgments—
to evaluate. Only as students become competent evaluators of
their own goals, experiences, and accomplishments do they
become truly educated (liberally educated, one might reasonably say) and capable of engaging in the individual judgmental
processes essential to a democratic society.

My fifth conviction is that any evaluation process is unlikely to be effective unless those involved in the process and in
the ultimate decision (and these may not be the same people)
have a thorough understanding of the instruments (tests, inventories) used and the data collected. Indeed, only those who have
attempted to develop evaluation instruments have an understanding of the complexities of defining criteria and collecting
evidence. Because such an understanding is a necessity, I am
hesitant about suggesting the use of already existing instruments.

My sixth conviction is that all too frequently educational
evaluation has been pursued without regard for costs. In great
part because of this, other forms of evaluation—such as program
budgeting, management by objectives, and cost-benefit analysis
—have been developed. Despite terminological differences, these
forms deserve to be added to the educational evaluation arsenal,
as I have attempted to do in this *Handbook of Academic Evaluation.*

My seventh and last conviction is that any evaluation process will never be entirely acceptable to the evaluators, to those evaluated, or to those affected by the evaluation. The evaluator would like more respect and appreciation and prompter action on reports than is commonly received. Those evaluated readily accept praise—as do we all—but they are naturally irritated when their judgments are questioned and their status threatened. And those who benefit from existing programs react strongly to termination or major changes which appear prejudicial to their interests. Realizing the inevitability of these negative reactions, I still am critical of those who look askance at formal evaluation and view it as a threat more than as an aid to rational decision making. I recognize dislike of evaluation as a human weakness, and I share it; but in attempting to develop an ideal of higher education as a self-critical enterprise, I cannot avoid an occasional comment about circumstances which cause us to fall short.

These strong convictions on the nature and role of evaluation in higher education are accompanied by equally strong convictions about the nature of the university as an academic community. Because these convictions influence the views I express in this handbook, I outline them briefly here.

First, the university must be dominated by a sense of reality and have relevance to the society which supports it. That the university should promote change is not in question, but there are widely differing views on the ills of society and on the means of correction. Education which would promote change must still take cognizance of and relate to the current scene.

Second, the university not only gets its support and its authority from society but must also take direction from it and be accountable to it. Its educational programs must be responsive to societal needs and concerns.

Third, the university, as an association of professionals, must have a degree of autonomy. Yet, there must be coordination and central control to ensure that autonomy is properly used. Autonomy is not absolute; it extends only to exploring and determining the most efficient way to perform assigned functions.

Fourth, the university must be committed to learning and

to instruction. Research is essential to the performance of instruction, but the university is not a research institute. Instruction focuses on motivating students to learn, while research continually modifies both what is to be learned and the means by which that learning is promoted.

Fifth, the university must be committed to continuing efforts to simplify its structure. The tendency of the university to organize along disciplinary lines results in the continual adding of new departments, new colleges, new curriculums, new institutes, new research projects, new public service programs, and, most of all, new costs with no internal assurance and increasing external doubt that this proliferating and complex structure contributes to the improvement of society. The proliferating disciplines require culling and regrouping to counteract this trend. Such reshaping will in turn permit flexibility in budgeting, allowing dollars to follow current needs rather than to be wasted by commitment to passé structures. Individual scholars or departments will be less likely to pursue their own interests without regard to costs or relevance.

The university must limit what it does to what it can do well. But such limitation requires evaluation, something the university has never done well. It resists self-evaluation and both resists and resents external evaluation. Yet, the time has come when external evaluation is of such magnitude that self-evaluation has become inevitable.

These convictions require a far broader approach to evaluation than is common in institutions or among evaluators. This *Handbook of Academic Evaluation* is thus dedicated to a reasonably thorough review of recent and current thinking about evaluation in the hope that evaluation efforts will be broadened to permeate every phase of institutional operations. Chapters One through Six discuss in general the reasons why evaluation is important, the various approaches to it, and the various concepts involved in it.

Chapters Seven through Twelve discuss particular areas which directly affect students, such as the selection of students, the learning environment, educational processes, tests, grades, and instruction. The emphasis in these chapters is on an analysis of the factors involved in evaluation rather than on the particular instruments or procedures used. This emphasis arises out of my fifth conviction regarding evaluation: Most evaluators have rushed too quickly into constructing or selecting instruments or data-collection procedures without careful consideration of the issues and alternatives involved. These prior deliberations are essential both for planning the evaluation and for educating those who will use or ignore the results. Instruments, no matter their technical excellence as measuring devices, and the data emerging from them can never be better than the analysis upon which they are based, and their results can be no more effective than the comprehension and readiness for change of those to whom they are given. Quick adoption of existing instruments merely postpones the discussion and argument until the data are in and leads inevitably to the accusation that the evidence collected ignores the real issues.

Chapters Thirteen through Eighteen are directed to evaluation of programs, personnel, and institutions. The areas covered are by no means exhaustive. Student personnel services, for example, require rigorous evaluation today, but I have ignored them because I have not thus far seen or been involved in an adequate evaluation in this area. Libraries and other learning resources also require attention, especially in respect to the manner in which they operate and are used by faculty and students. The business offices, clerical and technical staff, services, and maintenance on many campuses deserve a thoroughgoing analysis too. But the evaluator—even the institutional researcher— finds no enthusiasm for such ventures except among some members of the faculty.

The Epilogue takes the reader back to issues discussed in earlier chapters and attempts to synthesize these into a composite view. Rereading the Preface in conjunction with the last chapter will increase the reader's insights into the status and problems of evaluation.

The points of view in the *Handbook of Academic Evaluation* are largely my own except where I discuss alternatives in order to provide breadth of coverage or some comment on and criticism of my own views. I put strict limitations on specific references and attributions because I feel that, on the whole, the purposes of this volume are best served by straightforward treatment of the issues without copious, often needless, referencing. The scope of the Bibliography is evidence that I have read widely and profited from the thoughts of evaluators and other researchers in diverse disciplines. To them all, collectively, I owe a debt of gratitude.

I have attempted to write each chapter so that it is a reasonably self-sufficient statement. The volume is a reference, not a book to be read consecutively or at one sitting. But there are many interrelationships, and I have noted them in many cases by referring to other chapters.

The sensitive reader will distinguish some rather marked changes in style and in degree of specificity from one chapter to another. These differences are a result of at least three factors: personal experiences, the current importance of the topic, and the extent to which evaluation has been systematically undertaken on the topic. The chapters on grades and on faculty evaluation are lengthy, reflecting both extensive personal experience and a conviction that these two topics are, and will be for some years, of major concern. The chapter on institutional self-study also reflects extensive personal experience with many colleges and universities. In contrast, the chapters on the evaluation of administration and of state systems reflect both a lack of extensive personal involvement in such evaluation and a paucity of good materials to draw upon. Both chapters, therefore, are exploratory and analytical rather than specific.

Finally, the reader should be warned that although this volume is called a handbook, it is a handbook in the sense that it provides an understanding of and preparation for evaluation. It is distinctly not a how-to-do-it book. The Bibliography and the Bibliographical Notes at the ends of chapters provide ample reference to instruments and techniques.

This handbook is addressed primarily to administrators, faculty members, and others concerned with the higher education enterprise. Except in Chapter Six, which deals with technical aspects of evaluation, the discussion is nontechnical. Nevertheless, the scope of the treatment is such that even technically oriented evaluators may frequently achieve insights which will materially affect their approach to the evaluation. task. Too often, evaluators have developed and used machinery much too sophisticated for the nature of the available evidence or for the practical decisions which must be made.

Acknowledgments

No volume of this size could be brought to fruition without extensive assistance. Over the years, support made available from the Exxon Education Foundation through Frederick deW. Bolman, from the Danforth Foundation and later the Lilly Endowment through Laura Bornholdt, and from the Carnegie Corporation through E. Alden Dunham aided me in conducting studies which provided the background for the *Handbook of Academic Evaluation*. Papers and discussions by graduate students in my two seminars (curriculum and instruction and evaluation in higher education) have been helpful. Dissertations by several of my students have dealt in depth with various evaluation problems.

To Ruth Frye and Marion Jennette I am indebted for repeated typing of manuscripts, for editing, and for checking references. Charlotte Miller also rendered extensive services in this area. Ruth Lezotte has been of particular assistance; she helped with bibliographical matters, critically read the manuscript and made suggestions, and prepared the Bibliographical Notes.

East Lansing, Michigan   Paul L. Dressel
February 1976

Contents

Preface   ix

Part One: Basic Considerations
1. An Approach to Evaluation   1
2. Evaluation as Basis of Decision Making and Change   12
3. Starting with Objectives   27
4. Assessing Affective Outcomes   53
5. Accountability and Attainment of Social Goals   73
6. Some Technical Aspects   110

Part Two: Evaluation of Student Experience and Educational Progress
7. Recruitment, Selection, Classification, Placement   137
8. Learning Environment   164
9. Educational Processes   186

xvii

10. Examinations and Evaluation in Courses   208
11. Comprehensive Examinations   233
12. Grades, Credits, and Alternatives   256

Part Three: Evaluation of Programs and Personnel

13. Curriculum   297
14. Graduate Education   318
15. Faculty   331
16. Administration   376
17. Institutional Self-Study   401
18. State Coordination and Planning   433

Epilogue: Costs, Decisions, and Politics   450

Bibliography   461
Index   509

HANDBOOK
OF ACADEMIC
EVALUATION

Assessing Institutional Effectiveness,
Student Progress,
and Professional Performance
for Decision Making
in Higher Education

Chapter 1

An Approach
to Evaluation

An evaluation is both a judgment on the worth or impact of a program, procedure, or individual, and the process whereby that judgment is made. Such judgments can be reached in many ways. An administrator can make a judgment on the basis of a purely personal subjective appraisal. A group can make a judgment by mutual agreement or by compromise based upon individual opinions possibly reached after and influenced by the collecting and interpreting of extensive data. A researcher can make a judgment through elaborate statistical analysis of objective data which have been collected according to a complex research design and measured by instruments carefully chosen to ensure a high degree of accuracy, reliability, and validity.

Although such a research-based judgment may seem to be the preferred basis for decision making, this ideal is not often achieved—or desirable. Both the immediacy and the complexity

1

of many educational issues defy attack by rigorous research methodology. Pure educational research is concerned with basic theory development and with expanding knowledge and understanding. The possibilities for immediate application of such research findings are often limited because the researcher is concerned with long-range problems and seeks general principles and concepts. Educational problems, however, are frequently immediate and demand short-range solutions. Pure researchers frequently also make special arrangements (setting up control groups, for example) which destroy the reality of the educational environment and can lead to simple, unworkable solutions to complex problems. Such research also can seldom take into account in a satisfactory manner the value commitments of the individuals and groups involved. Many decisions about education are made under social, political, monetary, and time stresses which do not permit rigorous research and which, in any case, make such research irrelevant. Although controversy and displays of emotions are not unknown when pure research deals with sensitive matters, generally the researchers are apart from the current scene. They are protected by academic freedom and are subject only to the criticisms of their professional peers, not to the pressures of society in general.

Any educational problem in which many individuals and groups are involved and with which vast segments of society are concerned does not and never will have unambiguous and acceptable best solutions. But the fact that rigorous research design and methodology are impossible to use or are considered irrelevant for most educational decision making is no excuse for retreat to a pooling of ignorance by uninformed majority vote or to an enforced acceptance of the judgments and decisions of authority, however great the claimed or recognized expertise.

In an attempt to compromise, some evaluators (Suchman, 1967, for example) have advocated the development of evaluative research, which would be distinctive from and somewhat less exacting than pure research. Although sympathetic to the concerns which generate this attempt to define evaluative research and an associated methodology, I believe that it only adds complications and may still result in an unbridgeable chasm between practical educational policy formulation and unrealistically elaborate research. The issues involved are significant but not, I think, particularly relevant when one views evaluation simply as the best appraisal that can be made considering the importance and potential of the program evaluated and the constraints and pressures which exist. Although these pressures may occasionally permit some kind of research, usually they do not.

In attempting to discover an appropriate degree of rigor for projects, evaluators have used various models at various times. The measurement model, with its emphasis on reliability, validity, and objectivity, emphasizes the use of tests, norms, and standards and omits factors which are not operationally definable and objectively measurable. Values and other intangibles are ignored. Evaluation conducted on this limited basis is so restricted in scope that it is at times irrelevant to the central concerns of those involved and leaves no role for expert judgment. Because of its limitations, evaluation based on this model is now neither extensively used nor influential.

Using a second model, evaluators try to determine effectiveness in the attainment of program objectives. If there is unanimity on objectives, this evaluation process can be highly rational. With careful advance planning, student performance or other appropriate results provide feedback for diagnosing deficiencies and improving programs. Yet this approach may concentrate solely on results or on changes and ignore the procedures by which these results are achieved. Hence program analysis and improvement become impossible; only the global judgment of satisfactory or unsatisfactory is possible. Furthermore, concentration on objectives is not appropriate when the focus of the evaluation is an auxiliary or facilitative service (budget allocations, admissions) rather than a direct producer of change. And, finally, when the objectives are not specific (as they often should not be in education), evaluation is difficult. Many members of the faculty, for example, either regard specific knowledge and skills as the objectives or wrestle unsuccessfully with the relationship between course content and experiences and ultimate student behavior.

In a third model, evaluations are quick, broad judgments rendered with minimal data collection. Political and economic as well as social and philosophic views, values, and priorities influence such judgments. Hence generalizations based on them are not truly valid. When experts or professionals are involved in accreditation or site visits, for example, the summary judgments made on the basis of interviews, observations, and the materials provided lack objectivity. They may also be unreliable and invalid because of the abnormal circumstances surrounding a scheduled visit or because of differences in the values of the visitors and the goals of the institution. Ratings of graduate schools are also based largely on individual expert judgments, although they do use some data (Cartter, 1966).

In promoting a more thoughtful approach to decision making in higher education—one that both incorporates and goes beyond the models just described—I am mainly concerned with cultivating a recognition that most decisions are rather more complex than they appear on the surface. They are complex in the first place because values inevitably play a part in evaluation. *To evaluate* in fact means to place a value on or to draw a value out of an action, decision, or experience. Ideally, the values in an enterprise should be objectively identified in the initial stages because the final choice among alternatives depends upon the set of values which we hold or are willing for the moment to accept. In this fundamental, essentially philosophical, sense of the concept, evaluation is ever present in individuals. Yet many of the values which individuals have are implicit rather than explicit in behavior. When fully conscious of the values implicit in behavior, individuals may reject the values and alter their behavior—or continue that behavior for different reasons. (Curiously, this latter behavior is often called rationalization, suggesting that rationality is not always equated with sound reasoning.) Every part of the college environment also is based implicitly or explicitly on values, though these are sometimes unrecognized or unidentified. An essential responsibility of educational evaluation therefore is to bring about identification and examination of values and thereby to foster a rational approach to decision making in full realization of the values involved.

Decisions are complex in the second place because they usually involve more factors than are recognized and hence have an impact upon more persons, groups, and programs than anticipated. Those adversely though inadvertently affected are but little less disturbed than those affected by intent. And precipitate decisions with no rationale or supporting data are likely to be disruptive even to those who benefit from them.

Much of the often noted emotional reaction against evaluation results from external and tactless imposition. Imposed evaluation implies criticism and dissatisfaction and possible decisions to continue or alter a program. Since no educational situation ever has been or is likely to be ideal, elements of disapproval are inevitable and can be unreasonably inflated and used unfairly in competition for resources. Evaluation done with or for those involved in a program is psychologically more acceptable than evaluation done to them. When doubts already exist, when decisions are pending, and when concrete evidence is truly desired, the evaluator gains greater cooperation and finds a readiness to study and act upon findings. Evaluation carried out in this context usually brings gradual rather than radical change and is, accordingly, much less threatening. In fact, most change in education is incremental rather than radical, and advertising of this fact would improve the climate for evaluation. Evaluation, to be acceptable, must have some positive prospects. Elaborate and demanding evaluations done for departments or colleges with some promise of improving their position or increasing their resources have, in my experience, been given full cooperation. Similarly, evaluation carried on with students to assist them in improving and in reaching goals important to them provokes different reactions and has different results from evaluation which reflects only their deficiencies. Recognition of these complexities and rippling impacts justifies collection and consideration of as much relevant evidence as time permits. In this process, individuals involved or affected become aware that a decision is pending, and the rationale and bases for it can be communicated to them.

The rippling effects of evaluation reach not only individuals but every facet of the operation of a college or university.

Even if the primary focus of an evaluation is the impact of instruction, curriculum, and environment on student learning, attention to other areas may be required. Evaluation of instruction requires evaluation of the faculty, but the faculty members of a university are also heavily involved in research and in public service, which commonly so interact with instruction that they cannot be completely separated. Likewise, the promotion, reward, and support systems can scarcely be ignored if faculty evaluation is pursued in depth. And financial management and allocation of resources always enter the picture.

Despite the difficulties involved, every aspect of the operation of an institution should be evaluated at some time and its relationships with other aspects should be included. The various possible focuses of evaluation are the following: (1) educational programs including environment (physical facilities, equipment, human resources, and ideological factors), student learning (cognitive, affective, and psychomotor), curriculum (structured classes, objectives, informal unstructured experiences and requirements), instruction (goals, methods, and instructor traits), and instructional services (library, educational technology, and developmental programs); (2) research programs including discipline-based (or pure), applied (problem or task oriented), project (special grant or contract), and those involving curriculum, instruction, and student learning; (3) public service including dissemination of research findings, training and noncredit programs, and consultation; (4) institutional operations, management, and administration including educationally related processes and services (admissions, placement, library, student personnel, housing), business (fiscal and personnel related), and administration and management of resources (planning, budgeting, auditing).

In developing my approach to decision making, I am concerned not only that the complexities just mentioned be recognized and unraveled, but also that the process of evaluation itself be ongoing and continuous. This approach requires a priori consideration of evidence in an attempt to predict results, collection of evidence during the course of the program (or procedure or policy) to provide continuous feedback, a posteriori consideration of evidence to assess results, and continual review through recycling of this sequence as further evidence accumulates. During the a priori collection of information, the objectives and purposes of the program must be kept in mind. Educational programs are supported to achieve social goals; they develop educational goals; and they are usually committed to some set of objectives to be reached by those involved in them. Evaluators can play a part in the formulation of these goals and objectives. Surveys of social needs and of the views and attitudes of individuals involved in the program are frequently essential in developing a statement of objectives. Once these are agreed upon, decisions must be made regarding the programs and processes which will achieve these ends. Reviews of research and experience and limited experimentation will materially forward this effort and will permit insightful analysis later of the impact of various parts of the program on its ultimate success or failure. In this planning state, the criteria by which such success or failure will be determined should be explicitly stated.

In a formal research design, the program would then be left to run its course. No changes would be made until completion of the program and careful analysis of the results. But this sort of rigidity prohibits rather than promotes change. In my approach to evaluation, evidence collected and analyzed during the program may be used to clarify objectives and alter processes. Delay in so doing is likely to mean loss of impact and dissatisfaction; program alterations may then be forced on other grounds. From the pure researcher's point of view, the variables may be confounded; but the evaluator's concerns about internal validity in the real situation take precedence over those of external validity. Programs are generally in flux so that continuous and systematic evaluation is essential to provide the basis for improvement. Because information needs also change, timely and specific reports are required. Administrative and staff support for and influence on change are much more likely under these conditions of continuing feedback and discussion than after remote, mysterious, and cataclysmic reports. Such a procedure also prevents faculty members from arguing that a just-completed evaluation is useless because they have continued to innovate and alter their procedures during the program.

During the a posteriori consideration of evidence at the

conclusion of the program, evaluators must attempt to determine whether the criteria for success have been met and to explain why they have or have not. Have the objectives agreed on in the beginning been accomplished? What unplanned side effects have occurred? Which impacts of the program are a result of the program itself and which result from external influences? Once the degree of success in meeting goals has been determined, the resources expended can be related to the benefits received, and a decision can be made regarding continuation, revision, replacement, or termination of the program based on its value, benefits, or social utility.

Finally, all results must continually be reviewed as evidence of effectiveness accumulates. Few decisions or policies in higher education need to be or should be final. Structural or organizational decisions, because of personnel commitments and the vested interests of individuals, tend to become so imbedded that they are not easily altered. To counteract this tendency, the university must continually assert that structure, practice, and use of resources require review and adjustment as changes occur in the long-term role of the university and the educational goals of society. This is simply accountability in its most reasonable and undeniable form. But this review and adjustment need not and should not be characterized by the periodic and spasmodic replacement of one set of rigidities by another. Rather, it should be a continuing process quite analogous to the continuing search for truths never fully revealed.

In this outline of an approach to evaluation, the essential components or concepts involved in a definition of evaluation have appeared. Evaluation involves some or all of the following:

1. Identifying and examining the values inherent in the program, policy, or procedure to be evaluated.
2. Formulating or clarifying the objectives, goals, purposes of the program.
3. Determining the criteria for measuring success.
4. Defining, obtaining, analyzing, and interpreting data and other information.
5. Determining and explaining the extent of success and failure.

6. Indicating the relationships between experiences during the program and the outcomes of the program (impact of various program variables).
7. Identifying unplanned and undesirable (side) effects.
8. Determining the impact of the program and the impact of external, uncontrolled variables.
9. Recommending the alteration, replacement, or discontinuance of the program or of individual features of the program.
10. Setting up a continuing review of program results.
11. Assessing the value, benefits, or social utility of the program, objectives, and processes, and of the evaluation itself.

These elements effectively and comprehensively define evaluation. They imply that evaluation is the collection and interpretation, through systematic and formal means, of relevant information which serves the basis for rational judgment in decision situations. However, actual decisions frequently must go beyond these judgments because they involve social, political, financial, and other considerations which are not part of the immediate evaluation task. These value commitments may be as important as evidence in the ultimate decisions.

This approach to evaluation and decision making has two values. First, the university, by adopting it, provides a model of decision making which its students and society should emulate. Evaluation captures the very essence of education. It is involved in the planning of educational processes, in the definition of and agreement upon the outcomes of those processes, and in the determination of the extent to which those outcomes are achieved by the individuals involved. Evaluation also involves judgment both of the importance and of the priorities of the objectives sought, as well as judgment of the efficiency of alternative ways of achieving them. Education is successful only if each individual similarly acquires the ability to define goals, assess values, and weigh the worth of alternative courses of action in achieving those values and goals. Indeed, the central, pervasive goal of all education is the production of evaluators—individuals who are sufficiently self-confident and capable to make their own evaluations and act upon them. To achieve this goal, education must continually involve evaluation, encourage evaluation by students, and provide evaluative models to be emulated by students. Unless the evaluation practices to which the student is exposed day by day are good ones and invite emulation, education will always fail to achieve its central purpose. Imitation is and always will be the first level of learning, and it remains one of the most powerful.

Second, by taking this stance, the university encourages confidence in and understanding of its procedures and processes. Indeed, continuing evaluation may well increase the effectiveness of the university without necessarily inducing or requiring significant substantive change. For example, as the teacher undertakes to collect evidence of impact upon students, he or she is likely to find both undesirable as well as desirable impacts. Students may not clearly understand the objectives of the course and how teaching practices and assignments are related to expected outcomes. As the teacher clarifies these matters with students, the students arrive at a new understanding of the purposes of the course and the relationship of the processes to the objectives. As a result of this emerging rapport between students and teacher and the increased insights into the nature and purpose of their association, the impact of a course is greatly enhanced even if the essential processes of the classroom are unchanged. In many cases they will be, but the point is that the merits and results of any educational experience depend as much, and perhaps more, on the expectations and understanding brought to the experience as upon the precise nature of it.

Thus, evaluation promotes flexibility and adaptability but generates conflict with those who desire the security of continued stability. Evaluation both promises and threatens, and both are essential to its success. If no one is threatened, the evaluation is not sufficiently penetrating, and if it holds no promise to anyone of decisions leading to improvement, it is a waste of resources.

Bibliographical Note

The following books and articles address the issues surrounding evaluation, some directly, some obliquely. Some authors are clearly convinced that education can be measured, quantified, and rewarded according to appropriate formulas. Some apparently believe that education is a mystical art and any attempt at evaluation is folly.

The September 1974 issue of the *Educational Researcher* is devoted to questioning the original faith and subsequent disillusionment in the impacts of educational research.

Suchman's (1967) penetrating statement provides an excellent background analysis of the needs and problems of evaluation. It is especially valuable for its description of the concept of evaluative research.

Rippey (1973) presents a comprehensive discussion of transactional evaluation, as well as examples of evaluation projects. His approach emphasizes the internal conflict that accompanies change.

Provus (1971) gives an excellent analysis of one approach to evaluation, presenting both a carefully thought out theoretical base and a description of its implementation.

Chapter 2

Evaluation as Basis of Decision Making and Change

The purpose of systematic evaluation is simply that of bringing to a conscious level and in a form to expedite decision making, the assumptions and values inherent in educational programs, to relate these to anticipated procedures and expected accomplishments, and to compare these plans with actual functioning and results. I will discuss values and assumptions in Chapter Four. Here I wish to cover the role of evaluation in the collection and interpretation of evidence. This task facilitates the comparison of intended and actual means and ends—information essential in any decision.

If evaluation is ultimately justified as a basis for decision making, it becomes necessary to consider the types of decisions to be made. A program is undertaken with certain ends in view and some hunches or hypotheses about the best means of attaining these ends. Both the results and the processes however may differ from the intent. Let us look at the possible decisions required in each of these areas.

1. Decisions may have to be made regarding intended ends. Objectives may require alteration. They may require clarification. Some may be unachievable within existing constraints; others more realistic and equally desirable may have to be found. In this area, we are concerned with the determination of needs and with the general nature and objectives of a program designed to meet those needs.

2. Decisions may have to be made regarding intended means. Processes may be ineffective or require clarification and refinement. Better prepared teachers and revised materials may be needed. Costs may be too high. In this area we are concerned with tentatively selecting, designing, and sequencing procedures and with delineating and analyzing the relative merits of alternative procedures.

3. Decisions may have to be made regarding actual ends. Objectives may not be attained to the extent desired. Undesirable results may occur which need to be remedied or eliminated. When students do not meet objectives, the entire process may need replanning and restructuring. In this area we are concerned with appraising attainments, judging satisfaction, and establishing continuing quality-control arrangements.

4. Decisions may have to be made regarding actual means. The processes used may differ from or conflict with those intended because of conscious adjustments and improvements or a regression to habitual and inferior practices. More refinement and more control may be required. Following alterations and adjustments, a rerun might bring different results.

These are the possible decisions in all four areas:

1. Affirmation of the status quo (of the operating patterns, of the goals, of the staff). Such affirmation confirms program validity and implies that the program should continue and that cooperation and support should be given to it.

2. Reconsideration and possible redefinition of goals, purposes, objectives, or clients served.

3. Review and alteration of the means or processes used, including specific program elements, strategies, sequence, and format.

4. Redefinition or possible reassignment of functions, duties, responsibilities, and patterns of performance.

5. Review, clarification, or alteration of norms, rules, policies, standards.

6. Change in resource allocation (budget or staff).

7. Redefinition of roles and reassignment of individuals or alteration of organizational structure.

8. Reconsideration of priorities and ordering of activities.

An elaborate and expensive evaluation would be required to provide adequate bases for all these decisions. Hence, it is desirable to focus from the beginning on the specific areas in which decisions are to be made. Initial surveys of views and opinions of program participants and observers may be helpful. Even so, many of these decisions are interrelated in such manner that alteration of one markedly affects others. Thus an alteration in norms or priorities may require reallocations of resources or reassignment of functions. In addition, the issue of how decisions are made and who makes them could markedly influence the nature of the information sought and the form in which it is presented and interpreted. Some of these decisions are made by different persons or at different levels. Budget and staff reallocations, for example, may be made within the program or by external administrators. Concrete decisions and subsequent change therefore are by no means automatic results of an evaluation. The evaluation must be planned in relation to the decisions to be made and the processes involved in making them.

In doing such planning, it is useful for evaluators and those employing them to initially ask this series of questions: (1) What is to be evaluated? (2) Why is the evaluation being done? (3) What period of time is the evaluation to cover? (4) Who determines the goals, purposes, or objectives of the program? (5) Who determines the criteria or standards to be used? (6) What criteria or standards are to be employed? (7) What are the possible decisions or actions to be taken as a result of the evaluation? (8) What steps and procedures are to be included in the evaluation? (9) Who will make the decisions after completion of the evaluation? (10) Who will do the evaluation and how is this person related to program staff and institutional administration? (11) What preconceptions, commitments, or prejudices exist, in either individuals or groups, which may complicate or interfere with an objective appraisal and consequent action?

An understanding of the types of evaluation is useful in answering some of these questions. These types closely approximate the decision-making areas just described. In practice, a program evaluation will ordinarily include procedures of all these four types (Stufflebeam and others, 1971).

Planning, or developmental, evaluation is undertaken to determine needs or deficiencies and to devise objectives or goals to meet these needs. It facilitates decisions required at the early stages of developing a new program or of revising an existing one. It includes (1) defining and describing the environment (actual and desired conditions, conditions requiring adjustment); (2) identifying unmet needs, unused opportunities, and both needed and available resources; (3) identifying and diagnosing sources of deficiencies in meeting needs or in using opportunities in the past (including environment, personnel, and materials); (4) seeking to predict deficiencies in the future by considering the reasonable, desirable, possible, and probable relationships among inputs, processes, and outcomes (this has been called contingency evaluation). Planning evaluation requires a systematic, organized approach to the total task because it involves both a review of past practice and a prediction of desired and possible developments.

Input evaluation aids in making decisions about how to use resources to attain program goals. It does so by (1) identifying and appraising the potential of individuals and agencies; (2) comparing and analyzing possible strategies for achieving goals; (3) formulating designs for implementation; (4) estimating immediate staff requirements, other resource requirements, costs, possible difficulties; (5) projecting the requirements of (4) into the years ahead as the program becomes fully operative. Input evaluation calls for imaginative, creative thinking; it tends to be microanalytic in that it deals in detail and depth with many alternatives.

Process evaluation provides continuing or periodic feedback so that those responsible for program planning and operation can review and possibly alter earlier decisions. It (1) detects malfunctioning in procedures or their implementation; (2) identifies the sources of difficulty; (3) provides information for program revision and improvement; (4) appraises staff communication and adequacy in use of resources; (5) projects additional resource requirements not originally anticipated. Process evaluation must be specific to each process element if it is to be definitive on these points.

Output evaluation assesses the attainment, at the end of a project or at appropriate stages within it, of those goals which are self-contained and of those which are preliminary to entering another stage. Output evaluation includes (1) identification of the correspondence and the discrepancies between original objectives and actual attainments; (2) identification of unintended (either desirable or undesirable) results and suggestions as to possible causal factors; (3) provision of information and of suggestions for decisions to alter or replace previous planning, input, and process decisions; (4) provision for quality control by recycling the program to attain unmet objectives; (5) provision of basic information and suggestions for continuing, modifying, or terminating the program.

The terms *formative* and *summative* have also been extensively used to describe types of evaluation. Planning, input, process, and output evaluation, however, can be frequently regarded as both summative (providing a basis for decisions regarding continuation, modification, termination, or replacement of a program) and formative (providing a basis for formulation and reformation of a program). If planning evaluation leads to a decision that a program is not feasible, a summative decision has been made. Generally, however, planning, input, and process evaluation are tentative and formative—they are used in developing a program. Output evaluation, to the extent that it is used for feedback, development of alternatives, and improvement, is also formative. To the extent that it is used for retaining, modifying, replacing, or eliminating a program, it is summative. Thus summative and formative refer more to the nature and finality of a decision than to the role of evaluation. Since colleges and universities seldom act to eliminate any program, most evaluation is formative.

Let us look now at some specific changes in educational programs that can result from evaluation efforts. Such programs usually have four parts—input, environment, process, and output—which correspond roughly to the four types of evaluation.

The *inputs* include both tangible and intangible factors. *Dollars* provide facilities and staff. Social needs and preferences determine broad *goals*, while the specific *objectives* are determined by faculty and students. *Students* seek to become educated persons, capable of earning a living and contributing to society. But *faculty members* are also students engaged in learning (with research or service and faculty development as outputs).

The *environment* is made up of *people* (students, faculty members, administrators, clerical and maintenance personnel, campus police, cooks, residence hall personnel), *buildings, grounds and equipment,* and a *psychological and social climate.* This climate is a result of other components of the environment, of the criteria operative in determining the input, and of the interactions which constitute the next stage of the model. The environment, perhaps even more than the input, is the consequence of many decisions made in reference to different goals and value systems by many different persons over long periods of time. For example, residence halls have seldom been planned or arranged with reference to the educational goals and processes of a university; and faculty members are frequently selected by departments for their research potential even though their major task is teaching undergraduates.

The processes (transactions and interactions) bring together the input and the environment in various ways. Ideally, these processes are based upon an analysis of needs and goals and are designed to expedite the production of outputs in the most efficient and effective manner. These processes, as already noted, take place in an environment which they help to create.

The outputs, in the most general terms, correspond to the three major purposes and related functions of higher education: *instruction, research,* and *service.* An output at a certain level becomes an input for the next. Hence, desired *changes in institutions* (outputs) can, in themselves, be goals.

Table 1. Possible Changes Resulting from Evaluation

Parts of Educational Program	Changes
Input	
Students and faculty	In criteria for admission or selection
Dollars	In amount, source, allocation
Social needs and goals	In priorities or goals
Institutional goals and objectives	In priorities or objectives
Environment	
People	In characteristics, by intent or circumstance
Buildings, grounds, equipment	Alterations, replacements
Psychological and social climate	In relations of environmental elements
Processes (Transactions, Interactions)	
Educational (instruction, research, evaluation, planning)	In tasks performed / In mix, scope, priorities
Operational (budgeting, maintenance, management, administration)	In techniques used / In organization and governance
Output	
Educated persons	In goals, objectives, purposes
Research	In mix, scope, priorities
Services	In institutional aspirations

Table 1 suggests some of the changes which may take place in the several factors making up each of the four program parts. Even if no direct changes are made, maintenance of the status quo is usually a dynamic process in which minor adjustments must constantly be made. A pattern of drift, in which continuing minor adjustments are made without plan, is perhaps the most static pattern. Thus a college which fixes the number of students to be enrolled and modifies admission policies from year to year, or even week to week, probably faces less turmoil than one which makes no attempt to regulate enrollment to accord with assumptions on which the budget is based.

The role of evaluation in all these cases is to provide evidence on the exact state of affairs and to suggest the adjustments or changes which are required. Planning evaluation plays a role in decisions on the environment; it also concerns the interrelation of all parts of the program—input, environment, processes, and output. Input evaluation is especially concerned with the use of resources and with clarifying goals. Process evaluation corresponds to the process elements, but to appraise these one must reassess and analyze their contributions to the move from inputs to outputs. Output evaluation is concerned with discrepancies between intent and actuality and with analysis of the reasons or factors contributing to any deficiency or overrun. (Although it is difficult to imagine an institution or its faculty members admitting that the graduates are overeducated, this is, in fact, possible; a reduction in expenditures may force elimination of advanced course offerings which are acceptable elsewhere for graduate study or reduction in the extent of honors and independent study opportunities.)

Because the decisions resulting from an evaluation can be only as good as the evaluation itself, a final step in any evaluation process should be an evaluation of the evaluation. This second evaluation can be regarded as an audit and is increasingly stipulated in federal evaluation contracts. The auditor is asked to affirm to the grantor that the evaluation fulfills the intent of the contract, that the evaluation in fact addresses those issues stipulated in the contract, that the statistical analysis, if any, is correct, and that the conclusions reached in the evaluation report are warranted by the evaluation procedure. Such audits are a direct result of the increased demand for accountability by external funding sources, who are reasonably concerned that an audit made or directly arranged by the project administrators may be unduly lenient, highly biased, or deliberately selective to make the project look good.

The responsibility of the external auditor is often burdensome, especially when the evaluation is weak or contrived. The auditor's responsibility lies mainly with the contractor but is also tempered by professional considerations. For reasons already discussed, most evaluations are flawed from a research point of view, and yet many of these flaws are not readily overcome. The auditor who, to curry favor with the contractor, unreasonably flays an evaluation on such counts is hardly professional unless it is evident that the original evaluators neither recognized nor admitted the flaws. The criteria for these audits are thus both scientific and practical, and these must be kept in balance, for practical concerns weigh more heavily in evaluation than in pure research.

The scientific criteria for an evaluation audit are the validity, reliability, and objectivity of the evaluation; they interact with and support each other. These criteria are dealt with in greater detail in Chapter Six, but some preview is necessary here.

Validity is of two sorts. Internal validity is the correspondence between reality and the evaluation. Unless the evaluation produces results which relate outcomes to processes, the evaluation is misleading and useless because no information is provided to suggest improvement by alteration of the process. Thus, attempts at evaluating the quality of a program solely by appraising the input and process lack internal validity. External validity is the extent to which an evaluation is generalizable to other similar events. Such generalization frequently presents a problem in educational evaluation, especially at the college level, because of the autonomy extended to individuals and departments and the resulting differences in programs and resources. An evaluation which demonstrates that an individual professor attains astounding success with certain methods and students may be useful but limited in the scope of its application. In general, evaluation must exhibit more concern than does research about internal validity and less about external validity. Yet evaluation must strive for external validity; otherwise the results are only history. They provide no basis for planning.

Reliability concerns the replicability of either the program or the evaluation procedures and their results. Unless the details of the evaluation procedures and of the program being evaluated are recorded, replicability is not possible.

Objectivity requires that those responsible for carrying out a program do not make evaluations which are biased by their own involvement and that the evidence collected be available for examination and analysis by others. If these data are differently interpreted by competent persons, objectivity is lacking.

Practical criteria for judging an evaluation emphasize the need to relate the evaluation process and findings not only to the issues or problems but also to the possible decisions, the persons who make them, and the conditions under which they are made. In relating the evaluation to possible decisions, evaluators have to make critical choices. On the one hand, an evaluation should attempt to provide significant information relative to all aspects of the decision. On the other hand, evaluations seek, among other results, to encourage efficiency as well as effectiveness in programs, and an evaluation should itself be a model of efficiency. It is possible for an evaluation to be expanded far beyond any realizable benefits. Evaluators can, without help, develop extensive lists of desirable information, and program participants will add many others. Indeed, rejection of an evaluation can frequently be sensed in advance by the vast range of dubious criteria which some program developers suggest. For example, there are no good measures of enthusiasm, satisfaction, or success twenty years after graduation, and, in any case, their presence or absence is irrelevant to the issue of educational program effectiveness if other more concrete evidence is negative or even unavailable. Some trivia which might complicate the evaluation process can be eliminated simply by examining whether the evidence found would affect the decision. Much of what is suggested as "interesting" is irrelevant. A modicum of familiarity with prior research will also enable the evaluator to eliminate some suggestions. For example, attempting to ascertain whether students with four units of high school English will do better in a program than those with fewer units can and should be dismissed as wasted effort. Variation in high schools and in grades make the question unanswerable. This issue of coverage should be forthrightly confronted. Costs can become unreasonable and, in themselves, evoke negative reactions to evaluation. And the sheer amount of information amassed can so impede the process that the evaluation is never properly completed. Evaluation has as often been sidetracked by apparent enthusiasm for more and more information as by expressed antagonism and lack of cooperation.

Another practical criterion for judging evaluations is whether evaluation reports have reached all those involved in the programs evaluated or in making decisions about them. Withholding reports from those directly involved creates more antagonism and suspicion than a highly critical report. But widespread distribution to those who have no direct need for an evaluative report is often unwise; this procedure stirs up resentment which makes change difficult. If contacted by and serving program personnel, an evaluator works primarily with them, reports to them, and makes no report to others until it has been discussed in detail with them. If the evaluator is assigned by an administrator, the implications of this pattern, including the distribution of reports, require clarification at the beginning.

The evaluator must take into consideration too the conditions under which decisions are made. Whereas research tends to emphasize delay to attain perfection, timeliness is a must with an evaluation report. Decisions will be made with or without data. This situation does not excuse an incomplete or inadequate report which may be full of flaws and even misleading. An evaluation must be carried out on schedule in relation to other pressures. Failure to fulfill this obligation simply results in an increasing distrust of formal evaluation.

The evaluator should also produce evidence of the total cost of the evaluation, including direct expenditures, salaries, and time, which can be weighed against the results achieved. This requirement calls for an appraisal of the impact of evaluation not only on the project but on the views and skills of those involved and the later impact on other similar projects. In addition, an evaluator should assess the cost of implementing the findings of a study. In some cases, recommendations may have to be rejected simply because the costs of the programs suggested would be prohibitive. The subject of costs is discussed in greater detail later—notably in Chapters Five and Six.

The key point about evaluating evaluations is that evaluators must assume at least partial responsibility for unsuccessful evaluations; they simply cannot blame lack of success entirely on the recalcitrance of others. Evaluators who do not improve their performances by evaluation can scarcely expect to improve the performance of others.

Evaluation, viewed in the way I have described it in this chapter, is always forward looking. Each evaluation provides evidence for adaptation, alteration, expansion, or complete recycling of programs. It can also provide evidence for recommendations about the next steps for individual students, about changes in faculty behavior, or about reallocation of resources. But evaluation will be effective in these respects only if it is planned in reference to them. Evaluation has often been conducted on a haphazard, opportunistic basis with little sense of direction or of ultimate goals. It has been lacking in theory, structure, design, and criteria for effectiveness. It has not been adapted to the exigencies of particular situations, either in methods and procedures or in strategies for facilitating decision making. In this chapter I have shown how a good evaluation process can be planned to connect with the decision-making areas. The following outline sums up the essential elements of such a process and can be used as a checklist for planning:

A. What is the purpose and background of the evaluation?
   1. What inputs, environmental factors, processes, or outcomes are to be evaluated?
   2. What are the critical points at which evidence will be required for decisions?
   3. What rules, procedures, assumptions, and principles are involved in the decisions?
   4. Who will make decisions and what is the process by which these will be made?
   5. Does the overall situation suggest, require, or prohibit certain tactics and strategies?
   6. What timing considerations are involved?
   7. What are the limitations on costs?
   8. What are the specific evaluation tasks?
B. What information is to be collected?
   1. Are the particular items unambiguously defined and collectible by objective and reliable means?

    2. From where or from whom is the evidence to be collected?

    3. By whom is it to be collected?

    4. What instruments or procedures are to be used?

    5. Will the collection of evidence in itself seriously affect the input, environment, process, or outcomes?

    6. Will the collection of evidence become a regular part of the process, or is it an add-on for a one-time evaluation?

    7. What is the schedule for collection of information?

C. What procedures will be used for organizing and analyzing data?

    1. In what form is information to be collected?

    2. Will coding be required? If subjective judgments will be required in coding, are the criteria for these adequate? Who will do the coding?

    3. How will the data be stored, retrieved, and processed?

    4. What analytic procedures are to be used?

D. Is the reporting procedure clear?

    1. Who will receive reports?

    2. Will reports be organized by analytic procedures, by type of data, or by decisions to be made?

    3. Will reports include the practical implications regarding the various possible decisions to be made or leave these implications for the project staff or administrators to ascertain?

    4. Is the evaluator to state explicitly the particular decisions which he believes are supported by the evidence?

    5. When and in what detail are reports to be made?

E. How is the evaluation to be evaluated?

    1. Who will be involved—project staff, the evaluator, decision makers, some presumably more objective individual?

    2. What will the criteria used in this second-level evaluation be—costs, program improvement, impact on further planning of related enterprises?

3. To whom and when is this report to be presented?
4. What decisions are to be anticipated as a result of the report? Will they include improvement of evaluation processes in the future?

There exists an extensive literature on facilitation of change, but it offers little help to the evaluator or administrator. In theory, change on the campus should result from accumulation, assimilation, and application of knowledge, but in practice college and university personnel are strongly wedded to their views about curriculum, teaching, and evaluation. Some highly conservative and traditional professors continue to teach as they were taught. Others would replace all traditional practices with highly individualized and unstructured learning.

Since the evaluation process seldom throws any light upon the comparative effectiveness of approaches vastly different from the one under study, those who operate upon ideological rather than empirical or experimental bases exhibit the least interest in evaluation. Those who are more receptive to systematic evaluations, usually accept it for one (or a combination) of the following reasons: (1) Some see evaluation as a form of quality control and use tests and grades to maintain standards. Individuals in this group perceive continuing tendencies toward erosion of educational quality and they view standardized tests, comprehensive examinations, grades, and requirements as a means of controlling the erosion. Evaluation, for them, is thus a means of resisting change rather than encouraging it, although program revision can result. (2) Others seek continuous improvement through gradual change. Objectives and appropriate learning processes may not be clear at the beginning, but they become more specific and clear through engagement in evaluation. (3) Still others have definite objectives in mind and view evaluation as promoting progress in the achievement of stated goals through a rational experimental approach.

The evaluator faces a delicate task in effectively dealing with these various orientations. It is tempting to regard the extreme conservative, the ultra-liberal, and the doctrinaire as hopeless. Yet almost every program harbors a range of views and commitments both within and among individuals. Decisions for change can seldom be achieved if significant members of the faculty involved are actively antagonistic. And the decisions, once made, are seldom successful if indifference and obstructionism are exhibited by even a few faculty members. The evaluator's task is, indeed, a sensitive one if it is to be conducted as a persuasive educational experience for the faculty; and even the most tactful evaluators can succeed only if they are supported by others who are influential in policy formulation.

Bibliographical Note

The following authors present views about the role of evaluation in policy formulation, decision making, and the facilitation of change.

Rossi and Williams (1972) and Kopan and Walberg (1974) present analyses of the role of evaluation in identifying the need for and making large-scale policy decisions.

Popham's *Evaluation in Education* (1974) is a hard-bound collection of a series of American Educational Research Association training pamphlets directed toward educational researchers who are implementing evaluation programs.

Brick and Bushko (1973) discuss problems in the management of change.

Dornbusch and Scott (1975) examine the relationship between evaluation and the exercise of authority.

Hage and Aiken (1970) deal insightfully with the processes and difficulties of social change in complex organizations. Though not focused on higher education, the analysis is applicable.

House (1974) considers the politics of innovation. Though oriented to the public school system, including community colleges, his discussion covers many points relevant to higher education.

Chapter 3

Starting
with Objectives

Identification and elaboration of objectives has long been an early, if not the initial, step in evaluation. Tyler's (1949) contributions to this approach are well known. Identifying objectives is necessary because the array of possible experiences which can be provided to mold behavior is infinite (as are the behaviors themselves), and some choices must be made. Current demands for accountability (discussed in Chapter Five) also emphasize the need for objectives and demonstrations of program effectiveness in achieving them. (Unfortunately, accountability tends also to demand highly concrete and specific outcomes which may then displace more significant objectives.)

Despite the need for formulating objectives, doing so often meets with great resistance. The difficulties include confused terminology, basic philosophical differences in regard to the nature and role of education, difficulties in translating global

concerns into realistic objectives, and skepticism over the usefulness of stating objectives.

Attempts to define the intents and aspirations of individuals and institutions run immediately into a prolific and confused terminology. Words such as *aims, goals, objectives,* and
purposes are used interchangeably and hence obscurely. Institutional purposes, for example, are usually interpreted at broad
levels: "meeting the needs of society by interpreting and passing
on our cultural heritage to the young," "organizing and adding
to the cultural heritage," and "interpreting and applying knowledge for the alleviation of individual and social ills and the general improvement of society." These purposes lead naturally to
the functions of instruction, scholarship and research, and public service, but they are so broad that most any activity can (by
some interpretation) be justified in universities.

The diverse views which exist within institutional faculties
and among institutions as to the character and objectives of a
college education also create difficulties in attaining accord.
Heath (1968, pp. 274-278), in reviewing the goals of a liberal
education as propounded by various prestigious persons,
gleaned such phrases as "represent experiences symbolically,"
"self-insight," "allocentric," "firm set of convictions," "development of independence or autonomy," "inner freedom,"
"control over his own destiny." Bell's (1966, p. 152) list of objectives for general education include "overcome intellectual
provincialism," "centrality of method," "awareness of history,"
"civilizing role of humanities," "values infuse all inquiry."
Other persons, equally committed to liberal education, emphasize religious orientation, vocational preparation, and preprofes-
sional education. Other individuals in the university are concerned with increasing personal and academic freedom, encouraging innovation, expanding field services, improving the image
of the university, assuring financial soundness, increasing the
involvement of students and faculty in decision making, and
promoting egalitarianism (Uhl, 1971). It is not surprising that
external critics see a lack of direction in the educational establishment (and frequently too a tendency, characteristic of
bureaucracies—which many institutions of higher education

have become—to be more concerned with self-preservation and expansion than with service to society).

A refreshing note—though an irritating one to educators—is struck by those economists, program-budget exponents, and systems analysts who insist upon defining and assessing the benefits of education. The economist divides human activities into production and consumption, a dichotomy which many faculty members (especially those in the humanities) find irrelevant and even exasperating when applied to education. But if education is regarded (and quite reasonably so) as an investment in human capital, the production of human capital and of knowledge can be analyzed on a cost-benefit or cost-effectiveness basis. Unlike analyses of physical capital investment, however, analysis of human capital investment must recognize possible improvement in the quality of social and political life, which adds to the satisfaction of individuals. This is a significant benefit, although the economist finds difficulty in dealing with it. Clearly, personal and social benefits extend well beyond the economic benefits of increased income to the individual degree recipient. Economists differ among themselves as well as with educators on the relative worth of these personal and social benefits. The dollar value of personal satisfaction and of improvement in the quality of social life is not easily determined. Indeed, it will never be determined in a manner acceptable to everyone because of individual differences in values.

Adams and Michaelson (1971) go well beyond economic concerns in identifying career commitment, public concerns, quality of private lives, satisfying experiences, enlarged intellectual life of the faculty, and effective teacher preparation as possible results of innovative education. Yet evidence which would unambiguously demonstrate effectiveness in attaining such goals is not easily defined or attained. Indeed, widespread agreement on the goals is unlikely. Many persons face the necessity of changing careers several times. Quality of private lives is an ambiguous phrase, as is enlarged intellectual life of the faculty. Concern about public affairs can be overdone if it results in continuing confrontation rather than action, as, for example, has frequently been the case with ecological issues. Benefits approached in this way are not likely to satisfy the legislatures, the general public, or even most of the faculty.

This problem of defining and agreeing upon meaningful objectives is compounded when it becomes necessary to translate these global and transcendental concerns into specific objectives for which appropriate learning tasks can be found and adequate resources provided. Few persons would disagree that self-confidence, self-reliance, independence, respect for others, group cooperation, self-evaluation, concern for truth, creativity, and critical thought and judgment are desirable characteristics of individuals, but profound disagreement exists as to whether these can ever be defined in concrete operational, behavioral, or evaluatable terms.

That task is made even more difficult by the expressed doubts of many persons that the attempt is even desirable. Some thoughtful educators (Walcott, 1969, pp. 14-40) oppose the whole process of stating objectives on the grounds that (1) individuals pursue many and differing objectives simultaneously; (2) the effectiveness of instruction and learning may be at times decreased rather than automatically increased by awareness of objectives; (3) the worthwhile outcomes always outnumber those which can consciously be pursued; (4) specific objectives should not be imposed on all students; (5) at best, the attainment of any specific set of objectives is a series of approximations, and the movement at any point in time may be seen as forward or retrograde depending on the subjective views of individuals. Some critics believe in addition that no one should select objectives for another, that learning and subsequent change are always self-directed.

Goals of Higher Education

Support for this skepticism about objectives can be found when the overall objectives of higher education are considered. I have already hinted that an underlying difficulty in stating objectives is the diversity of sources from which they can be inferred or drawn. Another difficulty is that even the same goals can be variously interpreted. For example, at times some church-related colleges have viewed education primarily as a philosophical and moral experience. But moral values have changed, with youth now often rejecting the commitments of their elders as ill-conceived, impractical, bigoted, or insincere. And the goal of a "moral" education has correspondingly changed.

The role of a college education has most often been seen however as assisting in (1) learning facts about oneself and the physical, social, and cosmic environment; respecting facts and rejecting error, evasion, or deliberate misrepresentation; (2) developing the capacity for accurate use of language and clear thinking; (3) developing a critical realism which denies absolutes and yet rejects denial of all objective values; (4) developing personal value standards and the ability to evaluate alternatives and choose wisely among them; (5) overcoming provincialism and prejudice by seeing issues in a wide and deep perspective.

At some level, most people would accept all these goals as desirable, but distinctive orientations lead to contrasting and even conflicting interpretations and implications. In a college with a fundamentalist religion orientation, for example, a superstructure of beliefs, tenets, and even behaviors can lead to distinctive interpretation of clear thinking, values, and even "facts."

Even within the same institution faculty members differ markedly by disciplines (as well as individually) in their interpretation and acceptance of these five broad objectives. Some humanists emphasize study of the classics as the proven way to inculcate values and develop judgment. Scientists and mathematicians are inclined to emphasize knowledge of facts and principles and the acquiring of specific skills. Some social scientists consider unhampered development of the individual as the central goal of education and deplore detailed planning of educational objectives or experiences as inimical to personal development, which proceeds primarily out of affective experiences. And yet other faculty members encourage learning and personal development through practical experiences in travel, work, and problem solving. The preceding characterizations by disciplines are, of course, not entirely valid. But these differences do exist among faculty members, patterned either by their original choice of discipline or by their study of the discipline. The autonomy accorded colleges and departments in planning curricula and courses and the freedom of individual professors to adapt courses to their own priorities effectively discourage agreement on specific objectives beyond rough indications by credit-hour of commitments to the major areas of knowledge.

Goals in the Learning Process

Agreement on specific instructional goals is often as rare as agreement on the overall goals of higher education. College and university professors, other than those in education and psychology, have seldom given systematic attention to the psychology of human learning. Those who have done so find marked differences in theories and uncertainties in and disagreements among specific studies. Skinner's (1968) behaviorism, on the one hand, seems to ignore the possibility that humans might be much more complicated than pigeons and might respond to stimuli on the basis of cognition and affect as much or even more than on the basis of physical needs and gratifications. Carl Rogers, Nevitt Sanford, and other psychologists, on the other hand, emphasize affect, socialization, and personal development to such an extent that knowledge and cognitive ability seem, at times, to be ignored. Nevertheless, psychologists have provided concepts which are useful in planning student learning, among them: readiness, motivation, and reinforcement. Development of these concepts has led to the recognition that the assimilation or mastery of knowledge and the development or modification of attitudes, beliefs, and values are not automatic and are not ensured by the formal arrangement of classes or by other experiences which bring together professors, students, and resource materials. The tendency of some professors to assume that stupidity, indifference, lethargy, or recalcitrance underlies the inadequate performance of a student and hence to shrug off any responsibility for student failure is reprehensible. Some students are stupid, lethargic, or recalcitrant, as are some professors. But others lack readiness or motivation. Recognition of these and other concepts can improve the learning process and modify the statement of objectives. Hence a brief consideration of several of these concepts is relevant to the further consideration of objectives.

In structured cumulative disciplines such as mathematics and physics, lack of knowledge and of specific skills requisite in a course—lack of *readiness*—constitutes a handicap which few students can overcome. A student with no prior mathematics is unlikely to succeed in calculus. A student with two years of German in high school may not be ready for second-year college German. There is also a maturity factor in some circumstances. An individual may lack the experience to understand or to cope emotionally with aspects of the social sciences.

College students often also lack *motivation* for study. They view the degree as a key to opportunity and disdain the detail. Some psychologists apparently attribute to everyone the desire for self-improvement, but we can assume only that they have never tried to teach college students to write or do mathematics when they wish to do neither. Teaching basic science to medical students who view medicine as primarily a matter of human relations likewise involves the issue of motivation. Required courses, especially, reap a harvest of apathy. Some part of this difficulty certainly lies in the lack of clear course objectives and of interpretation of these to the student. When what is to be learned has no immediate relevance to the student, demonstration of its worth is a responsibility of the teacher. Students are seldom challenged either by a demand for memorization of definitions, facts, and principles, or by the search for truth. Memorized materials are unlikely to be retained for months and years until, in an appropriate circumstance, the meaning and relevance are suddenly clear (the ah-ha reaction).

Rather, instruction should actively involve students in reacting to ideas and in tentative formulation of their own possibly conflicting ideas. Only as students act or respond can the accuracy of their understanding be confirmed and *reinforced*. Students who have not fully assessed the meaning of ideas and confirmed their understandings are not likely to retain or to *transfer* their knowledge and skills to new tasks. Such transfer is an objective which must be consciously sought, as should the related objective of fostering critical and creative thinking.

Enough is known about how people learn to recognize that there are various *ways of "knowing,"* some of which impede rather than facilitate learning. Some people tend to hold tenaciously to views ("truth," superstition, prejudice) which they have always known to be "true." Authorities (rulers, scholars, religions, social mores, and folkways) support beliefs and behavioral patterns which are unquestioned by some people and which are rejected or disregarded only by persons sufficiently rash or resolute to brace the possible consequences. For some individuals, intuition and reasoning are methods of reaching truth, although rational processes can readily lead to rationalization rather than verification. Science seeks knowledge which is valid and independent of individual imperfections and biases (Cohen and Nagel, 1934, pp. 193-195). Much of the conflict over objectives is related to whether the scientific way of knowing should replace or be given priority over the other three.

Individuals also learn through *imitation* (sometimes conscious, sometimes unconscious) of others with whom they identify because of common interests. Some individuals, sensitive to the approbation of others, may change their values and habit patterns to bring the approval of those around them. Others are encouraged to accept attitudes and values tacitly by the threat of punitive action—low grades, for example. These (and other) agents can effect value change, but they involve submission, manipulation, or conscious adjustment, which make them inappropriate as change agents in an institution of higher education committed to the communication of knowledge and to the cultivation of intellectual abilities. Nevertheless, these agents of change exist, and often lead to unanticipated and undesirable results. Thus the teacher who forces students to accept values which are (to them) meaningless may succeed only in cultivating dislike for himself or herself or for the field.

Whatever the source of objectives (individual, society, psychology of learning, educational philosophy, religion), they have no educational efficacy unless they are known, under-

stood, and accepted by faculty and students. Many fine statements of objectives (presumably written by administrators)
appear in college catalogs, but faculty members and students are
either unaware of their existence or ignore them. Course out-
lines and syllabuses frequently include extended statements of
objectives which have been ignored in actual course development and in the instructional process. Objectives become significant as they are used as guides in educational planning and
learning. Unless learning experiences exhibit obvious relationships to the objectives, the objectives are ineffectual.

Too often also means which are remote from objectives
tend to become the ends and replace the objectives. For example, distribution requirements, the means, reflect an objective:
broad knowledge of the major divisions of knowledge, the disciplines. But the original concern is too readily forgotten as students work to cover blocks of content in specified periods of
time. The demand for specific knowledge becomes an end in
itself.

Types of Objectives

Objectives can fall at various points on several different
continuums. The immediacy-remoteness continuum goes from
immediate or short-range objectives to intermediate, terminal,
and long-range or ultimate objectives. The specificity-generality
continuum goes from narrow or broad subobjectives to major
objectives. And the isolated-sequential continuum goes from
single objectives to transitional objectives to auxiliary objectives
to a full sequence of objectives. A student's immediate goal may
be that of passing those courses in which he or she is presently
enrolled; the intermediate goal may be attaining a degree; and
the ultimate goal may be to become a successful lawyer. Narrow
goals may involve perfecting an array of techniques; the broad
goal may be to utilize these in creating works of art. Teachers
who emphasize neatness promote an isolated goal. Other objectives, such as acquiring techniques, may be prerequisites or
auxiliaries to the attainment of a whole sequence of objectives.
The place of objectives on these continuums can be disputed. A

literature teacher may require all students to memorize "Cowards die many times before their deaths; the valiant never taste of death but once," because he or she heard that a badly wounded soldier found comfort in recalling this quotation in the hours before rescue. The teacher has a long-range (though naive) objective in mind, but the students probably find the objective immediate, isolated, and irrelevant (Maxwell and Tovatt, 1970, p. 82).

Eisner (1972) provides one possible classification of objectives. He divides them into instructional, expressive, and problem-solving (my term for Eisner's Type III) groups. An instructional objective is explicit and prescriptive—"solve quadratic equations of all types." The goal is demonstrated and assessable student behavior. Expressive objectives are less structured. They cover experiences designed to develop patterns of thought and feeling which individuals can use in creative ways to express their own interests and individuality. Problem-solving objectives require students to use their own resources and imagination in solving a specific problem. Ingenuity in solution is the goal.

The most elaborate typology of objectives to date, however, is that emerging from the work of B. S. Bloom, D. R. Krathwohl, and their associates. This effort, fostered by Ralph Tyler, initially involved evaluation and examination experts from a number of universities. Indeed, the effort originated in part from a desire to expedite the exchange of test items and evaluation instruments by characterizing them according to the educational objectives which they covered. Work on the cognitive domain was completed first (Bloom, 1956). The taxonomy on the affective domain posed complex problems which delayed completion of that work (Krathwohl, Bloom, and Masia) until 1964. The psychomotor domain, neglected for a longer period, was finally attacked by Simpson (1971, pp. 60-67). Some question whether at least one other domain is required—an action pattern domain—since decisions are carried out in action, both physical and mental, with overtones of feelings. However, the addition of a fourth category to synthesize the existing three would only further complicate the situation. One should simply keep in mind that almost any human behavior is likely to involve aspects from all three domains.

The categories in the taxonomy of the cognitive domain (a condensed version of which is presented here) progress from knowledge through understanding, application, analysis, and synthesis to evaluation.

A. Knowledge
    1. General knowledge
    2. Knowledge of specifics
    3. Knowledge of terminology
    4. Knowledge of specific facts
    5. Knowledge of ways and means of dealing with specifics
    6. Knowledge of conventions
    7. Knowledge of trends and sequences
    8. Knowledge of classifications and categories
    9. Knowledge of criteria
    10. Knowledge of methodology
    11. Knowledge of the universals and abstractions in a field
    12. Knowledge of principles and generalizations
    13. Knowledge of theories and structures

B. Intellectual abilities and skills
    1. Comprehension (translation, interpretation, extrapolation)
    2. Application
    3. Analysis (of elements, of relationships, of organizational principles)
    4. Synthesis (production of a unique communication, production of a plan or proposed set of operations, derivation of a set of abstract relations)
    5. Evaluation judgments based on internal evidence, judgments based on external criteria)

The order is based upon the complexity of the task so that, in most cases, each level above the first requires some proficiency at the prior levels. A student cannot apply or use a principle or concept until he or she knows or understands it. Analysis of a problem requires understanding and application of concepts or principles. Evaluation can be insightfully made only after a procedure or problem has been fully understood by analysis and synthesis. Because no one can know or understand and apply every possibly useful idea or principle, evaluation is required in the choice of what is learned. Hence values enter in at the initial stages of cognition in the choice of those ideas, terms, concepts to which we attend.

The affective domain proceeds from receiving (including awareness of an idea, problem, or phenomenon) through responding (acquiescence, willingness to respond, and satisfaction in response) to acceptance of a value, preference for a value, and commitment. (A condensed version is presented here.)

A. Receiving (attending)
    1. Awareness
    2. Willingness to receive
    3. Controlled or selected attention
B. Responding
    1. Acquiescence in responding
    2. Willingness to respond
    3. Satisfaction in response
C. Valuing
    1. Acceptance of a value
    2. Preference for a value
    3. Commitment
D. Organization
    1. Conceptualization of a value
    2. Organization of a value system
E. Characterization by a value or value complex
    1. Generalized set
    2. Characterization

Commitment surely implies a considered judgment so that, at this point, the affective coalesces with the cognitive. The remainder of the domain includes organization and characterization (internalization) leading to a code of behavior or a philosophy of life. This domain is presumably based upon the extent of personal involvement with an idea, problem, or concern, but, upon closer examination, one finds the organization more complex. In its early stages, either cognitive or purely affective reactions may be involved. One may consciously elect to attend to an idea because it appears important or because it promises to clarify or resolve a concern or problem. But one may choose to attend simply because of pleasurable personal reactions or social interactions without considering the ultimate implications or effects. Value commitment seems clearly to imply the presence of cognition (evaluation) and a conscious decision. In the later stage of internalization, cognition appears to be suspended in favor of familiarity. This characteristic of the domain can be regarded as a virtue in the sense that the taxonomy is neutral; judgment as to whether the attitudes, values, or behaviors which are internalized are good or bad is suspended. But from the viewpoint of setting and achieving desirable educational goals, the separation of cognition and affect poses serious difficulties. Any educational procedure which fosters affective growth without awareness of implications and a conscious choice based on this awareness is simply a conditioning process or indoctrination.

The psychomotor domain (outlined here in condensed form) starts with perception, which is almost identical to awareness—the first stage of the affective domain.

A. Perception
    1. Sensory stimulation (sound, sight, touch, taste, smell, kinesthesia)
    2. Cue selection
    3. Translation (of perception into action)
B. Set (readiness)
    1. Mental set
    2. Physical set
    3. Emotional set
C. Guided response
    1. Imitation
    2. Trial and error
D. Mechanism (habituated response)
E. Complex overt response
    1. Resolution of uncertainty

     2. Automatic performance
  F. Adapting and originating (possible item discussed but
     not included in outline as presented by Simpson, 1971,
     p. 66)

Perception covers sensory stimulation including sound, sight,
touch, taste, smell, and kinesthesia (activation of muscles, ten-
dons, and joints). Selection of important cues essential to response and the translation of perception into action are also
parts of this first stage. The second stage in this domain encompasses readiness or preparation for an action. It involves mental,
physical, and emotional sets. Obviously, both cognitive and
affective elements appear at this stage. The third stage is a
guided response which may involve physical manipulation by an
instructor, imitation, or trial and error. At the fourth stage, the
response becomes a mechanism; it is becoming habitual and
requires less concentrated attention and effort. At the fifth
stage, the action becomes a complex overt response carried out
automatically and with confidence. Kapfer (1971) also suggests
that a sixth stage may be required in which the individual has
become so skilled that adaptations are readily made to unusual
circumstances or that a new and more effective technique may
be originated. This stage would also appear to involve cognition.
(For a different version of this taxonomy especially suited to
physical education, see Harrow, 1972.)
     As one moves from the cognitive to the affective to the
psychomotor taxonomies, there is a shift from abstract and
deductive mental processes to experiencing and inductive learning. The shift is from cerebral to physical activities, with the last
stage of the psychomotor domain, like the last stage of the
affective domain, involving routinization, habit formation, and
suspension of critical facilities. Kapfer's suggestion of a sixth
level for the psychomotor domain has merit; it would also be
applicable to the affective domain. By this addition, cognition
would be restored to a continuous monitoring role over performances dominated by affective and psychomotor objectives.
Thus the ultimate in all three domains would be effective, efficient behavior with sensitivity to changing circumstance and

with monitoring (low-level evaluation similar to quality control) to indicate the necessity of an evaluation in depth.

Critique of Taxonomies

Since these taxonomies and subsequent studies based upon them constitute one of the most exhaustive, continuing, and productive efforts in the statement of objectives, a detailed analysis of the problems, issues, and difficulties involved is instructive in understanding the task of specifying educational objectives.

The use of the term *taxonomy* stretches the meaning usually assigned in science. A taxonomy should first of all be made up of clearly differentiated, mutually exclusive categories. These three taxonomies are neither clearly differentiated nor mutually exclusive. Second, a taxonomy should be sufficiently comprehensive to provide bases for all possible decisions. Ambiguities make the taxonomies ineffective in this regard. Third, the labels of the categories should be consistent with existing usage. In these taxonomies, the category designations pose some difficulties because the language used in expressing objectives is idiosyncratic and hence inevitably rather loose. Terms such as *attitudes, appreciation, understanding,* and *application* are used in many different ways by writers of objectives. *Appreciation,* for example, is sometimes synonymous with favorable appraisal, at other times with critical evaluation, and at still other times with understanding. Objectives written for the humanities and for the sciences differ markedly in the words used. Furthermore, the attempt in the taxonomies to define terms and use them consistently imposes barriers to their use by teachers who prefer their own terminology and feel that rewording merely to satisfy some externally developed organizational pattern destroys the clarity and uniqueness of their concerns. Fourth, the structure of a taxonomy should define relationships among the subcategories. These taxonomies fulfill this requirement, but their structures are not always consistent with teacher or student perceptions.

Perhaps the greatest deficiency of these taxonomies is that

behavioral objectives usually cut across all three and also strad-
dle several subcategories within each taxonomy. The more complex the behavior desired, the more likely it is that this confusion will result. Nevertheless, the taxonomies do offer a useful
way to analyze the character of a given set of objectives and
then to rewrite them. The taxonomies may be even more effectively used if they are consulted and mastered before the objectives are written.

Problems arise in using the taxonomies as well as in their
definition. The taxonomies do not succeed in differentiating the
cognitive from the affective and psychomotor, and it is well
that they do not; indeed, it probably is not possible. Because
the resulting pattern of interrelationships is confusing, the taxonomies must be used with great care. There is no educational
objective worthy of more than incidental attention at the college level in which cognitive elements should not be the primary
concern. Activities combining cognition, affect, and psychomotor abilities and skills, such as using a complicated piece of
laboratory equipment or performing a surgical operation, are
certainly important, but cognition must be the dominating element.

Separating affective objectives from cognition is dubious
and even dangerous because it implies that emotions are uncontrolled by conscious application of standards or skills. Furthermore, college teachers in most disciplines are teachers because
of interest and ability in the discipline. They have not developed skills in dealing with affect, and many simply are not capable of dealing with it because of their own recognized biases and
conflicts. They are ordinarily reasonably well based in their disciplines, but this orientation makes them neither models nor
mentors for the character development of their students. Obviously, objectives cannot be limited to the cognitive, but all
college-level educational objectives must place cognition as a
central concern, while recognizing that cognition is always
affected by values and by psychomotor skills.

The addition of creativity to the range of objectives also
poses difficult problems for the evaluator. Creativity is always
subjective, and it is not necessarily understood or valued by

others. Creativity often results in products (pictures, literature, inventions) which are initially ignored or ridiculed. And, in any case, traditional learning patterns do not stimulate creativity; many professors are baffled or troubled when it appears.

Another difficulty with the use of the taxonomies is that objectives as stated by teachers tend to fall at the lower stages, particularly with the current emphasis on behavioral objectives (discussed below). Students are expected to learn certain facts, dates, and principles (stage A of the cognitive taxonomy). They are expected to pay attention to stimuli provided by the teacher (stage A of the affective taxonomy). Knowing a principle may mean only the ability to repeat or recognize it as originally stated (still stage A). Understanding (stage B) involves the ability to explain or recognize the principle in variant forms. Application (stage C) poses more difficulty. Since a specific application may have been learned, a task apparently at this level may be met by a stage A response.

Difficulties also arise in determining stages. A problem may be solved using alternative principles and therefore alternative stages. Students asked to find the value of x in the equation $x + 5 = 12$ may use the principle of subtracting the same quantity (5) from both sides of the equation; they may simply recall that $7 + 5 = 12$; or they may try several numbers until they find the correct one. In each case they solve the problem and find the answer, but the processes differ—the first response applies the principle; the second uses memory; and the third is trial and error.

Alternative solutions to problems can be based not only on alternative stages but also on alternative taxonomies. Even relatively simple problems may have various answers depending on the assumptions made and the attitudes and values developed out of past experience. A relatively simple problem, included several years ago in a widely used standardized test, ran as follows: "A father, working alone, mows his yard in one hour; his son, working alone, mows the yard in two hours. How long will they take if they work together?" Proffered answers were "less than one hour, one hour, between one and two hours, two hours, more than two hours." With two lawn mowers, presumably the answer is less than one hour. Alternating in the use of a single mower, the answer might be between one and two hours. Using only one mower, but assuming that weeding and trimming are included in mowing, the answer could again be less than one hour. But a lad who had found by sad experience that working with dad involves many interruptions, discussions, and reprimands might reasonably argue that more than two hours would be the realistic answer. The keyed answer, less than one hour, apparently ignored the number of lawn mowers and was based on the simple and sometimes correct principle that two people in cooperation can do a task in less time than one. This interesting and apparently simple problem thus involves all three domains rather than the cognitive only. Similarly, the objective of planning and preparing a luncheon for four persons, which may be appropriate for certain courses in home economics, involves knowing nutritional principles, aesthetic principles, and table settings. It also requires psychomotor skills; and it might require sensitivity to the tastes of individuals and knowledge of food restrictions because of diets or religious beliefs.

My own conclusion is that the taxonomies are useful tools for thinking about objectives and for analyzing them. I have not found them of much use in developing or categorizing objectives. Human behavior is simply more complicated than the taxonomies admit, and attempts to use them in developing or classifying objectives either put severe limits on the objectives adopted or result in a rather simplistic interpretation of the behavior sought.

Behavioral Objectives

Educational objectives indicate changes expected in students as a result of their participation in specific educational experiences—changes in knowledge, understanding, skills, abilities, and affective characteristics. Behavioral objectives are educational objectives stated in sufficiently specific terms for two interrelated goals to be achieved: (1) the planning of educational experiences can proceed directly out of the statement;

(2) the performance of the individual in attaining the specified behavior can be observed and evaluated. (Behavioral objectives are not new. The concept of operational definition, developed some years ago in an attempt to eliminate hypothetical concepts by phrasing definitions in such manner as to specify the steps—or operations—whereby the physical reality of that concept could be observed or measured, almost immediately led to operational objectives. Such objectives were intended to spell out precisely the performance intended so that it would be observable and evaluatable. Thus operational, performance, and evaluatable objectives may, in some respects, be equated to behavioral objectives.)

The emphasis on behavioral objectives arises out of the dilemmas already discussed. Global objectives such as critical thinking, good citizenship, internalization of certain values, mental and physical health, and preparation for a career have little to do with the planning of education on a day-to-day basis or with the evaluation of student performance. But, at the other extreme, teachers have continued to emphasize specific knowledge and skills for which students currently have no use and which they do not clearly see as relevant to their futures. Thus, objectives either are so broad and ultimate that they give no guidance for educational planning or evaluation or are so specific that education degenerates into a series of unrelated experiences which neither challenge nor give a sense of progress to any students other than those who, like their professors, are interested in the discipline or in knowledge for its own sake.

Most attempts thus far to spell out behavioral objectives have dealt with specific, low-level objectives attainable with limited effort in relatively short time periods. Although these are desirable contrasted with the esoteric, long-term objectives I have noted, the net effect is to convince many critics that the whole movement is a mechanistic, dehumanized form of behaviorism more suitable to rats or pigeons than to humans. Nevertheless, on balance, this pattern of analysis of educational objectives has been and will be useful. Its usefulness becomes especially apparent when the attempt is made to write objectives.

Writing Educational Objectives

A perfectly obvious point is that objectives should state how the learner will behave in the future and indicate the knowledge, skills, attitudes, and values involved in that performance. This is a distinct shift from emphasis on knowledge of specifics, which has frequently seemed to immerse the learner in the past rather than to prepare him or her for the future. Demanding that a student know details about certain authors and their works is quite different from asserting that a study of the authors' ideas and of the effectiveness of their presentation in these works can foster in the student improvement in communication, in sensitivity, in analytical capability, and in evaluation.

In order to evaluate whether these goals are attained and to what extent, the essential details of the behavior must be clearly stated. It may be appropriate to verify knowledge about certain authors and their works, for example, to assure that the student has sufficient background.

Evaluation also requires specification of the conditions under which learners perform. Will they be given a selection from some other author of the same period or genre with a detailed outline or set of questions? Will they be requested to develop their own treatment? Will they be asked to select a recent writer of special interest and adopt his or her insights? Are the insights gained to be applied to current social problems? Is student performance to be under close supervision with time limitations and security or are students to perform at their own convenience? Will answers be written or presented orally (individually or as a panel member)?

Evaluation also requires that there be established criteria. These criteria should be consistent with the behavioral specifications given to the student so that the feedback to the student can be directly related to improvement in performance.

To meet all these requirements when writing objectives, several rules should be followed: (1) Start with a verb (know, identify, describe, compare) that clearly and specifically suggests the exact nature of the student behavior desired. (2) State each objective as a student action, behavior, or product rather than as a segment of content. (3) State each objective as an end result of learning rather than as a learning process. (4) State for each specific objective one identifiable learning outcome which has sufficient generality to have practical meaning to the student. (5) State each objective so that it is attainable by several types of student behavior rather than by a single one. (6) When several objectives are combined in complex behavior, state the more comprehensive objective to avoid isolation and fragmentation.

In framing cognitive objectives, keep in mind that there are several distinct types: (1) content based (describe the nature of the federal judiciary system); (2) skill related (construct charts and graphs to present data in easily comprehensible form); (3) intellectual (relate principles to appropriate problem situations); (4) value related (distinguish good and poor literary selections and give reasons for so classifying them).

Gronlund provides a useful detailed breakdown of cognitive objectives (1970, p. 40): (1) Know basic terms as demonstrated by relating terms that have the same meaning, selecting the term that best fits a particular definition, identifying terms used in reference to particular problems, and using terms correctly in describing problems. (2) Understand concepts and principles as demonstrated by identifying examples of concepts and principles, describing concepts and principles in own words, pointing out the interrelationship of principles, and explaining changes in conditions in terms of the concepts and principles involved. (3) Apply principles to new situations as demonstrated by identifying the principles needed to solve a practical problem, predicting the probable outcome of an action involving principles, describing how to solve a practical problem by use of the principles involved, and distinguishing between probable and improbable forecasts. (4) Interpret data as demonstrated by differentiating between relevant and irrelevant information, differentiating between facts and inferences, identifying cause-effect relations in data, describing trends in data, distinguishing between warranted and unwarranted conclusions drawn from data, and making proper qualifications when describing data. (5) Use critical thinking as demonstrated by distinguishing between facts and opinions, identifying errors in reasoning, distinguishing between relevant and irrelevant arguments, distinguishing between warranted and unwarranted generalizations, formulating valid conclusions from written material, and specifying assumptions needed to make conclusions true.

Objectives which have the characteristics just described are generally longer and much more specific than those which teachers state. For example, a teacher of algebra may assert an expectation that students will learn how to solve linear, simultaneous linear, and quadratic equations. Does this teacher expect that all students will solve all such equations without error? Is it permissible for students to use the textbook or other resources in solving the problems? What are the conditions under which the work is to be done?

Specifically, the objective must indicate precisely what the student is expected to do, specify the tasks, and define an acceptable performance. This objective is phrased to meet these requirements: "Students will write a 300- to 500-word statement about their perception of the relationship of this course to their vocational and life goals." To complete the specification, the time, circumstances, and resources available should be stated. A minimum acceptable performance should also be described including requirements for grammar, spelling, punctuation, specific content, and demonstration of grasp of the course and its relevance to goals.

Because of the scope of objectives at this level, few teachers are likely to follow this prescription in detail. Yet the lack of clear specifications and the consequent lack of definite criteria for evaluation undoubtedly affect student performance. Consideration of these issues, even without the elaboration of objectives, assists the teacher in making clear statements of objectives and good assignments. The evaluation process, too, becomes objective and provides meaningful feedback to the student.

The following are some additional examples of cognitive objectives stated in behavioral-outcome pattern:

*By the end of the algebra course, at least 90 percent of the stu-
dents enrolled will show a 25 percent gain as measured by a standardized algebra test administered at the beginning and end of the
course.*

*By the end of the algebra course, at least 90 percent of the stu-
dents enrolled will be able to solve single linear equations in one
unknown, simultaneous linear equations in two or three un-
knowns, quadratic equations.*

*After ten weeks' study of botany, all students will be able to
specify the major characteristics of twenty plants, will be able to
identify them on sight, and will be able to sort unknown plants
into the taxonomic categories represented by the twenty plants.*

The statement of affective objectives is rather more difficult than the statement of cognitive objectives. Affective objectives can be interrelated with cognitive. If a student is asked to
write an essay on the relationship of a course to career goals,
expressions of affect are to be expected, including interests,
attitudes, and concerns relating to the course, to the projected
career, and to social and economic conditions.

If, however, specific tasks or actions which reveal affect
are desired, a different tack must be taken. The student may be
proffered choices or alternatives indicative of attitudes or interests. This should be done under circumstances in which there is
freedom of choice, no punishment or reward, and no cues or
factors influencing the choice.

Alternatively, behavior may be observed and inferences
made as to the affective qualities involved. This inferential approach is beset with irresolvable difficulties in that observation
or self-reporting can indicate what is done, but not why it is
done. The male student who reports going to three plays while
enrolled in or subsequent to taking a course on drama may only
be dating a young woman with strong interests in drama. The
individual who apparently ignores a crippled or blind person at
a street crossing may be insensitive to the needs of others or

may realize that intervention and assistance are a reflection on another individual's competence and a deterrent to developing it. Attending or not attending a concert is no sure clue to the value one places on music. An individual who does not attend may prefer a different kind of music, may lack the money for a ticket, or may simply dislike crowds.

Obviously, appraisal of affective behavior must not be graded. Evaluation must be directed to the impact of a course on students and be based upon the number, pattern, and range of behaviors (involvement or avoidance) exhibited by the entire group. Not many professors in the arts, sciences, and social sciences are likely to find assessment of affective behaviors by this approach either practical or of much interest. However, in professional fields such as social work, medicine, nursing, and administration, considerable significance is attached to such behaviors.

Summary

The statement of objectives in higher education often has had relatively little to do with instruction or evaluation. Broad institutional goals and purposes are often called objectives and indiscriminately mixed with highly specific learning outcomes. As a result, efficiency (the capacity to produce effective results relative to the efforts and resources expended) is unsatisfactory. Yet, if evaluatable objectives can be stated and clarified, communication about education among students, faculty, administrators, and the public is improved. And accountability, quality control, and budget planning can be directly related to educational processes.

Objectives, to have these effects, must be highly visible and realistic; appropriate, relevant, and related to need satisfaction; reasonably clear in their means-ends relationships; consistent with each other and with some view or philosophy of education; consistent with generally accepted principles of learning; stated at roughly the same levels of generality or specificity; comprehensive and balanced; distinctive; probably not completely independent; and attainable and evaluatable to some defined extent.

In addition, at some level meaningful across departments

and courses there should be a limited number of objectives which individually or collectively subsume all more specific objectives, thus providing for instructors and students a sense of direction, coherence, and continuity presently lacking in much of undergraduate education.

Many objectives are as much process as outcome—that is, they involve abilities and insights necessary for engagement in learning and self-development. If objectives are viewed in this manner, the reiterated objections to them become inconsequential (or perhaps indicative of the uncertainty, unclear motivations, and defensiveness of many instructors). If no objectives are permitted, then the central importance of the materials and documents stands unpolluted by any concern for utility. The discipline and course content are both ends and means.

It seems reasonable to conclude that the weight of evidence is clearly on the side of clear, stated objectives to guide teaching and learning. In colleges it is highly unlikely that objectives will be proliferated to the extent specified in some discussions of behavioral objectives. Indeed, such proliferation is undesirable because it distracts attention from substance and major outcomes. But, if neither teacher nor students have any sense of a destination and direction, no course can facilitate getting there, and, hence, each course will stand alone.

Bibliographical Note

Numerous publications deal with institutional goals and objectives. Much of the literature documents the need for setting institutional goals. But institutional objectives themselves have received thoughtful and deliberate analysis on too few occasions.

Beginning with Martin (1969), this problem has been given increasing attention. Both Martin and Bogard (1974) challenge the myth of diversity in American higher education and in doing so clarify the real issues surrounding institutional goals.

Greenbaum (1974) presents an excellent essay on the implications of the nationally professed ideal of pluralism in education.

Kerr's (1974) analysis of educational policies is not light reading, but should give pause to even the most ardent exponent of educational objectives.

Bloom's (1973) statement on mastery should be read, despite some doubts as to its applicability in higher education.

Cohen (1970), Kapfer (1971), and Maxwell and Tovatt (1970) present excellent analyses and statements about writing course objectives.

Chapter 4

Assessing
Affective Outcomes

Whether affective objectives (attitudes, beliefs, values) are either reasonable or defensible for formal educational programs is an issue upon which profound and irresolvable views have always and will always exist. That affective outcomes are associated with educational programs however cannot be doubted. Comments of students and graduates and studies of attitudes and values by many researchers provide supportive evidence. Even so, the precise nature of the impact of an educational program on values is unknown. It may be negligible or significant in unanticipated directions (the student who takes a profound dislike to mathematics because of a poorly taught course, for example). However, even if students become more liberal and value democracy more highly (commonly stated objectives) following or during a college education, the lack of a clear correspondence between that outcome and specific courses or experiences and the lack of knowledge about changes in other individuals not in the college make hypotheses of causal relationships both dubious and unverifiable. Unless these value changes are accompanied by and are based upon increased understanding of liberal versus conservative views or of democratic versus other forms of government, the change is hardly a credit to higher education. Furthermore, no experience is precisely the same for all involved because of differing backgrounds, values, and perceptions. Therefore, the nature, extent, or direction of affective change varies with individuals and is uncertain and unpredictable with groups.

It is equally true that objectives which specify the nature, extent, and direction of the affective changes desired are risky, dubious, and indefensible. They are risky because it is conceivable that individuals will move in different directions. An authoritarian-oriented individual may move to a position supportive of more extensive democratic participation in decision making. A person who originally espoused a completely democratic group-oriented approach to decision making may recognize the need for expert opinion and for increased coordination of the decision-making process. Affective goals are dubious when explicitly stated because many means of affective modification, such as persuasion, coercion, reward, punishment, imitation, and desire for social acceptance, might seem to be justified to produce the result. But only one—consciously self-directed and accepted affective change, based upon cognitive appraisal of supportive evidence, consideration of implications, and a desire to achieve harmony in knowledge, beliefs, values, and behavior patterns—is educationally defensible. Any other approach (insofar as it is deliberately planned to force or effect value change) varying from subtle direction to coercion and rejection or punishment constitutes indoctrination.

Nonspecification of affective outcomes does not mean however that instruction is value free; this is not possible. The instructor who proposes a value-free approach has thereby placed a value on value free but cannot carry it off. The offering of a course and the selection of texts, references, and topics are judgments in which values are inextricably involved. Even in a beginning chemistry course, the selection of topics, the time devoted to laboratory work, the credits allocated to the course are value judgments. So, too, is the decision as to whether chemistry (or a science) is to be required of all undergraduates.

Value commitments are so interwoven with our thoughts and conclusions that they are often not recognized as values or are confused with demonstrable conclusions. Public support of education is a value commitment widely but not unanimously supported. Whether the major benefits of higher education accrue to the individual or to society is a debatable issue, and those who see higher salaries and increased personal satisfaction as the most significant outcomes argue that individuals should pay all or at least a larger proportion of the costs. Politicians vacillate in espousing public support of higher education, depending upon resource availability, public pressures, and personal priorities. Required attendance through the twelfth grade is also widely supported, yet there are those (the Amish Dutch) who do not believe in schooling beyond the eighth grade. For many educated persons, value commitments in this area are so strong that they accept and interpret only evidence which supports their views.

Within an institution, the provision of courses in studio art, physical education, instrumental music, industrial arts, and home economics is a value commitment not unanimously endorsed by faculty members. Social science, natural science, and modern languages were accepted as suitable in college degree programs only after the prior and long-standing monopoly of the curriculum by the classics had been broken.

Course and credit requirements represent another value commitment. The recent increased availability of interdisciplinary concentrations and the discarding of specific course requirements involve a new set of values still strongly contested by segments of the faculty. This trend reflects a gradual move from a rigid conception of education for an elite to a highly flexible conception of higher education and of who should have access to it.

These trends may be viewed as a shift in view regarding the nature of knowledge and the respective roles of the teacher and student. Knowledge once was generally considered as a set of facts presented by the teacher in a fixed academic frame of reference to students whose task was that of learning correct facts and procedures. The teacher's role was to present facts and methods clearly and possibly to urge or force the students to master them. Some teachers still view education in this way; but as the view of knowledge has shifted from an absolute to a contextual and relative one, ideas of the teacher's and students' roles have also been altered. The teacher's role is more widely recognized now as instigator and supporter of the students' explorations of ideas, concepts, principles, and methods, as synthesizer of these and evaluator of their relevance and appropriate interpretation in relation to the concerns and aspirations of the students as they assume a role in society.

In simpler terms, the shift is from mastery of the liberal arts as a well-defined body of knowledge, attitudes, and values to a liberal education, which frees the student from unwitting acceptance of attitudes, beliefs, and values and thereby encourages and enables him or her to critically analyze ideas and develop a set of examined views and personal commitments. The original concept accepts a basic duality between right and wrong and good and bad and, in so doing, contrasts correct judgments of the faulty with erroneous views of others. There are absolutes and authorities, and obedience to or conformity with these absolutes and authorities constitutes mastery. The new concept vests in individuals the obligation to sort out of contrasting, contradictory, or independent views and beliefs those which constitute for them a consistent, coherent, defensible body of knowledge and beliefs. However, a conviction that everything is relative and that any commitments are therefore unwise and irrational is rejected as an unhealthy view which can result only in acquiescence to expediency, opportunism, and whims of the moment. One who neither stands for nor supports any pervasive values as a guide to behavior ends by standing for anything—and nothing.

Education in this new context is a series of experiences through which the individual moves from an all-or-none, right-or-wrong position to a relative one based upon recognition that the context of a problem or situation usually involves a constellation of values, often in conflict with each other. Some resolution must be achieved by the individual. Education, then, must foster and encourage analytical, synthesizing, and evaluative (or judgmental) abilities by which knowledge and values are organized by the individual into some coherent (though not necessarily consistent, as viewed by others) patterns of behavior based upon present but possibly changing commitments.

Commitment becomes a continuous process of adjustment by which the individual achieves a sense of equilibrium (dynamic and shifting rather than static and permanent) in what is otherwise a chaotic and irrational universe. The stance of the moment is consciously accepted or accorded faith rather than taken as truth. The position is one of considered conformity or judicious disagreement rather than blind conformity, zealous nonconformity, or revolt.

Life is complicated not only by the necessity of continuing reevaluation and alteration of one's commitments but by the various options through which individuals engage themselves with the realities around them. Uncertainty is both the greatest challenge and the most prevalent threat to man. The alternative of certainty, in the sense of knowing what the morrow will bring and being powerless to alter the event, is comforting to some, though frustrating to many who view this as loss of freedom and individual worth. Religions, which have exacted conformity in beliefs and behavior as the price of admission to life hereafter, have attracted devout followers who crave certainty and who thrive on flagellation and a sense of rectitude. Without such assurance of salvation, individuals are driven to make their own decisions on the basis of their own values, but find that any value which displaces all others becomes a vice. One who always says exactly what one thinks (tells the truth) is at least tactless and probably intolerable, yet tolerance itself is no longer a virtue when it necessitates debasing one's own values for the convenience or satisfaction of others.

Attempts to perfect man and society have foundered not simply because some reject the values projected but because the majority, despite inequities and discomfort, would rather endure what is than enter a new and unknown social order. A common error equates the desired with the desirable. What is becomes accepted as what ought to be. The majority preference becomes not simply the norm, but the desirable. Present needs and exigencies are more potent in influencing views and actions than are values, for even when the latter are generally acceptable, a majority agreement on the specifics (either means or ends) is seldom achievable. Only external and extremely threatening situations bring unification of views, and then only to the extent of resisting the threat.

Educational experiences which promote personal and social development should help the individual to move from simple and specific learnings to a realization of complexities in which these and other learnings are involved and ultimately to a grasp of these complexities as a basis for dealing coherently and effectively with specifics. Such an educational process does not involve manipulation or indoctrination. Rather, it is based upon the defensible view that students, through educational growth and maturation, should become sensitized to their own values, constantly reexamine them and attempt to make judgments, accept responsibilities, and enter into activities which reflect and support those values to which they are committed.

Kinds of Values

Examination of values quickly reveals that there are at least three ways of viewing them. First, values are (or can be) choices made by individuals. Second, certain values or interpretations of them become standards or norms in a society; the individual ignores or negates them only at some risk to status and acceptability. Third, some values are universals in the sense that all societies seem to have had standards in regard to these values. These have included beauty, truth, morals, and some set of guiding purposes and means of achieving them. As this sentence suggests, processes which are effective in achieving purposes or clarifying other values may also be regarded as values. Indeed, value has been attached to a process even when that process is not effective in reaching goal values. (The value of salvation and eternal life has been and continues to be sought in various ways with no objective evidence of success.)

The values to which people commit themselves are of various types ranging from affection or respect, desired from or given to others, to wealth and power, which may be used to the benefit or detriment of self or others. Knowledge, skill, a sense of well-being (health, pleasure, satisfaction), or a sense of rectitude have immediate worth to the individual, which is augmented by the respect or recognition of others. Basic needs such as food, clothing, and shelter can be subsumed under these broad values. When basic needs are unsatisfied, all other values may be compromised to attain them.

There is little agreement on absolute or ultimate values and less upon the behavior which supports or forwards them. Hence the values which immediately and directly motivate individuals and groups tend to be either instrumental or process values (power, knowledge, wealth, skill, affection, respect, and rectitude). These values assume importance both because of their instrumental nature and because of their self-reinforcing or mutually supportive character. Wealth, knowledge, skill, and respect all support and interact with power while power also reinforces the attainment of the other values. Any one or all of these values may be turned to attainment of ultimates or simply to self-gratification, pleasure, or satisfaction.

Some ultimate values such as truth, beauty, justice, and freedom have been regarded as absolutes transcending individual, racial, or national preferences. Certainly these values have been universally held, although there is no universal agreement of their best exemplifications. Truth is ever sought, but never fully found (and if this statement be regarded as true, it then negates itself). Standards of beauty vary with time, place, race, and individual. Justice as perceived by some is viewed as preferential treatment by others. Freedom is chaos unless balanced with responsibility and willingness to accept constraints which promote greater freedom for all. Complete individual freedom would signal the demise of any culture and would be as intolerable and repugnant as slavery.

Values involve both individuals and the interaction of individuals. Satisfaction is attained by receiving recognition, affection, or respect and is also attained by giving or withholding it from others. The individual may seek satisfaction or recognition of merit as an individual or as a contributor to the interests and needs of society. Thus the utility of values is found in part by analysis of the benefits conferred on the individual or on society. Values do not in themselves uniquely determine courses of action because more than one value and more than one person is usually involved. Rectitude for some has involved imposition of religious views upon others. The issue is joined in the long conflict between according human dignity to all or to an elect few.

Strategies for Value Change

Strategies for changing the values of others are limited in number. Coercion and persuasion are the major alternatives. Coercion, despite its undesirable connotations, is evident even in democratic societies. The views and values of individuals and minorities are frequently denied by the rules and procedures determined by the majority. Imposing values by coercion deprives the individual of choice or, at best, offers a choice between supporting the prescribed values or suffering deprivation, punishment, or elimination for not so doing. A range of sanctions exists. Deviations are deterred by threats, by punishment, and by banishment. Coercion is most successful and most insidious when individuals become acquiescent because this behavior is less harmful to self and to family or friends than nonacquiescence.

Persuasion, in many of its forms (advertising, for example), is primarily an appeal to emotion and may utilize other values such as a desire for affection, acceptance, power, or money. In its more acceptable form—convincing by rational argument and presentation of evidence—persuasion becomes the preferred strategy. Persuasion does not entirely deny alternatives; rather, it seeks to convince that a preferred value is best for all; and only the integrity of the persuader determines upon what grounds he or she argues for that best. If factual evidence is presented and the value is promoted by demonstration, proof, or rational argument, the appeal is to the intellect.

The distinction between coercion and persuasion is not always clear. When coercion is associated with withdrawal of benefits, it merges with persuasion. Persuasion which offers continued friendship or more tangible benefits in salary increases, promotions, or outright bribes then differs little from coercion. In one case, refusal is attended by withdrawal of benefits (undesirable consequences), in the other, rewards (desirable consequences) are withheld until acquiescence.

Instruments for change are closely related to the strategies of value achievement. Philosophical or religious conversion may result from coercion, from appeal to emotions, expedience, or rational examination. Social and political changes too may come about in any one or in a combination of these ways. Strategies for supporting values in politics are largely persuasive rather than rational. Political change may be indirect or devious in that the ends may not previously have been made explicit.

Ideally, education promotes change toward preferred values by clarifying objectives, by describing present practices and trends, by analyzing existing and alternative conditions, by projecting developments, and by formulating appropriate policy alternatives and practices. But the relationship of specific objectives, alternative policies and practices, and preferred values is usually complex if not obscure; hence policy decisions emerge as much if not more out of affect, compromise, and power than they do from analysis and evaluation.

Revolutions and education present contrasting extremes in ways of effecting change. Revolutions seek instant change, are motivated by intense conviction which has little to do with right or wrong, and usually void—at least temporarily—other values in the rush to change. Education, in contrast, presumably appeals to reason and seeks to bring change over time, recognizing that the ultimate change may be different in extent and character from the expectations of any one person or group.

Terminology

Terminology in the affective domain is not precisely defined. Authors vary in their usage of and in the meanings they attach to the terms. That is why, in the development of the taxonomy of objectives in the affective domain, Krathwohl,

Bloom, and Masia (1964) chose to depart from the traditional terminology by using the categories discussed in Chapter Three —receiving or attending—including awareness, willingness to receive, and controlled or selected attention; responding— including acquiescence in responding, willingness to respond, and satisfaction in response; valuing—including acceptance of a value, preference for a value, and commitment; organization— including conceptualization of a value and organization of a value system; and characterization by a value or value complex as a generalized set.

In more common usage are such descriptors as interest, attitude, fact, belief, opinion, motive, mood, personality trait, and temperament. An attitude is a tendency to evaluate an idea or construct in positive, neutral, or negative terms. An interest is a disposition to attend to (or, negatively, to avoid) certain ideas, activities, or constructs. Interests usually are regarded as involving overtones of pleasure or satisfaction, liking or disliking. Facts are presumably truths, but frequently involve hidden value judgments as in "Columbus discovered America in 1492," which ignores both existing Indian cultures and prior visits by other voyagers.

Beliefs range from matters regarded as factual to assumptions or operating hypotheses. Opinions imply views not necessarily factual or verifiable and probably less firmly held than beliefs. Motives relate to the reasons for seeking something; they are often covert and not necessarily clear to the individual, though guessing or deducing motivations is a favorite ploy of those who decry what someone else seeks. Moods are momentary and tend to fluctuate over time in relation to physical states, environments, and associates. A personality trait is a characteristic usually deduced from recurrent expression of views or forms of behavior which are observed and give rise to the characterization. Temperament is a rather more general term implying a more or less consistent and continuing combination of traits, attitudes, and beliefs. Obviously these terms are unspecific in definition and hence almost useless in attempts to specify and appraise the impacts of education.

Values are difficult to define if one starts from common

usage because they then must cover interests, opinions, attitudes, beliefs, and may be associated with personality traits, motivations, and temperament. It is more expeditious to start from the view that the values of an individual imply commitment to some goals (personal or societal) and a tendency to act in ways which are consistent with those commitments or which support and forward them. A value is belief in the worth of something to the extent that behavior is directed to achieve the ends implied. Some values are process oriented; some are goal oriented; some are pragmatic, utilitarian, or opportunistic; and some are simply self-indulgent. Critical thinking or scientific methods are goals valued as ways of seeking truth. Democracy is a process valued for resolving problems and maintaining social relationships. So are cooperation and compromise. A pragmatic, utilitarian, or opportunistic orientation leads to acceptance of whatever seems likely to achieve an ultimate value or to attain cooperation or compromise. Pleasure or gratification of the moment (rather than long-term good) exemplify self-indulgence.

Values may be aptly characterized as motivations to behave so as to achieve desired values, but in education, the intent is that persons emerge with values of such transcendent importance to them that the values become ends constantly and consciously sought by consonant means.

Values differ from attitudes in being more general or broader in nature, more central and pervasive as guides to behavior, less bound to specific situations, and less subject to moderation or extinction. Attitudes tend to be more superficial and more specific than values and hence are subject to modification—at least when expressed through reactions to words. The development of values is likely to take a longer time than is the development of attitudes and may result from more memorable or dramatic experiences. Values are thus not subject to short-term experimental change, which may explain the disinterest of psychologists who seek to emulate the methods of the natural sciences. They have tended to be interested in specific limited constructs which they designate as attitudes, motives, or personality traits. Values have been more frequently studied by anthropologists and sociologists, who see them as useful in differentiating among individuals and societies.

Assessing Values

In attempting to deal with values, evaluators face four distinct problems. The first is to determine a set of reasonably discrete values and express them by words or phrases which can be adequately defined. Adequacy depends upon whether one wishes to speak to other researchers or to people generally. If the latter, the chosen words or phrases must be those in common use. A second problem is that of characterizing individuals or groups by their value judgments. A third is to determine how people make value judgments. The fourth is to determine how changes in value judgments can be effected.

Assessment of values provides information which can be useful in selection of educational materials, processes, and techniques. In the extreme, presence or absence of certain values could be the basis for granting or withholding credit or even a degree, although the provision would be difficult to enforce and likely subject to legal appeal. Physicians or lawyers who crassly violate professional ethics (a set of values) risk withdrawal of their right to practice. But in the educational process itself, the most significant form of evaluation is formative in nature. By demanding that students reflect upon, verbalize about, and compare with others the value commitments which justify or which are implied by their behavior, we encourage, even force, them to become self-analytical and self-critical about their behavior and to become conscious of, though not necessarily guided by, how others view it.

Table 2 suggests the range of values and value categories to which appraisal might be directed. The categories are to some extent overlapping and the seventh probably could be divided into two or more subgroups. That many of these could be listed as attitudes underlines the difficulty of separating these concepts. Less evident is the fact that positive or desirable values may, if overemphasized, be undesirable. Complete certainty, compulsive cleanliness, and chaotic flexibility suggest the need

Table 2. Values and Value Categories

	Positive or Desirable	Negative or Undesirable
1. Purposive (telic)	Clarity as to ultimate ends and means	Lack of purpose
	Intention, goal orientation	Expedience, opportunism
2. Ethical (moral)	Good	Evil
	Honesty	Dishonesty
	Disclosure	Concealment
	Right	Wrong
3. Aesthetic	Beauty	Ugliness
	Taste	Vulgarity
	Order	Disorder
	Harmony	Discord
	Balance	Imbalance
	Symmetry	Asymmetry
4. Epistomological	Truth, verity	Falsity or error
	Coherence	Incoherence
	Conciseness	Diffusiveness
	Knowledge	Ignorance
	Certainty	Uncertainty
	Completeness	Incompleteness
	Clarity	Obscurity
5. Economic	Conservation	Wastefulness
	Wealth	Poverty
	Utility	Disutility
	Improvement	Deterioration
	Plan	Chance
6. Hygienic	Sanitary	Unsanitary
	Health	Disease
	Pleasure	Pain
	Moderation	Excess or deficiency
7. Social	Accord	Disagreement
	Freedom	Subjection
	Peace	Contention
	Security	Insecurity
	Altruism	Egoism
	Equity	Inequity
	Unity	Disunity
	Order	Disorder
	Reward	Punishment
8. Empathic (interpersonal relationships)	Love	Hate
	Liberality	Parsimony
	Courtesy	Discourtesy
	Friendship	Enmity
	Respect	Contempt
	Sensitivity	Insensitivity

(continued on next page)

Table 2 *(continued)*

	Positive or Desirable	Negative or Undesirable
9. Personal	Rational	Irrational
	Curiosity	Indifference
	Hope	Hopelessness
	Courage	Cowardice
	Wit	Dullness
	Cheerfulness	Dejection
	Content	Discontent
	Pride	Humility
	Vanity	Modesty
	Proficiency	Ineptness
	Confidence	Insecurity
	Success	Failure
	Caution	Rashness
	Sociability	Reclusiveness
	Honest	Dishonest
	Persevering	Capricious
	Motivated	Unmotivated
	Flexible	Rigid, compulsive
	Organized	Disorganized
	Democratic	Authoritarian
	Creative	Unimaginative
	Compassionate	Vindictive, ruthless

for moderation—the Aristotelian mean. Honesty is not always an unalloyed good; beauty can be wasteful; and excess freedom can destroy order.

This extensive list of values includes many that are readily assumed as objectives without full realization that they are values. Thus the epistemological group (truth, clarity, coherence, completeness) is so much a part of the educational process that few teachers realize that they are usually attempting to impose these values on their students. Aesthetic values (beauty, taste, order) are likewise taught rather than so approached as to develop these values in students. Good and right are, after all, relative terms, and judgment rather than knowledge must be the goal. The personal qualities of curiosity, cheerfulness, wit, flexibility, and sociability are also prized by many teachers who reward students for exhibiting them but do almost nothing in providing educational experiences to develop them.

Educators need to become much more conscious of their

own values and promote open discussion and opportunities for pursuing the role of values in thought and action rather than to simply assume that a set of desired values (presumably their own) is to be imposed upon students.

When we try to assess these various value commitments, we realize that neither attitudes nor beliefs (both expressions of values) can be equated to behavior. An individual holding an attitude or belief will not always behave in accordance with it. It follows that the attitudes or beliefs of individuals cannot be assessed from their behaviors. There are many reasons why this is so, but perhaps the primary one is that behavior results from the interaction of many factors including attitudes, beliefs, habits, conceptions of socially approved behavior, sensitivity to the well-being of others, respect for authority, and convictions about the long-term implications of behavior. Almost no behavior is so simple or so isolated that it does not involve some interaction or conflict among several affective elements.

For example, the husband asked by his wife to comment on a newly purchased dress may generally be a truthful person, but his answer at that moment may result from a quick weighing of several considerations. He thinks the dress is horrible, but he wants to read his newspaper rather than explain his dislike. He really doesn't want to hurt her feelings. He may habitually comment favorably on the tastes, statements, and actions of others because he believes doing so advances his status or social acceptability. He believes that he should speak the truth, but he has found it more acceptable to say what others like to hear. He is faced with the dilemma of every evaluator who must balance his integrity against arousal of enmity, which would destroy effectiveness.

Because behavior is not a reliable indicator, those who have undertaken to measure affective characteristics specify other more or less independent dimensions of measurement. Several are reasonably evident: (1) An attitude has direction; that is, it is favorable; neutral, ambivalent, or indifferent; or unfavorable. (Neutrality, indifference, or ambivalence are not necessarily identical, but all three represent a stage between favorable and unfavorable.) (2) An attitude has magnitude; that is, there are differences in the degree of acceptance or rejection. (3) An attitude varies in intensity—that is, in the degree of feeling, concern, or depth of involvement. (4) The generality or specificity of an attitude has much to do with its visibility, for the more extensive its applicability, the more apparent it becomes. (5) Commitment to an attitude involves a cognitive element, a tendency to consciously decide or plan on courses of action that are consistent with and that reinforce the attitude. Whereas intensity has affective overtones, commitment has intellectual ones.

Other dimensions which have been used, such as salience, centrality, flexibility, and imbeddedness (Robinson and Shaver, 1973), cannot be readily separated from the five just offered; and, indeed, the five above, though distinguishable in words, are not readily measurable in practice. Nevertheless, they have some utility in discussion of affective measures, if only in sensitizing us to the complexity of attitudes and values.

Attitudinal research is primarily the domain of psychologists and sociologists who seek to understand the motivations of individuals and groups, the bases for affective predispositions, and their effect on individual aspirations and human interactions. Much of this research is directed to the self-concept and to understanding certain attitudinal tendencies, such as alienation, anomie, helplessness, bias, and rigidity, which endanger the equilibrium of individuals. The research has implications mostly for psychologists, counselors, and therapists but can be useful also in educational settings.

One technique for measurement of attitudes employs reactions to carefully contrived statements. An approach developed by Thurstone (1959) uses roughly equal steps, as gauged by the responses of a norming group, from strongly favorable to strongly unfavorable reactions to the object chosen. This object must be rather specific such as belief in God, cheating, or racial bias. Such scales, being time consuming to construct, are primarily useful in research, although they can be used to assess the impact of an experience by noting the extent of shifts in the positions of individuals and groups before and after the experience.

Another technique (Likert, 1967) presents statements to

which individuals respond by "agree" or "disagree," with the possible insertion of "undecided" or "no opinion" and of more extreme positions such as "strongly agree" and "strongly disagree." Items reflecting a range of views and attitudes are readily written and combined into a single inventory. Several scores can be obtained from a single inventory by weighting and cumulating the responses on all items relating to a single attitude. For example, one set of items could relate to respect for or rejection of authority. One statement to which respondents would react might be: "The instructor should determine the topics to be included in a course." Another set of items might involve the balance between the rights of individuals and minorities versus the views or decisions of the majority.

Such instruments may have limited use in assessing course impacts, but they can be productive in discussions of the values and biases underlying contrasting positions. Both approaches share the weakness that the individual must react to an oversimplified and ambiguous set of statements. The views of business majors regarding the role of a mathematics instructor in selecting topics for a required course in mathematics for business students and the views of mathematics majors in an advanced course for majors involve quite distinct assumptions. The context in which a statement is placed often differs from student to student as well as from one class to another.

A somewhat more realistic technique specifies a situation and requests responses in that context. This technique can be used with considerable success in stimulating discussions about the value of respect for the worth and dignity of the individual, for example. One item might state that a freshman male called a senior woman prominent in campus affairs the evening before a major social event of the year and asked her to attend the event with him. Respondents are asked to indicate the nature and content of her response. Suggested responses might range from "telling him the facts of life" to "canceling her date to help one who obviously needs counsel" to "offering to arrange a date." Each respondent in some manner might defend the chosen response as consistent with concern for the worth and dignity of the individual, although others would disagree.

Apparently factual items can also evoke attitudinal responses. An item might ask what percentage of students is involved in the institutional committee structure. The range offered might go from 1 percent or less to 20 or 30 percent or higher if necessary. Those who have used the technique have found some evidence that the individual's attitude regarding the desirability of such representation and his or her view of the institutional position regarding student involvement markedly influenced the guess as to the actual situation.

Discussion and assessment of assumptions and values in such quasirealistic situations have far more potency in causing individuals to reflect upon their values than the scales earlier described. The scales may lend themselves much more to measurement, but the questions of just what is being measured and what relevance it has cannot be answered in any meaningful way.

The desirable characteristics of adequate measures of attitude are essentially those for other measuring instruments. They should have validity (that is, should measure the specified quality); they should be unaffected by irrelevant factors in the individual or test situation; they should not alter the quality in measuring it; they should spread individuals over a range (that is, differentiate individuals); the results should approximate those obtained by using other adequate instruments; the scores should possess reasonable reliability; and the tests should be reasonably easy to construct, administer, score, and interpret.

These qualities are surely desirable for research, but they are not essential in the teaching/learning context. An instrument used in an instructional situation alters the characteristic involved, invites reflection, and thereby encourages change. This is highly desirable. In fact, in the affective domain, it is difficult to construct instruments which do not affect individuals.

Individuals can never entirely predict their value priorities and interactions in specific situations. They perceive themselves (if they bother to think about it) as holding certain values, and they may perceive an ordering of these values (being right is more important than being accepted); but they find that new occasions involve new interactions and new truths. Actual values lie somewhere between personal ideals and adjustments forced by circumstances. The function of education in reference to values is to encourage reflection upon circumstances, self-perceptions, and ideals; to clarify the ideals sought; and to provide insights, modes of thought, and courage to bring actions closer to the accepted ideals. Thus individuals engage in self-direction and achieve satisfaction in so doing. At the same time they are concerned with how others perceive them. If two persons have similar ideals and values, their interactions should facilitate the development of both toward these jointly accepted ideals. If their values are unlike or even in opposition, their interactions may still contribute to clarification of self-perceptions and hence to differential personal development. Mutual respect may enlarge the commonality of values and cooperation in achieving them or may clarify the points of difference which require avoidance or compromise if continued cooperation is to be pursued.

The affective development of students would be enhanced if they were exposed early in their college program to some of the ideas here presented and if instructors in each course undertook to openly consider the role of their own values in the course, the values implicit in the discipline, the contrasting values of others, including those of individual students, and the values involved in applying the substance of the course to personal and social problems. In assessing the affective development of individuals, major attention should be given to the extent to which the individual becomes sensitized and committed to personal values after realizing, and to some extent accepting, that other persons are motivated by somewhat different values and may also interpret commonly accepted values and appropriate behaviors in distinctive ways.

Bibliographical Note

Numerous references in the Bibliography discuss evaluation techniques and list available instruments for assessing attitudes and values. For example, see Lake, Miles, and Earle (1973) and Pace (1972). Perhaps more important (and more difficult) is the development of faculty concern for affective out-

comes and of educational experiences designed to bring values to a conscious level in the instructional process. Handlin and Handlin (1970), in their discussion of the socialization function of higher education, provide excellent background reading. The books by Rokeach (1973) and Simon (1972) are instructive in identifying the nature and complexity of values. A special issue of *Phi Delta Kappan* (June 1975, *56* (10)), focused on moral values, is useful. Perry (1968) has produced perhaps the most elaborate scheme for identifying the forms of affective development and the nature and directions of changes which may be regarded as desirable.

Chapter 5

Accountability and Attainment of Social Goals

Evaluation and accountability, as applied to education, are interrelated concepts. Both imply a determination of the effects (planned or fortuitous) of educational programs and institutions. But whereas evaluation, as traditionally practiced, has been concerned solely with impact or outcome (effectiveness), accountability adds efficiency—the relation between outcomes and resource utilization. This added concern not only complicates the task but engenders confrontation between academics concerned with quality, traditions, ideals, and personal convenience, and the budget-minded, who focus on costs and have a practical view of educational benefits. Faculty members view those concerned with costs and practicality as external and unsympathetic (if not ignorant) critics who do not understand the

73

essential requirements for scholarly endeavor. There is truth on both sides.

Traditionally, accountability has been largely a legal concept defined by recommended or required procedures in record keeping and financial transactions. It requires clear channels of authority as well as procedures for enforcement and disciplinary action. Accountability may thus be regarded as enforceable discretion and effectiveness in the performance of assigned legal responsibility. It requires procedures for reviewing and disciplining individuals who violate professional ethics or standards. In an academic context, however, responsibility is voluntarily assumed, and performance is guided by adherence to a set of canons or ethics (often inferred rather than stated) and by peer review. External audit by nonacademics appears to academics to deny their own professional role.

In a more limited sense, accountability involves an audit to ascertain whether resources were used for specified purposes according to specified practices or requirements. This interpretation is consistent with current usage in education except that in education the accent is on results more than on the practices used to attain them. In the extreme, the results are guaranteed, and responsibility for learning shifts from students to faculty, administration, and institution. This interpretation has been most evident in the ventures (largely unsuccessful) into performance contracting, in which compensation is tied to results. This extreme view is distasteful and unprofessional in higher education. By analogy, the physician would collect only if patients were cured.

Accountability thus requires output-oriented managers who attain specified results at reasonable (ideally, minimal) costs. External evaluations or audits are required also to verify both outcomes and resource utilization. In addition, performance-incentive systems might be introduced to motivate and reward especially effective use of resources. (Awards for good teaching and research indicate that the incentive system is already used to a limited extent in higher education.)

Demands for accountability arise primarily out of fiscal

concerns. In higher education, until the 1970s, enrollments increased; new and costly programs were added; and faculty teaching loads decreased as faculty became extensively involved in research, political and social activism on and off campus, or profitable consulting activities. Simultaneously, salaries and the proportions of high-ranked and tenured faculty increased. The resulting need for funds could no longer be met in public or private institutions, and those responsible for providing funds began increasingly to ask for an accounting of how money was being spent.

The various other pressures behind demands for accountability may be summarized as follows: (1) student complaints about the irrelevance of their courses and programs and about indifference to their rights and concerns; (2) minority concerns regarding the unresponsiveness of higher education to their particular needs; (3) increasing taxes and inadequate evidence of the need for them and the resulting benefits; (4) widespread doubt about general and specific educational practices and their results; (5) concern that professors have undue control over their loads and working conditions; (6) impatience with the apparent antagonism of teachers and administrators to change or innovation; (7) recognition that administrators have lost authority to such an extent that only external intervention can correct the existing deficiencies and defects.

To some extent, institutions have recognized these concerns and have engaged in self-scrutiny. Offices of institutional research increased in number from 10 in 1955 to 115 in 1964 (Rourke and Brooks, 1966), and institutional research activities (not always so designated) have vastly multiplied since then. But since internal scrutiny tends to produce evidence of the need for increased funding, mandatory statewide coordination, evaluation, and planning have become the order of the day. New programs must be justified and old ones revised on the basis of costs, current relevance, duplication, and need. The demand is not simply for an accurate reporting of how resources are used, but for an analysis of the results obtained and evidence that as good or better results could not be obtained for less expense.

Social Benefits of Higher Education

Demands for accountability are, however, so frequently concerned with particulars that they underestimate or ignore the more general social benefits which higher education should be accountable for providing. Bowen (Bowen and Douglass, 1971) describes social benefits as "enhancing manners and refinement of conduct and beauty of surroundings and thus adding to the graciousness and reducing the tensions of social intercourse." These benefits are both internal (to institutions of higher education) and external (to the society at large). Internally, social benefits improve the character and quality of the interactions within the institution and thus indirectly provide a feedback mechanism to enhance the output.

The external social benefits can be divided (with some residual ambiguity) into contributions to the producer and contributions to the consumer. The producer benefits include (1) new knowledge and technology as a source of economic growth (increased productivity); (2) educated manpower (skilled, flexible, and innovative technicians and professionals) as a source of economic growth; (3) increased incomes, which collectively alter the demand for and use of publicly provided services (through decreases in crime and in welfare payments) and make possible allocation of resources to meet other social objectives; (4) vocational adaptability of employees; (5) identification of talent and consequent increased efficiency in hiring and placing individuals through use of such knowledge as college, major, rank, or point average.

Consumer benefits are reflected in improvements in the quality of social, political, and community life and in values, tastes, and attitudes, and also in educational opportunity. The university, being labor intensive, attracts scholars and researchers who affect the social and cultural life of the region. Industry may be attracted to the region and provide jobs. Educational opportunity is readily available.

The nature of educational benefits is depicted in Table 3. These benefits may accrue to the individual as well as to institutions and society. Many economists limit their attention to pri-

Table 3. Analysis of the Benefits of Education

	Private or Personal	Social
Production of capital	Differential in lifetime earnings	Productivity Identification of talent Knowledge Training of professionals Higher level of demand
Consumption	Personal development: sensitivity, awareness, insight, satisfactions (no monetary index of value)	Changes in social attitudes and norms Improvement in quality of social, political, and community life Educational opportunity

vate producer capital. Apparently they feel that the other categories of benefits are nebulous and nondemonstrable and must be accepted on faith. They argue, too, that the claimed impacts of education on individual and industrial capability, on values, and on knowledge do not closely correspond to societal demands and are not even clearly related to the activities in which the faculty and the universities engage. Yet if private producer capital became the sole concern of higher education, the quality of life would surely suffer.

Difficulties

In addition to not paying sufficient attention to broad social benefits, accountability presents other difficulties. Fundamentally, accountability involves a relationship between two parties in which one is expected to perform certain services or achieve certain results for which the other pays. Depending upon the precise nature of the agreement, accountability may require evidence that the service was conscientiously and fully provided, that the specified results were achieved, that any discrepancy between actual and anticipated results was due to unforeseen factors beyond the control of those providing the service, that the resources provided were used in accordance with original expectations, and that certain rewards were granted or penalties exacted for performance exceeding or falling short of specifications.

The immediate difficulties of accountability programs are readily apparent. The necessity for tight management of resources and personnel, inherent in the process, results in elaborate internal controls over use of time and funds. Specific goals, procedures, and performance standards must be agreed upon in advance so that both parties to the contract have assurance and protection. But because many desirable educational outcomes are unclear and difficult to evaluate, the tendency is for measurable outcomes to be overemphasized and other outcomes, including social benefits, to be ignored.

The opposition of those who are held accountable is another serious difficulty. Faculty members are not unaware of the need for accountability, but as scholars and professionals they view it in a limited and personal context. Faculty members are clearly accountable: to conscience, standards of integrity, and scholarship; to peers who judge scholarship and teaching performance in reaching decisions about promotion, tenure, and salary; to students for quality of teaching and for granting permission to freely and confidentially express their opinions and dissent; and to the institution for policies governing the academic program, for discipline of other faculty members, and for promoting a productive educational environment. Even certain of these elements however are not acceptable to all faculty members. On the whole, for example, they understandably reject the responsibility of policing their own ranks (and other professionals have not done much better).

Given this limited view of accountability, it is not surprising that faculty members reject many accountability programs. The programs have often also been imposed in an atmosphere of suspicion and distrust, not infrequently by those (legislators, for example) whose own accountability is suspect; procedures for assessing outcomes have been inadequate; and those administering the programs have sometimes been bureaucrats who comprehended neither the nature of their task nor its possible effects. Other reasons for failure include importation and use of policies and procedures without adequate discussion and preparation; lack of correspondence between procedures and anticipated results; an organizational rather than an individual orientation leading to misunderstanding, irrelevance, and undue busy work; inadequacy of measures caused by lack of clarity and specificity, irrelevance and oversubjectivity, bias, unreliability, shifting of meaning over time, and multidimensionality of tasks with a resulting lack of any acceptable way to combine evidence into a single index of effectiveness; and lack of correspondence between performance patterns and effectiveness.

Although the concepts of efficiency and effectiveness suggest areas where objective analysis may be possible, this approach also presents difficulties. The distinction between these two concepts is crucial. Steps that purport to increase efficiency may alter effectiveness. Economy drives focusing upon eliminating waste often reduce effectiveness because of the time involved and the irritation provoked. Increasing the number of students per teacher (an apparent increase in efficiency) probably lowers the quality (effectiveness) of education. Questions of cost, effectiveness, and satisfaction are often thoroughly intermingled. Accountability should imply therefore that steps taken to achieve economies will not affect the attainment of program objectives—a difficult task. Analytical methods—operations research and cost-effectiveness analysis, for example—are designed to deal with the complexities involved. Attempts to use such business methods of accountability in education however result in reliance on available data such as credits and degrees. These tell little about the complications of the educational process and nothing about quality.

The method needed is a merger of evaluation, which has typically ignored costs, and accounting, which has typically ignored qualitative values. But this method can pose difficult problems for all interested parties. There are grave deficiencies in the procedures by which colleges define and assess their goals. There are even greater deficiencies in the justification of goals in relation to social needs and to student and public expectations. Faculty members are seldom precise in stating course or program objectives and, with existing means of evaluation, are unable to validate the progress of their students toward educational objectives other than by counting credits and degrees. Clearly demonstrated causal connections between resources, patterns of experience provided, and results are therefore not available. The total impact of a college program on the individual is so uncertain and so fragmented by departmental, course, and program structure that the "value added" (achievement relative to initial capability) is unknown, though often effusively and ambiguously described in college catalogs.

A review of these difficulties readily suggests some requirements for an effective accountability program. These include (1) widespread involvement of all persons concerned in the task of framing goals and procedures and at least as much attention to goals of individuals as to those of the organization; (2) involvement of experts to reinforce the total institutional involvement and to assist in planning, operation, and evaluation of the program; (3) eminently clear statements of purpose and of standards and procedures consistent with those purposes; (4) identification of individuals to whom information will be directed; (5) identification of needs and of particular factors essential to program planning; (6) use of a systematic approach; (7) primary attention to improvement of performance rather than to accumulating information to support personnel actions; (8) inclusion of strategies for encouraging change; (9) allocation of resources in reference to the objectives of the accountability program and in such manner as to facilitate computation of costs; (10) an organizational structure and procedures which inspire confidence; (11) continuous assessment of operations and management, as well as of quality and quantity; (12) external audits of all aspects of the accountability program including the costs of the procedures used relative to the achievements; (13) continuing assessment and development of the staff to assure receptivity to and successful implementation of accountability procedures; (14) feedback to individuals reflecting concern for personal development.

Management

Effective management is essential if these requirements are to be met. But effective management imposes certain other demands: a program of institutional research to conduct continuing studies of operations and results; an effective budget system which relates resource allocation to expected outputs; and a management information system which permits quick, accurate, and adequate summarization and analysis of data. These requirements highlight the importance of using a wide range of high-quality technical experts. Even with the use of experts, a continuing program of education is required to develop the sophistication necessary for use of the results. The attainment of increased effectiveness and efficiency usually requires management to make changes which do not proceed automatically out of extensive analyses.

Management is a term to be used with some trepidation in the academic domain however. It is generally understood by professors and deans that residence halls must be managed in order to reduce indebtedness and that auxiliary enterprises, such as bookstores, food services, intercollegiate athletics, must be managed to avoid financial debacles. It is even accepted that research grants and contracts and off-campus educational community service must be managed to assure balancing of income and expenditure and accountability in the use of funds. Business managers, auditors, comptrollers, residence hall and food services managers are charged with such responsibilities. But there is an apparent hesitancy about attributing a managerial role to department chairmen, deans, academic vice-presidents, and presidents. The concept of professors as self-directed and fully responsible professionals supported to perform their self-defined roles in their own ways seems inconsistent with management, which is viewed as appropriate only to profit-making enterprises. Yet it is precisely this apparent lack of management —especially in the eyes of those external to education—that is causing many of the present difficulties in higher education. The entire paraphernalia of planning, program budgeting, and statewide coordination are attempts to force management upon faculty members and to provide means to determine both the effectiveness and the efficiency of that management in attaining goals which have been stated and given prior approval as the basis for providing resources.

A review of the various solutions proposed to overcome

inadequacies in management reveals some strengths in the solutions but mostly reveals their weaknesses. These various modes for assessment of productivity have sufficiently different methods and goals to require close examination. All fall under what is called a systems approach.

Concepts

A system is a set of objects and of relationships among them and their characteristics. A systems analysis seeks to explain relationships among objects by study of the objects as well as their places and relationships in the system or part of it. Such explanations are derived by building and analyzing abstract models which incorporate the necessary and sufficient relationships of the general systems theory. The task of the systems analyst is to ascertain the alternative decisions or actions available and to expedite decision making by appraising the outcomes and costs required by each.

The systems concept undertakes to unite the contributions of many disciplines. In the social sciences alone, numerous systems conceptualizations exist. Easton (1965) has developed procedures for analyzing political systems. Economics has generated a series of systems analyses (including input-output analysis, econometric models, and cost-benefit analysis); sociology has contributed theories of social systems through the writings of Parsons (Parsons and Platt, 1973) and others. Management has found uses for analytical systems techniques in operations research, management information systems, program evaluation and review techniques (PERT), the critical-path method, cost-effectiveness analysis (differing from cost-benefit analysis by its inclusion of nonmonetary objectives), and planning-programming-budgeting systems (PPBS). These approaches provide many logical, systematic, comprehensive, and, above all, rational ways to view problems.

The basic steps of systems analysis are the identification of objectives or goals (or, in the vocabulary typical of the fields of application, the benefits, returns, payoffs, effectiveness, and utility desired); the identification and evaluation of the alternatives in inputs and in processes required to produce the outcomes, including the determination of actions, strategies, and policies based upon the probable returns in relation to costs; the organization of an integrated, operating system with appropriate controls and feedback; the review, audit, and evaluation of the product and of the costs and effectiveness of the procedures utilized. It is apparent that except for terminology the preceding four steps are as descriptive of evaluation as of systems analysis.

A systems approach poses explicitly a problem also faced in evaluation. Just what is the scope or what are the dimensions of the task, problem, or system to be analyzed? Most systems are parts of still larger systems, and any complex system is composed of interrelated and interacting elements, subsets of which often form a subsystem. Complex systems must usually be broken into subsystems for analysis, but even these may be so complex and so affected by factors which are unrecognized or ignored for simplification that realistic models and modes of analysis are difficult or impossible. Accordingly, complex systems research is negated by the costs involved. Simulation by computer has probably been the most productive approach, but even computer models have generally been vastly oversimplified. The national economy, a state school system, or a large university are too complex for effective direct attack. Development of educational models requires attention to costs, student flows, dropouts, staff requirements, instructional processes, curriculum, and effects on the economy and society. Models involving some subset of these are possible, but, even with this attempt to simplify, such complexity remains that no institution or school system has carried out a systems analysis to the point of attaining and applying fully satisfactory models for prediction and control. The National Center for Higher Education Management Systems at the Western Interstate Commission for Higher Education (WICHE/NCHEMS), described by Haight and Romney (1975), has done by far the most comprehensive job to date.

Since systems analysis has developed more in a business or engineering context than in an educational one, there has been a tendency to use concepts not commonly occurring in discussions of educational evaluation. Nevertheless, the terms have relevance, and they assist in bringing into focus some decision points often missed.

Trade-off occurs when analysts attempt to determine the mix of inputs or resources which will achieve the greatest effectiveness. Some resources must be given up, or traded off, in this process. Effectiveness, here, might be variously defined in terms of unit costs (emphasis on quantity) or of quality. Alternatives might focus on maintaining (or reducing) unit costs and improving (or maintaining) quality. Thus two or more manpower mixes may be equally effective in achieving certain economic goals, but one mix may be less expensive than the others or result in superior quality. Trade-offs may also be made with regard to goals or objectives. If an objective is difficult or overly expensive to achieve, an alternative objective should be pursued.

The *pay-off matrix* exhibits the returns for the different actions which are under the control of the decision maker. The results may be compared with each other and with the effects of states of nature—that is, the variation resulting from variables not under the control of the decision maker may be determined. For example, the disabilities or disadvantages of the students in a program can overshadow the positive effects of various methods of instruction.

Feedback is an essential element in the analysis and operation of any system. Feedback should be provided at various stages as well as at the conclusion. Blind pursuit of a process without determining its effectiveness at various stages is wasteful in that too large a percentage of the final product will be unsatisfactory; the efficiency of various stages of the process will be unknown and, hence, not subject to correction.

The *constraints* under which a system operates must be identified. These constraints may be internally or externally imposed and may involve limitations of resources; space, equipment, personnel. They may involve attitudes and values which effectively bar certain approaches or the positing of apparently reasonable or logical principles or assumptions. Political considerations weigh heavily in any attempt to establish a system in an area affecting many people.

Education is provided with *resources* in the form of dollars, space, manpower, equipment, and time. These are joined and interact or are acted upon in *processes*—classes, laboratories, seminars, independent study—which involve both interpersonal activity and environmental impacts. These process elements are organized or structured by formats such as disciplines, fields, curriculums, schedules, calendars, and are administered by departments, institutes, centers, and colleges. And from these processes various *benefits* emerge: educated manpower, new knowledge, and a range of public benefits extending from the cultural impacts of an institution on the immediate community to agricultural and medical advances which have worldwide implications.

Productivity occurs when materials or people are subjected to these processes, which affect them so as to yield something different from the original in form or quantity and in utility, quality, or value. Productivity reflects the effective management of resources, processes, and organization to achieve specified objectives. It is usually desirable (and necessary) to view separately such factors as faculty productivity and the productivity of instructional processes and curriculum and course structures, as well as total program or institutional productivity. Productivity is constructive, not destructive; it is measured by the relation (difference or ratio) between the value of the original and the value of the new. The basic task of accountability programs therefore is the assessment of productivity by some procedure.

Productivity Model

To assess productivity five issues must be resolved. The first is the level at which productivity is to be examined. This decision depends in part upon the type of productivity considered. Student credit hours may be used as evidence of individual, departmental, college, or university productivity. Assessment of teaching effectiveness is most useful when applied to the department or individual.

The second issue is the type of productivity to be assessed: student achievement, research, or services. Both immediate results (cultural impacts) and deferred results (research, leadership) occur. Some types of productivity, such as faculty research and improved instructional materials and techniques, feed back immediately into the processes or structures, thereby increasing the efficiency of the operations. The third issue is the measures used: credit hours, degrees, test scores, achievement of graduates. The fourth issue focuses on the manipulation of the data, the computation of indices, and the formulation of a judgment regarding them. The fifth question is whether quantity, quality, or both are to be assessed. The difficulties in agreeing upon and assessing quality make for weaknesses in the assessment procedures and thereby determine the answer to the question.

There are many categories of productivity and a large number of possible data sources in each. Faculty activities include teaching, advising, research, professional development, and committee work, among others. Information about teaching is provided by credit hours, contact hours, clock hours, types and levels of instruction, effectiveness, and grade distribution. Professional activity in the broadest sense may be gauged by total hours of work, hours spent in various activities, percentage of time spent, or accomplishments. Faculty stature is revealed by awards and professional recognition.

Student-related outputs include cognitive, affective, and psychomotor learnings. But these are usually ignored for lack of satisfactory evidence, and evaluators concentrate instead on such matters as choice of career, completion of stages in preparing for that career, salary level, employment, community involvement, commitment to democratic principles, and motivation.

Institutional productivity is reflected in degree output, faculty-student ratios, research output, and benefits to the society and economy. Public service includes all activities in which university resources are used to benefit the general public: consulting, service of faculty and staff on boards and commissions, editing, accreditation activities, museum, library services. It is desirable to distinguish between services which are wholly or partially reimbursed and those which are not, and, further, to determine whether the reimbursement goes to the institution or to an individual.

Research outputs include expanding the horizon of knowledge and solving industrial, social, and political problems. Research may be sponsored or accomplished with university general funds. It may be a by-product or an integral aspect of graduate instruction or an independent activity. Creativity in the arts may simultaneously provide a cultural boon to the community, training for students, and recognition for the faculty and the university.

This already plentiful array of possible specific outcomes can be further augmented by adding such broad purposes as socialization of students, production of trained manpower, certification for entry into the professions, social mobility, and provision of a sanctuary for scholars and artists.

This range of outputs negates the possibility of full assessment of all contributions, yet limitation to any subset will be viewed as unfair to some institutions, departments, or faculty members. In some universities, a single output may be the product of an identifiable process or unit, whereas in another university that same output may be the composite accomplishment of several processes or units. And in still another a single process may have multiple outputs. Furthermore, the same outputs may result from quite different combinations of inputs. Hence, any attempt to define a subset of independent goals (in which alteration in the level of accomplishment of one in no way affects the others) will fail.

Thus, the assessment of university productivity is a complex task, and as long as the pressure for it is external and based on a single structure presumed appropriate for all, it cannot be equitable. External attempts at assessment also tend to shift from year to year as changing personnel veer from one scheme of management to another and from one mode of analysis to another. These shifts in emphasis cause continuing disruption and ensure that no progress is made in assessment of productivity. Meanwhile, productivity itself is threatened by the diversion of administration and faculty efforts to meet continually changing external demands.

Productivity is measured by comparing output with input. In higher education the inputs include many elements: labor (with many different levels of skills and many different special-ties within skill levels), capital, land, facilities, equipment of diverse and specialized types, knowledge, management skills, and raw materials. The outputs, also of many types, are analyzed in reference to the values added by the activities or processes carried on in the institutions. But there is difficulty both in agreeing upon the objectives and in assessing the stage of development of students at the beginning and at the end. There are gains in knowledge and in emotional and social development. And society and the economy reap benefits from the efforts of educated persons acting individually and cooperatively.

Weaknesses in this productivity model are caused not only by ambiguity in objectives but by uncertainties about the nature of the processes. Higher education is a labor-intensive activity, and, despite the available technology, faculty members pursue traditional patterns and students resist automation and speed-up. But education is also quality intensive. Professors, committed to quality although uncertain how to define it, insist that any attempt to achieve efficiency by altering the number, pattern, or rate of personal interactions destroys quality. Recognizing that animosity to change or discomfort with new procedures may have unanticipated impacts on both teachers and students, we can see why this lowering of quality may occur. Indeed, teachers cannot indefinitely increase productivity without endangering quality.

The productivity model also applies more readily to instruction than to other purposes and functions of higher education. Hence its use can overemphasize direct instruction and the teaching faculty, who become proxies for all instructional inputs. Credit hours, which in no sense reflect quality, become the most used output measure because they are the most tangible. The effects on productivity of technology, equipment, management, and facilities are seldom assessed because their interactions are too complex. The tendency, therefore, is to compute and compare output with number of full-time-equivalent instructors or with dollars. If the concern is with labor efficiency, output per instructor provides an index. Output per input dollar indicates capital efficiency, and input in dollars divided by units produced yields unit cost. If output is measured in student credit hours, the mean number of student credit hours produced by a full-time faculty member or the mean number produced per dollar are regarded as evidence respectively of labor and of capital efficiency. Cost per credit hour or cost per full-time-equivalent student tends to replace any measure of quality. With increases in numbers of students, increased funds are sought on the basis of costs. And since there are no accepted standards of cost per student based on carefully planned models and specifically defined outcomes, costs (actually partial or direct instructional costs in most cases) become the bases for program comparison.

In cost studies, a combination of assumptions and traditional practice effectively prevent significant change. These assumptions have to do with equity in faculty loads within and among departments and with a conviction that quality is related to workload and class size. Despite widespread rejection of the concept, for purposes of fiscal control, credit or contact hours taught commonly serve as surrogates for total faculty load. These simplistic procedures effectively discourage analysis in depth, adequate planning, and evaluation, which would permit effective communication with the public and justify the use of public resources.

Attention may be directed also to the marginal costs involved in adding a few students rather than to costs per student. Increased enrollment up to a point at which increases are required in faculty and facilities surely can be on a marginal cost basis. Indeed, if classes are small and some instructors have below-standard loads, an increase in students (properly distributed) can result in greater efficiency and in reduced costs. But increased burdens beyond the planned model may endanger quality by imposing a less efficient process or structure—that is, larger classes, crowded facilities, increased load. And at some point increases will require added facilities that do not seriously alter long-term costs but require an immediate major infusion of money if quality is not to be permanently impaired.

Higher education, apart from its utilitarian or economic benefits, is an investment in knowledge and value. Society becomes, in part, what educated people make it. Higher education is not a business; it is organized on entirely different lines. A more appropriate model is that of a group of professionals who choose to join together for increased efficiency and effectiveness. But this model also fails because higher education is not self-supporting; it depends upon continuing and increasing infusions of private and public funds. And it is here that the conflict is joined—accountability demands are justified by the support but resented by the implied negation of the professional role of the faculty. Because of both these built-in conflicts and the esoteric and uncertain nature of much of the product, productivity analysis tends to overemphasize direct instruction; view faculty time commitments as proxies for all instructional inputs; regard credit hours as outputs; ignore learning processes; disregard quality; and underestimate or ignore the contributions of capital inputs, technology, management, and equipment.

Furthermore, in education the distinctiveness of input, process, and output is not always clear, and, indeed, the definitions may undergo alteration in accordance with the emphases. If the university is thought of as including facilities, equipment, and faculty engaged in processes of manipulation, analysis, and synthesis, then the input may be viewed solely as students, dollars, and accumulated knowledge acted upon by the university to modify (improve) student capacity and to add to knowledge and adapt it to meet existing social needs. The processes are determined in part by the nature of the input and by the objectives which specify the nature of the products. Alternatively, the students, faculty, facilities, and even the objectives may be viewed as inputs. The processes are then defined as the interactions of these inputs to produce the desired outputs.

Either concept has mechanical or industrial implications which fall harshly on the academic ear. The idea that the faculty, whether regarded as input or as a component of the process, might be selected or modified to facilitate the molding of inputs into the desired outputs opposes the prevalent faculty view that faculty members selected for excellence in scholarship determine both objectives and processes.

In industrial processing, input is usually selected so as to minimize processing costs in attaining a desired product. Highly selective colleges have operated on a similar basis, but equal opportunity has become more important today than efficiency or expense. With open admissions, both processes and product may have to be redefined. More elaborate, more expensive processes and greater periods of time may be required to obtain products of equal merit. If alternative educational programs are to be compared in costs or effectiveness, the objectives—that is, the desired products—and the inputs of the program must be closely comparable. But there is no satisfactory way to compare alternative outputs, such as research with degrees. Only if all factors were definable in dollars could such comparisons become possible.

Much of the problem of input-output analysis as applied to higher education lies in the fact that the demand for it comes from outside the institutions. Suspicion of these external motives and concern about misuse of data do not provide a good basis for sound internal analysis. Neither faculty members nor administrators think in terms of alternative programs or processes; they decry emphasis on outcomes and objectives which are not easily agreed upon; and they usually ignore many unintended, incidental, or side effects considered of great value. Faculty and administrators, too, are united in resisting external incursion into university operations and react much more to crises in resources and their impact on programs and processes than to demands for statements of objectives and effectiveness in reaching them.

Input-output analyses also require some basis of comparison. Achievement of stated goals has little meaning until the goals are associated with historical data from the same institution or norms based on other institutions. But comparability raises many issues, some of which are at the heart of the difficulty in effecting input-output analyses in higher education.

Many persons (not solely educators) doubt that comparability is possible because of difficulties in definition and collection of data. Suspicion of misuse or unfair use of data, resulting in the reduction of all programs to some common level of mediocrity, militates against data exchange by educators. In contrast, proponents of exchange view it as the only course to more intelligent use of resources. There are some obvious requirements to be met if comparability is to be achieved. There must be common definitions and specified procedures for collection, analysis, and display of data; data must be relevant to major decisions; practical and relatively inexpensive modes of data collection must be used; effective collection and use of data should be encouraged and rewarded. And unless institutions are to be forced into some common pattern of organization, programming, and budgeting, there must be opportunity for explanation of atypical situations.

These requirements are not easily fulfilled because of inherent limitations in higher education. Differences in data are too easily accepted at face value without full understanding of possible underlying factors. Lack of accepted and valid indicators of the results of education carries with it the danger that inadequate indicators will be imposed. Problems of comparability arise both within and among institutions because activities or programs within an institution may undergo marked change over time and thereby destroy comparability. Even apparently similar programs within an institution may not be comparable in many respects because of distinctive histories, commitments, and quality. Standards or criteria common to units to be compared are essential, but do not always exist. Difficulties existing in one institution are multiplied in comparisons among institutions.

Yet, comparisons may well become the basis for supporting programs, and willingness to engage in comparison may be necessary to overcome public doubts about higher education. If adequate recognition can be given to the impact of diverse geographic, cultural, economic, and environmental conditions; differences in role, organization, and operational patterns of institutions; institutional and program history; interactions with other programs; program size and economies of scale, then valid and useful comparisons may be made. Even then, comparisons or differences should be analyzed to understand why they exist, and they should not be blindly used to force homogeneity and conformity and thereby destroy autonomy.

In addition, an assessment or inventory of outcomes should include all outcomes—intended, unintended. Although it would be desirable to define outcomes which are mutually exclusive and to relate them uniquely to particular programs, this is not possible. Graduate degrees and research are closely interrelated and interdependent. Any particular degree or research project may be the result of the combined efforts of several budgeted units. Overlap and a degree of redundancy in defining outcomes may be expected. Outcomes should also be so defined and assessed as to avoid value judgments. In a university, this is well nigh impossible since quality is not presently measurable and many other outcomes of value are unintended and unanticipated. Thus, the outcomes measured and used are those which can be counted or measured. But value judgments are involved in this measuring or counting process. When student credit hours are accepted as a major output, it is clear that arithmetic concerns have won out over qualitative ones. Naturally, if student credit hours pay off, the goal of the instructional staff becomes that of producing student credit hours; students will not be granted credits by examination since there is no payoff attached.

Since outcome measures influence both process and input, numerous criteria must be met by an outcome measure before it becomes acceptable for decision making. Any outcome measure should be valid. It should also be reliable—that is, yield consistent and reproducible results. The procedures, sources, and methodology for collection of data should be defined in depth to ensure comparability in time and among institutions. The measures used must be feasible both in time and costs.

Outcome measures should generally be chosen to avoid alteration of the process. If counting credit hours shifts the focus of instruction from learning to maximizing student credit hours, great damage has been done. However, if the emphasis on credit hours enforces a recognition that credit hours have been assigned to courses without adequate rationale and have been carelessly handled and accumulated, correction of these weaknesses may be strengthened by data-collection procedures and even cause some change in the definition of the learning process.

Data-collection procedures should not infringe on individual privacy, and they need not do so. A community college, for example, does not require detailed reports of grades and other information on all its transfers to senior college in order to assess program effectiveness. A particular research project might require such evidence subject to adequate controls. Regular follow-ups can be conducted on summary data for an entire group.

PPBS (planning-programming-budgeting system) is a form of input-output analysis which emphasizes consideration of alternative processes and a priori requires comparison of costs and values to facilitate a decision as to the product sought and the procedures employed. The alternatives may require different inputs and processes. Input-output analysis, in the more traditional sense, focuses on the relationship between input and output and would alter processes when the output is inadequate or the cost unduly high. Input-output analysis, in this sense, is more acceptable to higher education than is PPBS, for it tends to accept existing objectives and procedures. Moreover, it does not specifically call for long-term planning, which is a major purpose of PPBS. Quality receives largely verbal recognition in both patterns, although traditional input-output analysis tends to ignore quality entirely and to concentrate on unit costs.

The purpose of PPBS is to improve management decisions in allocating resources to attain specified objectives. This goal requires that activities be associated with programs for which both benefits (contribution to objectives) and costs or resource utilization can be determined. The number of programs identified should be kept within reasonable bounds to ease the task of analysis.

The primary phases of PPBS are these:

1. Planning includes both identifying needs and the priorities among them and defining the fundamental goals and objectives to meet these needs. Planning goals may be projected for five to ten years ahead, although any but the most general projections beyond five years are seldom of much value to a college or university.

2. Programming is concerned with specification of alterna-

tive sets of activities and services required to attain program objectives. A program is made up of a set of coordinated or interrelated services or activities which are intended to contribute to attainment of one or more of the accepted objectives. A program structure relates program activities to goals and objectives. The program budget sets expenditures for a specified period of operation, usually by year.

3. Budgeting involves the development, first, of a long-range financial plan related to goals and objectives and, second, of the details (including the next year's budget).

4. Evaluating initially involves choosing among alternatives and later involves assessing outputs, progress in reference to long-range goals and objectives, and efficiency and effectiveness in the use of resources.

Goals, as used in PPBS, are differentiated from objectives in being broader in scope and less specific in content. They may even be essentially timeless as, for example, the achievement of excellence. A college may be committed to the goal of developing character. This goal, while meritorious, lacks meaning, gives little direction, and cannot be evaluated without greater specification. Objectives are specific; they state who accomplishes what and when and in what time frame. An objective must be made sufficiently clear by defining criteria of attainment. Objectives do not specify how, where, or why. How and where relate to methodology or process. Why involves a value commitment which is usually included (implicitly if not explicitly) in the goal statement.

The process of program budgeting involves several identifiable steps, although they are interrelated and do not necessarily occur separately or in the order here presented.

1. Establishment of goals and objectives. Program budgeting uses institutional goals to compare alternate programs. Programs that best meet the goals using available resources are preferred. Translation of goals into measurable objectives is necessary for evaluation and determination of success as well as for the next step.

2. Development of alternative programs, strategies, or processes that might achieve the goals. In higher education,

some confusion is caused by this use of program. A degree program is regarded as a series of courses and experiences producing specialization or competence in a discipline, a problem area, or a profession. The program may be carried out through various patterns of courses and experiences so that alternative strategies or processes rather than alternative programs would be a more appropriate term in the university (Parden, 1972, p. 12).

However, if one of the goals is a broad concern for health, a number of alternative health science programs might be considered with choice among them being made on the basis of social needs and institutional capabilities and resources. The program selected constitutes an attempt by the institution to meet a selected set of objectives consistent with the broad goal.

An institution may seek to be unique or experimental in its objectives, programs, educational processes, and environment, or it may opt for a traditional approach. An educational institution, once committed to certain programs and its philosophical undergirdings, finds it difficult to eliminate the program or materially alter it unless new funds are available. Change can take place only over the long term as individuals die or depart and resources can be reallocated. The intent of program budgeting is to force review of all existing programs in order to compare them with new and needed alternatives.

3. Estimation of the total support or resources required for each alternative. In the university this task is difficult. A graduate specialization in counseling may utilize courses from the departments of psychology, education, and sociology; it may involve internships served in administrative offices, the counseling center, residence halls, the health services, cooperating colleges, and social service agencies; it certainly requires library facilities, offices, equipment, administrative services, and facilities for research. In some respects, the program yields services which must be balanced against costs. And costs may vary materially with the stature and rank of the faculty, the relative emphasis on practice or research, and the stipends and credits given for internships.

The decision as to whether an activity provides a program of its own or merely contributes to others may be a key one in the continuation and reinforcement of the activity, for activities whose benefits as well as costs are regularly appraised inevitably have a preferred position in acquiring new resources. Since the costs of an activity are usually assigned to departmental or college programs, the possibility of alternative uses of those dollars generates tension when resources are tight or even when programs are under routine review.

4. Estimation of the benefits of each alternative. This is a difficult, even impossible, task if one attempts to specify all benefits for all persons. Individuals achieve unique and unplanned benefits; and anticipated benefits do not accrue equally to all. Communities benefit from the presence of colleges, although these benefits are seldom adequately recognized or assessed. Both long-term and short-term benefits should be assessed, but the long-term ones, especially, can seldom be related to any particular program feature. Hence, the relationship of benefits and program alternatives has not been—and never will be—fully ascertained.

5. Consideration of the long-range fiscal implications of the plan. Program commitments have long-term implications usually requiring additional funds in each subsequent year. The introductory period for any new program (even though costly on a per-credit-hour base) generally tends to be much less expensive than in later years, when a mature faculty offers all phases of the program. Moreover, new programs interact with and may cause increased expenditures in existing programs. Proponents of new programs tend to overlook if not ignore the rapidly increasing costs of new programs in the immediately subsequent years.

6. Determination of the annual budget. The ideal, seldom attainable, is that the next projected annual budget be the initial one of the long-term projection. The difficulty is that actual budgets are almost invariably less than either the requested or the expected budgets. Yet corresponding reduction of subsequent budgets in the long-term plan to preserve the appearance of continuity encourages only further reduction the next year. This step brings out the major weakness of PPBS. It attempts to reduce to a logical, rational basis that which is, and always will

be, in large part, a political process even within private institutions.

7. Evaluation of program success by appraisal of both benefits and costs. The operation of the program must also be examined, for only as the specific program operations are related to success or failure is it possible to diagnose strengths and weaknesses and make recommendations for improvement.

8. Alteration of the program in one or more of the following ways: modifying objectives or expected levels of attainment; introducing alternative methods, policies, or processes; discarding the program as overly expensive or nonproductive; replacing the program by another of nearly equal priority.

9. Repetition of steps 1 to 8 with the new program.

Obviously, every university goes through something approximating these steps. However, development of a long-range program and continual updating in reference to changing social needs and pressures, institutional aspirations, and fiscal exigencies are time-consuming tasks. Moreover, they are ineffective unless large numbers of persons are involved and share in the visions created. But when many persons are involved, deliberations move slowly, and disillusionment may attend funding setbacks which destroy significant aspects of the plans. Those whose programs were not included may continue to press for alternatives or subtly move to sabotage accepted projects.

Drucker (1964) and McGregor (1960) have been credited with developing another form of input-output analysis, management by objectives (MBO), although there is basically nothing new in the concept. The experienced educational evaluator may marvel that a concept which has long been used by well-managed institutions with explicit goals and objectives should have been regarded as originating in business and industrial studies. There have been numerous reports and discussions of MBO, but relatively little evidence of success, possibly because MBO has been more of a slogan than a well-defined approach to management.

Early discussions of MBO emphasized the involvement of subordinates in specifying objectives or goals and developing criteria for performance evaluation. The typical pattern requires each administrator to develop objectives compatible with those for the overall organization as stated by the chief administrative officer. After the objectives, priorities, and required resources for a specified period (perhaps the next year) are approved, these objectives become the basis for setting objectives at still lower levels. Each level is then held accountable for attainment of the agreed-upon goals. Involvement of all levels in defining goals and individual responsibility for their attainment have been viewed by most MBO authorities as essential factors in motivation and ultimately in successful application. Goal achievement can then be evaluated, and the performance of personnel, in turn, can be evaluated and rewarded on the basis of attainment. Originally, it was anticipated that the imposition of goals would improve performance, but, in practice, the process of goal setting itself has become a method of achieving increased morale through interaction and unity of purpose. Thus, the emphasis of MBO has shifted from summative to formative evaluation.

Goal setting involving subordinates is closely associated with feedback and performance evaluation, but, again, the emphasis is less on accountability than on increasing effectiveness through the motivation which results from participation in assessing goals, roles, and achievement. As Odiorne (1965) indicates, MBO continues to be a procedure for defining common and interrelated goals of managers at various levels, for defining the role and responsibility of each individual in producing specified results, and for using the results achieved in evaluating individual efforts and increasing management effectiveness. However, these results now tend to be regarded as the result of improved working conditions and morale rather than of the rigorous imposition of goals.

One technique sometimes used with MBO relates compensation to results by granting merit raises for successful and timely completion of objectives. The impact and hence the appropriateness of this technique have been a subject of some discussion. It may not be relevant in all circumstances, especially in educational institutions. Tosi and Carroll (1970) note:

Goal attainment should be organizationally reinforced, and the reinforcement should be different for individuals, as a function of their own attainment. The use of an "objectives" approach in conjunction with a compensation program may also result in less dissatisfaction with the allocation of compensation increases made. Certainly there is virtually universal agreement among managers that rewards should go for actual accomplishments rather than for irrelevant personal characteristics and political or social standing.

The underlying concept of MBO is quite simple and analogous to that of evaluation in education: If you know what you are trying to do, you are more likely to accomplish it. The major accomplishments of MBO are seen as (1) providing common purposes and goals for the entire institution; (2) forcing top administration to constantly define and review goals and priorities and relate resources and individual assignments to these goals; (3) indicating specific tasks for each person, providing for accountability and relating individual efforts to the total task; (4) assuring that institutional goals are known and understood and that they continually provide direction for each individual.

Yet, the extent to which MBO has been successful is at best uncertain. Much of the writing and reporting have been, like that on educational evaluation, inspirational, optimistic, and prone to claiming results which are uncertain at best and probably related more to individuals and particular techniques or circumstances than to MBO. Such apparently reasonable generalizations as the following are presented: higher performance occurs when goals are specific rather than general or nonexistent; successful achievement leads to formulation of higher goals; participation in goal setting improves both performance and job satisfaction.

Ivancevich (1972), reviewing empirical research on MBO, found relatively few good studies. In his own study of two medium-sized organizations which implemented MBO, he concluded that the effects were short lived: "When perceived job satisfaction of participants was examined, there were no significant differences before external change-agent intervention and MBO training and measures twenty months after these events" (p. 126).

Alternative Models

The *investment* model views educational expenditures as investments in people which beneficially affect the economy. In contrast with the production model, in which educational expenditure is the input, education is the input, students are made into effective producers, and the outputs are consumer goods or manpower supply. Schultz (1963) and Becker (1964) have contributed to this approach. The crux of it is the determination of the rate of return for various levels of investment in education. Whereas the productivity model places much of the emphasis on costs and tends to ignore societal benefits in favor of individual benefits, the investment model suggests that careful management of the investment in education should increase the social returns. Reduction in welfare rolls, imprisonments, and protection services, which might conceivably result from more education, would reduce expenditures in these categories while permitting those persons on whom the money would have been spent to add other goods and services. Benefits would thereby be multiplied. This model shares with the production model the tendency to denigrate the importance of liberal education goals and replace them by concern about manpower and about the development of human resources to meet governmental and economic needs. Concern for and attention to individual development is either discounted or supplanted by concern for the preparation of individuals to fit various niches in the social order. The investment model, while encouraging educational expenditures, emphasizes materialism rather than individuality and humanism.

The *motivation research* model is more characteristic of business and industry in the United States than it has been of schools. Advertising on a grand scale, frequently highly dubious in both its appeals and its claims, has sought to create a demand for products to meet latent needs. The products may be demonstrably in no way superior to those attainable at less cost. Proponents of educational technology have at times seemed more concerned with motivation for use of their products than with the motivation or improvement of student learning. Some innovative educational programs, relying heavily upon group interaction and the stimulation of affect, have avoided formulation of educational objectives and argued that personal satisfaction and development of individuals in idiosyncratic ways should characterize the educational process. High cost and maximal flexibility are, apparently, to be accepted as synonymous with quality. Colleges have engaged in extensive advertising campaigns and used field representatives and alumni as recruiters to promote applications and enrollments. In proprietary institutions, in which the fees paid by students cover all expenditures (and perhaps yield a profit), successful motivation research which provides the necessary student population does indicate an effective operation, although it provides no evidence of quality. A commodity which sells and brings satisfactory returns to the seller is successful. In fact, many colleges and universities have regarded growth as adequate evidence of effectiveness and efficiency. But when increased enrollments require additional resources, the task becomes that of selling the program to others for increased support. And, at this point, those others can no longer be persuaded or motivated to provide support unless objective evidence of effectiveness and efficiency is provided.

However, motivation research is also directed to the problem of motivating employees in order to improve both morale and output in a manner analogous to that suggested by exponents of MBO. And, in this sense, motivation research can have an impact upon the operation of institutions of higher education. Indeed, the use of management tools and assessment procedures depends upon motivating the faculty to cooperate.

Policy Formulation, Planning, and Decision Making

Rational planning and policy formulation, which should provide the basis for decision making and accountability—especially, it would seem, in the university—are seldom pursued because the resources are usually inadequate. Consequently, agreement on assumptions, values, goals, objectives, processes, and environmental characteristics is not achieved. Meanwhile, some decisions are required by day-to-day exigencies. Major decisions, whether in the university or in other organizations, are often the result of the cumulative impact of these numerous minor, seemingly unimportant, actions necessitated by particular requests or problems. From the expectations and precedents set by these minor actions, policy emerges hazily and often with internal inconsistencies.

Policy making depends upon situational constraints and on trade-offs among competing groups with conflicting values or goals. No one strategy of policy formulation is likely to succeed in practice. Strategies must vary over time depending on internal and external pressures and must always be adapted to the units involved.

Compromise, distasteful as it is to those with deep-seated convictions, is essential, for a reasonable level of accord must exist to support collective action. Compromise, to be successful, must be based upon some common assumptions, understandings, and goals, although the specific elements of any compromise are often acceptable to various persons for different reasons. In compromise, no one gets everything desired; what one does get may not be in preferred form, and some part of one's acceptance depends upon what others lose as well as upon what is gained.

If policy analysis and formulation focus on the social and physical environmental constraints rather than on the internal motivations and behavior of individuals, the tendency to label decisions as prejudiced and irrational will be reduced. Thus the examination of constraints often leads to insightful analysis and understanding. Policy making, by this approach, never maximizes a single value other than, possibly, that of achieving accord. Rather, it identifies and reconciles conflicting values. Perhaps the major weakness of this approach, which fosters or flows out of a decentralized, incremental process, is that it does not meet the public demand for coordination and efficiency in higher education. But it does favor stability and results in gradual change, remedial rather than radical in nature. In contrast, the comprehensive, prescriptive paradigm emphasizes planning and draws upon such techniques as PPBS, systems analysis, and operations research.

Both the comprehensive and the incremental approaches to decision making have their proponents. Political processes, budget processes, and "market" economics generally reflect the incremental paradigm, and there is a well-developed rationale to support its use in these processes. But critics see this approach as not sufficiently flexible to permit rapid alterations in priorities. Many others fear that the comprehensive paradigm will lead to control by central, external authority. The incremental paradigm, operating through inefficient, somewhat obscure, processes, permits decisions to be reached which are not responsive to the public interest. If man were rational and society and political processes could become so, this paradigm might work exceedingly well. Because of the failures thus far of the comprehensive paradigm, the incremental paradigm may still be the only realistic approach to decision making in a democracy.

Planning (the comprehensive paradigm) requires agreement upon social norms, allows no serious disagreement, and relates ends and means by unambiguous prescription. Even processes are, to some extent, predetermined by the prescribed objectives and the budget allocation. Planning, especially when it becomes prescriptive and threatens to become self-validating, savors of authoritarianism. Yet the complexity of the problems faced in higher education, the rate of technological change, the success of science supported by an elaborate technology, the obvious shortcomings of incrementalism, and the apparent fallacy (even in higher education) of assuming that rational solutions based upon agreements on values are possible undergird continuing attempts toward imposing a prescriptive decision paradigm. Economists and applied mathematicians tend to favor this approach. Political scientists and sociologists, who are less taken with complex models and perhaps more in tune with reality, favor incrementalism.

The comprehensive prescriptive paradigm involves this logical sequence of steps: decision making—setting the values of outputs; programming—estimating required values of inputs;

implementing—processing according to specified plan; controlling—maintaining specified quantity and quality in outputs; researching—continual evaluating, studying, and developing of theory; forecasting—estimating needs, available inputs, and outputs.

One of the difficulties in planning is that the typical budget supports people and things. It reveals few of their interactions. The budget object classification exhibits wages and salaries, supplies, services, and equipment. The functional classification attempts to separate instruction, research, and services, although the phenomenon of joint products and the convenience of confounding assignments and funds by (for example) hiring a person on research funds to do teaching while the person released from teaching does research complicate, if they do not destroy, the validity of the classification.

The program budget should relate expenditures and output directly to the attainment of objectives, but universities do not usually budget by either program or function. Rather, they budget by organization, depending in part upon disciplines (which are not uniformly agreed upon) to set up departments which are variously organized into colleges and schools. New or developing disciplines or fields, such as the behavioral sciences or the political sciences, may be added to the existing roster, may replace existing departments, or may be placed in a new unit (center or institute) related to several existing colleges or departments. Even history is variously viewed as a social science and as one of the humanities. Other parts of the university organization depend on the existence of recognized professions (medicine, law), social problems and concerns (urban affairs, labor relations), and sectors of the economy (home economics, agriculture). In most universities, none of these units is self-sufficient; the programs of instruction and research are supplemented by the contributions of other units. Since university organizational patterns are idiosyncratic, the programs within institutions may not correspond at all to the programs defined in PPBS, which were developed to apply to institutions in general. Short of enforced uniformity, there is no satisfactory way of resolving these difficulties, especially since state and federal fiscal agents (regardless of their understanding of higher education) are preoccupied with their own difficult chore of analyzing budget requests with some degree of insight, sympathy, and fairness.

Budget reform, in which allocations would be directly related to programs and outputs, would be helpful, but the planning and execution would also need to become more systematic. PERT and the Delphi Technique, discussed in Chapter Six, are attempts to provide methodology to this end.

Summary

This chapter has introduced a confusing array of concepts and methodologies. If some overarching theory could be simply stated which would relate these and thereby provide a systematic and unified view of university-related phenomena, an explanation and prediction of the effects of changes in the variables would become possible. That this is unlikely must already be apparent, but a review of the essential ideas of this chapter will confirm it.

Educational institutions have purposes partly defined in charters, philosophical statements of educators, and aspirations of faculty members and administrators. They also have roles in the state and national systems of higher education, sometimes stated explicitly, but more frequently emanating from tradition. These roles, especially when limiting, are not always accepted by the faculty or the clientele of the institution. Long-term goals emerge, the intent of which is precisely that of defining a new role. There are also more specific goals or objectives for particular programs and for students completing them. Some of the more important outcomes, both for individuals and society, are inexplicit and unintended—too important to be called by-products, but too esoteric and uncertain to be claimed as set-offs against expenditures.

The institution provides a complex and costly environment consisting of students, faculty members, facilities, equipment, activities, and traditions. This environment is highly valued, continually changes, and possesses potential for influencing the processes of the institution in ways not fully grasped. Even the necessity of some aspects of that environment come into question with the increase in commuting and part-time students and the development of external degree programs.

An institution carries out the functions of teaching, research, and service and, in so doing, offers a wide array of activities, processes, and programs, some on and some off the campus. These activities, processes, and programs are, in many respects, clearer and dearer to the faculty than are the social responsibilities, purposes, goals, and educational objectives which presumably justify them. Hence the policies which guide the activities of a university relate much more to the processes which go on than to the outputs or the expectations of society. Leadership, which has come to be shared by boards, administrators, and faculty members, has far less to say about goals and decisions and the policies regarding them than would be desirable. This apparent lack of identifiable, responsible, and socially responsive leadership provides the excuse—one might say the necessity—for external intervention.

But external intervention, although possibly based, in part, on dissatisfactions with educational outcomes as well as with institutional efficiency and effectiveness in attaining them, tends to accentuate efficiency and effectiveness and thereby to intervene into management. Management involves planning and organizing resources to implement goals as well as evaluating, controlling, and revising them when required to maintain standards or improve them. But, if plans, goals, and objectives are not clear, then management inevitably is on an incremental (or decremental) basis, which does not satisfy the external critics. To the extent that management attempts to reexamine or force reexamination at lower levels of goals, objectives, and related activities and processes, it meets resistance by colleges, departments, and individual professors who regard these activities as their domain. With diffuse leadership, policy making and decisions are clearly incremental and not always consistent with universitywide goals. Management with sole emphasis on efficiency and effectiveness cannot achieve fundamental change, although it may provide an aura of accountability around an enterprise with unknown efficiency and effectiveness of outcomes by seemingly increasing the efficiency and effectiveness in the operations.

If identification and evaluation of outcomes and costs is made a continuing aspect of management, this process provides feedback which can produce exactly the accountability that is being demanded. But faculty members are reluctant about defining outcomes, resist evaluation, and some (a minority, I believe) decry any attempt by central administration and management to initiate a program review which might result in the elimination of, reduction in size of, or major change in any program. It is the lack of adequate central leadership, management, and control within institutions that leads to external criticism, intervention, and to statewide planning and coordination.

Higher education has been placed on notice that accountability is essential. In general, I believe, the institutions and their personnel accept this demand. Yet, it often seems that they procrastinate, quibble, and delay while holding firm to the myth that Ph.D.s know best. The difficulty is that none of the present elaborate systems provide either a workable methodology or a truly satisfactory answer to the complex problems of higher education. In the present state of knowledge, the best assurance of wisdom, equity, and accountability is a sensitive awareness of assumptions and limitations and evidence of responsible efforts to deal effectively with problems involved in the efficient use of resources.

Bibliographical Note

The role of management, accountability, and systems approaches in higher education is controversial and unsettled. If some of the most recent publications are any indication, the future is likely to bring more intensified and sophisticated arguments on both sides of the issue.

WICHE/NCHEMS is the best-known and most authoritative source of literature about and of activities concerning management systems in higher education. Many reports are highly technical analyses of systems or parts of systems. An equally large number of publications are of the persuasive kind. Numerous publications are listed in the Bibliography: the best entree to them is Haight and Romney (1975).

The Ford Foundation Program for Research in University Administration, operating out of the Office of the Vice-President for Planning at the University of California, Berkeley, produced a series of excellent monographs of which the one by Schmidtlein (1973) is an example.

Levin (1973) presents an analysis of the impact of an "accountability movement" on the education process. Baker and Popham (1973) and Windham (1972) also present thoughtful analyses of the implications and impacts of demands for accountability in education systems.

Kirst (1975) and Dresch (1975) point out some spectacular failures in the application of management systems to higher education. Both articles should be required reading for state and federal legislators who are contemplating legislation specifying certain management or budgeting procedures.

Chapter 6

Some Technical Aspects

This chapter provides an overview of some major technical concepts and criteria presently discussed and used by evaluators. Neither the inclusion nor the treatment is exhaustive. The treatment is geared toward those interested in evaluating and understanding evaluation studies rather than toward professional evaluators. Reading this chapter is not at all a prerequisite to understanding subsequent chapters, although reading appropriate sections will add significant insight to certain discussions.

Data Sources and Modes of Collection

The identification and definition of the appropriate variables and the specification of data-collection procedures are crucial to an evaluation. This process, when it involves a number of persons, can become something of a game in which the number of possible variables rapidly multiplies as individuals vie with each other in suggesting them and relationships worthy of exploration. Computer technology abets this tendency by making complex multivariate analyses practical. But such elaborate and undirected search missions, while possibly useful as a first exploration, seldom provide the information necessary for decision making. More focused approaches based upon specific objectives, hunches, or hypotheses, and a small number of key variables (with perhaps a few factors controlled or held constant) are easier to understand and to explain to those who operate a program or make decisions about it.

The variables which may be relevant to an evaluative study are virtually infinite. Some are qualitative, descriptive, and categorical (major, native state or region, race, sex, health, teaching style); some are quantitative, and these may be discrete (credits, courses enrolled in, class size) or continuous (age, time spent in study, costs).

Variables can be classified according to applicable scales or levels of measurement. On a *nominal scale*, objects or events are merely classified—sorted and counted. The categories or classes are not ordered, and the results are frequency counts. Here, the mode is the only applicable measure of central tendency. Distribution among categories can be checked by use of a statistic such as Chi Squared. On an *ordinal scale*, items can be ordered from smallest to largest; for example, percentiles and rankings have this quality but lack a unit of measurement. Medians and interquartile ranges are appropriate statistics. On *interval scales*, adjoining units are equidistant, making addition and subtraction possible. However, the lack of a true zero prohibits multiplication or division. Arithmetic means and standard deviation are the usual statistics. Temperatures (Fahrenheit and Centigrade) exemplify interval scales. *Ratio scales* are interval scales with a true zero, which permits multiplication and division. Most scales are ordinal, and most of the data with which evaluators deal are nominal or ordinal. Clearly, the nature of the data imposes limitations on the statistics and types of analyses used. Although test scores are commonly treated as interval scales, the range of difficulty of items usually assures that units are not equal over the range.

Variables may pertain to *inputs* (characteristics of students, economic level, age, ability, high school grades) or to *programs* (books and other materials, classroom structure, teaching methods). Program variables, which relate to educational processes, may also be designated as *independent, experimental,* or *treatment variables. Environmental* or *context variables* (community characteristics, political factors, social problems or crises) describe the setting in which the educational processes take place. Another set of variables, often ignored, relates to the *persons, instruments, or procedures* involved in data collection. These variables are part of the evaluation process and may greatly affect the amount and nature of the evidence collected. Unless unobtrusive measures (Webb and others, 1966) are used, the data-collection procedures can so influence the results as to invalidate the entire effort. *Outcome variables* (also labeled *dependent, output,* or *criterion variables*) are possible results of an educational program: achievement; employment; attitudes of students, parents, employers, and teachers; earnings; degrees granted.

The determination of appropriate measures and data-collection procedures for the chosen variables is a difficult and significant evaluative task. The range of collection procedures or instruments is large. Individuals may be requested to respond to tests, questionnaires, or inventories or to fill out biographical or personal-history forms. They may be asked to engage in actual or contrived decision-making situations or simulations. Logs, diaries, films, tapes, and interviews; archives and records (Wilcox and others, 1972); social indicators—measures of social condition derived from real-life behavior of people; and ratings, grades, observations, clinical examinations, and physiological measures are other means of collecting evidence. The human sources of information or data are also extensive: self, peers, students, teachers, parents, observers, and clinicians and other professionals who may have contact with an individual. Data can also be collected in many different locations and environments: classroom, laboratory, library, playing field, work, home, office, social situation, travel, and simulation. The evaluator's task is to sort out of these possible variables those which are likely to significantly affect results, those which characterize the processes involved in each situation, and those which give evidence of the results. The inclusion of too many variables is as likely to destroy the effect of the evaluation as is undue limitation.

Measures of Change

The measurement of change (growth) in students is attractive to those who first become involved in evaluation. However, it is a much more complicated and difficult task than it first appears. Increase in height or weight is quite simply determined in inches or pounds by taking the difference between two measures taken at two different points in time. But heights and weights are measured in standard units; have a fixed zero point; and can be added, subtracted, or expressed as a ratio. No defined units of measure for intelligence, cognitive abilities, or affective characteristics exist, and certainly (within the life span of an individual) no zero has been defined. For example, in a multiple-choice test, the items are commonly scored as right or wrong, and a total score is obtained by counting the number right, but differences in test scores over time ought not to be used to measure gains.

Several difficulties here are sometimes overlooked, and they invalidate the use of raw gains as change measures. First, there is usually both a floor and a ceiling effect. Since extremely easy items are usually excluded, a zero certainly does not mean "no knowledge." Neither does a perfect score mean "complete knowledge." Even with elimination of extremely easy or extremely difficult items, there will usually be a range of item difficulty such that those attaining high scores are doing so by answering (what are for that entire group) more difficult questions. Thus, even if the same test is used as a pretest and a posttest (an apparently identical measuring device which has, however, deficiencies in that there is the possibility of familiarity or recall and there is a restricted sampling of the domain of testing), the initially higher-scoring students are less likely to increase their scores than are the low-scoring students. Certainly, perfect or nearly perfect scorers have little chance of so doing. Were the ceiling raised by inclusion of more difficult items, that situation would be somewhat alleviated, but with the attendant difficulties of a reduced range of scores for the same length and harder test or a much longer and initially much more threatening test. Weighting of item responses by difficulty would appear to help in attaining a common unit over the entire range, but in fact this does not seem to materially help the situation.

Second, measurement errors, which occur in both the pretest and the posttest, reduce the reliability of an individual difference score calculated from tests with limited reliability to the point where the difference scores are virtually useless over limited spans of time.

Third, the regression effect—which, under conditions of dynamic equilibrium, operates to draw scores on retesting closer toward the mean—also confounds the meaning of the simple difference measure. To avoid these difficulties, residual gain scores (actual less predicted) and estimated true gain are alternatives developed in an effort to achieve a base-free measure. However, investigators such as Cronbach and Furby (1970), Werts and Watley (1969), and Linn (1965) prefer that measures of change be eliminated altogether and that posttest scores be used as the independent variable. Change scores are not necessary, and analysis of final performance (using various possibly relevant factors including initial status) is undoubtedly a more satisfactory technique.

The evaluator, who will be aware of these difficulties with raw gain scores, must usually educate his or her audiences, who typically regard gains as meaningful and appropriate measures because they do not grasp the shortcomings just noted.

Relationships or Comparisons

Evidence takes on meaning to individuals only in relation to their own value systems and those of their social groups. If we are told that a person is six feet tall, we probably will have little reaction. If we are then told that this six-foot person is female, we may be surprised. If we are told that the six-foot individual is a member of an African pygmy tribe, we will consider the individual indeed unusual. But if we know that the individual is a member of a professional male basketball team, we will think of him as relatively short in his milieu. The age of the individual raises still other associations and reactions. Thus, data and facts have little or no intrinsic meaning. They become meaningful only by association, by relationships or comparisons.

Comparisons can be based on specific standards. If an achievement test is carefully developed to cover all abilities and subject matter of interest, the performance of each individual can be directly interpreted on the achievement continuum measured. This performance might be reported as the total number or the percentage of tasks performed correctly on the entire test or on subsets of it relating to various abilities or content areas. Such a test would be *content referenced*. No norms are necessary. A specified level of performance to be attained or complete mastery (perfect performance) is the goal to be achieved by each individual. A stated level allows for some variations in individual performance; mastery specifies a (minimal) common level of achievement for all. *Criterion-referenced* measures pose a problem not found with content-referenced appraisals. The criterion usually cannot be directly measured or can be measured only at such great cost in time and dollars as to be unfeasible. Accordingly, criterion-referenced appraisal uses tasks which are judged to have or which have been empirically verified as having high correlation with the criterion. The criterion (a personality trait, for example) may be a construct (a hypothesized trait) whose reality, nature, and usefulness in explaining behavior are being explored. In another kind of measurement, factors are defined through factor analyses, and tests for each factor are provided. The result is a *factor-referenced* instrument which gives direct information on each factor.

It is also possible to carry on *ipsative* evaluation, in which an individual's level on one variable or characteristic is related to another variable or characteristic for that same person. This procedure compares traits within individuals rather than a single trait across individuals as does the *normative* approach. Whereas ipsative-referenced testing is idiographic (peculiar to the individual), norm-referenced testing is nomothetic, or at least approaches being so, by providing a distribution which can be regarded as a model or law to which all individuals can be compared. Specified standards of achievement or complete mastery moves one step further in permitting nomothetic interpretations of individual performance by relating that performance to a generally expected or uniformly required performance level. In practice, complete mastery is never fully achievable, since new knowledge is continually being extracted by scholars. The practical measure of a mastery standard cannot be perfection for all but the attainment in a reasonable time period and at reasonable cost of a previously defined acceptable level of performance. *Reasonable* must, of course, be defined in relation to costs, individual potential, and teacher resources.

Student Idiosyncrasies

Individuals possess characteristics which can profoundly affect their performances in the learning process or in evaluation. The determination of these characteristics and their possible effects is an intriguing task for the evaluator. It is especially challenging because of certain still unanswered questions: Should the teacher and evaluator accommodate these characteristics, or should they encourage and assist the individual to consciously modify the characteristics? Moreover, is the individual capable of changing; and even if so, do teachers and evaluators have the right to insist that he or she attempt to do so?

A *response set* is the attitudes and habits that affect an individual's performance on tests and in other contexts. Individuals may react positively or negatively to questions, to directions, to the tone or manner of the test administrator, to the number and type of alternative responses, or to the prospective use of the results. Thus, an individual's response in a given situation may be quite different from the response in another situation, where the same questions are presented in a different manner, form, or context. Personality traits such as caution or undue stress provoked by a test situation also may regularly affect performance. Similar traits include the tendency to guess, indifference, overconfidence, unduly critical attitudes, the tendency to take extreme positions, acquiescence to authority, and unwillingness to make judgments when lacking precise knowledge. Thus, one individual may respond quickly to test items; another may scrutinize each word or phrase, concerned that there may be a catch or hidden meaning. The proffered response "None of the above are correct" may attract the individual given to great precision and confident that no brief response can be fully accurate. Another student, reacting to a response pattern of "true, probably true, uncertain, probably false, or false," might regularly avoid the extremes. Even with the item stem "Gerald Ford is President of the United States," an exacting individual could argue that either "probably true" or "uncertain" is the best answer in that Ford might have succumbed within the past five minutes.

The types of response set which contribute irrelevant variance to individual performance are many. They include temporary but consistent reactions engendered by a particular instrument or session and stable tendencies which operate over all such situations. Some of the latter are inconsequential, including idiosyncratic word usage or aversion to particular types of questions.

The central element in all response sets is that they operate independently of the individual's knowledge and cognitive abilities. They reduce the reliability and validity of evaluation, and they may also reduce educability. It may be possible for any individual, once these sets are pointed out, to make adaptations, but extraordinarily sensitive teaching and evaluation would be required to achieve that modification. Surely the individual should come to know himself or herself in these respects, but alteration is the individual's prerogative and even then might require deep therapy and personality change.

Cognitive styles are usually regarded as more generalized than response sets; but there are many similarities between the two, and from the evaluator's point of view they pose similar problems. Cognitive styles are individual consistencies in manner or form of cognition. These, too, are independent of content or ability. They involve personality characteristics—preferences, attitudes, thought patterns—which affect or determine how an individual perceives, recalls, thinks, and solves problems. Psychologists working in this field have identified many such styles, including cognitive complexity versus simplicity, field independence versus dependence, tolerance of new or hypothetical situations versus intolerance, risk taking versus cautiousness, impulsiveness versus reflectiveness, rigidity in behavior versus flexibility, and use of broad inclusive categories versus narrow exclusive categories.

Cognitive styles differ from intellectual abilities in various respects. They relate to behavior rather than to content. Cognitive styles also are not usually considered as outcome objectives but rather as input variables which might limit the nature and the impact of an individual's education. Clearly, however, cognitive styles fall in the realm of values and, as such, may well be involved in educational objectives. Indeed, cognitive styles are not always clearly separable from intellectual ability. Impulsiveness, for example, is hardly consistent with sound scholarship in most substantive disciplines, and some modification seems essential.

Individuals differ not only in cognitive styles and response sets but also in achievement, ability, personality, interests, social class, ethnic background, and aptitudes; similarly, learning experiences can be varied in reference to disciplines, subject matter, instructional methods, teacher characteristics, schedules, standards, and evaluation practices. The concept of *trait-treatment interaction* arises from recognition that students with differing characteristics may learn more from one type of instruction or educational experience than from another; therefore, perhaps learning can be maximized if learner characteristics are matched with instructional methods and learning experiences. Certainly in medicine and in therapy it is known that some individuals respond to certain medications, treatments, or individuals better than to others; but just how far this individualization can be carried in education and how far it is desirable are issues of significance. Clearly, the blind student must learn through other than visual experiences, but should the sighted individual deficient in reading ability be encouraged or permitted to bypass this road to learning?

Awareness of personal idiosyncrasies is essential, for it reminds us that any program is likely to have differential effects on subgroups. Most students, however, are or can be flexible enough to benefit from a variety of patterns of learning experience, especially when the learning mode is inseparable from what is to be learned. For example, development of the ability to read requires continuing engagement with reading even though the facts of a given course might be learned through visual, tactile, olfactory, or auditory means.

Validity, Reliability, and Precision

An attempt to measure anything involves imposition of some structure, division into a set of categories, or use of some scale or units. And whenever any instrument of measurement is used, issues of validity, reliability, and precision arise. A physical education instructor who wants to separate students into four groups by height may do so visually; but this visual measurement is subject to various possible sources of error: head shape, amount of hair, coiffure, posture, thickness of shoe soles and heels, ground contour, and even the height of the instructor. Depending upon the definition of height which the instructor uses (top of head or top of hair, insistence on erect posture, and so on), the makeup of the four groups may differ markedly. At best, relative height is estimated; therefore, if a high level of precision is required, the possible sources of variation make the visual approach both invalid and unreliable in selecting groups homogeneous in height. If the concern is to measure individual height to provide a record over time and possibly to provide a check on appropriateness of weight to height, both height and weight must be taken under standardized conditions with reasonably well-calibrated instruments. If variation in height from hour to hour in relation to various length periods of rest, work, or exercise is under investigation, much more precise measurements may be needed.

For the unknown purpose or whim of our instructor, the validity, the reliability, and the precision of a visual approach may be adequate. If, however, the *tallest* group is assigned to play basketball, and the others to engage in other sports in which height is less relevant, the selection procedure may be regarded as unfair by some students. Even if height abets basketball prowess, the mode of selection does not measure either individual prowess or desire to play. Thus, even if the method were completely reliable in establishing four groups, it would be neither reliable nor valid from the viewpoints of those individuals barred from basketball by it. Validity, reliability, and precision always depend upon usage or purpose, which may in turn depend upon social or personal goals and values.

Validity refers to the extent to which the measures correspond to the characteristics under investigation. For a physical measurement such as length, a ruler, yardstick, or tape, whether calibrated in inches, centimeters, or other units, is a valid measure. For measuring achievement in a given discipline, the validity of an instrument or procedure depends upon the extent to which performance corresponds to achievement of the objectives specified by specialists in that discipline. In personality or attitude tests, validity depends upon the degree of correspondence between test scores or profiles and other evidence of the possession of certain traits or possibly upon the extent to which test results are predictive of behavior or views in specific situations.

Reliability refers to the reproducibility of a set of measurements. It has to do with consistency or stability of measures over time. Reliability does not connote accuracy or precision, for reproducibility can, at best, be at the level of accuracy of the original measures. An instrument that measures the heights of individuals to the nearest foot is a reliable measure (and also a valid one) if the primary concern is extremes of short and tall persons; but it certainly is not a precise measure.

Precision, or accuracy, has different meanings for educational measurement specialists and for scientists and engineers. Here it refers to the fineness of distinction or of measurement. Precision adequate for one task may not suffice for another.

Seconds constitute a rather fine time measurement, but track records are determined by fractions of a second.

Each of the three terms, *validity, reliability,* and *precision,* has several interpretations and alternative and distinctive procedures for measurement.

Content validity is appropriate when a present competency of an individual is to be assessed. The universe of tasks in which such competency is to be exhibited (usually too extensive for a complete demonstration) is sampled by some well-defined rules, and performance on the sample is taken as an index of competency in the total domain. The judgment of experts—supplemented by analysis and classification of the content, ability, and area of application tapped by each item—may be the best evidence available for the validity of the test relative to the domain.

Content validity is judged by the adequacy of the sampling of item types, content, and objectives, and of their possible and appropriate interrelationships. The universe of such items or tasks defines the achievements to be measured. In a sense, the procedure for developing the test becomes the basis for judging the adequacy of the definition of the domain and of the sampling of it. In some circumstances, the test itself may be regarded as the best definition.

Criterion-related validity is appropriate when future performance on the criterion is to be predicted from present performance or present ability or when present characteristics are to be estimated from an appraisal of other presumably correlated abilities or characteristics. In either case, the content of the test or of the characteristics measured is not (as in content validity) identical with that which is to be estimated. The measurements or scores are compared with one or more external variables—in the one case *predictive*, with data collected at a later date; in the other, with data collected *concurrently*. Some form of correlation becomes the common method of appraisal. Criterion-related validity is a two-step process: choose a criterion appropriate to the task and choose the appraisal procedure for the presumably correlated abilities in relation to the criterion.

Construct validity indicates the extent to which an appraisal permits an inference of the degree to which a person possesses a hypothetical trait, personality characteristic, or ability (that is, a *construct*) which is presumably operative in or reflected by the evaluation procedure used. Construct validity is especially relevant when the purpose is to achieve increased insight into the qualities involved in successful performance. It is also applicable when the implications of one or more hypothetical traits are pursued to the point of developing a theory which may, in turn, suggest how individuals will perform in certain situations. Thus, construct validity involves circular but reinforcing reasoning. The procedures for demonstration of construct validity are partly logical and partly empirical. If an attempt is made to identify and measure thinking abilities, individuals outstandingly good or poor, as perceived by faculty members, may be given a test of critical thinking which has been developed on the basis of an analysis of abilities involved and on construction of tasks or items in which these abilities are apparently required. To the extent that high and low performers are identified by the two approaches, the construct is verified. Alternatively, after individuals with high and low test scores are identified, hypotheses may be developed as to how the performance of these individuals will differ in other situations. If data collected on these other situations confirm the hypotheses, then the theory has validity to that extent. The investigation of the construct validity of a test is frequently pursued through determining relationships or correlations with other tests, data, or classifications. Viewed as a property of the test rather than as a property of the construct, this type of validity is most appropriate when one seeks a better understanding of the qualities or abilities which affect test performance.

Several different constructs may be required to explain complex behavior, and a single construct may be related to several different discrete performances. Factors derived by factor analytic methods illustrate this situation. Each factor is usually a composite of several different test scores or performances. Validity is inferred, not measured. From whatever evidence is collected, a decision is made that validity is adequate, marginal, or inadequate.

Whereas validity is an indication of the extent or adequacy with which available evidence accurately predicts or characterizes abilities or traits other than those actually observed, reliability refers to the consistency or stability of measurement. If the true heights of 10,000 persons were known within the limits of twenty-four-hour variability in height, correlation of these with another independent height measurement of the entire 10,000 persons would yield a measure of validity. The validity might be less than perfect because of inaccuracies in the scales used, inaccuracies in readings of the attendant, or other such sources. These sources may create either random or systematic errors. The scales may consistently overweigh; the attendant may consistently read a little high or low. If all heights in the second measurement are taken at the close of eight hours of work involving standing or walking, a systematic underestimate may result.

Obviously, then, validity requires consistency in measurement (reliability) and accuracy (precision). Without some degree of reliability and precision, there can be no validity.

If two different measurements (neither of them the true height) are correlated, an estimate of reliability is attained. This estimate might be designated as an index of reliability. Because it involves the entire population, it represents the upper limit of usual reliabilities as sample size increases, although only for those sample coefficients which involve the same sources of error.

In practice, we must deal with samples rather than populations. If new measurements on a *sample* of persons are correlated with their true heights, an *estimate* of validity is obtained which includes a sampling variation. And if still another measure of height is made for this sample, the correlation between these two sets of measures *for the sample* provides an estimate of reliability which can be no higher than the previous estimate of validity and will probably be lower because of other sources of error.

Several types of sampling may be going on simultaneously, and not all of them may be recognized. To characterize the competencies of high school graduates on a national basis, one must have a sampling of graduates as well as of the tasks which involve the competencies. If the ability to spell correctly one hundred specific words is the point of investigation, the *entire* hundred might be administered to a *sample* of graduates. The hundred items, defining an entire domain, do not contribute to sampling variation in repeated testing, but the sampling of graduates does.

The various types of sampling lead to numerous approaches to determining reliability because there are many sources of variation and of error, including: (1) variability in performance of an individual from one time to another (because of alertness, memory, state of health); (2) variability from individual to individual in whatever is being measured (individual differences); (3) variability in the administration of the tests (audibility, clarity, demeanor); (4) variations in testing environments (heat, light, noise); (5) variations in observers (when ratings are involved); (6) variations or errors in scoring whether by persons or electronic equipment; (7) variations in item types or presentation of tasks; (8) variations in test forms because of item or problem sampling.

The principal concerns with reliability have to do with consistency or stability of individual performance over time and over test forms, including different samples of items. Retesting the same students with the same form provides a measure of score stability over time. Retesting over time with parallel or alternate forms combines variation in time and in sampling. Variation in performance because of item sampling (without time lapse) may be estimated by separating a test into two parts and obtaining a split-half correlation, which can be adjusted for length by the Spearman-Brown formula (if one accepts the assumptions). The separation of a test into halves should follow the original procedure. If the domain of all items is at hand, the test can be made up of two parts, each randomly selected and alternated in the test. Alternatively, if the entire test is built by random sampling and ordered randomly, the items making up the two subtests should be assembled by sampling at the cell (intersections of objectives, content, and applications) level.

Test length and response time are closely related. Time, especially short time periods which require speedy response, may greatly affect reliability or, for that matter, validity and precision. Use of relatively easy items in a long test places a premium on speed. Reliabilities based on such a situation may be spurious. Speed, especially if many students do not complete a test, negatively affects validity and precision.

The previous discussion indicates that measures of reliability encompass many types of evidence which affect the consistency or agreement to be expected on successive testings or observations. The test performance is affected by many factors (sample, administration, time, scoring). Wise use of the scores or measurements requires some insight into how much each of the factors might have affected the results. Insofar as possible, irrelevant sources of variations should be controlled; if they cannot be controlled, the experimental design of the reliability study should provide estimates of the various factors. A number of different reliability coefficients differing in definition of relevant (true) and irrelevant (error) variance can be computed; each must be carefully defined so that the meaning and implications of reliability evidence are clear.

If a test is regarded as a measure of a trait or characteristic, a measure of internal consistency should be provided to assure that all items are related to the trait. The extensively used split-half or Kuder-Richardson estimates of internal consistency reflect as much as anything else the homogeneity of the test content. For a test which provides several subscores, both the reliability and the intercorrelation of the parts are essential to determine the meaning of the various scores. Cronbach's coefficient (Cronbach and Furby, 1970) and analysis of variance procedures are also useful. Criterion-referenced testing poses special problems in computation of reliability because of the limited range of scores. Livingston (1972) deals insightfully with this problem.

Precision (or accuracy) of measurement has frequently been confused with reliability or more specifically with the standard error of measurement (a measure of the variations about the regression line relating two measures). The reason for this confusion is that no units of measurement exist in the field of achievement or personality testing such as exist in physical measurements. In addition, in the usual norm-referenced testing, individuals are compared with other individuals rather than with a definite standard of performance. If mastery or a previously specified level of achievement less than mastery is demanded of each individual, then the judgment must be made on the basis of the score or of the percentage of a perfect score. The attainment of the necessary precision raises several new questions: Can the domain of competencies be broken into a series of tasks roughly equal in difficulty? For example, in the addition of all one-digit numerals, can 9 + 9, which is *one* sum, be regarded as of the same difficulty as 1 + 1? Perhaps not, but at least the number of the one-digit sums can be identified and mastery level can be defined either as complete accuracy or as correct performance on a specific percentage of all the possible combinations. Precision in this sense, then, involves the fineness of definition of all the tasks included in the domain.

Since this number can become very large when all possible tasks and all possible forms of these tasks are included, sampling is apparently necessary. We are back to a sampling problem. Perfect performance on the sample does not ensure perfect performance on the total domain. And for complicated behaviors, which require coordination, combination, or integration of several more elemental behaviors, the units necessary for precision measurement are lacking, and the entire concept of mastery, though not necessarily of criterion-related assessment, becomes rather unclear. There will be no agreement as to what mastery is and, because of time, costs, deficiencies or disabilities of some students, and performance errors, no prospect of determining it. Any lesser standard will be purely arbitrary. Clearly, the lack of precision in measurement effectively deters any significant progress toward mastery testing or complex goals, and it complicates and may destroy any prospect of developing criterion-referenced tests except in a highly subjective way.

Sampling

Sampling is a process of identifying a universe or population of concern and selecting from this universe the subset(s) to be studied. The population of concern and the population studied can differ because of sampling problems and response rates. For example, an attempt to study dropouts from a college after several years runs into difficulties immediately because of lack of current addresses. Whatever the intended population and sampling procedure, the population actually sampled is that for which addresses are available. And for those contacted, the response rate is usually low.

There are three broad types of sampling. The first is entirely fortuitous—using whatever data may be conveniently at hand. The second is subjective but is purposive and selective, guided by expert opinion. The range of faculty opinion on an issue, for example, may be gathered from phone contacts with a few knowledgeable deans, department chairmen, and committee members. Such a sampling is suspect as an indication of the frequency of various views but may serve a purpose in preparation of a statement or report. The third type of sampling, objective sampling, can be used to overcome the implicit and unknown biases of fortuitous or subjective sampling. Many patterns of objective sampling exist, each appropriate for various problems and constraints. A systematic sample, such as every twelfth name in a student directory starting with a randomly selected name on the first page, is an example. However, under this procedure certain combinations or samples are impossible; every item does not have an equal opportunity to appear in each sample. Other and better alternatives include simple random sampling; stratified random sampling, in which random sampling is done independently from each stratum; multistage random sampling, in which random selection is exercised in each of several areas—colleges, departments, courses, sections, students; and cluster sampling, in which all elements in the next to last area are included (for example, all students in the sections selected).

The mode of sampling used depends both upon purposes and upon available resources. When attempts are made to assess the achievement of large numbers of students over classes and institutions, the time requirements and costs can become exorbitant. The apparently simplest and most desirable procedure, requiring all items or tasks of all students, is impossible. A second approach is to select random samples of students and administer to them all items of a test. This procedure is regularly used in establishing norms for standardized tests. A third procedure is to administer a sample of items to all students. A fourth, matrix sampling, combines both procedures and uses random item samples administered to random student samples. Matrix sampling sometimes involves assigning subgroups of persons to respond to subgroups of items. Since the most serious sampling limitation is the time required of individuals, this procedure is an economical mode of assessment. If the samples of individuals are reasonably equivalent in backgrounds and ability, the composite scores on items over the samples permit some generalizations on overall group performance. Individual sampling may be random within a unit (usually a school or program) or based upon information about ability or prior grades, or the item subsets may include a few common tasks to provide controls. This is a convenient and effective way of dealing with appraisal problems. The method requires care in planning and use of estimation procedures. The problems and appropriate procedures are well and briefly presented by Sirotnik (1974).

In colleges, sampling in the area of instructional and curricular studies is attended by a unique series of problems which make generalizations risky. Students enrolled in a course or program in any one quarter or year may not constitute a sample from a definable population. Changes in requirements, in popularity of programs, and in the student body can, even within one year, effect significant change in results. Rotation of professors assigned to courses and the autonomy of professors in their teaching inject additional variables difficult to weigh. Hence, in any evaluation study in colleges and universities, consideration of sampling limitations is essential even if all students and all instructors involved in a program at a given moment are included in the study.

Costs

The difficulties in determining costs are formidable for several reasons. First, the definition of costs is a complex task. Second, customary records of expenditures do not readily permit determination of costs for programs. Third, there is a general ignorance about (and an indifference toward) the cost aspects of programs and of evaluation activities in colleges and universities. Fourth, costs in relation to decision making require predictions or estimates for the future, which are, at best, highly tentative and are also tenuous because of lack of specific information on the current scene. And, finally, the lack of acceptable quality measures makes it impossible to compare alternative program costs in any acceptable manner. Evaluation costs pose yet another problem, for evaluation carried out in the formative, feedback mode becomes so integral an aspect of a program that it is not fully distinguishable from it. At that point, evaluation becomes part of program costs.

The costs of a program are not found solely in the dollars directly expended, and some costs are not expressible in dollars. The cost of a program as viewed by one individual who loses something thereby is not comparable (as far as that individual is concerned) to a benefit gained by others. And, unfortunately, it is frequently the undesirable consequences that are associated with costs. A program has a variety of benefits such as improved learning or the satisfaction of students, teachers, and public. Obviously, there is no common unit whereby these can be combined to determine net benefits. With limited resources, every program has opportunity costs in that other benefits must be forgone. With the same resources, other benefits could be achieved. Thus, the cost of a program, from one point of view, is found not in the resources required to support it but in the values or benefits which would accrue from alternative use of those resources.

Costs, too, lie in the future and must be estimated. Though benefits and costs can be estimated at a point in time, the final decision should always be made by a projection into the future. Later program improvements or expansion may add significantly to past or current costs.

Cost factors include time of faculty and administrators, equipment, supplies, and use of space. Developmental or start-up costs include investments in needed space or equipment and operating costs which are continually changing. All of these can be expressed in dollars. The time of students is also a cost often ignored or taken too lightly. Heavy demands upon student time may be rebuffed or may be subtracted from other efforts.

When costs of new or expanding programs are being estimated, it is not always evident what costs are relevant. The costs of decisions already made (*sunk costs*) are not usually relevant, since the expenditures have been made and are not retrievable. Only incremental costs caused by the program such as those for remodeling and new equipment, are relevant. Expansion of a program may take place on a *marginal* cost basis if existing staff, facilities, and classes can accommodate more students. But marginal costs (and decreasing overall costs per student) hold only until enrollment forces expansion of staff and space. Fixed costs in administrative salaries, overhead, and maintenance are not relevant to program costs unless the program is of such size or of such complexity as to require increases in these areas. Marginal costs are low simply because fixed costs do not materially change until a critical point in student growth requires an expansion in facilities, staff, and supervision.

The several functions of faculty in research, public service, and instruction pose a problem in *joint costs*. A demanding new program may result in increased time in instruction, with consequent decrease in research. Unless this consequence is noted and taken into account, costs are underestimated and possibly quite seriously so. Some costs, such as salaries and maintenance, are recurring. Remodeling and new equipment are nonrecurring.

Program costs can be external as well as internal. Some external degree programs depend heavily upon the gratuitous services of faculty paid by other institutions. Off-campus service and study programs frequently thrust a significant burden upon others who are not paid for the task; but such services take the time from other efforts. Medical program costing efforts systematically undertake to assess the dollar value of contributed services.

At least four different costs are involved in a program. First and most obvious are the direct dollar expenditures in salaries, supplies, and equipment. Second, there are costs which are not reflected in expenditures, yet they are real and interpretable in dollars. Depreciation in facilities and equipment is an example. Unrecognized redistribution of faculty efforts from one function to another is also a cost. Third, there are costs which are quantifiable although not readily expressible in dollars. These include student and volunteer time, use of facilities, and use of the contributed services and facilities of agencies which provide service and internship experiences. Fourth are costs which are nonquantifiable and often exceedingly difficult to assess: faculty and student morale, effect on other programs, reputation of the institution, academic and public reactions to the program and personnel.

A complete cost assessment covering all these points is unlikely within most evaluative studies in higher education. Indeed, such assessment is impossible with any accuracy if the future reference for costing is kept in mind. Nevertheless, costs must be dealt with in evaluation if in no other way than by indicating why they are ignored. When major program decisions are to be made, every reasonable effort should be made to provide estimates of program costs and alternatives in relation to benefits.

Evaluation Design

Evaluation in the higher education context does not often lend itself to elaborate experimental projects and designs. Projects to be evaluated are ongoing and are seldom subject to the variable manipulation and controls required for comparative analysis using the sophisticated techniques of statistical analysis. Because evaluation in higher education is largely formative and relates to practices and programs which, in some form, continue, the lack of elaborate designs is less of a defect than would be true if major decisions using summative evaluation were being made. Evaluation can and should be a continuing component of programs rather than an incident. And the most important impact is certainly on people, with improvements being introduced by them or perhaps resulting spontaneously and simply because of new insights, confidence, and enthusiasm.

Much of the evaluation activity in any venture, especially

in its early stages, is descriptive and historical. In some cases, such activity is enough to muster support for a change. For example, the history of the foreign language requirement in American colleges in no way supports the often expressed faculty view that competency in a second language is a traditional and sanctified aspect of liberal education. A report showing that less than 50 percent of classrooms are in use after 3 P.M., coupled with information on departments and individuals with no classes scheduled after 3 P.M. over a span of several years, clearly points to one solution to the complaint of inadequate classroom space.

In planning evaluation, ex post facto "designs" are unfortunately too common. New programs are put into effect, and only after a period of time is evaluation demanded, occasionally out of curiosity, but often to meet external criticism or to gain recognition. Since the factors involved in the choice of the program and the details of its operation are often unknown and unrecoverable, an evaluation can do little more than indicate matters deserving further study in the current scene. The fact that many present- and future-oriented faculty members are little interested in or influenced by studies of past operations also supports this view. The costs of such an enterprise are high, and the ultimate results may not justify the cost even when the study results are clear; few people are impressed by statistical analyses which they do not understand, especially when the results do not conform to their own convictions or to their own habits and patterns of thought. Stufflebeam and his associates (1971) provide an extended and excellent treatment of these issues.

One of the recurring tasks of an evaluator is that of describing complex, multivariable phenomena in terms which assist in development of instruments and in interpretation. Typically, an extensive array of scores, ratings, or other data is to be analyzed with the expectation that a smaller number of components can be identified, interpreted, and named. Correlation and regression analysis, factor analysis, discriminant-function analysis, the Stephenson Q sort and its adaptations P, O, R,

S, and T (Mulaik, 1972) are all useful for this purpose. Multivariate analyses of variance and covariance are also powerful tools for analysis of sources of variance and determining the significance of various factors.

The applicability of these techniques and the validity of their interpretation require rigorous advance attention to design and the use of experimental or quasiexperimental designs. Such designs are frequently impossible because of conditions and constraints, but ignorance and failure to consider design early in a project probably account for improper or complete lack of design as much as do the constraints. Consideration of alternative designs relevant to the decisions to be made has several benefits: (1) Variables, problems, constraints, and possible relationships will be identified and clarified by the deliberations about design. (2) Consideration of designs, whether or not adopted, will inject an element of objectivity into a process fraught with bias and emotion. (3) When designs are carefully planned and executed, decision making will be, to some degree, removed from feelings or beliefs to demonstrated facts or principles. (4) Selection of design will be based largely upon the issues raised and the nature of the data. Applicable statistical methodology will be related to and limited by the design. (5) Designs can always be discarded or made less specific if circumstances make this necessary. Movement in the opposite direction is not possible.

Even sophisticated designs and statistical methodology, however, may yield ambiguous data. Many well-planned studies are inconclusive—"no significant difference." "Educationally significant" and "statistically significant" are entirely different in implication. Statistical significance does not mean educationally significant, especially when costs are taken into account. And a procedure or innovation which is educationally significant does not necessarily produce statistical significance. Evaluation always has a heavily subjective component, precisely because it does deal with values; but that inevitability does not in itself excuse slovenly design or statistical analysis. The intent should be always to move as far as possible toward objectivity.

Delphi Technique

The Delphi Technique, developed mainly by Olaf Helmer (1966) and Norman C. Dalkey, is a method for collecting, organizing, and sharing "expert" forecasts of the future. The procedure calls for collection of individual conjectures and judgments to form a composite group judgment. The original intent was to define a probable set of scientific and technological events and to predict the time of occurrence. Although based upon the speculations of experts, the procedure does not reveal the judgments one to another, thus barring undue influence by prestigious individuals.

In response to a questionnaire, respondents first submit conjectures as to likely events and later (second round) submit a guess as to the probability of each event's occurring. At this second stage the initial responses have been screened, edited, and combined. Following the second round the results are summarized; on the third round, the respondents are asked whether they want to revise their estimates after viewing the summary of predictions made. On the fourth round, persons whose judgments fall outside the interquartile range of the composite responses are asked to justify their responses. They may still change them at this point. Other questions or tasks may be proposed: (1) How desirable or undesirable is each of the events? (2) What are the probable or possible results of the events? (3) What policies or intervention procedures might be developed to discourage, encourage, or deal with the consequences of an event?

Several attempts have been made, with somewhat dubious results, to apply the Delphi Technique to educational prediction. However, the approach may be useful in forcing awareness of change and of the assumptions, ambitions, goals, and factors which influence it. Major criticisms of the Delphi Technique are the following: (1) No substantive explanation of the forecast is provided. It rests solely on consensus, which is neither a necessary nor a sufficient condition for plausibility. (2) The technique involves judgments, but those judgments, in turn, may alter the likelihood of the changes. (3) Propositions about the future are matters of rational persuasion or of emotion—they are not subject to scientific proof. Even a correct forecast does not validate the technique. (4) Most informal judgment about the future, even by informed persons, is little more than guess-work. (5) There is a distinction (not always conscious) between hopes or goals (which are ideals) and expectations, probabilities, or likelihood (which are based on reality). (6) The technique may be more useful as a teaching strategy than as a research instrument—a way of studying how people think about the fu-ture, a way to force thinking about the future. It might also serve as a planning tool to probe priorities of individuals and constituencies.

Summary

The diverse technical aspects of evaluation presented in this chapter have been dealt with relatively lightly to provide some insight into several of the more difficult and controversial aspects of evaluation. So diverse are these topics that it is doubtful that even a skilled and experienced evaluator will be knowledgeable about all of them. Those concepts or problems which appear especially relevant to an evaluation study should be pursued further through the references. Both the study and the understanding of it will be enhanced by the insights gained, even when the concepts or issues noted are more complicated or sophisticated than the study demands.

Bibliographical Note

Individuals seeking to pursue further some of the technical aspects of education will find many sources in Anderson and others, *Encyclopedia of Educational Evaluation* (1974). The Thorndike (1971) volume on educational measurement is also an excellent source. Other items in the Bibliography will also be useful, although by design the technical aspects have been underplayed to provide materials more suitable to students, pro-fessors, and administrators interested primarily in an overview of the nature and role of evaluation. Cronbach (Cronbach and

Gleser, 1965; Cronbach and Furby, 1970; Cronbach and others, 1972) deals with many of the issues raised in this chapter. Hambleton and Novick (1973) undertake to integrate theory and method for criterion-referenced tests. Shoemaker's (1971) volume on multiple-matrix models is a useful reference. Gronlund (1965) deals with many of the topics in this chapter in a manner appropriate for the nonspecialist.

Chapter 7

Recruitment, Selection, Classification, Placement

This chapter deals with a series of interrelated topics which some evaluators completely ignore and which others regard as only remotely related to the mainstream of evaluation. It is my conviction that the admissions, classification, orientation, and placement of students are crucial in determining the character and quality of an educational program. The need for and role of evaluation are apparent in many ways. First, the institution faces a series of decisions about admitting individuals, about the programs and courses for which they are qualified, and about prior educational experiences and credit for them. These decisions require extensive evidence on students and appraisal of it. Second, the processes of recruitments, selection, classification, and placement themselves require continuing evaluating as personnel and student preparation change. Third, prospective students should be deeply engaged in evaluation of themselves and of institutions and programs. Fourth, recruitment, orientation, and counseling should be viewed as both encouraging and increasing the capability of the individual to engage in evaluation. Fifth, the costs of the admission procedures should be examined in reference to the persistence of students and the character of the student body. Sixth, admissions procedures should be consistent with the educational philosophy, programs, and practices of the institution. Faculty members must be informed about and involved in the several stages of induction of a student into college. Furthermore, the respective roles and interactions of faculty members and administrators, student personnel staff, and admissions personnel in developing policy and in implementing it provide significant insight into the internal governance patterns of the institutions.

From the viewpoint of the institution, there are four distinct stages in the initial relationship between a college and a student—recruitment, selection, classification, placement. Recruiting is discussed less openly than the others, but recruiting in some form, varying from active face-to-face recruiting by admissions personnel to less formal contacts by mail or alumni, is always present. Elite colleges engage in recruiting to maintain quality and a desired degree of diversity. Even an institution with open admissions which seeks a reasonable student mix in geographical origins and social and racial characteristics often recruits minorities and women students.

Filing of an application for admission does not assure admission (except for National Merit Scholarship Award winners and those who have signed athletic tenders). After an institution has selected and notified applicants of their admission, all but a few institutions rest uneasy (even after receipt of acceptance) until the individual appears and enrolls. For many colleges, admissions must run well above desired enrollments to account for those who choose to go elsewhere. Consequently, it is necessary to evaluate the reasons for no-shows.

Concurrently with or after selection, the problem of classification must be faced. The student may not have a definite program in mind or may choose one for which prior preparation or aptitudes are inappropriate. Program classification interacts with course placement. If prerequisites are lacking for certain courses, extra or remedial work may be required. Advanced placement, with or without credit for prior work in certain fields, is also possible.

These four stages require evaluation as related processes. In the areas discussed in this chapter, therefore, evaluation must include (1) evaluation of the student and the records; (2) continuing appraisal of the processes used and their effectiveness; and (3) assessment of student, faculty, administrative, and public attitudes toward the processes, their fairness, their relation to the maintenance of standards, and their costs.

Recruitment, selection, classification, and placement are matters of ever increasing concern in higher education because of the increasing competition for applicants, the proliferation of specialized curricula in response to the continually expanding range of occupations, college-level courses offered for gifted high school students, and the increasing numbers of community college graduates transferring to four-year institutions. The complexities of the decisions forced by these developments have given rise to much research but few definitive answers. My aim, therefore, is to present the issues involved, suggest some alternatives, and point out by comment and bibliography references the need for evaluation and improvement of these processes in each institution.

Recruitment

Despite widespread recruiting by institutions, the recruiting process has not been studied in depth—possibly because different institutions recruit for different purposes: to maintain quality, to change the institution's image, to raise the intellectual quality of the student body, or to upgrade athletics or music or other programs. Many institutions have recently made special efforts to recruit minorities and the disadvantaged; others engage in extensive recruiting simply because their administrators view size, quality, and resources as interrelated. At times, institutional needs take precedence over the needs of the prospective student.

Recruiting can be expensive: the costs vary from a few dollars per student recruited by mail or by volunteers to several hundred dollars per student recruited by full-time recruiters. And recruiting can have adverse effects when students who might have gone elsewhere are unduly pressured to change their minds by recruiters who misrepresent the character of the institution. The distinction between students enrolled only because of recruitment activity and those who would have enrolled in any case is not easily made. In any event, when many recruited students transfer after one year or drop out, something is basically wrong with either the recruitment process or the educational program.

Furthermore, when many recruits transfer or leave, recruitment costs are inflated, as becomes evident when recruitment costs are related to total student years rather than simply to the number of students recruited. This can only be done finally after a lapse of four years, but a similar approach can be used for lesser periods. Comparison of the effectiveness of individual recruiters is facilitated by relating each salary plus expenses to the years of attendance and the satisfaction of those recruited. As with all attempts to quantify, caution must be observed. Rigid application would encourage recruiters to concentrate on students already favorable to the institution rather than to seek new prospects and develop new territories. Recruiting then would be an added cost with uncertain benefits. Effective recruiting must bring students who would not otherwise enroll, but they must also be students who remain at the college.

Selection

From those students who apply for admission, an institution must select those to be formally admitted. Selection, however, is a gradual or cumulative process. Many initial contacts are informal (made by personal visit or by telephone). Lack of enthusiasm or active discouragement at that point may eliminate the necessity of formal action on an application. Institutions which admit almost all serious applicants may argue for their selectivity on the basis of these "informal rejections," although the institution rather than the applicant is rejected. Indeed, in some institutions, nonappearances may run to 50 percent or more of those admitted, and they may be more able than the students who enroll. Presumably, most of the no-shows make multiple applications and are admitted to more selective and preferred institutions.

Selection does not cease when the student appears on campus. Some rather selective institutions have, in the past, eliminated as much as 30 percent of the freshman class by the end of the first year. Public institutions with coarse admission screens can become selective institutions by the elimination which occurs within the first year or two. Indeed, whatever the care and the criteria used in the admissions process, the error is such that, were it not for the costs, selection by trial might be preferable to provide all individuals with a reasonable chance of success the opportunity to prove themselves. This is the role of the community college, and it is also consistent with open-admissions practices.

Most of the emphasis in selection prior to the present attention to minorities and the disadvantaged has been on cognitive evidence: previous grades, high school ranks, test scores, and patterns of courses. Courses taken appear to offer some evidence of student interest, but may only reflect conformity to presumed college preferences. High school grades or ranks generally have given somewhat higher correlation with college grades than have any other data. Various types of academic aptitude tests and achievement tests, however, run a close second; and the combination of grades or ranks (which depend upon the particular school in which they were attained) and test scores (which are independent of the variations in schools) yields somewhat better predictions than either taken alone.

The correlation of grades, ranks, or test scores with first-term grades ranges over the interval from .4 to .55; a combination may occasionally reach .70. Although Bloom and Peters (1961), using data from a selected group of schools, found that a somewhat higher correlation might be achieved by a progressive adjustment of high school grades for differences in high schools and of college grades for differences in colleges, other studies (for example, Lindquist, 1963) cast doubt on both the utility and the generality of that finding. The expectation is that, regardless of the combination of cognitive evidence used, no more than 50 percent of the variation in first-term college grades will be accounted for. Some students do better than predicted; others do far worse. Some students who are admitted fail despite the selection process, and some persons not admitted would have succeeded. In colleges in which grades have become markedly inflated in recent years, prediction may have become worthless. Admission and persistence, joined with financial support, yield a degree.

On the whole, secondary school course patterns are not significantly related to success in college, although there are obvious exceptions. The student with no mathematics is in difficulty in engineering or science. The student whose work is entirely in vocational or business courses may, despite high grades, have difficulty in college. For transfer students, the best evidence is the record at the previous institution. Transfers frequently suffer a slump in grades during their first term after transferring, and a rather higher mortality occurs among transfer students than among the native students at similar levels—possibly because transfers seldom receive the attention given to freshmen. However, an institution may wish to establish a differential in the prior performance of transfers or to require demonstration of competence equal or superior to that of native students at the same class level. Community college administrators usually resist such action as a reflection on the quality of their program.

For graduate students, the undergraduate record plays much the same role as the high school record of the new freshmen. Here again the disparity in standards among disciplines and among colleges leads many institutions to require the Graduate Record Examination, the Miller Analogies Test, or some other test or battery of tests as a supplement to grades in making decisions about admission. If only pass-fail grades are available, test results become essential.

Affective factors, such as interests, values, and personality, have been much studied with a view to improving the selection process. Insofar as prediction of grades is concerned, the weight of the evidence is that affective assessment adds little. One of the problems is that college grades either take little account of affective factors or take account of them in an unsystematic way, depending upon the idiosyncrasies of individual instructors. Or perhaps other factors in selection result in a reasonably close matching between the affective characteristics of an individual and those prevalent in an institution, so that the resulting spread and mix is tolerable to the institution and to the individuals. However, individuals with atypical values, interests, or personalities are often among those who change their curriculums and whose academic performance is markedly lower than predicted. Often, too, they are among those who drop out during the freshman year even though their academic performance is satisfactory. Some colleges require an interview, and experienced admissions personnel often insist that, from an interview, they can make accurate assessments in the affective domain. However, extensive use of affective measures raises serious questions about equity in the process. Can imposition of affective requirements ever avoid the appearance of bias or prejudice? Research evidence thoroughly discredits the interview as a selective procedure, but it may prove useful if the institution desires students who favorably impress its admissions officer. At the present time, there is considerable concern that colleges depend too much on cognitive qualifications and pay too little attention to the creative area. There is surely validity in this concern, but it is also true that the typical college emphasis on cognitive outcomes yields an environment less than fully hospitable to the highly creative individual. Clearly, further evaluation in this area of affective criteria is desirable, but unambiguous results are not to be expected.

Psychomotor factors, such as athletic prowess, artistic talent, musical skill, and social competence, may also be taken into account in the admissions process. For instance, within a specified range of cognitive ability, an institution may wish to diversify its talent so as to include athletic ability, artistic skills, and social skills, and thereby build a community with a wide range of cultural, recreational, and athletic activities conducted at a high level of excellence. Or an institution may decide to accept lower cognitive standing when this is balanced by unusual talent in physical, social, or arts areas. The risk is that these individuals may lack the interests or ability to meet scholastic standards in required courses in science and language, although special tutoring and careful selection of instructors and sections can overcome this difficulty. Conceivably, talent in art or music could yield sufficiently high grades in these fields to counterbalance less than satisfactory grades elsewhere. Probably, however, an institution that decides to include in its student body individuals with a high degree of creative ability, athletic prowess, artistic talent, and the like will have to adjust its curriculum and its requirements to suit these individuals. In effect, the music major in many institutions is already a vocational rather than a liberal arts experience.

Mature adults returning to school after several years of work present complicated admissions problems. The usual criteria are unfair and irrelevant. Maturity, motivation, and goals should be assessed by specially selected and sensitive admissions personnel, and consideration should be given to individual programming, including the waiver of irrelevant undergraduate prerequisites and requirements.

An institution wishing to evaluate the effectiveness of its recruitment and admissions should collect data on each of the following points for each recruiter and admissions officer: contacts made with prospective applicants; applications filed; admissions granted; initial enrollments; continuing enrollments for one, two, three, and four years; transfers to other institutions; degree candidates still active; and degree recipients. Only then can the costs and effectiveness of the early stages of this sequence be critically examined. The conclusion might well be that more effort expended after initial enrollment would pay greater dividends than increased effort in recruitment and admission. The most selective institutions graduate only 85 to 90 percent of those initially enrolling, and less selective ones may graduate 30 percent or less.

Classification

Classification of a student into an appropriate major or curriculum may be part of the selection process. At the graduate level, it almost inevitably is, for applications are for specific programs and admissions are by schools or departments. In complex institutions with numerous specialized undergraduate programs, differences in requirements may cause selection and classification to be combined. For the student with deficiencies in mathematics or science, admission to engineering is impossible, at least until the deficiencies are removed. In many cases, however, classification is separable from admissions because the student is qualified for any of several majors or curriculums and is seeking evidence to assist in making a choice. Students, counselors, and colleges and departments all have a stake in this choice, and procedures for assisting students in appropriate choices should be a cooperative effort.

At times, university personnel may also have special concerns which are not altogether in the student's interest. For example, coaches may insist that athletes known to be marginal scholars major in an easy physical education program. Continued eligibility may be much more easily guaranteed both by the nature of the courses and by influence upon the instructional staff. Such practices should be identified and carefully scrutinized.

Classification can be conducted on a probabilistic or mechanical basis employing objective data, or it can be based upon a clinical and individual approach. One objective approach uses the technique of regression analysis, whereby a number of variables are combined to predict the average grades of a student in each of several fields. A different set of regression weightings is determined for each field, but the same basic variables (if sufficiently extensive) are used throughout. Presumably, then, the predicted grade averages indicate those fields in which the student is most likely to do the best work. This approach may differentiate effectively among such broad fields as the sciences, social sciences, and humanities. However, since verbal ability or general academic aptitude plays a significant role in success in all college fields, relatively few variables are the determining factors in prediction in all fields, and the differences in prediction are relatively small. In a few curricular areas, moreover, courses are relatively easy and grading is generous, so that almost all students make satisfactory grades in these areas, and many individuals find that their highest predicted performance is in one of these areas. Such information is almost useless and possibly dangerous, for it may encourage ill-advised choices. Although systems of *comparative* prediction have been worked out in a number of universities, their use for determination of the field appropriate for an individual is inappropriate. The results, however, may be useful in providing individual counseling.

Another type of prediction, *differential* prediction, focuses on the differences in performance in fields. Ideally, in this type of prediction different test batteries would be used for each field; or else an unusually comprehensive and unwieldy composite, covering all fields but containing information irrelevant to many, would be used. As already indicated, the actual difference in grade point averages for groups of students with the same general level and pattern of ability may be small. Indeed, the distinctiveness of programs may be limited to a few courses in which, however, success is essential and special abilities are required. Thus, in differential prediction the study of abilities or aptitudes which may not make a major contribution to over-all prediction of the grade point average, but which may contribute to successful performance in a few requirements or courses distinctive to a particular field, becomes necessary. One insuperable difficulty with the differential predictive model is that students seldom, if ever, complete the requirements for a number of different fields. Thus, in practice, no data on differential performance of individuals in different fields exist, and differentiated prediction based upon empirical evidence is impossible.

Another model which may be used for classification is that of the multiple-discriminant function. Both comparative and differential prediction require quantifiable data and use a regression model to predict success in one or more fields. The multiple-discriminant-function model takes into account a wide range of information, some of which involves only classification into categories, and attempts to determine whether distinctive subgroups of individuals are characterized by a distinctive array of traits. It then sets up a weighted combination of these which maximizes the spatial separation of these groups. The information on a given individual may be utilized to determine his or her location in reference to these various subgroups. Thus, individuals are placed with those persons whom they are most like in respect to whatever characteristics have been used in the original analysis. The multiple-discriminant-function approach may provide usable information where the regression approach does not. Thus, an individual might have similar predicted grade averages in physics and in engineering, but might be found by a multiple-discriminant-function approach to be much more like majors in physics than majors in engineering. Several studies have indicated distinct differences in student groups enrolled in the pure and in the applied sciences. Whether perpetuation of these differences by selection based upon them is desirable is an issue worthy of more attention than it has thus far received. Since we lack statistical confirmation of the role of these characteristics in ultimate success, the decision would have to be a subjective one.

There is, of course, a classification approach based on specific requirements. Admission to engineering requires a certain number of units in specific mathematics and science courses. The student lacking them will not be accepted in the engineering curriculum. Some advocates of this approach argue that students do not pay the full cost of their education and the institution cannot afford to subsidize the extra time in school required to make up deficiencies. Further, they argue that the student who has not taken such courses in secondary school has, in some way, betrayed a lack of motivation or commitment and therefore should be discouraged. The inequity of such an approach is most obvious when one recognizes the vast range of competence among students who have completed requirements. When requirements are general—that is, when they are not specific prerequisites to further study in the same field—classification based upon them should be viewed with suspicion; at the minimum, alternative bases for a decision should be provided. For instance, if in a certain field two years of high school mathematics are required, but no further mathematics is to be taken in college, the significance of that requirement is dubious. Even when the student plans to continue in the same field (such as mathematics or a foreign language), units taken in high school are not satisfactory evidence of ability to proceed with curricular requirements in that particular classification. Further testing is necessary. I return to this point under the discussion of placement.

A second approach to classification is the clinical or individual approach. In fact, as already noted, the data resulting from comparative prediction have been, in most cases, used as part of a counseling process with individuals rather than as a definitive basis for stating to a person that he or she can or cannot enter a particular field. The multiple-discriminant-function approach can similarly be used. In fact, the multiple-discriminant-function analysis corresponds more closely to counseling procedures than does the prediction approach because the counselor encourages an individual to consider a wide range of interests and personality traits and physical competences as well as intelligence and to explore the relationship of these to several possible fields of work. Some counselors utilize a rather directive approach in analyzing aptitudes and interests relative to curricular and vocational possibilities and suggest specific possibilities to an individual. Others urge that individuals engage in self-examination in depth and perhaps in an exploration of curricular or vocational possibilities in order to reach their own conclusions. The individual may be encouraged to try out a possibility for a semester or a year to determine the extent of interest and the adequacy of ability. One difficulty with this procedure in college is that many fields require a firm basis in the basic arts and sciences, and the courses which are distinctive to a special curriculum are not available in the freshman and sophomore years.

The counseling approach to classification may also put

remedial work in an appropriate light. People continually find that new developments require knowledge or competence which they lack. Individuals must decide whether they are willing to take the time and apply themselves to the extent required to develop such competence. They must decide where they want to be at the completion of college and what they must do to meet the standards set for the completion of a particular program. If an individual and flexible approach is possible, there is no undergraduate program that an *able* student could not finish in four years, whatever his or her status with regard to specific requirements at the time of entrance.

The clinical or individual approach can be expedited by curriculum requirements which emphasize general education and orientation. Thus, a program in which the first year or two consists of core course requirements coupled with an introduction to the various special curricula makes possible student exploration of alternatives. Ideally, the general education courses should open up the possibilities in the more specialized curricula and thus simultaneously provide a basis for specialized work as well as experience helpful in making a choice. However, the student with a definite vocational objective may be irritated or unchallenged by the general education requirements and may therefore leave. If this period does not provide opportunity for exploration as well as for general education, students may progress no further than they were at admission. Students interested in the sciences and technical fields can keep open a wide range of possibilities by concentrating on mathematics and science in the first year or two. Obviously, the possibilities raise many issues deserving of study in any college.

Some persons have proposed that counselors actively discourage individuals from entering fields in which an oversupply of workers presently exists or is predicted in the near future. But because our society regards education as an opportunity for individual development, counselors and admissions officers give only minimal attention to economic and social needs. Students may be informed that there are shortages in certain areas and possibly oversupplies in others, but they are seldom overtly pressured to choose on this basis. There is even a definite lack of interest in American higher education to tying undergraduate financial aid to a vocational field, although this has been done to some extent—as, for example, in the forgiving of some portion of a loan to teachers who engage actively in a teaching career after graduation. At the graduate level, initial preponderance of support for study in scientific and technical fields generated demands for equal assistance in other fields. Promotional material dramatizing needs and increased salaries in response to needs is no doubt effective in motivating choice. Ultimately, though, there exists a widespread belief in this country that a person well educated in any field can adapt to demands and find a suitable niche. Yet opportunities for reeducation to meet changing demands are limited, and education for adaptation is more a banner than an actuality.

The quality of the counseling provided on these matters deserves recurrent evaluation. Students should have the opportunity of evaluating their initial choices both by experience in some courses and by appraisal of their interests and aptitudes. They should also have information on employment prospects and career development possibilities. And they should know that changes in college or even in mid-career are often desirable.

Placement

Subsequent to selection and classification there may still be a problem of placement. For example, the mere fact that an entering student has had chemistry is not an adequate basis for placement of the student in a chemistry sequence since high school chemistry courses vary greatly in quality. Testing may indicate that some students should be placed in the second or third quarter of a freshman chemistry sequence or occasionally at an even more advanced level. It may also be desirable to section the first term of chemistry, not only to distinguish between those with or without previous chemistry but also to recognize those who have superior background in mathematics and in sciences other than chemistry.

Foreign language and mathematics involve similar problems, perhaps of even greater intensity because these fields may be pursued for three or four years in the secondary school. Students with two years of study of a foreign language may vary from a level suggesting almost no experience to a level approximating two years of study in college. Similarly, some entering freshmen show no mathematical aptitude, whereas others can take relatively advanced undergraduate mathematics.

Development of local placement tests is expensive and time-consuming; and, unless expert assistance is available, such tests may be of poor quality. Furthermore, the task is never done, for frequent revision is essential for security and for maintaining a proper relationship between the test and the course, which usually changes somewhat from year to year. Tests available from the Educational Testing Service could be used, but their acceptance by faculty members is often a matter of expediency rather than of conviction. The Advanced Placement Tests of the College Entrance Examination Board are usually taken only by students who have had special programs in secondary school. Therefore, in spite of the difficulties in developing local tests, institutions that accept large numbers of students from a variety of secondary schools will find that a locally developed testing program (which may include some commercially available instruments) is required to appropriately place students. In highly sequential disciplines the task of placement may involve quite comprehensive testing to determine whether knowledge and skills basic to continuation in advanced courses are present. In fields which are not so highly cumulative or sequential, vocabulary level, wide reading, and excellent reading ability may be the significant indicators of the appropriate level at which an individual can function.

With adults and with transfer students, where the concern in placement is largely that of determining the appropriate class level (freshman, sophomore, junior, senior) rather than the particular course sequences, the problem is even more complicated. How does one evaluate the educational level of an intelligent adult who had read widely, traveled extensively, and held responsible positions in higher education? In higher education we have tended to emphasize knowledge of specifics even though we know that these do not long remain with individuals. We do not have adequate equivalency examinations which measure whether one has the insight, the power, and the ability to learn —qualities that remain after specifics have fled.

One sensitive issue in respect to placement is the granting of credits. Colleges and their faculty members are much more willing to grant advanced placement than to give credit for the courses waived. External degree programs and state programs for granting credit by examination and other forms of appraisal bear witness to the reluctance of the traditional college to engage in this activity. The granting of credit by examination runs counter to the deeply seated convictions of many faculty members. These convictions are based upon several somewhat distinctive views about education. One view is that there is no satisfactory substitute for taking the course and for completing a full complement of credit requirements in the institution which awards the degree. Thus, a course offered in a secondary school, taken by correspondence, or completed by unsupervised individual effort can never be the equivalent of one offered in the college. Associated with this view is the concept of the professor as a scholar who provides to students an experience available only through another professor-scholar in the same discipline in the same or another college. Another view is that the four-year period and the degree-credit requirement are fixed and that each student should advance within that framework. Accordingly, advanced placement is acceptable, but without credit, so that the student simply takes additional courses— perhaps even graduate courses in unusual cases. The concept of a degree as a well-defined level of achievement and of placement as a determinant of the progress of an individual toward that level has not been widely understood and certainly has not been a part of the faculty view.

Foreign language facility is a notable example of the attitudes and problems involved. Foreign students who must demonstrate sufficient facility in English to study in an American college are not, in many colleges, granted credit for their native language facility. When facility in two foreign languages is required for the doctorate, foreign graduate students often find that neither English nor their native language is acceptable. As foreign language requirements have been liberalized or discarded, somewhat greater flexibility has appeared.

Honors work has been, too frequently, a device to justify retention of undergraduates who display capability for study well in advance of the average undergraduate. And in some colleges, an honors college accepting outstanding students at an early phase of their college career has also served to extend their education for the full period and credit quota, thereby avoiding the issue of early completion of the degree. In some colleges now pursuing a three-year degree, the principal devices are summer study and heavier schedules rather than acceleration or advanced placement.

Students differ in their views on advanced placement, credit, and acceleration. Many are degree seekers, but they also view college as their last four years of pleasant living prior to assuming the cares of adulthood. They have no desire to reduce the four-year term, and neither have they any desire to enter advanced courses which would require intensive effort and possibly result in a lower grade. On the whole, these attitudes are supported by faculty, although for somewhat different reasons. Those students who display ability which would indicate advanced placement, credit, and acceleration are encouraged to take other courses, honors work, independent study, or any other work which ensures continuance for the full period. Acceleration is acceptable to most faculty members when it involves increased credit and course loads, summer school attendance, and a constant record of A's. In six trimesters (two years) a student taking 20 credits a trimester could finish the 120 semester hours required for a degree.

The mature individual returning to school and concerned with time and responsibilities finds difficulty in obtaining consideration from a faculty oriented to an education described in the credit-time mode. Even when adjustments are made, they may be accompanied (as students have frequently reported) by a tolerant, condescending attitude suggesting that not much can be expected from a person who does not attend college in the traditional way.

We need widespread acceptance of the view that ascertaining the amount of work needed for a college degree is a matter of assessment and prescription. Initial assessment of an individual seeking a degree should ascertain knowledge, skills, and abilities, not simply in existing courses or disciplines but in the broad sense of knowing concepts and principles, thinking clearly, and having good communication skills. This initial individual assessment should then be compared with the outcomes or expected status. To a considerable extent, this must be a subjective decision based in part upon the individual but in large part upon the consensus of the faculty. The discrepancies between present status and ultimate status require decisions in regard to experiences or treatments required to achieve the objectives—treatments such as individualized materials and objectives, pacing, and enrichment. Those making such decisions should consider the interests and learning patterns of the individual; aptitudes, knowledge, and competence; continuity and sequence of educational experiences; time required; anticipated personal satisfaction and persistence; objectives or outcomes; relationship between personal traits and particular experiences (trait-treatment interaction); side effects; costs; and the possibility of correcting decision errors.

This model, as Willingham (1974a, p. 10) points out, would put decision making in the placement and program areas into the context of decision theory. In this context, the three major variables are time, cost, and individual achievement. Cost is divided between the individual and the institution, and both have reason to keep costs within bounds if not to minimize it. Time and cost are interrelated; if one assumes that cost both to individual and institution is a function of time, the variables are reduced from three to two. Whereas the faculty would keep time constant (four years) and maximize achievement, an alternative is to fix a minimal acceptable level of achievement and also to minimize the time required to reach that level. In fact, the problem is further complicated by the varying costs of treatments or experiences and by the necessity of keeping the student in a program which provides a degree of personal satisfaction. The problem posed then might be: How do we minimize the time required to achieve a degree by appropriate selection of treatments which do not exceed a specified cost? Perhaps the time, treatment, and cost might be jointly varied, with more expensive treatments reducing time and with some individuals meeting the standards in short periods of time and with unusually low costs. However, some individuals might not be able to meet the standards under the cost limitations because of inadequate preparation or ability. As Willingham points out (1974, pp. 10-16), trait-treatment interactions hold the key to effective adaptation to individual differences. Assignment to treatments by a placement test requires that the test have different regression slopes for each treatment or that different tests be used for each treatment and that the student take all of them. We are back to the problem of differential prediction discussed earlier.

In fact, however, the complications of the placement-test approach, including the personal and social values involved, are such that mathematical decision theory will not play a significant role in placement. The major difficulty is that no dollar value can be assigned to learning outcomes or degree standards. Nevertheless, the concepts of and the mode of thinking in decision theory have real value in thinking about placement problems. The need for extensive evaluation of the placement process is apparent.

Orientation and Counseling

The orientation of a new student to a college is frequently confined to an orientation period in the summer or just preceding the fall term. Orientation includes such diverse events as a series of tests, inventories, biographical forms; a presidential welcome; college or major convocations; residence hall orientation or social functions; campus and library tours; health examinations; student government and student activity presentations; counseling and advising contacts; enrollment; registration; and payment of fees. Transfer students are ignored, are required to participate in some of the sessions for new freshmen, or are given special sessions. In large universities, this group may be so diverse in background and extent of preparation (one or two courses to three years of work elsewhere) that no common orientation for all transfers is feasible. Once a pattern of orientation is set, bureaucracy tends to make it an inflexible requirement for all. Yet much of the typical orientation program is inappropriate for advanced undergraduates and for adults; indeed, much of it is untimely if not inappropriate for the entering freshmen.

An evaluation of orientation, in order to clarify its purposes and its relation with other activities, would lead to its reshaping in many institutions. Assumptions such as the following may be the starting point.

1. Orientation is a continuing process, starting with admission and extending over at least the first year; for students unsettled in a major or beset with various problems of adjustment, it may continue into the second, third, and even fourth years.

2. Orientation is a phase of a continuing counseling-advising process.

3. Incoming students vary so markedly in interests, ability, and maturity that what concerns some does not concern others.

4. Talking *at* individuals in large groups, especially when other matters are more pressing to them, is not effective in communicating information, conveying a welcome, or offering assistance.

5. For freshmen living away from home for the first time, living conditions, social opportunities, and friendship can be almost as important as orientation to the academic programs.

6. Parades of personalities across a platform or in a reception line probably do more for the ego of those thus exhibited than for the students.

7. Heavy testing programs, which have neither an immediate feedback nor a reasonable explanation, are time-consuming, wearisome, and even frightening to some students.

8. Materials sent to new students prior to arrival on campus, if carefully done and limited to essentials, are more likely to be an effective method of communication than materials handed out or oral statements made after arrival. Excessive and uncoordinated mailings of diverse materials are counterproductive.

All these are assumptions; but some, such as 4, 6, and 7, have also been validated by interviews or questionnaire responses of students. If the students find little or no help from the experiences or are confused or worn out by them, the effects are largely negative. A major deficiency of such programs is that *all* students are told about something (remedial reading, tutoring services, or student paper opportunities) at a time when *none* is really concerned. Later, when the information would be useful, it may not even be readily found.

Altering orientation programs to account for such weaknesses is not easily accomplished. Student-run orientation programs are generally deadly, but the student leaders change from one year to another, and all the incoming leaders are likely to react strongly against any diminution of their role. The same (in all respects) holds for the typical parade of deans (personnel and academic).

Such questions as the following need to be asked and honestly answered with regard to each activity considered for inclusion in orientation:

1. How many students need to know about this activity prior to enrollment?

2. What evidence is there that inclusion of this activity in the program is successful with students?

3. What individuals or offices particularly benefit by the inclusion of this activity?

4. Does convenience or ego massaging of program participants outweigh benefits to the institution and the students?

5. What are the costs of the inclusion of this activity in dollars, in confusion of objectives, and in possible elimination of more desirable alternatives?

6. Could this activity be held at some other time and place with less difficulty and with greater gain for the target audience?

If orientation is viewed as merging into continuing counseling and advising, evaluation should include an examination of this relationship. In some colleges, a seminar or course is assigned a continuing orientation role. Classification, placement, and career development are natural extensions of orientation and should be evaluated in this context.

Advising and counseling are used interchangeably at times, but some distinction is desirable. Advising is typically a responsibility assigned to a faculty member to assist students (individually or in small groups) in selection of courses and fulfillment of degree requirements, to monitor academic performance, and to respond (to whatever extent the adviser's interests and capabilities permit) to student concerns or questions about electives, major, preparation for examinations, study habits, mathematical deficiencies, reading difficulties, career development, and personal problems. However, few faculty members have any special competence beyond assisting in choice of a major and then only within their own discipline or field. Study habits, reading difficulties, and deficiencies in mathematical skills require special services which are not available on all campuses but may be provided in a counseling center or elsewhere. The adviser's competence stops at knowing when, where, and how to refer the student. Advice or preparation for examinations may come from many sources including the instructor, remedial reading courses, a study habits clinic, or another and more able student in the same class.

As interdisciplinary programs have become common, as programs generally have become flexible, and as students display concern for career planning, the typical faculty adviser has little to offer to many students. Yet concern about majors causes faculty members to insist on their prerogatives; at the same time, if advising is considered an extra burden, the efforts to evaluate faculty performance in this role are negated. The costs of faculty advising are hardly calculable because of the overload concept, and hence attempts to recapture dollars for support of an alternative advising system are defeated. Only when the advising role has been directly subsidized by extra payment to advisers or by a reduction in teaching load is there a substantive basis for renegotiation. Costing in reference to opportunities forgone is also an uncertain enterprise. Advising seriously undertaken may reduce time for other professional activities, or it may only replace some other less directed form of socializing with students. Hence, an alternative to faculty advising usually adds to total costs but demonstrates little or no gain in other faculty activities. There may be some loss also in that removal of student advising contacts may (whatever the quality of the advising) render the professor less sensitive to students and hence less effective as a teacher.

If an extensive evaluation of advising is to be undertaken, there are numerous types and sources of evidence and many ways of collecting it. The sources of evidence include the students, the advisers themselves, colleagues, departmental chairmen, academic deans, personnel deans, residence hall personnel. Students, by use of rating forms (analogous to those used for teaching) or by interview, provide information on adviser contacts, on the nature and worth of the contacts, and on satisfactions, problems, or deficiencies. Advisers can report on contacts and their difficulties and satisfactions as advisers. Colleagues and administrators—through their observations, awareness of student comments, and overall appraisal of the cumulative effort of individual faculty members—are another source of appraisal. Unobtrusive measures—for instance, errors and changes in enrollment, requested changes of advisers, delays or failures in completing curriculum requirements, use by advisees of special services, time of declaration of major, later changes, and completion of degree—also can be used to assess the effectiveness of advising. Whatever might ultimately be done about alteration of advising assignments or selection of advisers, such evidence cautiously communicated to individuals or used in in-service training programs should assist in improving advising.

The significance of the advising assignment in many colleges is demeaned by certain policies and practices. For example, if advising assignments are limited to one or two years, with the expectation that the chairman of the major department become the adviser upon declaration of major, both the nature of the advising function and the extent of contact with the adviser are thereby limited to inconsequentials. Likewise, when advisers are viewed as necessary primarily to enforce requirements, they have a menial role. In contrast, if advising is viewed as something approximating a tutorial role or as a key continuing contact to foster unity in the undergraduate program, a different result is attained.

The faculty advising role is also complicated by the presence of other sources of advice. When residence halls include advisers or counselors who do not have adequate background for that role, the students become understandably confused about who does what for or to them. Student personnel workers, in their desire to assist individuals, may also enter the scene. Professional counselors, usually working on the fringes of the students' academic programs, often detect adviser errors and may, with no mean intent, cast aspersions on advising.

In brief, the advising role is usually ill-defined; it has few prerogatives and is inadequately rewarded and undersupported. It is often undermined by criticism and by competing services, yet it is regarded as essential. Formative evaluation is more likely to be successful than condemnation by summative evaluation, but such evaluation necessarily has to be continuing and aimed as much at altering administrative policies and practices as at the advisers themselves.

Counseling, as earlier defined, differs from advising in that counselors have specialized training and assume a responsibility for facilitation of personal development, including dealing with personal, emotional, social, and career problems as well as academic matters. Persons with problems which interfere with functioning but are not disabling constitute a significant part of the counseling clientele. With those who have more serious problems or difficulties, referral to health and psychiatric services becomes a significant and sensitive function. Some students resist the referral, some counselors hesitate to make it, and some physicians and psychiatrists are convinced that counselors overestimate their competence. Thus, counselors operate in a situation in which their activities, too, are peculiarly subject to skepticism or criticism from many sources. Hence, any attempt to evaluate counseling runs the risk of arousing anxiety on the part of counselors that a reappraisal can result only in criticism and in redistribution of some portion of their resources. Yet an evaluation conducted by counseling staff, as with any other university unit, leads only to the conclusion that more resources are required.

An evaluation of counseling should look at the following:

(1) history of the rationale for establishing a counseling program; (2) changes in conception and role over time and the relationship of these to changing needs, policies, and requirements in the institution; (3) the interrelationship (formal arrangement and actual operation) of the counseling staff with student personnel, health services, academic deans, faculty, central administration, residence halls; (4) the role of the counseling staff in instruction, internships, off-campus services, research; (5) views of students, faculty, and administrators; (6) the source, characteristics, and problems of counselees and procedures for dealing with counseling case load; (7) qualifications, reward system, and retention of counseling staff; (8) evidence of successful counseling as reflected in counselee evaluations; case histories, reactions of deans, faculty, and others who have referred students to counseling; (9) case loads to determine whether undue time and resources are being used for individuals requiring intensive long-term therapy or lacking interest in and capability for satisfactory performance in an academic milieu; and (10) costs and benefits. This evaluation can be a time-consuming procedure. The estimate of costs and benefits is particularly difficult. Counselors quite understandably prefer voluntary or self-referrals, so there is always a question whether the clientele is that most needful of the service. Yet any appraisal must take into account that sound educational policy asserts that any student with a problem should be able to take it to someone. Reduction or elimination in counseling services only reassigns that burden elsewhere, with the possibility that it will be less adequately assumed or entirely ignored.

Summary

Underlying the processes of recruitment, selection, classification, and placement and the associated functions of orientation, advising, and counseling are several basic values relating to individuals and to the institution. *Equity* or *fairness* to the prospective student is rightfully a major concern. Yet an institution does a disservice to the financially or educationally disadvantaged when it recruits individuals to whom it is unable to offer adequate financial assistance, special services, or educational programs. There must be a suitable *fit* between institutional programs and the needs and aspirations of students. Undue allocation of resources to individuals with special needs may be unfair to the other clients. The suitability of this fit is, in great part, revealed by the *retention* of students until the completion of an appropriate program. A brief stay in a college may be beneficial if the dropouts or failures have been sensitively treated or redirected, but there is an equal possibility that only an additional indignity has been laid upon individuals who are already victims of social inequities. Fairness is also involved in the extent to which the institution extends to each student the opportunity to make decisions which affcct his or her college program. The manner in which recruitment, selection, classification, and placement are conducted can involve inequities. Arbitrary assignment to special programs or treatments fall into this category. In most colleges, departments play a major role in final decisions about advanced placement and granting credit. Variations in attitudes on these matters among departments lead to inequities. Evaluation of variations in execution of stated institutional policies is thus highly desirable.

Efficiency is desirable but is always somewhat at odds with equity and perhaps with quality. The most efficient way to meet social and economic requirements appears to lie in selection of well-prepared students who successfully complete high-standard educational requirements in minimal time and with minimal costs for special services. Yet this may be a short-sighted view. Equity, through removal of injustice and indignity, may be attained only when appropriate proportions of the previously disenfranchised are found in each of the many vocations and professions required in our society. *Quality*, defined in relation to service potential in a heterogeneous society, is not necessarily the same as quality defined by grades, cognitive ability, or even professional skills. Sensitivity to and experience with certain problems may be significant components of success with certain segments of society.

In particular, no evaluation should assume that high *costs* indicate either quality or inefficiency. The social costs of achieving efficiency through reducing costs, even if quality in some sense is maintained, can be high, though the costs may be (as they have been) charged elsewhere: to police protection, welfare, and other sectors of public expenditures.

Evaluation which attempts to relate equity, fit, retention, efficiency, quality, and costs will not be easy. Collection of relevant data is difficult, but much more difficult is the task of resolving the semantic complications and the value conflicts involved in those criteria. Some prefer to leave well enough alone, but surely careful examination and reflection can lead to policy statements which clarify and justify existing procedures or lead to others which can be openly adhered to with good conscience.

Bibliographical Note

The following issues were not addressed directly in the chapter but are important in the overall treatment of students in higher education.

Huff (1975) and Leslie and Fife (1974) address the large-scale impacts of federal and state student financial-aid policies. Both articles reveal surprising effects of these policies which hold significant implications for the future.

Tinto (1975) presents an excellent analysis and synopsis of the literature relating to dropouts. His article should be the first of many studies analyzing the college student from a realistic and ultimately meaningful perspective.

Willingham's report (1974a) is a definitive study of placement practices in higher education. It also includes an extensive bibliography.

Chickering's (1974a) research is disturbing in that he reinforces traditional ideas about the commuting student and points out that the proportion of commuting students is high and rising.

Chapter 8

Learning Environment

Prior to the development of large municipal universities and community colleges, the prevalent pattern of college attendance required leaving home and residing on a campus for four years. The college was usually small, rural, residential, and liberal arts in emphasis. Students were regarded as naive and inexperienced, so the college was expected to accept parental responsibility, to impose regulations assuring a protected environment, and to monitor conduct during the student's transition from childhood to adult status. A college education was viewed as a twenty-four-hour-a-day, seven-day-a-week experience which had to be carefully guided and controlled. Character development was accepted as an obligation, and the environment was shaped not so much to mold character as to force conformity to the accepted conception of good character. Effort was made to absorb the few students who maintained a local residence into the college environment.

Thus, in an earlier era, residence halls and even private rooming and boarding houses were under rigorous supervision and students were subject to rigid rules regarding hours, week-day chapel and Sunday church attendance, dress, and sociali-zation between sexes. In their time, these practices were re-garded as aspects of character building. Moreover, it was ex-pected that these requirements would eliminate many distrac-tions and encourage focus on scholarly pursuits. In theory at least, residence on the campus provided interaction with the faculty on many fronts; campus residence also permitted col-leges to schedule and possibly to require attendance at various musical, artistic, dramatic, and other events. Just how effective this pervasive environmental approach to higher education was is not possible to say. There was little or no alternative.

Since 1950, the continuing rapid growth of higher educa-tion has shifted the mass of enrollment, so that well over 70 percent of the students are enrolled in community colleges, large urban universities, or public colleges and universities. The year 1974 marked the first in which part-time enrollment ex-ceeded full-time enrollment. The day of the four-year stay on a small campus is gone. Many students now attend class and use campus facilities between classes but are otherwise not involved. Residence halls have, to a large extent, become little more than rented facilities for many inmates, who apparently prefer it that way.

In this same period several other trends have called into question the importance of the sustained environment as a sig-nificant element in higher education. First, the increasing num-ber of graduate students and professional students limit their campus contacts to faculty and facilities unique to their special-ties. For professional students, off-campus facilities used for field work, hospital experience, and service may be much more significant than those on campus. Second, the temporary popu-larity of the living-learning concept as a theme for new colleges provides evidence that residence halls and extracurricular pro-grams have become remote from academic life. Third, the popu-larity of off-campus work and service programs and of travel and study abroad indicates that the campus environment is in many respects an unrealistic one which hinders rather than assists the relating of student learning to the world scene in which it must ultimately be applied. Finally, the surge toward external degree programs and the granting of credit for informal learning from life experiences arise out of the conviction that an extended campus residency is an expensive luxury and may not even be as motivating (at least for some people) as active involvement in work, family, and community.

In some sense environment does play a vital role in all these alternatives, but not quite in the manner envisaged in the efforts at environmental assessment to date; in approach and in substance, these efforts hark back to an earlier concept of a unified total campus experience. But, before pursuing environmental assessment further, we need to consider just what is meant by the term *environment* as used in education. Environment, as usually defined, refers to the conditions, circumstances, and influences which surround and affect the development of an organism or a group of organisms. Another term, *climate*, frequently used interchangeably with environment, is similarly defined as prevailing conditions affecting life or activity. Both these definitions differentiate organisms and life from conditions, circumstances, or influences. This differentiation corresponds to a concept of environments and people interacting in or through processes designed to achieve certain objectives. The environment thus includes such psychological, social, and physical components as these: campus mores, traditions, rules; acceptable standards of behavior and achievement; innovative-conservative balance; issues and controversies; grounds, architecture, facilities; value orientations and priorities; organizational structure. The difficulty in separating these components from people is obvious, but these seven components can certainly be regarded as long-standing characteristics of a campus. It is possibly appropriate, consistent with the views of others who have attempted to assess environments, to add to the environmental components the characteristics of the students, faculty, and administration.

The relationship between groups and environmental characteristics is one of the important aspects of environmental assessment. The heterogeneity of the student population in a large institution likely means that there is not one but several environments, induced in part by the characteristics of the various subgroups but perhaps even in greater part by the selectivity in exposure of these subgroups to different aspects of the environment. I have already noted that undergraduates, graduates, and professional students may be immersed in distinct environments within the same institution. Within these groups, but more especially within the undergraduates, dichotomies may exist between traditional and nontraditional students, residential and commuter students, full-time and part-time students, men and women, minorities and nonminorities. Nontraditional students may be immersed in one or several programs or colleges; full-time and part-time students seldom intermingle; and some subgroups (minorities, foreign students) often, either by their own choice or otherwise, use different facilities.

To a considerable extent, programs and services may also become part of unique environments or, at least, constitute a unique subset of processes (people-program interactions). Tutoring and other individualized services (including special counseling) have, on some campuses, become oriented to the needs of the economically and educationally disadvantaged. Professional schools frequently develop their own counseling and personnel services and have separate social programs for students and faculty. Residence halls, especially those assigned to living-learning academic units, may operate almost as isolated entities within the larger institutions.

Clearly, environmental assessment is a complicated task in that any unitary approach to it within an institution may only gloss over distinctive factors, so that the generalizations which emerge have no validity either in describing reality or in affording bases for change or adaptation. Perhaps the best way to gain insights into the problems of assessing environment is to critically review the various procedures which have been used.

Environmental Assessment Procedures

A demographic approach to characterization of environments quickly demonstrates that institutions vary in financial affluence, in intellectual characteristics of students and faculty, in size, in sex of the student body, in the homogeneity or heterogeneity of offerings, and in technical emphasis. These identifiable quantitative and qualitative descriptors of an institution are all subject to change but only as a result either of major decisions to alter the character of an institution or of catastrophic events which force such alteration.

A second approach to environmental assessment starts with the question "Who lives here?" The answers lead to characterization of students by intellectual abilities, origins, values (academic, collegiate, vocational, nonconformist), goals, and occupational interests. A third alternative is to ask the question "How do individuals behave?" Here the evidence collected seeks to determine how people (students, faculty, administrators) use their time as well as the motivations, goals, and concerns which dictate this use of time. A fourth approach solicits views about the environment or the interactions and processes taking place in the environment. Still another possible approach is to determine the needs which exist in an institution. Several possibilities exist here. The needs might be those identified by experts (usually the faculty) based upon standards derived from their own experiences, beliefs, and aspirations; they might be derived from an assessment of the demands or wants of the students, faculty, public, or employers; they could result from determination of the extent to which various existing services are used, abused, or neglected; or they might be derived by comparisons with other institutions, through the use of norms from an extensive survey of like institutions or ones that the institution wishes to emulate. An institution's approach to need identification tends to determine the patterns of environmental assessment which are likely to have utility. For example, faculty members who regard the definition of campus character as a professional obligation and prerogative are not much impressed with student views until their own livelihood is endangered by decreasing enrollments.

A review of some of the instruments for assessing aspects of the environment indicates the various approaches and definitions used as well as some of the problems involved.

Astin (1968) views an environmental influence as any characteristic constituting a potential stimulus capable of changing the student's sensory input. In his view, environments are transmitted by people, and the environment depends upon personal characteristics of students, faculty, administrators, and staff. To describe a college environment one must identify and measure those observable institutional characteristics that are likely to have some impact on student development. The existence or occurrence of these characteristics must be confirmable by independent observation.

Earlier (1961), Astin and Holland used the following characteristics as a basis for describing environment: selectivity (number of able students who apply for admission divided by number admitted), size (total full-time enrollment), realistic orientation (percentage of degrees in agriculture and several other applied fields), scientific orientation (percentage of degrees in natural science), social orientation (percentage of degrees in education, nursing, social work, social science), conventional orientation (percentage of degrees in accounting, business, economics, library science), enterprising orientation (percentage of degrees in advertising, business, history, political science, prelaw, journalism, international relations, foreign service), and artistic orientation (percentage of degrees in fine arts, language, music, speech). One may quarrel with some of these groupings and even more with their labels, but they do yield definite distinctions among institutions.

In his Inventory of College Activities, Astin (1968, pp. 8ff.) attempts to identify environmental stimuli observable by students and reportable in a questionnaire. This instrument includes items developed under these headings: college environment—peer, classroom, administrative, and physical environment; college image—subjective impressions, ratings of environmental traits, evaluations and satisfactions; personal characteristics of students—educational and vocational plans, self-ratings, ratings of roommates' traits. Astin found some inconsistencies among these several approaches, but he did find extensive institutional differences. He ignored the impact of environmental stimuli upon faculty and administrators and regarded each institution as a single environmental entity.

Another significant weakness from my point of view is that this approach seems to confuse experiences, processes, and interactions subject to academic planning with environmental characteristics and student characteristics not readily subject to modification.

Another instrument, the College and University Environment Scales (CUES), was developed by Pace (1969) to "aid colleges and universities in defining the atmosphere or intellectual-social-cultural climate of the campus." Atmosphere, as used here, refers to people, traditions, policies, programs, physical environment, attitudes, values, sense of awareness, involvement and controversy, and interactions among these. The items on the scale call for student perceptions and are viewed as characterizing the institution when either 66 percent of the respondents indicate that the item is true or 33 percent indicate that it is false. The items are categorized in five basic scales: practicality—enterprise, organization, material benefits, social activities, knowing right people, good fun, school spirit; community—friendly, cohesive, group-oriented campus; awareness—search for meaning (personal, poetic, or political), tolerance of nonconformity, expressiveness, questioning, and dissent; propriety—polite, considerate, thoughtful, cautious, proper, conventional; scholarship—intellectuality, scholastic orientation, disciplinary emphasis. Two additional scales, dealing with campus morale and with quality of teaching and faculty relationships, bring together items used in the other scales. The term *atmosphere* rather than environment is advisedly used in describing this instrument in that it deals more with people and interactions than with environment per se.

The instrument is not scored for individuals in the usual way. The score for a scale is the number of items answered by 66 percent or more of the respondents in the keyed direction less the number answered by 33 percent or fewer in the keyed direction. To this, 20 is added to avoid negative scores. The item rather than the individual is the basis for scoring. The result is a count of dominant collective perceptions. This is an excellent instrument in many respects, and because it is, it is a useful tool for considering many of the issues involved in environmental assessment.

Although the results can be productive for discussion, neither the categories used in this scale nor its student perception approach deals with those issues of most vital concern on most campuses. The underlying assumptions and values which give rise to institutional differentiations on the several categories are not ones upon which there is faculty or student consensus as to either meaning or desirability. Hence, the use of the instrument is unlikely to produce significant change.

The student perception approach has several weaknesses, as various samples selected from CUES reveal. Item 12, "Most of the professors are dedicated scholars in their fields," forces the student to render an overall judgment with limited basis for so doing. Except in the smallest colleges students have no first-hand basis for judging the scholarship of "most professors." Moreover, small colleges frequently play up certain professors as outstanding scholars when, in fact, they are not. Asking students to make a generalization for which they lack adequate evidence encourages a dubious pattern of overgeneralization. When the words used, such as *scholar*, take on different meanings according to the quality and character of an institution, the item itself has no fixed meaning, and interinstitutional comparisons become suspect.

The extensive use of such words or phrases as *most, almost always, frequent, lot of,* and *typically* in the items reflects a loose language usage which is deplorable. Certainly such usage is thoroughly discouraged by teachers, whether in humanities, social sciences, or science. Should we require students to react to statements which we otherwise discourage and disparage? I think not, unless we can relate the responses to subsequent discussions in which the dangers of overgeneralization are considered. Clearly, a college should not set objectives for critical analysis and reasoned judgment and then encourage or force dubious responses, especially if these are to be used to bring about change.

Item 53, "Everyone has a lot of fun at this school," poses the same problems as the previous item, but with the added difficulty that the only reasonable response for any school is "false." There will certainly be a few persons who do not have a lot of fun. An individual who might make this statement informally may have difficulty in accepting it when it is presented to him in a formal way. The same criticism can be made of the statements "A controversial speaker always stirs up a lot of student discussion" and "Concerts and art exhibits always draw big crowds of students."

Such a statement as "This school has a reputation for being very friendly" poses another problem. The student is asked to react to a perception attributed to others—a second-level perception. This becomes an impossible item for the critically minded person who knows that the school's reputation is promoted and widely believed but who doubts its truth.

Item 58, "Students must have a written excuse for absence from class," is ambiguous in that it is not clear whether policy or practice is at issue. Experience would indicate that even if a college had such a rule, some instructors would not enforce it. What does the student do when he knows that the rule exists but is not enforced?

The manual argues that a majority response can scarcely be wrong, but in fact a majority *can* be wrong in its perceptions; the reality or truth of some of the issues presented is complex. Segments of the faculty might differ, and the administrative perceptions might be at odds with both student and faculty perception. In my perception, faculty, student, administrator discussions of many of these perceptions get absolutely nowhere, but my perception is not necessarily either true or shared by others. And if perceptions of individuals and groups do not accord with reality, what does one change—the perceptions, by education or indoctrination; the perceivers, by revised selection procedures; or the reality? That the perceptions are real in a certain sense is surely true, and individuals act on their perceptions. But prestidigitators, psychologists, and college administrators have demonstrated that illusions are readily found or produced.

Most of these difficulties could be removed if the students were asked to indicate their own personal experiences and first-hand observations. Students can, with honesty, state that they attend art exhibits, that they have been late to class, or that one or more of their instructors takes attendance. Whether it is desirable to use this approach and generalize from individual perception or ask the students to generalize in their response is not only an evaluation issue but also an educational one.

Another scale, the Institutional Functioning Inventory (Educational Testing Service, 1968), describes an institution's values and commitments: (1) intellectual, aesthetic, extracurricular, (2) freedom—academic and personal, (3) human diversity—heterogeneity, (4) improvement of society—solving social problems, (5) undergraduate learning, (6) democratic governance, (7) meeting local needs—educational manpower, (8) selfstudy and planning, (9) advancing knowledge—research and scholarship, (10) innovation—commitment to innovate and explore, (11) institutional spirit—sense of shared purposes and high morale. Categories 4, 5, 7, and 9 relate to institutional goals or purposes, whereas 1, 2, and 3 involve value commitments regarding the institutional environment. Numbers 6, 8, 10, and 11 relate to the way in which the institution goes about its business. That institutions differ in the profiles derived from this instrument is to be expected. If "is" and "should be" responses can be acquired, gaps or disagreements could be productive of discussions leading to changes. Various subgroups, such as students, faculty members, administrators, and board members, can be asked to respond to this inventory with the expectation of considerable variance in perceptions, both within and among the groups. Comparisons among institutions are also possible. The instrument, by title, would seem to focus on processes, but in fact its coverage includes goals as well as processes. The responses are perceptions, and the profile can be regarded as an environmental characterization.

The Institutional Goals Inventory (Educational Testing Service, 1972) is an attempt to provide a means for assessing priorities among various outcome and process goals in such manner as to promote study of intergroup and interinstitutional comparisons, as well as within-group variations. The goals are divided into the following outcome and process goals:

Outcome Goals

Academic development: acquisition of knowledge, high intellectual standards

Intellectual orientation: attitudes about learning and intellectual work

Individual personal development: personal goals, sense of self-worth, self-confidence

Humanism/altruism: respect for diverse cultures, peace, moral issues, welfare of man

Cultural/aesthetic awareness: appreciation of art forms, humanities, student participation in such activities

Traditional religiousness

Vocational preparation: specific occupational curriculums, career fields, and career planning

Advanced training: availability of advanced graduate education

Research: extension of the frontiers of knowledge through research

Meeting local needs: continuing education for adults, cultural and resource center

Public service: commitment of institutional resources to solution of social and environmental problems

Social egalitarianism: open admissions, educational experiences relevant to the evolving interests of women, attention to the needs of minority groups

Social criticism/activism: criticisms of prevailing American values, working for basic changes in American society

Process Goals

Freedom: academic freedom and freedom for faculty and students to choose their own life styles

Democratic governance: responsive and participative government

Community: mutual trust, interaction and communication, and respect among students, faculty, administrators

Intellectual/aesthetic environment: intellectually exciting campus

Innovation: ferment, experimentation

Off-campus learning: travel, work-study, credit by examination

Accountability/efficiency: concern for program efficiency and
   accountability and effectiveness

Again, it is evident that various types of institutions should
yield differing profiles on these goals. Although these goals do
not directly provide or even describe an environment, they
surely influence it and must be consistent with it. If goals and
environment are not reinforcing, then action is required to
avoid conflicts and low morale, which will certainly result.
Nevertheless, most institutions, even small colleges, accommodate individuals with vastly different goals and priorities and
provide reasonably congenial subenvironments for them.

   Such matters as protection of academic freedom, open
communication, rich program of cultural events, although they
refer to processes, do characterize an environment which is
more hospitable to some processes and people than to others.
Careful reading of this goals instrument shows that tight categorical delineations of people, environment, processes, and goals
are virtually impossible, though some distinctions are certainly
used. Such distinctions involving process goals are more prob-
lematical than are those involving outcome goals.

   The College Student Questionnaires (Educational Testing
Service, 1965) provide a means for collecting extensive biographical and attitudinal information about students. Part 1 is
intended for use with entering students prior to the opening of
the academic year. This part includes sections covering educational and vocational plans and expectations, secondary school
activities, achievements and perceptions, family background,
and personal attitudes. Part 2, to be administered near the end
of the academic year, has sections on educational and vocational plans (identical with the first part of Part 1, except for
deletion of items on anticipated activities, satisfactions, and
problems); college activities, covering satisfactions, problems,
study techniques, attitudes regarding faculty, rules, major field,
and other aspects of the college experience; and personal attitudes (identical with the fourth part of Part 1). The use of this
instrument facilitates studies of entering students, student
plans, dropout and retention patterns, sources of satisfaction

and dissatisfaction, student typologies, and student change. Interinstitutional comparisons, intrainstitutional comparisons of various groups, change over time, and identification of particular concerns or trouble spots are all facilitated by use of this instrument. Repeated administration to successive entering groups permits detection of changing characteristics of incoming students.

Another instrument, Student Reactions to College (Educational Testing Service, 1974), is in many respects analogous to the College Student Questionnaires but is designed especially for use with community colleges. Four broad areas are covered: processes of instruction and studying, goals and plans of students, administrative regulations and problems in scheduling classes, and student activities and general problems of living (housing, finances, transportation). In addition, an extensive set of item categories (twenty-five in all) covers activities and attitudes in regard to such specifics as studying, counseling, extracurricular activities, library, faculty contact, program planning, living problems, scheduling, and registration. Again, these various subsections include both environmental processes and interaction patterns.

Centra (1968) developed the Questionnaire on Student and College Characteristics for use with College Board member colleges which elected to use the instrument as a possible aid in describing themselves to prospective students in the 1969 *College Handbook*. Although the colleges made limited use of the results for the intended purpose, Centra's analysis of the instrument and some of his findings are important.

The instrument included student perceptions of their institution, self-reports of activities, interests, and demographic-family characteristics. This approach contrasts with the perceptual approach developed by Pace and Stern (1958), which relies on students' reports of activities and emphases but does not include their own behavior or preferences. Centra also included in his study objective published data on the institution—such data as average academic aptitude of students at each college, enrollment, faculty/student ratio, and college income per student.

A factor analysis of the student perceptions identified the following factors: restrictiveness (rules, regulations), faculty-student orientation (extent of interest in and contact with students by faculty), activism (protest, controversy), nonacademic emphasis, curriculum flexibility, challenge (standards), laboratory facilities, and cultural facilities. Centra found that these factors were useful in describing distinctive college climates.

Centra made a further analysis of the eight factor scores based upon student perceptions, thirty-four student self-report items, and eleven objective institutional characteristics taken from public sources. From this analysis, six factors were derived: athletic versus cultural pursuits; size, cliquishness; elitism; activism, flexibility; student satisfaction; social life. Again, institutional differences were amply apparent. However, the various factors tended to be specific to the method of assessment, a finding corresponding to that of Astin (1968), who previously found that self-report and perception data apparently involve somewhat different aspects of institutional differences.

Centra further pursued his analysis using a multimethod factor analysis (1970, pp. 31-35). This further analysis produced another set of factors: 1—female, cultural, versus male, athletic; 2—enrollment, student-faculty interaction, faculty-student ratio; 3—academic stimulation, challenge; 4—student-perceived activism, self-reported involvement, civil rights activities; 5—highly regulated, few students going to graduate school, versus less restrictive, high percentage of students going to graduate school; 6—curriculum flexibility, percentage of students in residence halls, and student self-reported involvement in dating and social life; 7—fraternity, sorority; 8 and 9—no factors clearly emergent; 10—laboratory facilities and self-reported involvement in science.

From this elaborate analysis, Centra concluded that four factors were independent of the method of assessment and reflected valid differences among institutions: athletic-cultural; size, faculty-student interaction; elitism, academic stimulation; and activism. Some overlapping was found among the three methods (perceptions, self-reports, and objective data), but it is amply clear that the three approaches cannot be expected to yield the same descriptions of college environment. Student perceptions of what goes on around them may not coincide with their own involvement and first-hand knowledge, and objective descriptors of a college may not determine perceptions or activities. By an extension of this argument, it might be unreasonable to expect that students, faculty, administration, and the public will hold the same views about a college. Perhaps it is not even desirable that they should.

Utility of Environmental Measures

The utility of environmental measures in evaluation (though not in research, which is quite different in focus) depends upon the identification of decisions to be made, which will be improved by using evidence provided by such measures. If this definition is accepted, environmental measures available to date have been largely a waste of time and money. Such a brash statement requires some explication. As Baird (1974, p. 307) points out, current measures are unsatisfactory because they are so "atheoretical or global as to be unrelated to concepts suggesting pragmatic actions." To gain insight into this contention, it is necessary to consider the possible decisions that might be made. One of the arguments for provision of detailed information about a college was that such information would facilitate intelligent choice of a college by a student. Coleman (1969) argues for a symmetry principle in which the demand of the college for information on the individual applicant would be matched by information provided to the applicant by the college on the social and intellectual climate of the college as well as other qualitative and quantitative information. An attempt to move in this direction by encouraging the use of a questionnaire met with discouraging results (Baird, 1974, pp. 314, 315). Colleges are not much interested in and some are markedly antagonistic to the approach. Many presidents cannot tolerate any critical comment, especially in published form. Most administrators and admissions officers (even some of the faculty) are interested in portraying aspirations rather than actuality. And most institutions are concerned with altering and improving their image rather than with perpetuating it. Furthermore, a degree of heterogeneity in an institution is essential to producing ferment. If the public reporting of institutional characteristics were to promote increased homogeneity, both students and institutions would lose—students, because interaction with others of different views and new experiences are a significant part of education; institutions, because heterogeneity is one of the forces causing ferment, challenge, and innovation.

An approach based upon student perceptions—particularly when vague, ambiguous statements are used in the assessment instrument—no doubt provides evidence of perceptions but not of their validity or accuracy. Such perceptions are, therefore, to be treated with care and should not be overinterpreted. Although perceptions do influence behavior, it is doubtful that the perceptions recorded by individuals lacking direct experience have much effect on their own thinking or actions. Certainly any attempt to make program alterations based on such data requires faculty and administrative analyses which will almost surely result in disagreement both as to realities and ideals.

I prefer an approach requiring individuals to report actual experiences, thereby permitting researchers to put together a composite based upon facts rather than perceptions. Students can report whether they have had to present excuses to get back into class after an absence. They can even provide a crude estimate as to whether this has usually happened to them. The summing of either type of response is certainly a more accurate picture than is a vague perception of general practice. But a survey of student experience or reaction alone is insufficient. College rules or policies, faculty views and practices, and administration views and practices all must be consulted to resolve even such a matter as excuses for class absences. Action may come more quickly if a few such issues are identified by discussions or interviews than if a large number of items are reacted to on an inventory and summarized and reported by categories which conceal rather than reveal the specifics. Discussions of global categories quickly become bogged down in semantics.

The use of published or other objective data about an institution as a means of characterizing its environment is not promising. Undoubtedly there are subgroups of institutions based on such variables, but any implications drawn from such evidence about either the environment or the nature of student experience are so uncertain that neither change nor research on educational impact can be implemented by such evidence.

The major difficulties with any practical use of such information, however, are of a different kind.

1. There is no unique or clear relation between the various desired objectives or outcomes of higher education and any single pattern of either environmental or process characteristics. Hence, such evidence is impossible to interpret in reference to improvement of education; it often generates heated discussion but no constructive action. And this is no doubt for the best, for with present limited information any attempt at far-reaching changes based on such evidence would be unwise. The history of false starts and the short lives of some of the experimental colleges bears witness to this conclusion.

2. It is not even evident that the items studied by probing the environment have any significant impact on the cognitive outcomes of primary concern to the faculty. The trend, in fact, is clearly away from the type of campus environment which views college living and learning as an integrated experience to one in which learning is much like a job—something engaged in eight hours a day for five days a week.

3. To some extent, measures of environment based upon student reports seem to assume that students should be satisfied and happy with their experiences and that changes should be made whenever students are unhappy. This assumption, if carried too far, is dangerous. Part of going to college is the development of a sense of dissatisfaction with what is, whether in the college or in society. Moreover, students are concerned with immediate problems and irritations for which they expect a quick solution. Faculty and administrators are rightly concerned with long-range goals and purposes.

4. Even if actions seem to be required, it is not easy to decide what should be done. If an engineering program is panned by the students as too theoretical, the possible changes are manifold: seek a different type of student; alter the program

and probably the faculty as well; seek support for the program from employers and convey this attempt to students; interpret the program more carefully to the students and add a course or seminar on applications.

5. We should recognize that common or widespread concerns are seldom fatal to anyone, but unique individual problems often are. In short, counseling of individuals with serious problems should not be dropped in favor of attempting to alleviate mass but often low-level or minor irritations. Sensitivity to individual concerns and flexibility in dealing with them will resolve many of the concerns and irritations even of those who react primarily to the problems of their friends in communicating impressions.

6. Most decisions or actions are taken on the basis of political considerations or emotional reactions rather than on the basis of carefully collected evidence. A careful study of costs of and needs for footpath crossings of a campus railroad track has little impact compared with one student's being killed at an often-used but undesignated point of crossing.

7. The several instruments earlier discussed offer, as one of their advantages, data permitting comparisons with groups of institutions of similar or different character. Such comparisons have limited significance and should be used with great caution, if at all. Even if the comparisons dealt with more specific matters, such as construction and characteristics of residence halls, rules, regulations, and requirements, there is no assurance that (1) these are the source of success where already used; (2) transfer to another institution will be effective; or (3) change in some aspects of an institution without compensating changes elsewhere may not simply add a new problem. No college that I have known well has ever solved a local problem by alterations undertaken to change its position relative to national norms. There is no substitute for thorough local study of all factors and of possible impacts of change prior to renovation or innovation.

8. Attempts to promote discussion and change by asking any group to react to a set of statements on the bases of both actual and ideal are intriguing, but not as useful as evaluators anticipate. Not only are there different perceptions of what is,

but there are also different perceptions of what should be. And even those who state or select an ideal do not necessarily desire it. To many administrators and faculty, an ideal university would have few freshmen and sophomores, but since relatively cheap instruction at that level is the source of support of expensive advanced programs, few institutions have ever undertaken to achieve that pattern.

As I noted before, I find the overextended concept of environment used in most instruments detrimental to careful study, understanding, and alteration designed to improve a college educational program. The difficulty starts with the definition. Pace (CUES manual) states that an environment is what people perceive it to be. This view is reminiscent of the blind men attempting to describe the elephant. Even complete unanimity on their part would not necessarily describe the elephant as seen by others. Others have suggested that the people who live in an environment determine its nature. An environment (a desert, for example) may go far to determine who lives in it; it may also affect the behavior and views of people who live in it.

Astin (1968) argues that the task of defining a college environment is that of identifying and measuring those observable institutional characteristics that are likely to have some important impact on student development. I tend to agree but would alter "impact on student development" to "impact on those residing in it." Ideally, an educational institution is supported by society to achieve certain results. These are not specifically determined by society, but, in a broad sense, they correspond to the several purposes of higher education discussed in Chapter Three. To achieve these results, certain educational processes are required. These processes are selected because they hold promise of generating educated persons to fill needed roles in society, because they encourage research, and because they provide the public services which are part of the institution's obligation. These processes take place in some type of environment, although not necessarily that afforded by the traditional college campus. This environment, however, must permit a variety of interactions with various groups of persons as well as with materials and equipment. As the Open University in Britain has shown, even laboratory experience does not require central campus laboratories. A carefully selected kit of materials can be sent to students to use in their own living quarters. But educational processes do require some kind of environment, and they do require people (students, teachers, administrators) and a planned schedule of interactions among people in the environment. People and an environment are essential to create processes to produce desired outcomes.

With this model, people, environment, processes, and outcomes become the four identifiably separate elements in defining an educational program. Students can be students wherever they are, and they are always in some environment. The characteristics, needs, backgrounds, and aspirations of these students are important considerations in developing a program for them. Faculty members must certainly exist in some sense, but not necessarily in the role of teachers in laboratories or classrooms. Books, videotapes, films, pictures, libraries, museums, and art galleries (which house the outputs of people) may supplant live teachers. But the characteristics of these people or materials provided should be known in detail if the processes in their usage are to be defined in reference to the attainment of certain outcomes. In this view, librarians, clerks, and technicians are essential intermediaries between the teacher and the student. Their potentials and roles must also be understood.

In this model, what is the environment? Surely it is not necessarily defined by the students, who need not see each other; it is not a set of face-to-face interactions, for there may be few or none. It is not the residence halls and living arrangements on a campus. It is not the behavior of the instructors except insofar as this may be revealed through the materials or medium which brings their thoughts or demonstrations to the student. The following elements are, however, present: a set of rules, regulations, and policies governing the way in which materials and learning experiences are made available to the students; living arrangements and places of residence; physical facilities in which the student engages in learning; and a philosophy of education, covering its nature, outcomes, and the purposes for which it will be used. Since these elements of the environment can be available in many different ways, and since learning can take place in different environments, a college campus may not be a necessary or even desirable learning environment.

In this model, then, the following general questions are posed: What are the outcomes of education? What processes and interactions are deemed essential to attaining these outcomes? What are the characteristics of the people involved in these processes and interactions? What are the characteristics of the environment in which these processes and interactions take place? To what extent is it possible, desirable, or necessary to modify the environment to increase the efficiency and effectiveness of the processes and interactions?

Such an approach readily encompasses both traditional and nontraditional concepts and forms of education. The environment no longer appears to be (as it now seems to be in approaches to assessment and as it actually is on some campuses) an end in itself but a means or set of circumstances subject to limited adjustment for facilitating educational processes and goal achievement. Perhaps studies using this approach (and consistent with interest in external degrees and nontraditional educational approaches) might reveal that some efforts at environmental enrichment (for example, through extensive residence hall programs, faculty-student interactions of various types, or social and recreational programs) weaken rather than reinforce the education of students. The traditional ideal of an integrated college experience may postpone rather than facilitate a student's maturation into an educated, self-reliant, socially and economically contributing citizen in a democratic society. I do not assert that this is so, but I suspect that it well may be.

The environment is effective only as it facilitates processes which bring about changes in people in accordance with specified objectives. But this use of environment is appropriate only if students enter into or avoid that environment, or aspects of it, in accordance with their own values and objectives. To date, the instruments available for environmental assessment offer almost no assistance to pursue this conception, and hence they do not serve local institutional evaluation and institutional research needs, though they have (as the discussion in this chapter indicates) contributed to the understanding of higher education.

Bibliographical Note

Sturner's (1972) article about the changes effected by a physical restructuring of a campus plan contains an excellent discussion of the impacts of the environment.

DiMarco's (1974) article explores interrelations among life styles, learning structure, and attitudes.

Leslie and Satryb (1974) discuss the changes in student-discipline practices since the early 1960s and the implications for both students and institutions.

Barker's (1968) volume on ecological psychology develops concepts and methods for the study of environment.

Baird (1971) and Centra (1970) provide unusually insightful discussions of environmental factors, with Baird concentrating on the functions of environmental measures.

Adams and Michaelson (1971), in an attempt to assess the benefits of collegiate structure at the University of California, Santa Cruz, throw considerable light on the practical difficulties of environmental assessment.

Chapter 9

Educational Processes

In the preceding chapter, environmental assessment techniques were reviewed, culminating in the view that these approaches have taken such a broad view of environment that much of the educational process is subsumed under it. If the environment is defined in the more limited sense proposed at the close of that chapter, including more or less permanent features such as traditions, institutional goals and priorities, range and characteristics of facilities and equipment, and campus layout and architecture, then the educational processes can be more meaningfully and realistically defined as those arrangements which characterize how people interact in this environment and how they use its resources to promote learning. In this model people (students, faculty, administrators, staff) are brought together in an environment (which may include distinctive subenvironments) to engage in educational processes designed to facilitate the attainment of educational and social goals, not only for students but also for faculty members and the institution.

Educational processes are not limited to a campus or to the more or less traditional patterns of experience common to campuses. They may take place in one's own home, on the job, in a variety of community facilities, in field work, in work-study programs, or in travel and study abroad. Each of these environments may have features that limit or enhance learning. Educational processes are also aided or deterred by the materials, equipment, and people with whom learners are brought into contact by design, by their own devices, or by circumstance. Objectives, too, are affected by the people, the environment, the materials and equipment, and the nature and range of interactions, since these factors may facilitate the achievement of certain objectives while negating the possibility of achieving others. Thus, the study of educational processes requires evaluation of the relation of the processes to these other factors.

The processes that facilitate learning can be divided into those external and those internal to the learner. However, since all learning ultimately depends upon internalization by individuals, the external aspects of educational processes are effective only as they positively influence internal ones. The most obvious external factors are the instruction, evaluation, and interaction patterns of students with people, things, and practices. These are usually in large part specified by teacher or staff in advance, but they are also markedly influenced by the predilections and preferences of individual teachers, by the discipline or field of study, by the students, and by the objectives. For example, mathematics classes are seldom conducted with emphasis on student discussion, but social science courses frequently are. These differences result from differences in the disciplines as well as in those who study them.

Differences in Learning Styles

Some psychologists argue that learning experiences (and even objectives) should be adapted to individual differences in learning styles. For students with apparent physical deficiencies, such adaptation is obviously necessary. Deaf individuals, unless unusually skilled at lip reading, do not learn much from lectures. Blind students do not gain from films and demonstrations unless these are accompanied by extensive and varied verbal comment. And even then, the nature of the learning is different from that originally intended. Handicapped persons may require alternative tasks or omission of some or simply observation of the work of others. But the internal learning styles of individuals generally are not apparent to the teacher, as is best seen by examining the nature of some of these differences in individuals and in their learning patterns.

Some individuals have a strong verbal orientation, whether by nature or experience is uncertain. They are adept at grasping ideas, concepts, principles, or modes of thought but are inept at or dislike laboratory or other learning approaches requiring manipulation or strenuous physical effort. Should these students be excused from those components of a course or from any courses requiring such activity?

Some individuals have a strongly emotional orientation. Because of personal beliefs, sensitivities, or values, they reject, for example, certain types of art, literature, and music. They may have a strong aversion to quantitative methods. In some cases, students disliking (or incapable in?) algebra or geometry have been permitted to occupy their time producing designs and have been graded on this output. When records do not reflect such a deviation from the usual pattern, a lapse in professional ethics is apparent. At the college level, adaptation by waiving segments of a course, providing alternatives, or excusing individuals from courses triggering emotional reactions is possible but at the risk of perpetuating biases rather than educating the individual.

Individuals differ in their personal-social orientation and hence in the type of learning situation in which they feel most comfortable. Some are strong minded and self-directed, quite capable of independent study. Some prefer interaction with peers and dislike lectures or the instructor-dominated classroom. Still others find peer interaction and student discussion either threatening or a waste of time. Others are authority oriented and cherish "the word" as presented by the instructor or the text. An individual who is strongly goal directed may require only occasional suggestions and evaluatory feedback;

another blooms under continual social approval or recognition by authority. Individuals may be motivated, persistent, organized, and responsible, or the opposite, and they usually are not consistent in their behavior in all learning situations. These statements are not simply observations. There is evidence to support them. There is also evidence that those who, for example, prefer discussion or other forms of group interaction to the traditional classroom hold somewhat different values, have different priorities in goals, and are generally more people oriented than content oriented. Should instruction in science or mathematics be adapted to these characteristics? Or should all students be encouraged (if not required) to engage in a range of distinct learning experiences to correct their weaknesses and enable them to adapt to changing social and vocational circumstances in later life? Specifically, should the dependent, other-directed, disorganized individual be required to carry out at least one independent study project? Clearly, adaptation to learning styles or preferences and educational objectives can be in conflict.

Some individuals are quite sensitive to physical environmental features. Sound levels, conversations, street noises, and other distractions unnoticed by some persons are intolerable for others. Lighting and heating, either in amount or type, affect the concentration and performance of some persons. Chalk dust provokes allergies; drafts caused by blowers in air-conditioning or heating equipment may do the same. Crowded conditions affect some individuals by forcing closer contiguity with others than they like. The aesthetics and even the layout of a classroom may have a beneficial or a malign effect on individuals. These environmental features are frequently beyond the control of instructors, but they should be aware of them, make adaptations when possible, and make their awareness and concern apparent to students.

Obvious physical impairments, such as blindness and deafness, have already been noted. In addition to sight and hearing, physical impairments in taste or smell and differences in tactile sensitivity can be impediments to certain types of learning and performance of some jobs. There are also physical differences in people in time adaptation (night owls, early and late risers) and in the tendency to be physically active or passive. Pictures, diagrams, working models have different learning impacts depending on individual strength or deficiencies.

A good teacher should be sensitive to these differences in characteristics and to their association with various learning styles. But how "real" and how "permanent" are these differences? If they are real but not permanent, the goal of instruction may well be that of planning experiences to remedy the deficiency. If they are permanent—that is, irremedial—alternatives adapted to individuals should be sought both in learning experiences and in ultimate career. It is not my concern here to take a position on this matter but, rather, to point out that evaluation of student achievement has to take into account the educational processes and their relevance to the inherent abilities or disabilities of individuals. Evaluation can thereby help instructors clarify their responsibility and options in adapting teaching styles and instructional processes to the learner. Equally, evaluation may help learners reassess their own learning styles and, if necessary, develop others which are desirable or essential to the fullest attainment of desired objectives of learning.

Any meaningful evaluation of educational experience, then, must recognize differences in individual potential for attainment of the objectives; it must also recognize that these objectives may most readily be attained if learning experiences are adapted to individual interests and ability. The motivation and capabilities of the instructor as well as the characteristics of the environment and the available equipment must also be taken into account in the evaluation. Finally, costs, institutional reputation, and social needs must also be weighed. A high-cost individualized educational experience for one who will still perform at an inferior level is unjustified because of the excessive resources required and because of the social obligation of the institution to train fully competent practitioners.

Other Factors

The college and university concept of learning requires that people (learners and teachers) be brought together in a complex environment to engage in various processes and interactions presumed to encourage learning. But is it necessary that learners and teachers be brought together in a room for learning to ensue? The answer comes at two levels. Almost everyone will admit that learning can result from individual efforts through observation, reading, listening, conversation, feeling, taste, and smell. But many persons assert that few persons learn much or learn the right things in this manner; for most persons a structured environment and set of experiences and constant direction and supervision by a teacher are so ingrained or so gratifying that the processes become ends in themselves. A professor enjoys giving a lecture and finds it so satisfying that he or she considers no alternative. In a broad sense, however, printed and recorded materials and other objects may bring their creators into the role of teacher without physical or visual contact yet with an interaction far deeper than that of the classroom, in which most teachers are at best mere intermediaries between students and the ideas of others.

The typical college environment probably contains as many elements to impede learning as to promote it. Athletic facilities, student activities, planetariums, museums with moldy specimens and specimen cases loaded with unorganized and unused materials, libraries with limited access and lost or dislocated material, residence hall programs and personnel vying with faculty for the attention of students—all these elements use time, space, and dollars but may contribute little to or may interfere with faculty effort and student learning; yet these elements are often considered just as important as the academic functions. It can, of course, be argued that these experiences are educational in a limited sense, but it seems quite unreasonable to argue that they are a necessary part of education or that they even complement it significantly. In fact, the noninstitutional experiences of a student may provide better reinforcement of education than the rather insignificant, time-wasting, and irrelevant experiences systematically provided, publicized, and urged upon students on some campuses.

By encouraging study and travel abroad, community work and service experiences, cooperative work-study programs, internships, and other off-campus experiences, many colleges and educators have, in effect, admitted that the campus is not well adapted for many significant learning experiences. External degree programs, which recognize educational accomplishment however attained, deemphasize the highly structured environment as an essential component of learning and recognize that it may be so contrived and artificial and multifaceted as to deter learning. These programs accept the view that any environment can be the basis for insightful study and application or that individuals can rise above any environment to achieve learning. The learning process itself can provide its own environment through the people involved, the innovative components introduced, and the materials used. Yet other external elements may intrude and neutralize the previous ones.

For example, the educational processes are never entirely separable from the people involved. Differences in individual learning habits, styles, and motivations assure that no process is ever quite the same for two learners. Differences in teachers result in differences in processes, even when verbal characterizations and superficial observations appear to indicate that the same instructional technique is in use. The statements of administrators also may markedly affect the educational process by encouraging unrealistic expectations of a program; students and teachers are attracted to the program but soon find that the reality does not accord with the description; so they further modify the reality, and it then corresponds even less to the stated ideal.

Likewise, innovative educational processes introduced in one or a few courses can be rendered completely ineffective by traditional practices in other courses, which place demands upon students in the way of routine tasks and recurrent examinations, and these immediate demands must take precedence.

Again, the materials used in a course, the equipment provided, the availability and use of educational technology, and the evaluation procedures are all, in a sense, part of the educational process, yet any one of these may be so used or misused as to destroy the impact of what was expected to be a particularly potent educational experience. For example, expensive and potentially excellent aids to learning, such as programmed materials, computer-based instruction, and language laboratories, can be and have been so misused as to reinforce rather than revolutionize traditional learning.

These comments highlight the necessity of relating process and results. Although evaluation of the results of learning can be done without regard to the learning process, provided objectives are both clear and accepted, such evaluation is unlikely to assist in improvement of the process. Only when that process is known in detail, and when alternatives are considered and used, is evaluation of the learning process possible. When the commitment of the faculty is primarily to a process, change is not easily induced. Poor results may be attributed to either the failure of the evaluation or the inadequacies of the students. At times the satisfactions of both students and teachers with a particular process foretell the failure of any evaluation other than effusive endorsement. To be sure, enthusiasm and satisfaction are desirable concomitants of learning, but they provide no assurance that the process is better than others. The nature of a process is often so uncertain and highly variable that generalization to other students or instructors is impossible.

Components

The evaluation of an educational process requires identification of its various components and of their interactions. One segment of an analysis should scrutinize the processes and the agents used to facilitate learning. In the large—that is, in curriculum or program structure—there are such factors as requirements in courses and for credits, range of programs (majors, minors, and concentrations) available, academic calendar, schedule, and the manner in which requirements and programs are not solely specified by disciplines, problems, or themes.

Requirements are not solely a matter of catalog specification. They are more sensitively identified by a study of advising and enrollment procedures or of the courses taken by students. Announced themes or problems as a basis for course offerings may only thinly veil traditional courses built for disciplinary majors. Much is made of calendar innovation, such as a three-to-five-week winter term which would provide a change of pace;

but careful scrutiny may indicate that most students see these innovations as the same old packages in a more concentrated form. Periods of off-campus study, travel, or service can readily become only boring or stimulating vacations which interrupt rather than forward the student's education. Only a probing in depth of the views and activities of individual students and faculty members yields meaningful evidence as to just what the educational experience is and how it is related to objectives. But the enthusiastic advertising of such program innovations has often resulted in an indisposition to view the actual process and results in any critical way. In fact, there is no evidence that these structural adaptations of educational processes are particularly effective. Having viewed many of them, I believe that a certain amount of enthusiasm is created by innovation and that temporary enhancement of learning probably results, but these patterns, too, can readily become a humdrum experience enlivened only by the continuing and usually ultimately successful efforts of traditionally oriented faculty members to return to a more familiar pattern.

The smaller adaptations—including such characteristics as class size and instructional method (lectures, discussion, library-centered education, practical experiences, use of technology, new patterns of interpersonal interactions and interactions with equipment)—receive attention in particular courses and occasionally in a total college program. Here, again, the tendency is for the enthusiastic innovator to prescribe the new pattern for all students, for all fields of study, and for all teachers. The process becomes the focus of attention, and the seeming gain in flexibility and adaptation often becomes only a new and temporary rigidity, which shortly recedes toward traditional practices as the innovators are replaced by others who have no commitment to the innovation and find it difficult to accept or inconsonant with their views of education.

Because of these regressive tendencies, I believe that evaluation of the educational process focusing upon these structural and procedural matters cannot yield results of permanent value. A more fundamental approach which relates to the motivations and learning processes of individuals and to the learning sought (the objectives) is required. These are informal processes and psychological components of learning and teaching; they transcend the structural and methodological adaptations which appear, disappear, and reappear because they are only superficial attempts to cope with the fundamental problems of learning. The essence of a nontraditional approach to education is a focus on the individual student's progress toward and achievement of educational objectives.

The planning of an effective educational program requires attention to motivation and individual initiative, not to facilitate traditional learning but rather because the motivations and the initiative of the individual are, in themselves, characteristics to be modified by learning. The truism that an educated individual is recognized by what he or she can do rather than by what he or she knows is a profound observation. Individuals' motivations and initiative, in the long run, determine what they become, how satisfied and confident they are with their own capabilities, and how they contribute to society. This is not to say that the motivations and objectives of individuals should determine or control their education. An educational program worthy of support by society must educate individuals who accept that some motivations and objectives are superior to others.

Individualization

Improvement of educational experiences or processes can be undertaken by many different routes. One is course reorganization based upon discipline restructuring and a sequence of experiences which provide practice and understanding for the students but with the focus still on the discipline. In a course in algebra successfully so modified, the student might be able to (1) solve more problems of a given type in a specified period of time, (2) solve more difficult problems of a particular type, (3) solve problems of types not previously included, (4) demonstrate some understanding of the methodology used and the assumptions underlying it. Course objectives may be made more specific but otherwise are virtually unchanged. For students with strong interests in the discipline, this disciplinary elaboration procedure may also constitute a form of individualization in that it provides a wider range of more challenging tasks and some insight into the underlying structure of the discipline. For other students, such reorganization may only heighten confusion by presenting more material while completely ignoring any connection with matters of interest to them and by requiring more time to master irrelevancies which soon disappear without leaving a trace.

Another approach to individualization encourages students to set their own objectives. In the fullest literal meaning, this approach is intolerable. Chemistry is not offered by a college to train individuals to make nitroglycerin and blow safes. Neither is a course a form of entertainment to be attended for superficial edification by those who put forth no effort to achieve its goals—a situation which pass-no grade appraisal encourages.

However, individuals may have personal objectives beyond those stated for a course or which are adaptations of course objectives. Those who take a course in an attempt to explore its relevance to their own concerns have specific objectives well beyond those of the teacher and course. Indeed, the students' concerns may be quite unfamiliar to the teacher. But such individual variants do not require complete revision of a course or of its objectives; neither do they require such flexibility that individuals engage in completely individualized activities pursuing individual goals. When such changes are imposed on a course, the unity of the course is destroyed. It becomes a form of independent study. There is a place for independent study; there should be more of it; and each student should have such an experience. But a student's exploring alone or in a tutorial relationship a highly structured course outline is not fully individualized study. The fully individualized experience should be planned by the student with stated objectives in mind and reviewed and approved by the instructor serving as mentor for the project.

There are other forms of individualization: individually prescribed instruction, well-defined sequences of behaviorally defined objectives, and differentiated progress for individuals at their chosen or appropriate rates. The specification in detail of any procedure inevitably erodes individualization in some degree, and the lack of any specification imposes the impossible task of complete individualization. Hence, it is desirable to explore the parameters which can be adjusted to achieve individualization and to consider which of these adjustments can be made within a structured course.

Duration (the amount and time spread) of instruction is the simplest form of individualization but the most difficult to use. It is simple because it requires only time flexibility in the completion of tasks and continuing effort until success is achieved. It is difficult to use because courses and degrees are time bound, with required fees and grades; degrees are also time bound by our social mores. Practices which materially extend the time of completion of courses and, ultimately, of a degree are rejected by those concerned with fee collection, by records and reporting officers, by financial officers who tie aid to satisfactory progress, and by faculty members who find it a burden to keep track of students whose progress does not fit neatly defined enrollment, examination, and grade-reporting practices, as defined by a calendar. Duration, too, can cover completion in less than the standard calendar time. Here again there are problems. Students find more difficulty in working at a faster pace than the average because instructors tend to assign them more work or insist on a higher level of mastery. Those who work at a slower pace are simply ignored and given low grades or failed. Few instructors are comfortable with the idea that some students can complete course requirements in less than the scheduled time, and the system does not readily permit increasing the credit hours for those who do more work.

Rate of progress refers to the progress made in a period of time rather than to the time required to cover a fixed amount of content or attain a specified level of competence. Ideally, students capable of advancing at accelerated rates should pursue a program which is less course bound and more goal oriented than the usual program. When progress is encouraged with no regard for calendar, the student becomes goal oriented rather than time bound in pursuit of an education.

The extent to which *objectives* can be chosen or defined to individualize education has been briefly discussed. Some of the disagreement and confusion here is in the interpretation of objectives. As used here, an objective is a skill or an ability; a set of views or values; a method for collecting, evaluating, and using evidence. Objectives are subject to modification in particular disciplines, problem situations, and with individuals, but they are not to be rejected except when sheer physical disability eliminates a certain capability, such as the ability to make visual distinctions.

Learning can also be individualized by adjusting the *mode of learning or type of instruction* to individual styles through individual selection of special topics, themes, problems, materials, or tasks, or even through selection (by the individual or others) of classmates whose aptitudes and traits are similar or different in ways which promote educationally significant interaction. Such sectioning or ability grouping is a much-debated practice. There is no conclusive evidence one way or the other about its effectiveness in given circumstances. Either extreme homogeneity or extreme heterogeneity can be stimulating, depressing, or disruptive, depending upon purposes and the interpretations of those involved.

A pattern or mode of learning can be selected in expectation of facilitating learning, or a prescribed or already selected pattern can be modified for or adjusted to individuals. Indeed, to some extent, this happens without planning. The same instructor leading two separate discussion groups on the same topic usually finds marked differences in views, emphases, and dynamics. But individualization of classes which results merely from the presence of different individuals and distinctive group dynamics is not to be construed as planned individualization, which encourages individuality of thinking and activity for all rather than simply adaptation to whatever direction is taken by a group under the domination or leadership of a few expressive individuals.

Individualization is not simply adapting learning to individuals but to some traits, qualities, interests, or aspirations of individuals. Accordingly, attempts at individualization can run into difficulty because of conflicts within an individual or discrepancies between individual desires and academic or social realities. The individual who seeks to become a doctor but dislikes science has no reasonable claim to an individualization which would adapt medical training to that bias or deficiency. Individualization should not become a way whereby the individual avoids the hard work necessary to acquire essential knowledge and competence or whereby the institution avoids social responsibilities for maintenance of standards.

Individualization of *standards* is also possible. Objectives are closely related to standards, and both are subject to some adjustment. Those students taking a course with the intent to major in the discipline may be entirely content with learning terminology, attaining skills, and memorizing facts because they see these as steps to further study in the discipline. Other students who might be interested in the basic methodology, structure, concepts, and values of the discipline as a way of seeking and organizing knowledge seldom find relevant experiences provided in introductory courses. Indeed, many Ph.D.s lack these perceptions because they are specialists in knowledge rather than in acquiring it. Individuals concerned with acquiring relatively simple skills or with increasing adeptness in certain behaviors often find that the emphasis on knowledge precludes adequate practice for such skill development. And those who seek to understand subject matter for which the discipline provides a useful tool or mode of study may find only discouragement with a "pure" disciplinary approach.

Any approach to individualization ultimately succeeds or fails depending upon how it is used by teachers and learners. A book can be read for recreation, for painstaking identification, for location and memorization of major points, or as a dialogue with the author. Furthermore, learning in life is not neatly packaged, and any procedure which cultivates continuing dependence is to be avoided.

Individually prescribed instruction, programmed instruction, and computer-based instruction can be and have been reduced to serving highly traditional instruction. Moreover, at best, any such technique is an aid—a crutch—to be dispensed with as soon as independence in learning can be established. Thus, new individualized learning technologies which are enthusiastically praised by their developers and disciples should be reviewed with a full measure of skepticism. None of these turn out to be a solution. They are usually more effective in promoting specific knowledge and low-level skills and abilities than in promoting high-level analytical, synthesizing, and evaluative skills. Moreover, they follow paths already delineated in detail by their developers. Hence, some individualized approaches are individualized to a limited extent. They permit variation in progress, in working with the materials, and in the sequence of experiences, depending on performance. But this is individuality within a structure imposed by others; it does not allow the individual to pursue completely original or creative methods or unanticipated ways of proceeding within a structure. In this broad sense, individually programmed instruction is itself something of a straitjacket from which individuals must be released as soon as they can accept and use complete freedom without harming themselves or others.

Individualized instructional approaches, accordingly, can be regarded as simply another way in which a teacher's views, traits, or characteristics define and limit the range of educational experiences available for students. Teachers who view their sole responsibility as dispensing their discipline in a rigorous way may use new materials and techniques, but they will use or misuse them to support their view of learning. A teacher's ability, cognitive style, interests, motivations, and aspirations limit the approach to teaching, just as these same characteristics limit the student's approach to learning. And with the teacher, as with the student, these characteristics may require modification if improvement in teaching and learning is to result.

In the typical course, the teacher is the center around which individualization must revolve. This requires an ease with discipline, with students, and with learning materials and procedures which many teachers lack. In the tightly controlled classroom the teacher plans in advance what is done or said in the class session. The unanticipated can be deferred, and the teacher need never display lack of assurance, either in knowledge or in thought. When students learn on an individual basis, familiarity and a confident mastery of all phases of the course are requisite if the instructor is to preserve an image of omniscience. And he or she may be caught up even then in the necessity to think through a problem or question, thereby modeling what is expected of the student. But thinking about something while trying to teach an individual can be threatening to some teachers.

Interactions

Interactions of various types and durations make up the substance of the learning experience. The interaction can involve an almost infinite number of combinations of people, materials, equipment, objects, and disciplines. Methods of teaching (lecture, discussion, seminar) imply certain patterns of student-instructor interaction. Such evidence as we have indicates that a child raised with no interaction with people would lack all semblance of learning in human terms. Learning by people is always an interaction with materials, ideas, or people. Some social and behavioral scientists insist that interactions among individuals and groups are essential to learning—to personal and social development. It is obvious also that improvement in human relations and in group problem solving is fundamental in a democratic society. Group interactions can also result in personal enrichment through development of communication skills and a sharing of knowledge. Person-to-person interactions can contribute to learning in any field, but they seem to have less value in highly structured disciplines such as science and mathematics than in the social sciences. Most of the instigators or leaders of "new" colleges, which highlight human interactions, have themselves been social scientists or humanists. Scientists, mathematicians, artists, and musicians tend to interact more with physical objects, theories, or concepts, and commune with each other only to clarify and extend their abstractions and models. Indeed, individuals provided with materials and equipment have pursued study in disciplines with almost no interaction with other people.

Some writers on instruction believe that the teacher, in

various ways, provides a model, a sounding board, and a guide essential to individualized learning. Having interacted with thousands of academics for over fifty years, I have high respect for them as scholars, but I find them no more truthful, noble, self-sacrificing, socially conscious, compassionate, or even intelligent than individuals in other fields. College teachers seldom become teachers because of deep interest in young people; most enter the field because of interest in a discipline and in a scholarly life which permits them to pursue it. They provide models for others who would pursue that life—no more.

Educational interactions involve factors much more profound than provision of a model. Several key concepts relate to aspects of interaction. One is a continuum of active-passive involvement. This continuum is often mistakenly interpreted to distinguish overt action or expression from lethargy or indifference. In fact, interviewing students shortly after a class confirms that some who seemed to ignore the professor and their fellow students are more deeply involved in assimilation and analysis of a lecture or discussion than those who gave overt signs of vigorous participation. A well-organized and well-presented lecture, sensitively developed for the audience, usually achieves more active involvement of students than does a student-centered discussion, which too frequently becomes a superficial exchange or pooling of ignorance by unprepared individuals.

Practice and feedback are necessary aspects of any interaction. They can occur in groups, but they can also occur when an individual engrosses himself or herself in an essay or lecture and develops a hypothesis about what the presentation is teaching and the implicit values which direct it.

The dichotomy between student-centered and instructor-centered instruction is much used in characterizing interpersonal class dynamics. In my judgment, this dichotomy is often perverted by those who view extensive and overt student participation as desirable in promoting individual learning. In some circumstances, student participation is essential. But what appears to be instructor dominated may in fact be student centered when instructors are aware of student concerns, when they clarify issues in which students are interested, and when they are sensitive to facial expressions, physical movements, and other signs of intense involvement. A good actor is audience centered, though audiences say nothing until after the play. An instructor can be totally instructor centered, and there are some pompous, vainglorious, insensitive examples. An instructor can also be discipline centered, devoted to presenting in an effective, scholarly manner the substance of a discipline. With an appropriate audience, he or she can be a tremendously challenging and effective teacher.

A democratic-authoritarian continuum has some utility in describing classroom interactions, but this too must be used with caution. Instructors should be authorities in their fields. They have an obligation to present course objectives and to organize learning experiences in a sequential manner. But they should do so in full regard for the students, recognizing individual differences in motivations and goals and adapting to them as far as is consonant with reasonable standards of achievement. Being democratic does not require turning a course over to the students. Indeed, anarchy rather than democracy may ensue. Respect for students as students is essential to effective teaching, but this does not require engagement in amateurish psychiatric therapy, big brotherism, or camaraderie, first names, and exchange of irrelevant intimacies.

Evaluation of Processes

Many of the attempts to analyze, evaluate, and improve educational processes have failed to acknowledge the fact that these processes are extremely complex. Thus, we have had a profusion of studies suggesting that a type of instruction, a new structured approach to learning, or a new college program is superior to traditional approaches, with possibly some qualification as to the objectives sought. The evaluator will do well to peruse this literature lightly and start anew, for it offers no useful generalizations which can be applied directly to a specific teacher, course, or group of students.

Educational processes must be evaluated by their impact on learning. Learning is the development of capability, flexibility, and adaptability in assimilating and applying knowledge and skills in full recognition of the values involved in their application and in the situations to which they are applied. Implicit in this statement is a set of educational objectives from which specific criteria can be drawn to direct evaluation of educational processes.

Every educational experience has some affective components and contributes to the formation of affective qualities. If these qualities are desired, the experience should contribute to and reinforce them. If it does, several principles or generalizations can provide a basis for evaluation.

1. The students, individually and collectively, and the teachers should enjoy the experience. This does not mean that it is fun or that it does not require hard work. Students, on the whole, are not in class for fun; the vast majority, having paid fees and given time, expect some concrete, worthwhile return. But achievement that is fostered by continued threat, harsh grading, and contemptuous treatment of student errors is unlikely to have long-term desirable effects. It is quite likely to have undesirable ones—such as avoidance of future contacts with the field and emulation of the instructor's pattern of behavior. Enjoyment of the process merges into satisfaction with the results, and satisfaction is, in large measure, contingent on enjoyment.

2. If the instructor does not enjoy the experience or is dissatisfied with the results, some aid or intervention is desirable. This could be directed to reeducating the instructor, altering the course or objectives, or assigning the instructor to other responsibilities. Reaching the appropriate decision in a manner fair and satisfactory to the instructor may require extensive study.

3. Satisfaction with the results on the part of both instructor and students suggests that the course has been effective to some extent. If the objectives have been carefully stated, it should be possible to acquire evidence of student achievement, but this is evaluation of results rather than of process. Evaluation of the process should scrutinize the experiences provided in the course and those engaged in by students in relation to the course in order to probe their relevance to the objectives. This

apparent relevance of learning experiences to intended outcomes can be further assessed by canvassing student opinions and by relating them to instructor expectations. When these do not coincide, alteration or clarification may be required.

4. The stated objectives should (but may not) explicitly indicate the desirability of increments in student independence and self-direction in learning—learning how to learn. This can be addressed by reviewing the nature of the assigned tasks and of those voluntarily undertaken by students. Do these reflect increasing responsibility offered to and accepted by students in their course-related activities? Perception of the relevance of course-related experiences and attempts by students to apply these experiences to problems beyond the course confines are also informative. There may also be some unrealized expectations of students which could be met by the course without alteration of its stated intent.

5. The absence of undesirable side effects should be investigated. Have students been encouraged by lack of specificity and clarity in expectations to slough off any effort directed toward the course in favor of other, more interesting or demanding activities? Have they, because of views presented by the instructor, come to feel that society is so decadent and chaotic that the accomplishments fostered by the course are useless? Have they been led to appraise other disciplines, professors, courses, or the institution as a whole as inferior or wasteful of resources? Such results are seldom intended, but they are not uncommon.

6. When the instructional model is relatively expensive, the experiences provided should be scrutinized with even greater care. What apparently good aspects of the course could be maintained in a less expensive model? Are the experiences provided justifiable?

7. Few of these questions can be investigated in a rigorous statistical model which would at best demonstrate statistical significance. What is needed is practical significance, based initially on an informed judgment of instructors and evaluators, to be validated by further evaluation. In this evaluation of process, an assessment of the relationships (perceived and empirically vali-

dated) between the several distinct processes and the outcomes is needed. With people, perceptions and expectations weigh heavily as determinants of results. Highly beneficial side effects do happen fortuitously, but a course cannot be planned or justified on that basis. Reproducibility is desirable and is possible only when the relation of processes and outcomes is both posited and verified.

8. Individualization is desirable, but it tends to be costly and it presents some complexities in assessment, in counseling of individuals, in providing a wide range of alternative experiences and assignments, in managing and directing the program, and in evaluating it. As an alternative, diversity and flexibility in instructional patterns, objectives, and learning experiences somewhat accommodate individual differences.

9. The development of increasing independence is an objective to which all courses should contribute. This capability for self-directed independent study is the single most important goal of education. Independent study opportunities require special assessment. In too many cases, independent study is perceived by both instructor and student as a way to learn only about a subphase of a discipline not covered in a course. There may be justification for this in some cases, but the true objectives of independent study should be increased insight into and mastery of the methods of a discipline by independent effort, coupled with increased self-direction and self-reliance in learning. Interviewing students to discern the nature of their experience and reviewing the results of their efforts will aid in determining whether independent study is truly that or simply another course with consequent increased burdens or high costs and diminished benefits.

10. The focus in evaluation of educational processes should not be to determine the best process for any particular instructor, student, course, or objective but, rather, to bring processes and desired outcomes into such close relationship that processes (or parts of them) are clearly identified with objectives and promote student development in the competence involved.

The approach to evaluation of educational processes presented in this chapter holds more promise for improvement than the usual evaluation devoted to assessment of outcomes. The usual procedure readily leads to a confrontation between teachers committed to a process and results interpreted as inadequate. Only when the processes are viewed as a range of alternatives available to instructors and subject to planned alteration without any implication of poor teaching is the evaluation of processes likely to be accepted and effective. To be successful, processes must be related to outcomes, but in the context of alteration and improvement rather than of condemnation—formative rather than summative evaluation.

Bibliographical Note

The evaluation of learning processes is such a wide field that only a few aspects of it can be touched by a limited set of references. Cooley (1974) has developed four major process dimensions: learning opportunity, environmental enhancement of motivation, quality of curriculum structure, and effectiveness of instruction. This may provide a useful approach to thinking about processes. Hodgkinson and others (1974) have produced a manual for evaluation of innovative programs and practices which should be a helpful introduction to the variety of approaches possible. Hartnett's (1971) discussion of problems in assessing college impacts is an excellent statement.

Discussion or evaluations of more specific processes are found in the following: Dressel and Thompson (1973), independent study; Jamison, Suppes, and Wells (1974), effectiveness of alternative instructional media; Teachey and Carter (1971), evaluation of programmed instructional materials; Wilson and Lyons (1961), work-study college programs.

Chapter 10

Examinations
and Evaluation
in Courses

Although this chapter focuses on course examinations, because they are the most frequent experience of students and teachers, most of the discussion is equally applicable to comprehensive or other examinations designed to assess the broad or cumulative aspects of a student's educational development. Indeed, the course, despite being the fundamental instructional and learning unit, has severe disadvantages when evaluation is conducted with a desire to measure fundamental educational accomplishments. Specifically, the tendency in course examinations is to pose the question "How much do you remember of what has been covered?" rather than "What can you do with what you have learned?" Such examinations tend toward a provinciality which reflects and reinforces the specific phraseology of a text or the idiosyncrasies of the teacher. Consequently, an examination given in one section of a multiple-section course might be deemed inappropriate or unfair in another section and inapplicable in a noncourse context.

This is only one of the complexities and deficiencies of course examinations. A course, instructor, or department may take a distinctive approach to material which, if too strongly present in an examination, handicaps able individuals who have mastered much of the essential substance but have not entirely shed former habits or accommodated the prejudices inherent in the approach. The test environment itself affects persons differently; some find their concentration adversely affected by closeness to others, by the patrolling instructor, or by external noises. In brief, some students do not perform at their optimum in the typical classroom test situation. Recognition of this problem reinforces the tendency of many teachers to pose largely recall rather than thought questions.

Schedules and calendars can also have a negative impact on testing. Reasonable sampling of the range of materials covered, which is essential to fairness, almost forbids many thought questions in a one- or two-hour period. Several tests are usually thought to be desirable to permit students to overcome a poor performance, but if tests are regarded by the instructor as depriving him or her of adequate time for covering course materials, testing readily becomes a perfunctory activity. The typical pattern of a one-hour midterm and a two-hour final illustrates the point—and in some cases even the midterm is omitted. Certainly testing in courses is laden with so many difficulties that it is not surprising the quality of such testing is often poor.

Purposes

The improvement of testing is also handicapped by the purposes for which it is used. The suggestion "You had better know this because it will be on the next examination" is commonly used by teachers who are aware that some students are exerting little or no effort. Thus, testing becomes a reward-punishment situation even to the extent that teachers give many low grades in early examinations to force greater effort. And, once again, this tendency encourages a heavy concentration on facts and recall to drive students to read the text carefully and review and memorize their lecture notes. Cheating in various forms is a result, for students resent the pressure to memorize what has little significance and will soon be forgotten.

The route to improvement of this situation is to view examinations as an essential aspect of the learning experience for the student and of the teaching experience for the instructor. More evaluation rather than less is the crying need in most courses. An examination is an excellent means for clarifying course objectives and for sifting out the important from the unimportant aspects of a course. The teacher, in preparing an examination, ideally is driven to ask how class activities are related to the objectives; the student confronted by the examination has a similar experience and is, in addition, brought to a realization of teacher expectations. The passive, receptive demeanor of many students is overcome because of the necessity for an independent response. Only as the student attempts to respond does he or she become aware that what seemed obvious has not been assimilated. And only as teachers find that material has not been assimilated can they realize their own deficiencies as teachers. If this view be accepted, examinations can be regarded as learning experiences, and even the grades can be useful feedback to the student. But this is not the case when each examination is given solely for the purpose of recording a grade.

The use of examination exercises for instruction and feedback requires more time than some teachers are willing to give to the task. Computer-assisted instruction, programmed instruction, and individually programmed instruction are alternatives. But these, too, are tasks which can be indefinitely postponed or done reluctantly. Without tests in a course however, many students simply put their efforts where the pressures are greater and the payoffs more imminent.

A distinction is needed between examinations for assessing progress toward mastery and examinations for assessing knowledge at a point in time for grading. When progress or lack of progress is the focus, the examination should be diagnostic or at least should lend itself to analysis of the reasons for student failures. The student still has to assume the primary responsibility for diagnosis, unless the instructor or the paper readers have the time to annotate incorrect responses and procedures. For multiple-choice tests in which wrong answers correspond to some common error or misconception, the feedback can be readily supplied by a printout which indicates the number and percentage of students selecting each response.

Examinations viewed as learning experiences need not be given grades, and comparative performance indices need not be provided to students, though many will want them. Examinations as learning exercises can highlight absolute performance, pointing up how far even the best student falls short of the goal rather than how much better he or she is than others in the class. Even if ultimate grades are relative, motivation should be toward excellence. The examinations or exercises need not be identical for all students; if mastery is truly the goal, repetition until that goal is achieved should be permitted. This repetition again poses problems for the instructor, who soon finds that repetition of examinations at will by the student is demanding in time spent with students and in time required for preparing and processing examinations. And the ultimate examination for the record must still be given under secure conditions and have an achievement standard for all students if equity in grading in large classes is to be achieved.

This extended concept of examining and evaluating as a continuous and inseparable part of instruction requires a rethinking of teaching responsibilities and a change in the lecture, read-the-next-chapter, one-or-two-examination pattern found in many college courses. It requires some shifts in view: an examination is no longer regarded as a threat and a culminating appraisal but as an aid and motivation for directing learning and teaching; a course is no longer regarded as something to be passed or failed in a fixed period of time but as a segment of knowledge, a set of skills, a list of objectives to be successfully completed at a defined level of mastery.

Types

In this view of examinations and evaluation, every assigned task related to a course or educational program involves evaluation, whether that evaluation is recorded or not. If the task is rejected or failed, the individual cannot avoid self-depreciation. When students are expected to complete certain tasks in preparation for a class, their doing so or not is noted and recurrence of their performance may lead to a judgment of their motivation. Attendance records kept by some instructors influence— and occasionally provide an automatic deduction from—the grade. Work at the blackboard, still occasionally used in some small classes, permits informal evaluations. One occasionally still hears of an instructor who attempts to make a grade entry for each student each day based on an oral response to a question, homework, a few objective test items completed in class, a written response to a single question, or the effusiveness of the student's laugh in response to a pet joke. Mannerisms, eye contact, questions, or compliments after class are an informal means by which impressions are formed and evaluations made. In small classes grades are typically higher (perhaps in this era of inflated grades one should say they *were* higher) at least in part because the increased range of interactions, even though perhaps irrelevant to the course, tempers the appraisal. This perhaps undue elaboration of the incidental occurrence of evaluation suggests that evaluation often is a continuous process of appraisal—an accumulation of impressions, some relevant and some irrelevant to student progress. However, if this continuous appraisal is well planned and judiciously used, at times for motivation and at other times for determination of progress, formal examinations need not be used.

Most teachers, however, prefer to give several formal examinations. Here too there is a much wider range of possibilities than is used in many courses. Large classes and heavy instructor loads result in extensive use of objective tests. Good objective tests are not easily constructed, and the typical ones place undue emphasis on facts. Thus students are driven to memorization. The ability to recall, at appropriate moments, terminology, facts, principles, definitions is desirable, but recall alone is no indication of ability to use what is recalled. And ability to select a correct response among several alternatives is not a sure indication of ability to recall without cue. A problem involving more than recall may not test what was intended. The student asked to solve the equation $x^2 + 5x + 6 = 0$ may factor or may simply substitute the list of proffered answers to find which ones satisfy the equation. The latter procedure indicates some insight in itself but does not indicate ability to solve the equation. There are situations in life, such as voting, when one must select from a proffered list, but occasions for such behavior are limited.

Carefully constructed and validated objective items can, in theory, be used repeatedly, but this practice has two major defects. One is that it is difficult and perhaps impossible to maintain security. Some instructors build up large files of such items and make them available to the students, who know that any examination will be made up of a sampling of these items. Testing the ability to apply, analyze, or synthesize is impossible with this procedure. The second difficulty with secure items is that students have no chance to review their responses and learn from their errors. Neither can they recheck the scoring of a test on which they scored lower than they expected to. Secure final examinations are possibly justified, but only if security is guaranteed. The chance of surreptitious access, which invalidates some scores and is inequitable to those not in on the collusion, is always present.

Essays are strongly defended by many professors as the only adequate approach to testing. But essay questions have several severe deficiencies. First, despite the vaunted emphasis on writing, such questions may require only a repetition in but slightly altered language of a numbered list presented in a textbook. When essay responses are read simply for the presence or absence of specifics, they may become little more than objective tests.

Second, the question may not be carefully thought out and worded. "What were the major immediate causes of World War I?" Unless that question is qualified explicitly or implicitly to refer to a particular authority, it requires a very lengthy answer.

A third deficiency of the essay question is the probability that the question writer does not have a clear idea of the best answer. Some testing authorities recommend that the writer develop a model answer or an outline, but, in practice, this is seldom done. Lacking that prior specification, an instructor should read all answers, developing a list of criteria to be applied to all, and possibly at the same time sorting the responses into preliminary groups on the basis of a tentative judgment of excellence. A second reading applying the developed set of criteria is desirable to obtain reasonable reliability. Ideally, these steps should be done with names removed or covered to prevent bias.

A fourth deficiency of the essay is that responses vary in grammar, spelling, punctuation, choice of words, and sentence construction. Most of us are prone to react more favorably to statements expressed in our own style and to depreciate responses which are hard to read and understand. Perhaps basic composition skills should be weighted in rating the responses, but, if so, this weighting should be made known to students. Unquestionably the student who writes easily and quickly and has an extensive vocabulary has an advantage on essay examinations. And the clever, creative individual may take a word or phrase as a jumping off point to write eloquently about another topic.

A fifth problem arises out of the possibility that students are differentially prepared on various aspects of the course. In attempting to overcome this sampling problem, some professors like to offer several essay questions from which the student chooses a subset. Commendable in some ways, this practice complicates reading and marking by introducing still another variable. A further adaptation to overcome the sampling problem permits a student to both pose and answer one or more questions. If a regular practice, this permits students to write part of the examination in advance. Another related practice permits students to write the essays for two or three questions before coming to the examination. From these the instructor agrees to select one question for the examination. Class discussion of the questions prior to the selection may also be encouraged.

Subjectivity in the reading and rating of essay responses is a sixth problem. The use of several readers is usually recommended if rater unreliability is to be corrected, but the time involved both in reading and in devising a set of criteria makes this impractical even if instructors were favorably disposed toward having others rate their students.

Oral examinations are favored in some colleges and are extensively used in graduate programs. These require the presence of at least three professors, generally must be limited in time, and pose even more problems than the essay. Some students (graduate and undergraduate) are so awed by the oral situation, especially when one or more examiners are unknown and the performance is public, that the examination deteriorates to the search for questions which the individual can answer. Other difficulties with orals include (1) the lack of prior planning of questions by the examiners either collectively or individually with consequent lack of focus and lack of balance, (2) the asking of obscure, poorly worded questions for which the questioner apparently expects a precise answer, (3) the tendency of some examiners to pose and ultimately answer questions to impress colleagues, (4) the expression of differences of opinion among examiners, which diverts attention from the student, (5) the impact of personality and fluency on examiners, (6) variations in emphasis and judgment among raters, which make it difficult to get a consensus of deficiencies to be communicated to the student; this is less of a problem though still not a negligible one when the facility in oral communication is itself the ability being appraised. A prepared oral presentation to a seminar or other group on an assigned topic, followed by discussion and questions, is an alternative to the formal oral and avoids some of its weaknesses.

Although most discussions of examinations consider only the objective, essay, and oral patterns, the range of tasks which provide opportunity for evaluation is as great as the range of possible learning experiences. Were these all regarded as examinations in the formal sense, learning would be impeded and disrupted, but if they are not regarded as opportunities for evaluation, then learning is also impeded. The student needs to become self-evaluative, and the instructor needs continuing evaluation of student success as feedback for assessing his or her own success.

Laboratory projects (routine or special), art works (paintings, sculptures), music recitals, clothing and food (prepared in home economics courses), reports of travel or field trips are all also appropriate for evaluation. Generally, the projects will be more effectively completed if the criteria for evaluation are available in advance, and if the student assists in their development or is aware of what they are. This foreknowledge of the criteria for evaluation, properly used, should not only result in better performance but also remove or diminish the repeated complaints of students that they are uncertain what the instructor wants. Also, as students are encouraged to continuously evaluate their own efforts and as their criteria increase in sophistication and approximate those of the instructor, both learning and increasing capability in self-direction and self-evaluation are promoted.

Such issues as open- or closed-book examinations, examinations taken in or out of formal class sessions, fixed or flexible time limits are relatively insignificant in this broad concept of evaluation. Yet they are apparently important to some teachers. Open-book examinations present two problems: (1) They lead some students to assume that because they are able to look up anything they need, no depth of study is required and nothing need be memorized in advance. (2) Overuse of the book in a limited time reduces the amount of work completed. Whether an open-book examination is different from a closed-book examination depends upon the nature of the questions. Questions primarily of recall demand memorization in one case, facility in locating the appropriate page in the other. Questions demanding original thought—analysis, synthesis, evaluation—are not materially altered by the circumstance. In an open-book examination, a book (text or other) may be seen in its proper role as a resource needed at critical points.

Whether examinations are taken in class or elsewhere depends upon their nature, the purposes for testing, and the concern about cheating. The classroom situation provides some controls which minimize cheating, but has constraints which eliminate the assignment of tasks requiring extended effort, creativity, or power. The external examination, despite required certification of no assistance, is uncontrolled, with the usual problem that honesty, threatened by dishonesty, sometimes itself succumbs. External examinations followed by an oral provide some control—at least to the extent that the student is pushed to understand rather than simply copy answers from others. If each student receives different questions, the possibility of receiving help is diminished, but not eliminated. Comparability of grades is also reduced.

More generally, examinations can be classified as criterion-referenced or norm-referenced measures. In norm-referenced evaluation, the performance of each individual is compared with that of other individuals. The teacher scoring tests and ranking and grading individuals according to the score distribution is using norm-referenced evaluation. Achievement tests developed for sale or for testing programs commonly use percentile or standard scores derived from testing large groups. The percentile or standard scores of individuals thus tell something about how they compare with the norm group, but it tells nothing about specific things they have learned or what they can do with what they have learned. Norm-referenced testing encourages the coverage of large segments of subject matter. No student is expected to master everything; but he or she should learn enough in a given period of time to compare favorably with others. What "enough" means is uncertain.

Criterion-referenced testing shifts the attention to individual proficiency. Performance is evaluated on the basis of an external absolute standard. Successful performance of the task is based upon a description of student capability. The ideal criterion-referenced test yields different characteristics from those the ideal norm-referenced test yields. For the norm-referenced test the mean score should be approximately 50 percent of the total score; for the criterion-referenced test it should be close to a perfect score. Variability should be large for norm-referenced tests and small for criterion-referenced tests. Test reliability, measured by traditional means, should be reasonably close to 1 for the norm-referenced tests and low for criterion-referenced tests. Correlation with aptitude measures should be modest but significant (.40-.70) for norm-referenced tests and very low for criterion-referenced tests. In fact, assuming that deficiencies in ability and that human frailty in response could be eliminated, the ideal for the criterion-referenced test would be a perfect score for everyone. For such a test, then, there is no variance in scores, no reliability as usually defined, and essentially no correlation between aptitude and achievement. Given sufficient time, everyone can achieve the level of proficiency specified.

The ideal for criterion-referenced testing is that the score indicate exactly what tasks an individual can perform in a defined domain. The ideal is impossible in practice. Field sports events illustrate the situation. The individual who wins the mile run is not greatly concerned that he or she did not beat the local, state, national, or world record. Performance takes on meaning in relation to the performance of competitors. The winner may do better or worse the next time. The world record is itself an individual performance, and the individual who seeks to beat it indirectly competes with another. Minimum short-hand and typing speeds for employment are assessed by performance standards (criteria), but ultimately these are based upon cutting points in the distribution of actual speeds of individuals. Only if a specific performance is described as mastery does a criterion-referenced objective connote mastery. Criteria emerge from performance data. Criterion-related performance is not simply a one-time performance; it must convey reasonable assurance of continuing ability to perform at that level. Licensing or certification requirements in the health sciences make evident the rationale for this requirement.

Criterion-referenced behavioral objectives and testing thus permit the emphasis to be on each individual's attaining a high level of mastery. Bloom (1973) discusses this prospect. The focus, for him, should be on individualized instruction using a wide range of learning materials and a pace suitable to each individual rather than on standardized classes running for specific periods of time. This view of education is as refreshing as it is idealistic. Most students enrolled at any level, from primary school to advanced graduate study, do not have the ability and the motivation to master all tasks embraced in a reasonable set of objectives. Sequential, cumulative disciplines present a special problem. Except for a relatively few devoted souls and geniuses, learning (and especially mastery) in these fields is hard work. Teachers surely have some responsibility for motivation, but as one who has taught mathematics and statistics from the seventh grade to the doctoral level, I am certain that mastery of a reasonable range of tasks by all or even 95 percent of the students is unrealistic. And I base this statement not so much on problems with time, individualization of learning, and costs as on problems with motivation.

In deciding upon the appropriate type of examinations (both the nature of the tasks and the attendant circumstances), the instructor must be concerned with time, costs, convenience, student motivation, fairness, and validity. Reading and marking examinations are never delightful tasks, particularly when concentrated in a few days between a final examination and the grade-reporting deadline. Costs generally rule out use of commercially available tests, and those which are secure prohibit detailed feedback to students. Good objective tests are time-consuming to produce and may be somewhat expensive to reproduce. Essay examinations are quickly written and quickly reproduced, but time-consuming to read.

General Problems

Four general problems are associated with examinations, each sufficiently complex that no formal resolution satisfactory to all faculty members or all students is possible. The first problem is the coverage (sampling). Complete coverage of everything in a course is not possible and any structure for sampling is subjective. Elaborate sampling structures involving several elements can be generated. One element is the course objectives: facts, understanding, application, analysis, synthesis, and evaluation. A second element is the topics covered in the textbook or lectures. A third element is application to new problems or materials. When questions or test items include various combinations of these elements, the course itself is seen as a sampling of a larger body of knowledge and of problems with respect to which the student is expected to develop a capacity for effective involvement.

This extended conception of sampling induces a second set of problems with reliability, validity, and fairness. Recall items tend to have much higher reliability than thought questions; in essay format recall responses are more reliably read. More complex questions may be invalidated simply because of their structure. And some faculty members and many students think any item novel in content or in structure is unfair because no direct experience in resolving the problem was provided in the course.

Obviously, we have here a set of tensions and anxieties resulting from the conflicting purposes of examinations already noted. The third problem area of time and the discontinuities in courses caused by examinations is, in a sense, an extension of this conflict. Examinations interrupt learning rather than promote it, or they encourage delay in learning until the examination requires it. The giving and grading of an examination are unpleasant to teacher and student alike, yet in too many courses the examination alone forces students to exert effort, misdirected and unprofitable as it may be.

The fourth problem is the conflict of counseling and improving individual achievement versus accepting social responsibilities and maintaining standards. Whether a weak, slow, or disinterested student should be encouraged to pursue a course over a longer than normal time span, achieve even then a minimal level of competence, and enter a career in which this background is essential for successful performance is a complex issue. The extra costs (including the inconveniences and difficulties caused in the usual program structures), the possible compromise of standards, and the possible misuse of scarce resources are not excused simply by an appeal to equity and equal opportunity for each person.

Components of Questions

An examination question has four substantive elements. Three of these were already mentioned in the discussion of sampling problems. A question has an objective (the first element) —a cognitive reaction ranging from simple recall of a fact or term to an exceedingly complex evaluation. The question usually requires this cognitive reaction within the framework of the concepts, principles, methodology, and structure of a discipline (the second element). If the question requires cognitive ability beyond simple recall, it involves application of knowledge to a problem or context (the third element) not previously covered. For example, an individual presented with certain data may be required to consider the characteristics of the data provided, decide the summary generalizations which would be useful, consider and select the appropriate analysis from a range of possibilities, carry out the analysis, and interpret the results. The selection of an appropriate procedure for considering the properties of the data presents an expansion of content beyond the in-course experiences, which usually cover procedures separately and do not involve the student in choices among them.

The fourth substantive element is the task or the item structure. There could be some argument as to whether the item structure is substantive or incidental, a personal preference or a conscious decision. With direct questions calling for an answer formulated by the respondent, the structure is so simple as to almost evade notice: "What is your name?" "Who was the first president of the United States of America?" Either question could be a request from a person seeking that information. Either could also be a question to determine whether the individual addressed knows and can express the answer already known to the questioner. Rather than being helpful to the questioner, the student is placed in a temporarily inferior position because capacity to respond is in doubt.

The further questions—"Why were you so named?" "Why did Washington become the first president?"—introduce other factors. One's name, being a combination of surname and given names, requires a complex answer and could lead to discussion of different cultural practices and legal requirements for names. For given names, the reason for parental choice is often not clear and may not, in any case, be known by the child. So any answer from "I don't know" or "my parents picked the name" to an elaborate explanation of the process would suffice with questioners who have no basis for doubting the response.

The second question introduces the concept of an authority as well as the judgment of the teacher and the student. The student may correctly respond: "because he was elected" or "because there had been no president before him." More likely the student anticipates that the teacher expects several reasons relating to Washington's reputation and prior service and seeks to recall what the teacher or the textbook said. The student then is answering the question in someone else's terms or at least in a manner to satisfy someone else. Whenever a question is posed by one who is presumably completely informed to one who is incompletely informed, this artificiality of response is inevitable. Instructors seldom ask students questions designed to obtain information of importance to themselves. If they did they would have difficulty grading the answers.

Even when a question asks for a student's opinion or appraisal of a statement, work, or idea, the concern about the basis for the instructor's reactions pushes the student in the direction of seeking a structure for response which conforms with that of the instructor or the textbook author. The open-ended essay question then implies or is seen by the student as implying a set of assumptions or views which constrain the answer. If the student did not so view the question and succeed in identifying the structure, most essay questions would require a lengthy article or book for a reasonably complete response.

For objective or multiple-choice items, the structure is imposed by the item format: "Michigan State University was founded in (1) 1700, (2) 1855, (3) 1900, (4) 1920." Students have only to have learned the date 1855 to respond without thought. If students do not know the date, they may recall that the institution advertises itself as the pioneer land-grant institution and that central Michigan was still unexplored by white men in 1700. The combination would lead, with reasonable certainty, to 1855.

"Michigan State University was founded in (1) 1835, (2) 1855, (3) 1857, (4) 1862, (5) 1955." This item is in the same format, but differently structured by the alternatives presented. The University of Michigan was founded in 1835. Michigan State College began classes in 1855. Classes began at the Michigan Agricultural College in 1857. The land-grant act was passed in 1862, and the Michigan Agricultural College was designated as the land-grant college. In 1955, Michigan State College became Michigan State University. The correct answer depends on the exact meaning of *founded*. A series of five true-false questions presenting each of these events with the correct or an incorrect date would require exact knowledge and would deemphasize the meaning assigned to founded. Thus, item structure does determine response patterns.

If a series of statements interpreting exhibited graphs is to be answered by a choice of "true, probably true, uncertain, probably false, false," the student's interpretation of the data is completely structured by the items. Characteristics such as trend, interpolation, extrapolation, sampling, reading values, indication of reasons for collecting the data or actions to be taken because of them are patterns of interpretation imposed on the data which may or may not have been adopted by the student making his or her own interpretations. Recognition of or even willingness to use the distinction between true and probably true (or their opposites) involves insights and attitudes which may affect the results. If the student has not seen this structure before, making distinctions among the five choices is formidable. If this structure has been used but a full range of possibly correct and incorrect interpretations has not been considered, the structure will still be exceedingly difficult. If both alternatives and statement patterns are familiar, the task is reduced to applying a familiar and useful structure to a new set of data. If even the graphs or data have been carefully studied, the response may be entirely rote. Thus, unless the structure of an item in some way conforms to a pattern previously studied and found useful, the structure complicates or alters the intended behavior. The goal should be to use an item structure which, if not previously used and known to the student, is so related to the objectives, content, and discipline that it facilitates rather than confuses.

In addition to the four substantive elements of objectives, content, discipline, and item structure, several human elements are interwoven with examination questions. Individual instructors have characteristic ways of phrasing materials and questions; so has the textbook author. Students trying to phrase questions or respond to them have their own patterns, which must usually be overridden to accommodate instructor expectations (to whatever extent these are evident or guessable). Every attempt should be made to reduce the impact of such idiosyncratic phrasing and expectations unless they are relevant to course objectives, as perhaps in creative writing. Students are being educated to deal with life and not with particular college instructors. They should be encouraged to seek clarification or make their own interpretations rather than guess at someone's intent. The instructor rating the work of students has a similar problem. Rather than holding tightly to preconceptions of an answer, the instructor should rate a reasonable and internally consistent interpretation on its merits. Both instructor and student can learn from the experience. And this is true with both essay and objective materials. The need for this practice is illustrated in the extent of interchange in oral examinations before a question is clearly phrased for all parties.

Criteria for Answers

The criteria for the intended response to either an essay or objective-test question are not always obvious even upon close scrutiny. (Objective-test items are the referrent here, but with some rewording, this discussion is also applicable to essay questions.) The jargon of testing speaks of right and wrong answers. Since *right* answers are counted as *correct*, no distinction in the use of these two words is possible. (One is reminded of the cab driver's comment that giving him exactly the correct fare isn't right.) Answers may be right or correct, but differ in accuracy. To a request for a characterization of Albany, "Albany is the state capital of New York" is a more accurate response than "Albany is a state capital" or "Albany is in New York." An exact answer for the value of x in $x^2 = 2$ is $\pm\sqrt{2}$ although ± 1.4 might be correct and ± 1.414 rather more accurate.

The Albany example may also be considered with reference to completeness. The characterization of Albany as the state capital of New York identifies it uniquely and more completely than do the other responses. This matter of completeness opens the option of a best answer among correct answers. Best must be determined by applying a set of criteria or values. If the problem is to find the area between two concentric circles with respective radii of 49 and 51 inches, any of the following expressions will yield the correct (and exact) answer.

$$\text{difference} = A_2 - A_1 = \pi r_2^2 - \pi r_1^2$$
$$= \pi(r_2^2 - r_1^2)$$
$$= \pi(r_2 - r_1)(r_2 + r_1)$$

However the last expression immediately yields 200π, which is surely the quickest and most accurate answer whatever value of π is used. The best answer can also be determined by application of such criteria as completeness, clarity, sensitivity, efficiency, or display of an awareness of alternatives. But usually these subjective judgmental factors are not readily incorporated in multiple-choice test items. Even the synonyms for right have some value overtones. A right answer need not be complete; it is right as far as it goes. A correct answer indicates absence of error; an accurate answer implies concern for exactitude; and a precise answer further implies minute accuracy perhaps even beyond any need or justification.

Whatever the criteria used by a teacher in judging responses, he or she must specify these criteria in advance and in as concrete a form as possible. If not, the student may see the teacher evaluation as unduly subjective, biased, and even haphazard. The student cannot be quite certain what is expected and lacks clues as to how to improve performance. Without a firm grasp of the judgmental criteria, the individual is unable to progress to self-evaluation through either mastering the teacher-developed criteria or proposing, applying, and defending his or her own.

Except possibly for final course examinations, every student performance should receive sufficient feedback either by notations on papers, by class discussion, or by provision of model responses to ensure that every conscientious student becomes aware of his or her deficiencies and learns what further must be done to fully correct them. Anything less coupled with a passing grade constitutes teacher approval of a less than satisfactory performance.

The test performance of a class also constitutes feedback to the teacher. I would not go as far as to state, as did one dean, that any student failure is a teaching failure, but when many students do poorly, the teacher must share the blame. Poor presentation, too fast a pace, inadequate practice by students, lack of feedback by the teacher, failure to clarify standards or criteria for success, poorly constructed examinations, or application of unrealistic, biased, or unduly rigid criteria are all possible problems. In examining students, conscientious teachers examine themselves.

Structure of Multiple-Choice Questions

Multiple-choice questions appear in a variety of patterns, but all share certain common parts. One part of the item presents a problem or stimulus: a question, statement, concept, picture, array of objects, or construct about which a judgment is to be rendered by use of a proffered set of responses. The most common pattern presents the stimulus followed by four or five responses from which the one correct or best response is to be selected. Though seldom done in standardized tests, more than one correct answer can be included, posing the somewhat more difficult task of indicating all correct responses. The objection to this multiple-response pattern is that all right answers are seldom equally specific or precise and the student is left in doubt as to where to draw the line. The task is essentially identical to a true-false response in which the false is omitted. Generally, such an item might better be broken up into several true-false items.

A reverse multiple-choice pattern places the responses ahead of the stimuli. This pattern is especially appropriate when a set of responses embodies a desired method of discrimination or analysis. Thus the responses "true, probably true, insufficient data, probably false, false" can introduce a series of statements purporting to interpret a set of data. A series of stimuli each comprising a statement and a possible reason or condition may be headed by a response pattern such as the following: "Statement true if condition holds. Statement true regardless of condition. Statement false if condition holds. Statement false regardless of condition. Insufficient evidence to decide." Such responses are excellent if they incorporate distinctions or analytic processes which have been taught to and used by students. Otherwise they become difficult simply because of the time required to grasp and apply them. The preceding is a relatively simple pattern; more complex ones can readily be developed. Responses in the reverse multiple-choice form can also be art works, book titles, authors, or philosophers. The stimuli, which may be philosophical points of view, historical eras, characterizations of art works, or distinctions among definitions, assumptions, empirical evidence, hypotheses, and theories are readily perceived in this pattern. Responses and stimuli can also be interchanged in many cases.

Thoughtful item writing requires analysis of the aspects of a course to be included; the types of problems to which the disciplinary methods, concepts, and principles are to be applied; and the objectives to be tested. In addition, the type of item or the task presented to the student should not inject some additional irrelevant structure. Rather, the item should provide a structure which approximates the natural behavior of an individual engrossed in the task.

The range of behavior used to answer multiple-choice questions is limited, but less so than is often thought. The simple recall multiple-choice item requires (for the student who knows the right answer) only that the alternatives be scanned to locate the answer. The best answer requires a careful examination of all alternatives to separate those which are correct (or partially so) from those clearly incorrect. The correct answers are again scrutinized to determine the differences among them. The student then selects the best answer on the basis of the differences found. The underlying structure or assumptions from which the alternative responses were developed must be determined by analysis of them.

In contrast, the response pattern itself may present the analytic structure to be used and that structure may be deemed to be of such importance that it is extensively used with sets of items sampling various materials, problems, and objectives. For example, the designation of a series of data-interpretation statements as "true, probably true, insufficient data, probably false, false" could be any one of the following tasks: (1) Recall of correct answer for items which reproduce classroom exercises or textbook examples. (2) Selection of correct answers for a set of new or different interpretations for data already familiar to the student. (3) Selection of correct answers for a learned pattern of interpretation applied to new data. (4) Selection of correct answers for unstructured interpretations of new data, exhibited in novel ways. Other variations are possible, but these already range from simple recall of learned responses to a generalized application of a classification structure to completely new materials. The injection of a pattern of interpretations changes the reaction pattern of many students.

Statements which suggest courses of action or decisions go beyond the data to indicate uses. Such statements may be characterized as value statements, and students may have learned that "should" or "ought" are often found in such statements. But behaviors predicated on recognition of value statements and those predicated on the presence of "should" or "ought" are of quite different levels of sophistication. And apart from a learned structure and response pattern, the decision as to whether a possible use of data is indeterminate because of value implications is one upon which scientists disagree.

The construction of a test item which requires a specified type of behavior can be an exacting task. For example, the possible relationships between one statement or proposition A and a second possibly supporting statement B can be analyzed as follows: A can be true, false, conditional, or indeterminate; B can be true, false, conditional, or indeterminate; B can support A, contradict A, or be irrelevant. The possible combinations are $4 \times 4 \times 3 = 48$, a rather formidable number around which to develop test items.

However, there are many ways to simplify this problem and reduce the possibilities.

Example 1: Let A be true or false but possibly conditioned by B. Let B be an imposed (and possible) condition. The alternatives reduce to (1) A is true if B holds; (2) A is true regardless of B; (3) A is false if B holds; (4) A is false regardless of B; (5) Insufficient data to decide. This pattern can be applied to any number of statements followed by a condition, with the relationship to be characterized by an appropriate choice of response.

Example 2: Let A be true or false. Let B be a possible "reason" which may be true or false and supporting, contradicting, or irrelevant to A. The following twelve possible alternatives emerge:

	Statement A	Statement B	Relationship
(1)	True	True	B supports A
(2)	True	True	B contradicts A
(3)	True	True	B is irrelevant to A
(4)	True	False	B supports A
(5)	True	False	B contradicts A
(6)	True	False	B is irrelevant to A
(7)	False	True	B supports A
(8)	False	True	B contradicts A
(9)	False	True	B is irrelevant to A
(10)	False	False	B supports A
(11)	False	False	B contradicts A
(12)	False	False	B is irrelevant to A

Many of these alternatives have no meaning or are impossible. We can eliminate (2) because B true cannot contradict A true; (4) and (5) because B false neither supports nor contradicts A true; (7) because B true cannot support A false; (10) and (11) because B true can contribute to establishing the falsity of A (8) but otherwise B whether true or false is irrelevant. Thus the twelve alternatives reduce to (1), (3), (6), (8), (9), (12). This pattern can be revised into a cause-effect appraisal: both A and B are true but have no cause-effect relationship; both A and B are true and are related as to cause and effect; A is true and B is false, and they are related as to cause and effect; A is false and B is true, and they are related as to cause and effect; A is false and B is false or irrelevant.

Items using these structures present quite complex tasks. The first two alternatives are straightforward, but the remaining three are not. If the fact that A is true makes B false, the cause-effect relationship is clear, although it is between the statements as evaluated rather than as stated. But, although the fact that B is false may cause A to be true, B as stated is not the cause of A. Had B been so stated as to be true, it could be the cause of A. Responses (3) and (4) share this difficulty. If either A or B is true and if the other then be false and regarded as irrelevant, there is no available response. Either (3) or (4) must be revised to include "irrelevant" or the pairs of statements to be evaluated must be carefully selected to avoid that prospect. Even so, as the discussion indicates, agreement on correct responses may be impossible even by those who share in the development of such items. Such a format might conceivably be used for instructional purposes, but it is not a good format for final examinations. It has been included only to demonstrate that reasoning-type multiple-choice items can readily become extremely complicated or ambiguous.

Summary

If only one type of evidence were available for evaluation of a course and of the instruction provided, the examination would surely be it. It reflects the instructor's conception of what is important, and it also reflects his or her intellectual sensitivity and scholarship. In addition, it reflects course content, objectives, and the extent to which the course is viewed as providing abilities to deal with broader issues or problems than those specifically covered. An examination, more than anything else, determines the extent and nature of student effort in the course. It is essential, however, that examination here be interpreted as including all types of required student work which is evaluated to determine accomplishment.

The next most significant type of evidence is the performance of the students on these examinations—in actuality and as appraised by the instructor. Some instructors have unrealistic expectations, which are reflected in the level of the examination and in the severity of the grading. Others are extremely lax in both areas.

The third type of evidence, which surely reveals more than anything else connected with examinations the character of the instruction, is the manner in which student performance is used as feedback to the students to assist and encourage their efforts and as feedback by the instructor to direct and adjust his or her efforts and the materials chosen to the needs and deficiencies revealed.

Because a course is a segment of the student's broad education experience, it must be perceived by students and by the teacher as contributing to the development of insights and abilities which transcend the course—that is, which can be transferred to other areas of endeavor both in other courses and beyond the campus. Examinations (in the broadest sense) and the appraisal of student performance on these examinations by the instructor reveal much about this possible transference, but good teachers recognize and cause students to recognize that some desirable outcomes cannot be assessed in formal ways for grades and that, indeed, attempts to do so may destroy any prospect of achieving them. Accordingly some course evaluation should be avowedly motivational, encouraging self-analysis and evaluation and clearly separated from grades.

Bibliographical Note

Individuals interested in the use or development of examinations in a course should usually look for publications dealing with evaluation in their disciplines or fields. There are numerous general treatments; see Gronlund (1965), for example, which provides technical background and examples and suggestions for item writing. Bloom, Hastings, Madaus (1971) contains chapters on testing in a wide range of fields as well as other excellent material. Thorndike (1971) is probably too technical for many persons interested in achievement testing in a particular field, but it does contain many chapters—for example, one on essay testing—which are appropriate.

Buros (1972) contains extensive references including references to works on test development in particular fields. Several of the most widely known volumes of this type are included in the bibliography: Berg (1965), Colwell (1970), Nelson (1967), Shields (1965), Nedelsky (1965), and Lado (1964).

Chapter 11

Comprehensive Examinations

The original, classical curriculum of the early American college was a sequential, cumulative program required of all students. At one time, a professor or tutor taught the same group of students throughout their stay in a college and demonstrated by his or her example the expectation that each individual eventually be able to integrate and apply the total college curriculum. As that classical curriculum was gradually replaced by electives or alternative programs, instructors adhered closely to covering only the material in their own courses. Thus the degree came to be an accumulation of independent courses.

At Harvard in 1909 (Harvard University, 1934), a committee recommended that "a student must take courses enough in some one field to lead to a degree with distinction and must distribute the rest of his courses so as to leave none of the chief branches of learning wholly untouched (p. 4). This provision

233

was meant to restore systematic organization to the undergraduate curriculum. In his annual report for 1908-1909, the president hoped that "under the new rules for the choice of electives, some form of general examination at the end of the college life on the principal field of study will be more commonly required" (p. 5). The stage was set for comprehensive examinations of two types: first, a broad general examination of knowledge of the distribution, or general education, aspects of the degree program; and, second, a general examination of knowledge of the field of special emphasis (pp. 10, 11).

Although the term *comprehensive examination* appears to be virtually restricted to the educational system of the United States, examinations of a comprehensive nature have long been used as an incentive to and a check on educational achievement. Such examinations were extensively used in the universities of the Middle Ages. Cambridge and Oxford, as a means of education reform and to maintain high standards, introduced examinations prior to 1830. Apparently the innovation was somewhat successful in achieving its purposes, for the use of examinations became widespread. By 1858, the University of London was awarding degrees to candidates who successfully passed examinations, regardless of where or how long they had previously studied (Clapp, 1959, pp. 41-42).

In the United States, examinations have generally played a somewhat less significant role. Jones (1933, p. 13), in his survey of comprehensive examinations, notes that "the emphasis on one great effort, one decisive exhibition of mastery, has not been present in the typical American college." Jones further comments (p. 15): "In considering American and European systems, one significant difference in attitude should be mentioned—the tendency abroad to consider examining as a major function apart from instruction. One suspects a minor revolt on the part of a number of American educators against giving prominence to all kinds of examining. This is in part due to the obvious inadequacy which they witness in most examinations given in this country—the fact that they are hurriedly made up, that they are based primarily on hashed over textbook items, and that they do not sample enough data to ensure mastery of the material."

Comprehensive examinations in varying forms have been extensively used in some American colleges. From a survey of a limited number of colleges and universities in 1955, Steible and Sister Rose Agnes (1955) report that in sixty-eight of the eighty-two institutions questioned comprehensives were in use. An unpublished survey of 101 selected liberal arts colleges and universities made by the members of the DePauw University faculty revealed that thirty-seven of seventy responding institutions were using comprehensives. A more extensive letter survey which I made in the spring of 1959 included 700 liberal arts colleges and evoked 466 interpretable replies (Dressel and Associates, 1961). Of these 466 institutions, 301 used some form of comprehensive examination. Among the 165 negative replies were 46 reports of study of the possibility of using them, 30 reports of plans to inaugurate a comprehensive examination program, and 49 reports of strong interest in such examinations. In 18 of the 165 nonusing institutions, a program of comprehensive examinations had existed, but had been discontinued. The reasons for discontinuance varied, but increased numbers of students and insufficient faculty were given as reasons several times.

A review of current practices as reported in *American Universities and Colleges* (Singletary, 1968) indicates a continuing but decreasing interest in the use of comprehensive examinations in higher education. Of 946 institutions, 180 (19 percent) reported use of the Graduate Record Examinations, 12 (1.3 percent) reported use of sophomore comprehensive examinations, 1 use of junior comprehensives, and 310 (33 percent) use of senior comprehensives for one or more groups of students. Only 16 explicitly mentioned oral examinations, usually as part of a senior comprehensive. (It is impossible to know how accurate an indication these figures provide of the current use of comprehensive examinations, but the suggested format and past use of this reference suggest that most institutions which make any consistent use of comprehensives so report.) The 310 using senior comprehensives were, with one or two exceptions, relatively small private liberal arts colleges. The groups involved in taking such examinations varied: honors students only, students in only some departments, everyone except those in departments which exercised the option of substituting projects or special seminars. Examination in the minor was rarely noted. Advanced Graduate Record Examinations were occasionally included as part of the senior comprehensive and, in a few cases, the Graduate Record Examinations and departmental comprehensives were alternatives.

In 1959, I found (Dressel and Associates, 1961) that approximately twenty colleges had interesting features in their comprehensives. I contacted these institutions to gain up-to-date information on current practices and received responses from eighteen. Twelve of the eighteen reported that comprehensives have been dropped. Four indicated that a few departments continue to require comprehensives, but no general requirement exists. The remaining two reported a continuation of the comprehensive examination requirement in some form. Those institutions which had discontinued the requirement offered various explanations. The general easing of specific requirements and the flexibility allowed in defining broad concentrations rather than departmental majors were factors in several cases. Student resistance, supported by many faculty members, was also reported. Seminars, projects, theses, and senior essays were listed as replacing comprehensives, but with essentially the same intent: providing a culminative, integrative experience. Comprehensives for honors candidates are maintained in some cases even though the general requirement has been dropped. Apparently, from these reactions, the comprehensive examination is on the wane, although the concerns which originally justified it continue and are manifested in other forms. This development is not surprising, for earlier surveys suggested that comprehensives never fulfill their intended purposes in most colleges and are sources of irritation, constantly discussed and modified, and a heavy burden on both faculty and students.

Nevertheless, my informal correspondence with college deans suggests that the lack of an essential unity in programs and a concern about pervasive educational objectives are causing some faculties to review the need for and role of a culminating, integrative requirement. Accordingly, an analysis of the nature, intent, and procedures of comprehensives is still timely.

Purposes

Despite wide differences of opinion on the nature of comprehensive examination programs, some agreement exists on the purposes. First, liberal education has multiple objectives which are not adequately met or assessed in any single course, but which can be assessed by comprehensive examinations. If communication skills are a prime goal, English proficiency examinations may be regarded as comprehensive examinations. The writing or oral expression demanded in other comprehensives is also a means of assessing communication skills. Other broad objectives such as the ability to analyze, to form judgments, and to assess values are often required and prominently displayed in comprehensive problems or tasks not assignable in any single course.

Second, education is recognized as being cumulative and integrative, and comprehensives reinforce this recognition. Breadth, depth of knowledge, and increasing insight into the relationships of accumulated facts, concepts, and principles are essential aspects of liberal education. Yet emphasis on discrete courses and credits suggests that the only purpose of a course is gaining a satisfactory grade. Because professors of mathematics and science see their disciplines as essentially cumulative in nature, they generally have been less favorable to comprehensive examinations. Jones, in his study of comprehensives, noted this tendency, and it was confirmed in my 1959 survey. One college, for example, reported that the departments of chemistry, mathematics, and physics required two additional courses in lieu of a comprehensive.

Nevertheless, the comprehensive is still widely viewed as a device to encourage continuing student review and interrelating of current and earlier studies. A similar impact upon the faculty is expected, for if instructors do not relate teaching to other courses, the student is not likely to do so. The comprehensive examination may be viewed as a final assessment in which the student has the opportunity to demonstrate competence to a tribunal of higher authority than the individual teacher. In this sense, the professor and the student may find a common ground for working together to ensure that both come out of the comprehensive examination with the best possible record. Ideally, a high degree of student-faculty interest and mutual helpfulness can be developed through the introduction of the comprehensive examination system. Likewise, the enforced cooperation of faculty members both within and across departments in deciding upon the details of individual comprehensives develops a set of mutual concerns which weld the faculty into a single unit. In the opinions of administrators and faculty in institutions with successful programs, the comprehensive examination does inject a unifying element into the total educational program which is not otherwise attainable in this day of emphasis on grades and courses. To achieve this unity, it is necessary that the comprehensive examination requirement and its purposes be continually interpreted to students not as a threat or a hurdle, but as a chance to demonstrate finally whether they have truly acquired an education during four years at the institution.

Types

A comprehensive examination may be a single examination comprehensive by virtue of the range of material covered, or the comprehensive quality may be invoked by combining several examinations. A single one of the many course-related achievement tests available from the Educational Testing Service would scarcely merit designation as a comprehensive examination, even though its coverage would generally exceed that of a single course. A combination of several such achievement tests might, however, be so designated by a college. Four distinct types of comprehensives exist: examinations on courses or course sequences extending over more than one term, examinations on the general education (or breadth) components of curriculum requirements, divisional examinations covering a related group of disciplines, and examinations limited to the major or field of concentration.

In some institutions, an examination based upon completion of a sequence of courses has been required. From 1944 to 1954, Michigan State University used comprehensive examinations in each of its basic course sequences. The student's grade and credit (with or without formal enrollment) in each of the seven three-term sequence courses then offered were based solely on the results of a four- to six-hour examination covering the materials of the course. Several other institutions, including the University of Florida and the University of Chicago, followed a similar practice. Ultimately, faculty resistance, based on the feeling that separation of grading responsibilities jeopardized their control of students and reduced them to tutors, combined with administrative impatience with the record-keeping complications, led to abandonment of this system. Many students and parents also expressed strong opposition. The pattern of course grades and comprehensive examination grades seemed to some to be a case of double jeopardy.

In other institutions the comprehensive examination program has included broadly conceived examinations in social science, science, or other fields, with most students completing a series of courses in preparation for these examinations. The course requirements, however, are often not explicit, and the number and nature of the courses taken prior to passing or attempting to pass an examination may vary with the student's needs as determined by prior experience and study. Thus the examination becomes the significant requirement, and courses are viewed as means rather than as ends. This expanded conception of course-sequence comprehensives merges into the broad general education comprehensive requirements.

General education comprehensives have usually been required at the close of the sophomore year, on the assumption that the first two years of college are devoted mainly to breadth and the last two years largely to specialization. Even if breadth and depth educational experiences are viewed as parallel rather than sequential, the close of the sophomore year is a natural point for appraisal and planning of the remainder of the college experience. However, placement of general education comprehensives at the close of the sophomore year has not been universal. Many colleges have required a general education comprehensive at the close of the sophomore year and have also included a general education phase in the senior comprehensive.

In one college, for a time, the comprehensive examination was given at the beginning of the freshman year and retaken at the end of that year in an alternative but equivalent form as a basis for advising and program planning. At the end of the sophomore year, performance on the same examination was used to determine whether the student had satisfactorily completed the requirements.

Existing attempts to measure all of liberal education include accepting as a comprehensive the final examination of a senior seminar, individual laboratory projects, creative work in the arts or literature, and recitals for music majors.

Divisional comprehensives (humanities, social sciences, natural sciences) may be regarded as a phase of the general education requirement or (if divisional concentrations, or majors, are permitted) as major comprehensives. When part of the general education requirement, the comprehensive is typically a college rather than a divisional requirement, but divisions or departments sometimes require a divisional comprehensive to ensure breadth in the division which the major is part of.

The term *major comprehensive* is not synonymous with senior comprehensive. The latter may include more than the major, and major comprehensives are sometimes scheduled for the end of the junior year. The term *senior comprehensive*, however, is in common usage. In my 1959 survey of liberal arts colleges, 243 of the 301 reporting use of comprehensives indicated that these were at the senior level.

Major comprehensives differ greatly in length, form, and coverage. The total time required for senior comprehensives has varied from a few hours to several days.

Commercially available examinations may be used along with locally prepared material. Oral, written, and multiple-choice tests may be combined in various patterns. When written and oral examinations are required, the orals may emphasize breadth of comprehension, interrelation of the major with other disciplines, and problems and issues of current significance. One college, at the end of the senior year, used examinations consisting of the following parts: Undergraduate Program Area Tests and appropriate Advanced Placement Examinations (APEs), a departmental written examination, and an oral. The final examination of a senior seminar course has also been accepted as fulfilling the comprehensive requirement—a curious twist in which the integrative role of the examination is played by an integrative senior seminar. Numerous colleges have used a senior comprehensive similar to the final oral for a graduate degree in that the student presents a paper, report, or creative work which must be defended before a committee composed of two persons besides the major professor.

Minors and related fields as well as the major may be covered. In one college departments are encouraged to require related courses in other departments as part of the preparation for the comprehensive examination. In another college, seniors were examined in the liberal arts program for a minimum of six hours and in their major areas of concentration for a maximum of eight hours. Another combination called for an hour written comprehensive in the minor in addition to the six-hour written and oral examination in the major. A recurring pattern is that of a departmentally posed but broadly conceived examination based upon both departmental offerings and a reasonable amount of peripheral reading. The pattern of senior comprehensives in a foreign language may be somewhat different. Frequently, the comprehensive for majors covers the total study of the language, literature, and culture of the country. Oral examinations may also be considered an essential part, the obvious though not sole intent being to determine the facility of the student in speaking the language.

Commercially Available Examinations

The Buros yearbooks contain detailed information and critiques on commercially available examinations. Hence there is no need to elaborate upon them here. Moreover, such examinations are continually under revision and the entire field is in a state of flux. In the current scene, the following examinations are worthy of attention for use in comprehensive examination programs: Undergraduate Program Area Tests, Sequential Tests of Educational Progress, Graduate Record Examinations,

Teacher Education Examination Program, National League for Nursing Tests, Modern Language Association Tests, American Chemical Society Tests, National Occupational Competency Testing Institute tests. Conditions of availability, detailed descriptions, and costs are all available in Buros (1972) or from the respective agencies.

The use of commercially available examinations for comprehensive purposes has both advantages and disadvantages. The faculty is spared the task of examination construction. The examinations are far better technically than those that most faculty members could construct. However, faculty members hesitate to put much faith in such examinations, and their attitude tends to be reflected in their students' attitudes. Outstanding performance relative to available norms is cordially received as evidence of excellent instruction, but poor performance is usually excused on the grounds of the irrelevance of the items covered. Unless faculty members can be induced to review the examinations thoroughly in advance of administration and commit themselves to counseling, program appraisal, or other uses, the effort is likely wasted. And so are the time and money expended.

Procedures and Types of Questions

It has long been recognized that *objective tests* can measure critical thought and mature judgment. Chapter Ten of this volume discusses the problems involved and gives some examples. Faculty members lacking skilled assistance however have not commonly found much satisfaction in their efforts at constructing such tests; hence, they retreat to the use of standardized examinations, although with no great belief that such examinations are entirely relevant or adequate in coverage.

Constructing good objective examinations requires a vast expenditure of time; unless the number of students to be tested necessitates equal or greater time for reading essays or participation in oral examinations, there is no net gain for the faculty.

A second problem posed by the use of objective tests is that of security. Because of the difficulties involved, faculty members are forced into continuous writing of new ones. This extra effort makes secure programs such as those provided by the Educational Testing Service look attractive.

A third issue posed by the local development of objective tests is the lack of standards for comparison with other colleges. Such a lack may be of little importance in large institutions, but smaller colleges concerned with accreditation, with placing students in graduate schools, or with internal comparisons and improvement of departments may find the norms of a standardized test of some use.

Although the practice of using only objective tests is not uncommon, not all the significant objectives of a college can be assessed with such a practice. A combination of objective tests and essay tests, orals, and projects is generally viewed as essential to provide full coverage of important outcomes.

Although *essay tests* of a comprehensive nature are easier to formulate than are objective tests, the repeated effort to develop guidelines for such questions is evidence that this ease is not absolute. Commonly, questions have to cover not only the required courses of the major sequence, but also the elective ones. At one college, for example, the seniors were told: "(1) Emphasis . . . will be placed upon the major, although 'related subjects' may also be included in the examination, and the examination will involve pertinent subject matter, relationships, problems, and interpretations; (2) the examination may also include other fields of study in those respects in which there is a reasonable interrelationship of subject matter, problems, and attitudes." In addition, problems or questions often must be ones about which the student has not been specifically taught or coached.

One solution is to select a current issue such as racism, the conflict between communism and democracy, or colonialism and to develop questions around that issue. Such questions are formulated to draw upon the total educational experience of undergraduates—core courses, courses in the minor, and elective courses. This essay test can be given as a take-home or open-book examination to be completed within a two-week period. This type of written examination is seen primarily as a method of requiring the student to review, to integrate, and to bring knowledge and understanding to bear on a current issue. Some persons initially attracted to this approach have finally rejected it because it requires individualized questions and permits the student to solicit undue assistance from others.

Of those programs reporting the use of essay or *oral comprehensives* in my 1959 survey, 236 used written examinations and 104 used orals; 60 programs employed both. Although the oral examination was thus used rather extensively, the replies suggested that it is most commonly a part of comprehensive examinations for honors students rather than a required part of general comprehensives. The use of orals seemed also to be concentrated in the smaller, more selective institutions.

Oral examinations vary markedly in length and (one would infer) in importance. They are often closely related to written examinations and may even constitute a follow-up of the student's written responses. This procedure permits adjustment for those students who are more adept at writing than in oral communication and vice versa.

External examiners are occasionally used in preparing and reading essay examinations, but this practice is much more frequent with orals. In some cases, the external examiner participates in the development and grading of both written and oral phases of the comprehensive, although this participation is not readily accomplished if the written phase must be evaluated prior to the oral. Use of external examiners may be required or may be approved if requested.

The difficulties of assuring that oral questioning is comprehensive are no less complex than those of assuring the written examination is. An additional difficulty is that it is neither easy nor desirable to structure an oral examination as tightly as a written one. The requirement that oral examination questions be submitted in advance destroys one of the major advantages claimed for the oral: that the later questions may grow out of the candidate's performance in the early part of the examination. Screening by the chairman of the examining committee can ward off unreasonable questions, but it cannot ensure good ones.

Projects can be substituted for all or part of the comprehensive examination procedure. Projects include preparing a thesis, planning and carrying through an experiment, exhibiting artistic productions, or giving a recital. In some cases, the project, much like the doctoral dissertation, becomes the basis for the final comprehensive examination—usually oral in these circumstances. Projects have the advantage of directing the student's efforts over a longer period of time than does preparation for a comprehensive, which is usually restricted to a few days. Projects may be chosen to accommodate a great deal of individuality and creativity. In turn, there is the recurring concern that this advantage raises problems in assuring uniformity of procedure and comparability in grading.

Use of Results

Essentially five distinct uses of comprehensive examination results are identifiable. The first is in the process of remediating deficiencies, placing the student, planning of a program, and checking on progress. The second is as a graduation or honors requirement. The third is in the evaluation of instruction and curriculum. The fourth is as a measure of long-term student development. And the fifth is as a partial basis for awarding external degrees.

Repeated use of comprehensive testing first for detection of deficiencies, next for program planning, and then for a check on progress is attractive; but an examination serving all these purposes is difficult to construct. The detection of deficiencies as a basis for further course requirements is frequently a result of the use of sophomore comprehensives and junior comprehensives. In some cases, the comprehensive examination is held in September of the student's senior year. If performance is unsatisfactory, a planned remedial program is inaugurated so that the student may remedy any weaknesses in time to pass the comprehensive for graduation. This procedure also avoids the embarrassment which results from last-minute failures just before commencement.

One college, for example, reported that the sophomore

comprehensive examination covers general education; the results are given to the student and the student's counselor. In some cases, parts of the comprehensive stand as indicators of progress in particular areas, and the passing of the examination may result in the granting of credit and thus in the waiver of course requirements. In this sense, the comprehensive examination plays the role of an advanced placement test as well as a check on progress. Too often the comprehensive examination is a final hurdle which can yield only bad news for the student. If it instead offers recognition and reward, it gives the able student an incentive. (The whole issue of credit by examination is discussed in the next section.) A few colleges apparently use the sophomore comprehensive examination results as a partial basis for selection of the major, but such selection is done more on a counseling basis than on the basis of attaining a minimum score or meeting standards for acceptance.

The use of the senior comprehensive as a final degree requirement is the second and most common manifestation of comprehensive examinations; however, the specific provisions for the examination and the treatment of the results vary markedly. The embarrassment caused by failure just prior to commencement has led to a confusing variety of policies about the time at which examinations are given and the conditions under which they may be repeated. Moving the examination to the late junior or early senior year tends to delegate the comprehensive to a relatively minor role.

The relationship between the comprehensive examination requirement for graduation and the honors requirement also varies from institution to institution. Indeed, the policies are not entirely clear in single colleges. For example, one college has a comprehensive examination requirement for all seniors and a comprehensive examination requirement for candidates for honors, but it also allows combining the two if this procedure is approved by the adviser. In some colleges, the award of honors is based on high performance on the senior comprehensive examination required of all students, whereas in others the comprehensive examinations are required only of candidates for honors. Thus, an honors degree may mean either a difference in quality of performance or a fundamental difference in the kind of work done.

Evaluation of instruction and curriculum is a third purpose of comprehensives. Colleges that use objective examination programs, such as the Undergraduate Program Area Tests, frequently feel that the results are most helpful in the evaluation of the curricular and instructional program. For this purpose, norms which provide comparability from institution to institution and, to some extent, even from department to department within an institution are considered valuable. Colleges have required additional course work in certain areas or introduced new courses because seniors have demonstrated weaknesses in certain phases of comprehensive examinations.

Although relatively few institutions provide direct evidence on the progress of the individual from the beginning of a college program until its close, attempting to assess long-term development is a fourth frequent use of comprehensive examination results. If senior-year data are related to similar data accumulated earlier, the impact of a sequence of courses or of the total college program can be assessed. The Undergraduate Program Area Tests of the Educational Testing Service are often given at the end of the sophomore year and repeated at the end of the senior year; locally developed objective examinations may be used in a similar pattern. The results at these two stages give objective indications of change in the student. Comparison of essays is equally possible, although more difficult. The final oral examination itself may be planned to take on this evaluative role for both the faculty and the student. Occasionally, elaborate case studies in which all information on the development of the student is discussed in relation to performance on the final comprehensive examination have been developed. Even though it is not possible to do such case studies for all students, the preparation of such an analysis for a limited number of students helps faculty members understand comprehensive examination data.

A fifth possible use of comprehensive examination results is for awarding degrees, independent of formal study. This use has seldom been accepted in the United States, although a few colleges have, on paper at least, stated that intent. Generally, the comprehensive has validated course work, rather than replacing it, but a few colleges have explicitly stated that the comprehensive is the fundamental requirement and that passing it at an appropriate level constitutes one basis for granting a degree.

Credit by Examination

Although the comprehensive examination concept, fully developed, could provide a basis for granting degrees, this has not happened. Comprehensives have been add-ons rather than a means for granting credit, and most comprehensives in use would not be adequate for granting credits or degrees. Nevertheless, credit by examination is more like comprehensives than course testing, and I therefore treat it in this chapter.

Bersi (1973) reviews the nature of time-shortened degree programs in the United States. Out of 1400 accredited colleges and universities contacted, 1008 responded, and of these 243 reported proposed or operating time-shortened activities. Of these 243, 76 reported use of the College Level Examination Program (CLEP), 43 the granting of credit by examination, 41 the use of the College Entrance Examination Board Advanced Placement Examinations (APE), and 6 the use of departmental examinations for credit. In a smaller sample of 62 (some incomplete), 34 of 60 reported granting credit by use of CLEP or APE or both. Twenty indicated the use of challenge examinations; in these cases, a student has the privilege of challenging a required course, and if the department offering the course believes the challenge to be well based, a special examination is prepared and evaluated by the department. Practices as to waiver or credit and recording of a grade, as usual, vary not only with institutions, but with departments as well. This use of various examinations, such as CLEP, for granting credit can be regarded as an extension of the concept of comprehensive examinations, although departmentally constructed challenge examinations and the APE correspond more to course examinations than to true comprehensives. (In fact, the APEs were constructed to appraise the achievement of students taking advanced placement courses developed by secondary school teachers.)

CLEP is divided into two parts: first, a set of five general examinations in English composition, humanities, mathematics, natural sciences, and social sciences-history, and second, a set of thirty-four college-level subject examinations. Whereas the APEs were constructed as common, centrally graded examinations corresponding to planned courses, the CLEP examinations attempt to recognize unconventional, out-of-classroom study. The CLEP general examinations in their full scope are a definition of liberal or general education, and the thirty-four subject or discipline-based examinations correspond to a broad, comprehensive view of each subject rather than to any one course. Hence the CLEP examinations, especially the general examinations, are comprehensive.

Both the APEs and the CLEP were devised to assist colleges in granting credit to students for study prior to or independent of college attendance. Many colleges and universities have preferred to give advanced placement without credit, although many of those in Bersi's report were granting credit, usually with a limitation on the maximum permitted. The following allowances indicate the patterns: up to sixty quarter hours on CLEP and APEs; up to forty-eight quarter hours on CLEP and specially prepared departmental examinations; up to forty-eight credits by examination in areas other than foreign language, twenty-five in foreign language, and no limit on challenge credits. The majority of the institutions held credit down to one full year, with a few allowing another half year by special examinations.

There was also marked variation among the institutions in the standards required for credit. The APEs are assigned grades: 5 (extremely well qualified), 4 (well qualified), 3 (qualified), 2 (possibly qualified), 1 (no recommendation). Some colleges grant credit only for 4 and 5, some for 3 and above, and some for 2 (after individual consideration) and above. Minimum standards for award of credit on CLEP vary among institutions from the twenty-fifth to the seventieth percentile. One university (not included in the Bersi report) indicated that, for a time, performance at the ninetieth percentile was required for credit, although this requirement has since been reduced. Most reported the fiftieth percentile as the minimum for credit. Certainly the twenty-fifth, though recommended by the American Council on Education, appears unreasonably low (not far from a chance performance on random marking), and the ninetieth is unreasonably high.

Since Bersi's report focuses on time-shortened programs, it is not surprising that relatively few of the colleges (twelve to fourteen, depending on interpretation) reported the use of comprehensive examinations. In several of these colleges, the comprehensive examinations were available to fulfill general education requirements. The Undergraduate Program Area Tests were used in several colleges for this purpose. Others indicated use of tests of foreign language proficiency; alternate routes for general education by tests, work samples, or faculty judgment; comprehensive area examinations for disciplines or segments of disciplines; field examinations at elementary and intermediate levels, with a research project or scientific demonstration in the senior year; and departmental comprehensives.

Problems and Benefits

Most of the recurring issues and problems faced in the use of comprehensive examinations have been dealt with incidentally in the preceding sections. These can be briefly summarized:

1. Comprehensive examinations conflict with both departmental autonomy and the widely prevalent course-credit emphasis. Though intended as a partial antidote to this emphasis, the requirement may only generate opposition.

2. The development of good comprehensives and the appraisal of them is a time-consuming task and one for which most faculty members are not well prepared.

3. The recurrent issues about content, procedures, timing, and use of comprehensives are never fully resolved. Rules which are generated tend to rigidify the process and raise still other problems which breed dissatisfaction with the program.

4. If tests are especially purchased or rented for comprehensives, and especially if outside examiners are employed with attendant transportation costs and honoraria, the direct finan-

cial outlay may be no small item. A quick and crude estimate of the cost of giving a battery of foreign language tests (220 minutes of testing time) to one hundred students is six dollars per student for test materials, faculty time, and scoring. The costs of elaborate programs involving outside examiners and oral, essay, and objective tests have been estimated to run as high as one hundred dollars per student. And to this cost must be added the forgone benefits of instructional hours and the diversion of faculty from other pursuits.

The claimed benefits of comprehensives are difficult to assess. Faculty, administration, and student opinions constitute the major evidence cited, and frequently there are marked differences among as well as within these three groups. The claim that comprehensives force students to accept responsibility for learning is denied by those who point to the many preparatory programs (seminars, theses) that must be introduced by the faculty and to the tendency of those programs to replace the examination. There is a continuing disagreement as to whether the focus of a comprehensive should be on synthesis and integration in the major field or over the entire college experience, whether it should be retrospective and summative, or prospective and formative. The claim of providing a unifying influence on the curriculum is hard to demonstrate when segments of the faculty deny either the validity of the concern or the relevance of the comprehensive in meeting it.

In my 1959 survey, the students reported that comprehensives motivated them to study for a long-range point of view, to review and try to integrate their education, and to keep all their texts and notebooks at hand. However, ten years later I (Dressel and DeLisle, 1969) found a small increase in the use of comprehensives, but no indication of widespread enthusiasm. Indeed, there was evidence that such developments as tutorials, senior theses, field work, and community service were regarded as replacing or even as being superior to comprehensive examinations in providing students with an opportunity to demonstrate how well they could apply their education. There are hints also that student reactions to comprehensive examinations in the 1970s may be much less cordial than they were earlier. Administrator comments indicate an increased antipathy toward comprehensive examinations because of the rigidities and extra work involved. Requirements have thus been liberalized or dropped, and new broad concentrations have been made available. With an increasing number of students discontinuous in attendance or transferring to other institutions after two years, the ideals of continuity, sequence, integration, or unity of knowledge are more difficult to maintain. In a sense, comprehensives are needed more than ever before, but the current scene is not the most hospitable for such emphasis. A few institutions which were once strongly committed to comprehensives have completely abandoned them. Yet the interest in external degrees and in appraisal of the educational benefits of informal unplanned experiences, combined with the possibility of greater discontinuity in the pursuit of higher education, may bring once again to the foreground the need for comprehensive examinations. And this new approach may well be psychologically better in that it provides recognition rather than imposes an additional burden.

Characteristics of Successful Programs

The first characteristic of a successful program is clarity of purpose, of use, and of the educational objectives to be attained. The comprehensive examination then has meaning in that tangible and significant educational decisions can be based on it, and in that it adds a new dimension to the program rather than being another routine requirement which is largely anticlimactic. One may debate whether clarity emerges from definition of purpose or from overall educational practices and the decisions made on the basis of the results of the comprehensive. The argument is largely moot. Explicit purposes may not be accompanied by a program which reflects them. In a well-planned program the purposes, although largely implicit, may emerge clearly. For example, the integrative purpose of the comprehensive examination is often emphasized, but the examination often does not accomplish this integration. Integration must be implicit in curriculum and instructional practices and in tangible evidence that the student has to demonstrate this ability to achieve a degree.

The second characteristic of the successful comprehensive examination program is effective coordination and availability of technical assistance. In those colleges in which comprehensives are almost entirely a departmental matter, the disparities in the operation and decisions on these examinations from one department to another are a continual source of frustration to everyone involved. Although coordination is sometimes supplied from the dean's office or even the registrar's office, the most appropriate source seems to be a strong all-college policy committee on comprehensive examinations. In addition to coordination, technical assistance in the preparation and handling of examinations is desirable. A full-time examiner is not necessary. Persons with training and experience in the field may be hired in certain departments, such as psychology or education, and provide, as committee members, a coordinating role in the examination program. Alternatively, those who are in fields relatively unrelated to efficiency in evaluation may, through workshops, self-study, or a combination of interest and experience, become rather highly proficient in many phases of the examination program. Such individuals can be an excellent resource to the total program. Their reception by the faculty at large may be much better than will that of a person trained in evaluation.

The third characteristic of a successful comprehensive examination program is a close relationship among curriculum, instruction, and the examination program. (This characteristic follows closely from the first noted characteristic, clarity of purpose.) The many seminar review sessions, reading periods, theses, and the like which have to be developed to support the comprehensive examination system point to a general recognition of the fact that students cannot be expected to do in a comprehensive examination what curriculum and instruction have not provided experience in doing before that time. As I have pointed out, the introduction of any of these various devices may simply add a new unit to the total program without in any way affecting the general curriculum and instructional practices. For this reason, some faculty members constantly oppose the idea of introducing any courses or other formally planned experiences to help the student prepare for the comprehensive examination.

The fourth characteristic in a successful program is found in the highlighting of its importance. Assuming that the reasons for the comprehensive examinations are clear and that the decisions to be made by reference to the results are reasonably specific, it is necessary to continually reiterate these purposes to students and faculty and generally to the clientele of the institution, including the parents. The relationship of the comprehensive examination to the total experience provided by the institution is important. In those institutions where comprehensives have long held sway and have been most successful, the interrelated features of the program, to which the comprehensive but supplies the final punctuation, are a matter of pride and of extended explication in a variety of publications. This continuing interpretation involves emphasizing discipline or rigor, motivation of the student, review and retention, integration of subject matter, individual initiative, and increased cooperation between students and professors as results of the use of comprehensives.

Continuing interpretation, however, also demands continuing assessment (the fifth characteristic) to see whether these values are achieved. In particular, examination results need to be analyzed and interpreted to the faculty in relation to the curriculum and instruction and the purposes of the program, as well as in relation to individual student performance. A generally unsatisfactory performance on certain questions or in a certain field may become the basis for reexamination of the course requirements or the instruction provided in the particular area of deficiency. Ultimately, a decision may be reached to change the requirements or to use a different pattern of instruction. If faculty members instead become highly critical of the inadequacies of the students, consideration of student performance on external tests, such as the Undergraduate Program Area Tests, may restore to both faculty and students a reasonable perspective on the ability of the students and on their preparation. Thus, the interpretation of the examination requires analysis and summarization of the results of student performance in ways which make it possible to point up the deficiencies of the program as well as those of the individual student. Unless a comprehensive examination accomplishes both these purposes, it fails at being comprehensive in its significance, even though it may be comprehensive in its coverage.

Bibliographical Note

As this chapter suggests, the use of comprehensive examinations in the traditional sense is limited largely to private liberal arts colleges. Accordingly, the literature on this topic is restricted. Jones (1933), though dated, is still worthy of reading by those interested in comprehensives. Dressel and Associates (1961) includes numerous examples of practices as of that date, which are still of interest, though probably no longer current in the institutions cited. Kreplin's (1971) review of the literature on credit by examination has some relevance. Volume II of *The Seventh Mental Measurements Yearbook*, edited by Buros (1972), in its books and reviews section, pp. 1533-1846, contains annotations on many books which will be useful to those pursuing the topic. The lists of published tests and critical reviews of them effectively cover the range of those which might be used in a comprehensive examination program.

Chapter 12

Grades, Credits, and Alternatives

"The present age is one of transition in higher education: the American college is on trial. Condemnation is heard on every hand. The capital charge is preferred that there is a general demoralization of college standards, expressing the fact that, as the college serves no particular educational purpose, it is immaterial whether the student takes the thing seriously or not. . . . The college is charged with failure in pedagogical insight at each of the critical junctures of . . . education, so that a degree may be won with little or no systematic exertion, and, as a result, our college students are said to emerge flighty, superficial, and immature, lacking, as a class, concentration, seriousness, and thoroughness."

This paragraph, written by W. T. Foster, president of Reed College, appeared in 1911. The reference to standards clearly indicates that either the standards themselves or the means of

256

assessing student accomplishment relative to those standards had become faulty. The complaint echoes today, although others argue that the imposition of standards and the associated tests, grades, quality points, and credits are in themselves the explanation of the difficulties of colleges. Grades are seen by some professors as the means of maintaining or enforcing standards and by others as destroying student motivation or channeling it narrowly into achieving grades rather than into significant learning. Some members of the latter faction would go as far as to eliminate all formal evaluation, arguing that students must evaluate their own efforts in achieving their own goals. Others would substitute other forms of evaluation which emphasize feedback and incentives for further effort and development.

Contrasting Views

Numerous psychologists such as Carl Rogers, Earl C. Kelley, A. H. Maslow, Arthur Combs, and Phillip Clark embrace a self-actualization view of motivation. They argue that human nature is essentially good, that each person has unique and almost infinite potential which, under proper conditions, he or she will seek to attain. The optimistic assumption is that almost everyone is rational, ambitious, and both self-motivated and self-directed. Those who have such convictions see the traditional approach to grading as capricious, autocratic, and antithetical to mental health, to ambition, and to the development of independence and individuality; it encourages rote memorization and recall rather than mastery of concepts, use of higher mental processes, and creativity. In this view, teaching facilitates learning by encouraging and assisting rather than by directing and grading. Instruction should emphasize individualized learning, recognizing differences in readiness, in learning rates, in goals, and in appropriateness of materials, learning experiences, and methods. Adaptation to individual differences and mastery (at individual rates) of criterion-referenced goals and materials of interest to the individual should, in this view, replace structured classes, uniform assignments, and the imposition of norm-referenced grades.

This highly humanistic view of education is attractive and plausible. The difficulty is that, for many years to come, we probably shall not find or train teachers who either accept or are capable of executing this ideal. Such schools as have been based upon this approach appear chaotic and are even disruptive to the neighborhoods in which they are located. It is doubtful that legislatures or the general public would long support colleges which attempted to operate on these principles. And the question remains as to whether the ideas and findings of social scientists who are based in soft, noncumulative disciplines and who put an emphasis on human development are entirely applicable to the learning of tightly organized, well-structured, and sequential material such as in mathematics and the natural sciences. One further and highly personal comment: These humanistic views about schooling, although presented forcefully and with back-up research, are not essentially different from those presented by some educators and psychologists of fifty years ago. In preparing for teaching in the late 1920s and early 1930s, I was exposed to and, in some measure, was indoctrinated with similar views. Yet it seems to me that we are no closer to and in many ways are further from their realization than we were then. The constant flow of new knowledge, new technology, and new methodology raises serious doubts that an undisciplined and undirected approach to education based on intrinsic individual motivation will suffice or that society will long support colleges which adopt this course.

Those who damn grades or any formal critical evaluation are concerned with affective development, originality, creativity, and individual freedom. Whatever individuals do is acceptable if they so evaluate it, although they might be subtly led to engage in more critical evaluation. Yet who really decides when a program is successful? On the job, a person's self-appraisal is rarely the basis upon which he or she is promoted, given a raise, or retained. Rarely even is the individual completely satisfied unless others also value the effort. In music, art, and literature, critics, sales, and the test of time combine to make an appraisal from which there is no appeal except to more time and other critics. True it is that these fields are perilous for the untalented student who cherishes praise and good grades. In this creative arena, compromise in grading by taking effort into account may well be condoned. Pass-fail, credit-no credit, or sympathetic appraisal may be preferable to more rigorous grading in these circumstances.

In the area of sports and physical activities, grading shows up in its harshest form, with little or no acknowledgment of individual differences, and yet apparently causes little concern. In running the mile, only time counts; form is relevant only if it affects time. In gymnastics and in ice skating figures and dances, form, grace, difficulty, and timing are essential elements of the performance. Although presumably competent judges may disagree in their ratings, the criteria are reasonably clear.

Observation of the eagerness with which individuals enter competitions seems also to belie the view that competition is destructive to ego. While it is true that, for some, coming in second is a momentary failure; for others, it is a joyous and unexpected success. And even those who fail would not be content to perform without the stimulation of audience and competition. Initial and even repeated failure is, for some individuals, the stimulus for renewed effort, whereas success often is accompanied by retirement from competition, gradual atrophy of the skills which led to success, and perhaps a shift to a new field of competition.

The view that competition is bad because it imposes external and stultifying standards on the individual results from a limited conception of competition and decision making. There are several forms of competition, as demonstrated by the following list. Competition may be (1) with oneself and one's past performance either for self-satisfying improvement or for attainment of a personally imposed goal or ideal; (2) with friends and associates either for mutual stimulation and motivation or for forwarding the goals of the group; (3) against others either for inclusion in an elite or for top rating and attainment of personal prestige; (4) against fixed standards for one of several reasons: to minimally qualify for certification, recognition, inclusion in a group; to achieve a recognized level of proficiency; to set new standards.

Each of these forms of competition requires some form of grading and some form of decision making, but differs in decision-making agent and in the interests served by the decision. An evaluation is useful for decision making only when an interpretation is imposed upon it. This interpretation and the decision may be made by (1) the individual (and others whose advice he or she seeks) with the individual's best interests in mind; (2) the individual and immediate associates with the group's best interests in mind; (3) others with their best interests in mind.

Ideally, one might hope that what is best for the individual is best for others and society. But individuals are not always motivated to accept the reality of their limitations or to sacrifice their aspirations for the sake of a better world. Unreasonably high aspiration can lead only to ultimate disappointment and disillusionment. Self-evaluation must, therefore, ever be attended by recognition, understanding, and acceptance of the evaluations of others or of personal performance in reference to external standards. These external standards may be either relative to the performance of others or absolutes accepted and recognized by others.

The idealistic views summarized above nevertheless provide valid criticisms of existing evaluation and grading practices and of the character and quality of instruction in our colleges and universities. If we cannot put these views into practice as enunciated, we can learn from them and move in the direction of recognizing and promoting individual aspirations rather than denying or negating them by irrelevant comparison.

Grades and other evidence of satisfactory or praiseworthy performance are facts of life with which we all contend. They serve as a desirable antidote to recognition or reward based on family, money, or social connections rather than on personal merit. Grading is not inherently objectionable or harmful, though many manifestations of it clearly are. In this chapter, I discuss the problems of, purposes of, and approaches to grading, pointing up the weaknesses, but also suggesting how grading practices might be improved. My view, quite simply, is that success and failure are always relative, that they are always, in part, based upon the judgments of society as well as upon those of the individual. Furthermore, judgments of the effectiveness of individuals perform a social function in selecting those most capable, especially in professional areas. Consider the implications if teachers continually reward and encourage ineffective performance and thereby encourage an individual to enter a field for which he or she has little capability. Resources are wasted; others may be denied access because of the presence of incompetents. Regardless of immediate emotional implications, knowledge of relative performance is both humane and essential for an individual and for society. Our problem with grading in education is that it is not done well, and that the systems used are mixed, are subjective, and do not permit unambiguous interpretation.

Credit Hour

The classical curriculum of the early American university was essentially a required common experience for all students, culminating after four years (three years, originally, at Harvard) in the baccalaureate degree. This required curriculum could not, of course, ensure that all students either had identical experiences or learned the same things. Later, some colleges introduced alternative curriculums, but the total program continued as the unit for educational planning. With the advent of alternative courses and especially of extensive electives, neither a required total program nor a compilation of completed courses indicated progress toward a degree. The introduction of credits was an attempt to meet the need for equating student work regardless of electives and alternative courses taken. The credits assigned to a course were a rating of the worth of the course in working toward a degree; all students completing the course satisfactorily received the same number of credits. Individual grades were added to reflect differential achievement.

Today the publications of colleges are cluttered with explanations, rules, and requirements regarding hours, credits, quality points, courses, majors, units, student loads and fees, faculty loads, degree credits, and grade point averages. Such paraphernalia provide a facade of specificity and accuracy which is misleading and detrimental to sound education, yet these requirements are so convenient and so well geared to departmental structures, to faculty interests, and to record keeping as to destroy most efforts at critical review and significant alteration.

The credit describes in part the organization or structure of the educational process. It reveals nothing about student learning, and an accumulation of credits, even in a single discipline, provides no assurance of knowledge. Only as those credits are related to grade and course requirements is it possible to determine an individual's progress toward a degree. Thus, credit hours represent at best exposure and time serving by students; and, with the demise of attendance checks in some courses, they no longer assure that. Despite these shortcomings, credits have only expanded and systematized the pattern implicit in the earlier required college programs. Though this required curriculum provided superficially common experiences, time serving was and still is the route to a college degree. Today there are simply many more confusing ways of serving time.

Credits do provide some permanence and security not present in the earlier patterns. A student dropping out of a required sequential program after three years had difficulty in returning to complete the fourth year. A major in mathematics, science, or a foreign language would still face those difficulties today because credits dating back more than a specified number of years may not be counted, especially in cumulative disciplines and at the graduate levels. In noncumulative areas, such as history, literature, and the social sciences, however, it may be relatively easy to acquire the additional credits needed for a degree despite discontinuity in attendance and probable loss in specific knowledge and competence.

A unit of measure must indicate a fixed amount of some aspect of whatever is measured. On this basis, the credit is not a unit of measure, though it is made to serve as such. A fifty-minute lecture three times a week for eight to ten weeks and the traditionally expected two hours outside the classroom for each hour spent in it yield three quarter hours of credit for the student. A laboratory credit may require anywhere from two to six hours in the laboratory or in preparing or completing reports. Credits for field work have generally been far fewer than the actual hours involved. Required field work and internships may receive no credit.

The credit hour has nothing to do either with difficulty. A five-credit mathematics course may be difficult and require many hours of study for some students, but little time or effort for others. Another course, lacking in substance but filled with petty requirements, may be made time consuming though not difficult.

Despite these drawbacks, credits are widely used for various purposes. They provide the basis for prescribing degree requirements, for balancing areas of study in a degree program, and for laying out the student's schedule. Credits play a role in advising, counseling, and placement in courses. Credit loads may be adjusted to student difficulties or to outside work requirements. Course prerequisites are frequently stated as a specified number of credits in related courses. Credits weighted by the quality points assigned to grades become the basis for awarding scholarships and for dismissal. The quality of the credits awarded by a college has been, at least theoretically, the basis for accreditation, both regional and professional.

Numerous additional uses make evident how essential the credit hour has become in the structure of higher education. Transfer from one institution to another depends heavily on course-credit correspondences. Predictions of student success utilize the course-credit structure as well as grades. Credit (and course) requirements provide the basis for certifying professionals. Student credit hours are the basis for both internal budget allocations and state appropriations. Departmental, faculty, and student loads are determined by credit hours. Student progress or class status is based on credit hours. Student fees are assessed according to the credit-hour load.

Credit hours are also used to distinguish between evening or extension courses and regular course offerings. This distinction has little to do with quality or with the amount of work involved for either instructors or students. But the insistence that credits be granted only for courses offered through the traditional structure provides one of the most effective barriers to developing external degrees, granting credits by examination, or recognizing the educational merits of informal life experience.

The use of the credit hour in graduate and professional education is even more harmful than in undergraduate liberal education. Doctoral-level education has always been predicated on research competence in a discipline, but accountability and budget allocation by credit hour have forced many universities to insist on a correspondence between credit-hour load and faculty responsibility at this level.

Indeed, credit hours play a major role in budget allocations at all levels. In some states, auditors are already inquiring into discrepancies between student credit hours reported after three weeks and those reported at the end of a term. They note that drops, no grades, deferred grades, and incompletes account for a significant number of the credit hours which are counted in budget requests. Legislatures, too, have become concerned that independent study and credit by examination may be used to produce credit hours which (they believe) require little faculty effort. Thus the traditionally antagonistic view of many faculty members toward such activities may be reinforced by external insistence that a credit hour involve direct faculty contact with students. Indeed, it appears that budgeting officers and legislators are becoming more concerned with contact hours than with credit hours. An auditor's report in Michigan recommended that courses giving more hours' credit than class hours scheduled should be reported to the legislature at the class-hour figure.

The unintended consequences of preoccupation with credits are evident when departments and colleges encourage or insist that students (both graduate and undergraduate) take most if not all of their credits in the college and department of their major. In fact, there are so many problems with the definition and use of credits that the credit hour lacks both validity and reliability as a measure of effort, achievement, or exposure: (1) Credits usually imply time, but when granted by examination they may be indices of achievement. (2) Because there is no way to ensure equivalence of courses in content coverage, in difficulty, or in goals achieved by students, there is no way to ensure equivalence of credits. (3) Credits wrongly imply a direct relation between processes or experiences and learning. (4) Grades and their weaknesses contribute additional confusion to the meaning of credits and point averages. (5) Credits have little value at the graduate, especially at the doctoral, level. (6) Credit requirements do not adequately describe programs nor do they reflect degree time, time in class, or effort expended by students or faculty. (7) The credit concept is not useful in non-traditional approaches to education and, in fact, tends to freeze traditional patterns and make them unchangeable.

But alternatives to credits will be difficult to introduce in the face of both faculty reluctance and legislative rejection. The review of extensive portfolios or the use of comprehensive examinations for award of degrees is time consuming and requires specialized assessment facilities and procedures. These reviews are not readily reflected as credit hours in the traditional sense. Assessing the results of diverse, unplanned educational experiences is a task different both in nature and in procedure from assessing the results of regular courses.

Before we turn to a discussion of the problems of assigning grades, the relationship of credits and grades deserves some comment. Credits reflect time serving and exposure to the experiences and content specified in course descriptions. They reflect neither quality nor mastery—a role reserved to grades. If a credit reflected a level of achievement, variation in credits awarded would more effectively reflect accomplishment than the present combination of fixed credits and variable grades. In this sense, variable credit and no credit (or fail) could replace the present confused system and satisfy those who seek a credit-no credit system.

Purposes of Grades

The purposes and the uses of grading are inseparable. Indeed, past uses of grades have regularly been presented as reasons for their continuance. For example, since graduate schools depend on grades in admissions, the elimination of grades jeopardizes the graduate school prospects of students. Grades are directed to or are used by students, parents, sponsors, the college, researchers, other colleges and professional schools, the government (draft status, veteran benefits), and prospective employers. For the student, grades serve variously as motivation, feedback, reward, and punishment. Grades have also been extensively used (and often misused) in prediction studies, in counseling, and in selecting individuals for educational programs and jobs.

Some uses serve both the student and the institution: assessment of academic progress; award of honors, scholarships, fellowships, assistantships; admission to graduate and professional school; selection for honorary societies. Grades, in many cases, are also the primary basis for written recommendations. Additional uses are less defensible. The requirement of a minimum average for admission to social fraternities is certainly debatable, as it is for participation in extracurricular activities and athletics. A grade requirement in the latter case is protection for the individual against the ambition of coaches and colleges that would use any capable athlete regardless of ability to do college work. Yet easy courses, cooperative instructors, and graduation rates of athletes indicate that grade requirements can be and are ignored when it is to the apparent advantage of the institution.

Nature of a Grade

Grades are symbols or sets of symbols which indicate a level of achievement or conformity to a set of standards. Grades are a condensation of the results of evaluation. Many factors may enter into a grade, but the grade does not in itself reflect them, nor can one infer the evaluation process which generated the grade. Grades form an information system and, as with all information systems, there are concerns regarding fidelity, recording, costs, retrieval, and adequacy of information conveyed.

A teacher's grades involve unknown factors and unknown weightings of those factors. Fidelity (capability of reproducing the original work from the record grade) is obviously low, especially when a single grade is used for each student. A test score reveals neither the items answered correctly nor the thought processes of a student. But, before lack of fidelity is used to reject grades, it should be noted that lack of fidelity is inherent in any condensed record, for it can only in part produce the original.

A single grade (commonly A, B, C, D, or F) is easily recorded by hand or by data-processing equipment. It can be speedily processed for large numbers of students and teachers at reasonable costs. It is easily and flexibly retrievable and reportable. The information provided is limited, but suffices for many purposes. It probably is at least as accurate as the grading of eggs, meat, and fruit, which markedly affects their prices.

If the process of evaluation can itself be systematized, the grading process can easily be expanded to achieve greater fidelity and convey more information. Several grades could be given to each student for each course, covering such items as knowledge of facts, ability to apply principles, relevant attitudes, and laboratory performance. A single letter grade could be extended to include subscripts and superscripts (drawing upon a practice of mathematicians); the subscript and superscript would refer to particular characteristics, and the letter grade itself would be an average determined from these characteristics. Thus B_{23}^{21} could indicate an overall grade of B, based upon (superscripts) a generally good attitude (2 on a 1-to-5 scale) and very hard work (1) and upon (subscripts) good knowledge of facts and principles (2), with fair or average ability in applying them to new problems (3). Computers could readily be programmed to handle such grades, and researchers would glory in the studies which would result. But the evaluation task of the professor would become complex, and the possibility of confrontations with dissatisfied students would be multiplied. Costs inevitably would increase, and fidelity would be increased only if faculty members could make and defend the judgments required.

Beyond the qualities of grades already mentioned (fidelity, retrieval, adequacy of information, and cost) are the usual ones of validity, reliability, and objectivity. A grade is valid to the extent that it measures whatever it purports to measure. If the grade is a clearly defined composite of a complex set of characteristics, it may be valid without having high fidelity. To have high validity, it must have high reliability—that is, it must be reproducible. A repetition of the process by which the grade was assigned should yield the same grade. If it does not, the grade is neither reliable nor valid. A grade based upon several examinations limited in scope may be both reliable and valid relative to that limited scope without necessarily being reliable and valid relative to a broader conception of what the student actually has learned. This deficiency is one of the basic concerns about grades. There is also a high degree of subjectivity in grading. Objectivity and a resulting degree of comparability, though highly desirable, are not easily attained. In most institutions, a degree of uniformity in grading across instructors and courses is attained by conformity to institutional practices in grade divisions, definitions, and distributions. Despite the lack of uniformity, grade averages of students do show some consistency and stability from term to term (at least up to a year) and have some utility in making comparisons within and even among institutions. The treatment of academic performance as a single dimension represented by grades is somewhat justified by this evidence. A grade, however, conveys at best a limited amount of information; no one is quite sure what that information is, but many people try to use it for purposes for which it was never intended.

The number of dimensions upon which grading policies can vary is rather larger than has been reflected in college practices. Grading can be continuous, recurrent, or culminative; that is, grades can be recorded day by day; they can be recorded at intervals; or they can be based upon a final course examination or even a comprehensive examination. Continuous or recurrent grading can also be used as feedback (or formative) evaluation with recorded grades based only on a culminative performance.

Grades can be numerical, literal, or descriptive. Numerical grading may be based upon a 0-100 interval (percentages perhaps) or upon arbitrarily chosen intervals such as 0-10 or even (as has been the practice in a few institutions) upon a 0-400 interval. Literal grading may be of the common A, B, C pattern or some other designation, such as *E*xcellent, *G*ood, *S*atisfactory, *U*nsatisfactory, *F*ailing. Literal grades are frequently associated with a numerical rating, such as 4, 3, 2, 1, 0, or 3, 2, 1, 0, −1, for convenience in computing point averages. Descriptive grading uses a specified set of words or phrases or the idiosyncratic phrasing of individual faculty members. Descriptive grades are difficult to interpret, essentially impossible to combine, and time consuming for the instructor who undertakes the task conscientiously. In practice, they are not even informative to the student because instructors are not adept in brief characterizations of the strengths and weaknesses of individuals.

Grades can be single or multiple indices. Descriptive and literal or numerical grades can be joined by agreeing upon a specified set of characteristics and entering a separate grade for each. A composite or average grade combines single, multiple, and descriptive grades.

Grades vary also in the number of categories used. Since the descriptive approach is almost unlimited, variation in the categories of literal or numerical grading is more easily summarized. Pass-no record or credit-no credit is essentially a single category. Pass-fail is a two-category system. Three categories are typified by superior, pass, fail, and four by excellent, very good, qualified, incomplete. All of these have been used at some time and place. The five-category pattern of A, B, C, D, F (or 4, 3, 2, 1, 0) is the most prevalent. These five may be expanded by the addition of pluses and minuses, thus extending the basic five to fifteen categories. Michigan State University currently uses a 4, 3.5, 3, 2.5, 2, 1.5, 1, .5, 0 nine-category system.

Distribution recommendations or specific limitations may accompany a system. One college, using a three-category distribution, specified 80 percent in the middle category and 10 percent in each of the extremes. Another college recommended that grade distributions for large classes follow this pattern: A, 0-10 percent; B, 15-25 percent; C, 40-60 percent; D, 5-15 percent; and F, 0-10 percent. Such recommendations are useful and probably justifiable when grading is on a relative basis, as it usually is in large classes. (For an explanation of relative and absolute grading, see the discussion of test scores in the section on improving grading practices later in this chapter.)

Substance of a Grade

What should be included in a grade? What tasks and what aspects of those tasks should be evaluated in arriving at a grade? Alternatively, are there some important objectives which cannot and should not be graded? Disagreement on the answers to these questions lies at the heart of any discussion of grades and their uses.

Educational objectives have been grouped into three categories: cognitive, affective, and psychomotor. The trichotomy is unrealistic and unfortunate, for much of significant human behavior encompasses all three. Study of mathematics obviously involves cognition, but in some sense (whether immediate or remote) enrolling in mathematics involves affect, which may be reflected in a liking for mathematics as a discipline or in a desire for a degree in a program requiring mathematics. Students who have little liking or aptitude for mathematics also appear in mathematics courses (even in advanced ones). Mathematics requires psychomotor skills too—vision, writing, drawing, some facility in simple arithmetic, and perhaps the use of a calculator. Should the grade in a mathematics course therefore reflect (1) evident like or dislike for the course (or instructor), (2) ability to do the simple arithmetic involved, (3) quality of sketches or drawings, (4) degree of multidimensional visualization, (5) originality in method versus conformity to textbook or instructor expectations, (6) time required to perform specific tasks, (7) ability to explain a proof or problem solution to others, (8) regularity and accuracy of completion of outside assignments, (9) number of problems solved or seriously attempted, (10) average of several tests or performances on a culminative final task or examination, (11) quality of written or oral expression, (12) performance of supplementary or additional tasks or reports perhaps only remotely related to the course, (13) ability to read mathematics versus dependence upon instructor explanations, (14) regularity of attendance, (15) whether the student is majoring in mathematics, has elected the course out of personal interest, or is required to take the course?

These several possibilities have no doubt affected grades given by instructors. The conviction that this is the case more often than is admitted by instructors is a major factor in the reaction against grading. But as long as grade assignment is the prerogative of the individual professor with little or no recourse, even in those few but painful cases of obvious prejudice, there is no infallible way to resolve the difficulties.

On some points there is reasonable agreement. Few persons would support the position that dislike of a course or an instructor-student conflict should directly influence a grade. But there is no way to ensure that they do not. Indirectly such factors do affect student motivation, effort, and performance. An instructor can undertake to evaluate papers or tests anonymously, but may soon recognize the handwriting of certain students and almost unconsciously modify judgments. With small classes, especially when instructor and student become well acquainted, objectivity is harder to maintain. Attempts to adjust for dislike of an individual may lead to overcompensation.

The instructor who suggests supplementary tasks for those who have difficulty with the course may be seen by his associates as weakening if not destroying standards. Individualization of instruction and learning to the point where objectives become idiosyncratic to the individual student has merit, but fairness to other students and to those who use the record dictates that the record, whether a grade or a comment, reflect what was done as well as how well it was done.

If a grade is to have meaning, it must be defined in reference to objectives which are clear and subject to objective (valid and reliable) judgment. In turn, students should be encouraged to take courses for which the objectives are consonant with their own. Required courses with specified objectives destroy individual motivation and reduce the grade to a substitute for such motivation.

Attempts to overcome these deficiencies by restricting grading to purely cognitive objectives do not correct the situation and may further sap the quality of education. Grading based solely on factual recall, facility in solving certain types of problems, rote repetition of textbook or lecture explanations reflects such a narrow and rigid conception of education as to be revolting to thoughtful and able students, as well as to many teachers and the general public. Indeed, so-called facts are themselves frequently judgments laden with value commitments.

To eliminate judgment and evaluation would be to eliminate education. The essence of evaluation is that there are some values which, because of their transcendent nature and widespread recognition, are superior to others. Becoming educated requires both an awareness of these values and of one's own status or position in regard to them, not solely through one's own eyes, but also through the eyes of others. Evaluation is always ultimately in some sense relative and comparative, and so is the grade resulting from an evaluation. The essence of grading is in relating individual performance to an external standard, which again ultimately is based upon the performance and judgment of others. Hence to eliminate all grading is to eliminate all evaluation and ultimately to eliminate education, which is itself a process of induction into a value-laden society.

Weaknesses of Grades

Grades are often condemned because of the anxiety they cause students. In extreme circumstances, this is a matter of concern. But those students who become distraught with grades have other problems which require attention. Eliminating grades would not eliminate their difficulties. From another point of view, a certain amount of anxiety or uneasiness about one's performance is desirable. After all, people have many kinds of activities in which they can engage. Those which are significant to the individual and which also generate some unease, some concern, some threat of failure are more likely to be given a higher priority than those in which any performance is acceptable and praiseworthy. Anxiety at this level is little more than motivation, and the motivation is as much within the individual to do well, to perform respectably, as it is in the external pressure and threat. Arousal of this normal anxiety might well be regarded as one of the main reasons for grades. Only abnormal, neurotic anxiety is a serious problem; such anxiety may be attributable either to a grading procedure which is vengeful and ruthless or to weaknesses within the individual. Either of these has to be dealt with in other ways than by changing the grading system or eliminating it.

A second argument is that grades frequently involve undesirable motivation or inappropriate emphasis. This criticism certainly cannot be denied. When the grade is based upon an examination which involves rote recall of a large number of specific facts, the student is motivated to memorize, at least for a time, as many facts as possible. This motivation is certainly undesirable, and the emphasis is inappropriate. But again, this is not a problem of grades per se; it is a problem of the bases upon which grades are assigned. Ultimately, it reflects poor instruction.

A third area of weakness of grades has to do with the fact that they may involve unrealistic standards for individuals. Credit in a required swimming course, for example, may be based upon a minimum time for swimming one hundred yards. Obvious physical deformities are the bases for exempting a person from the requirement, but the requirement is unrealistic anyway because it is irrelevant to individual needs for a college education. Some teachers are content that an individual work to the level of aspiration consistent with self-concept. An individual who desires insight into an area without desiring to spend the time required to attain a level of performance equal to that of students with special interests in the area should be accommodated. But this accommodation can be made through the use of pass-fail or credit-no credit grading or in independent study rather than by a complete change of the grading system.

A fourth weakness of grades is that they have a superficial objectivity, which encourages faculty members, employers, sponsors of fraternities, and others to believe that grades should be readily available for any reasonable purpose. In other words, the nature of grades makes them less obviously confidential than medical records are. They appear to tell something definite about an individual's motivation and level of performance. To avoid misuse, it is necessary to make grades available only to those who are qualified to use them and have responsibilities which require their use.

Inequities in Grading

Juola (1968) examined and documented several aspects of grading which demonstrate inequities in the process. He found, as have others, that instructors tend to impose a grade distribution on a class rather than determine grades by class performance. During a period of several years in which the student ability level increased, grade distributions remained essentially unchanged. In a few cases in my own experience, emphasis by a dean or president on the increased quality of admissions led to an increase in the percentage of low grades given by the faculty. Apparently the reasoning was that better students require higher standards which are evidenced by more failures. This reasoning would eventually lead to accepting only a few top prospects and failing all. Juola also notes that grade distributions over sequential courses tend to be almost identical, so that, for example, 14 percent fail the first quarter of chemistry, and 14 percent of those passing are failed in the second quarter. Such practices result in an attrition which is artificial and unjustifiable.

Teacher bias is a second effect suggested by Juola's data. In the extreme, it appears that grades may depend more on the instructor one gets in the registration lottery and on his or her grade distributions than on the amount or quality of work done.

Juola also points to a third effect—variation in grading in reasonably comparable courses, for example, first-year foreign language. He found the mean grade point averages for the first term of nine different foreign languages to vary from 2.10 to 3.19 and the difference between mean grade point average in foreign language and mean grade point average in other courses to range from −.62 to +.78. Correlation between these means was negative (Rho = −.20). Juola suggests that by taking Italian instead of German, for example, a student could exchange a C for an A. German has a reputation for being a difficult language, but it should not be made so by harsh grading.

Juola also comments upon the effect of grade distributions in special sections. He found a tendency for honors sections and remedial sections to yield the same grade distribution. Apparently, students would be wise to avoid honors sections and to seek remedial ones if they want high grades. Juola also notes that trailer sections, composed in large part of previous failures and students attempting to raise D's, received the normal distribution. Apparently, advisers in large universities would do well to urge marginal students to complete requirements in trailer sections. Indeed, by utilizing such information on course sections and instructor vagaries in grading, coaches and advisers have kept marginal students in college. These observations suggest that grade distributions are imposed upon classes rather than derived out of the class performance.

Another obvious problem lies in the differences among students in intellectual ability or aptitude, prior relevant experience, motivation and interest, goals, and extent of outside involvements. The following specific situations make evident the quandary. How should each of the following individuals be graded? John obviously does not work and is a nuisance in class, but writes A examinations. Sarah works hard, wants an A badly, but makes only B's on tests. George has a poor background, works hard, progresses from F to D to C to B on successive examinations, and writes an A final. Elizabeth has an excellent record but is so involved in activities by her senior year that she lacks time to maintain that record. The varying decisions in these situations lead to accusations of arbitrary and capricious grading.

Another source of inequity in grading is the personality traits of students and instructors. Conforming, rigid, insecure students are more likely than nonconformist, flexible, and self-directed individuals to observe signals of and closely adhere to obvious biases and preferences of the instructor. Some instructors are complimented and pleased by such imitation and grade conforming students higher than those who depart from the phrasing, emphasis, and views of the instructor. Differential student performance on instructor grades and independent comprehensive examinations bears out this observation. Also, students with a large measure of common sense and a gift for expressing their ideas can frequently achieve grades from instructors which are better than actual mastery of the course content would justify. These inequities are virtually impossible to eliminate, and some instructors would not even agree that they are inequities.

Cheating constitutes a grading inequity of a different type. Cheating is usually viewed as an attempt, using unfair or illegitimate means, to obtain a grade higher than that merited. The devices for cheating are numerous: copying or buying the work of someone else; stealing copies of examinations; carrying hidden notes to class; writing on one's hand, arm, or clothing; copying from another's paper; signaling responses for objective-test questions to friends; obtaining and using a key (set of correct answers) to an objective test. The obvious ways of reducing or eliminating cheating depend upon the actions of faculty members, not all of whom accept the responsibility. Few faculty members condone cheating. A few who are antagonistic to examinations and grading regard it simply as a natural and inevitable part of the system. Others are unwilling to adapt police tactics which might reduce or eliminate it.

Some idealists have thought that cheating could be restrained by use of an honors system, in which individuals are required to report others whom they know to be cheating or to report themselves. Episodes at the service academies suggest that the honor code is not effective. Some argue that cheaters hurt only themselves. This simply is not true. Grades, honors, and awards are basically competitive, and those who cheat hurt those who do not. Thus the instructor who ignores cheating and thereby abets it injures all students and the reputation of the institution as well.

Cheating is a special problem in mass testing situations because individuals are essentially anonymous; no prior and no continuing contacts provide a ready check on individual performance. Nationally available examinations for credit may shortly be driven to using fingerprints for sure identification. On a university campus, the need to give large lecture or multiple-section examinations and the use of machine-scorable examinations make it difficult to prevent cheating. Several forms of an examination, even if they differ only in the order of items, can be distributed so as to discourage copying or to render it unprofitable. Careful and continuous proctoring by individuals in constant and erratic movement rather effectively discourages use of illegal aids. Caution and security in preparing examinations eliminate some practices. All these efforts cost in time, in money, and most of all in loss of the scholarly atmosphere which should pervade a university community. Yet, distasteful as they are, such measures are essential to maintain a reasonable degree of integrity in the examination and grading process.

The grading behavior of some instructors increases this list of inequities. Some simply avoid or minimize responsibility for grading. Examples are found in the indiscriminate all-A grade reports for some courses with no requirements. Although possibly appropriate for an advanced graduate or even undergraduate seminar made up of highly motivated students, the practice cannot be condoned for large classes in which the instructor does not even know whether students are present. Such grading practices, unmodified after warning, constitute an adequate basis for termination of an instructor's appointment since widespread use of the practice would debase the college degree to the point where payment of tuition for the required number of credits would be all that was necessary.

Other instructors avoid grading because they believe the practice to be unfair to students. They ignore the fact that not grading is equally unfair to students, for it becomes impossible to recognize and reward merit. The criteria or standards rather than the practice are unfair. Others grade nothing but performance on a single final examination, a paper, or other task. Although this practice is viewed with horror by some, it may well be a superior practice. To make it so, there must be adequate feedback evaluations during the term, and the final task itself should be a sufficiently comprehensive, valid, and reliable measure. If it is, individuals should then be able to complete the requirements and obtain the credits solely by acceptable performance on that culminating task.

Those teachers who give bonuses or deductions for effort, neatness, handwriting, artistry, or deportment may be, but are not always, simply yielding to natural human tendency to allow irrelevancies to influence judgment. In some circumstances, effort may be an appropriate factor in grading; it should be so specified in advance. Neatness may be relevant or irrelevant. Part of science is recording data and manipulating it in ways which can be checked and replicated. Neatness, to this end, is relevant in laboratory reports. Neatness in typing is essential for the prospective secretary. An illustrative drawing may add clarity to a paper in science, mathematics, or history, but an original, even though excellent, portrait of a mathematician or historian on such a paper is an irrelevant bit of creativity. Deportment and attendance are perhaps the most inappropriate bases for grades. Yet I have seen A-level performance on examinations reduced to F for nonattendance or for what an instructor regarded as effrontery. Even today, with various routes of appeal open to students, such injustices are not easily remedied.

The shifting of grading rules or policies part way through a course is inexcusable unless done following discussion and acceptance by the students. The most common reason for such behavior is the sudden recognition that an "unseemly" grade distribution—one with an excessive proportion of high or low grades—is developing. Adjustment amounts to lowering or raising grades after they have been received, an alteration which unfairly affects some students. The individual who has devoted many hours of extra effort to attain an A is not likely to be pleased when it becomes evident that far lower achievement is being upgraded to an A. And, regardless of feelings or motivations, the change is not fair if the grades are used for graduate or professional school application.

Some instructors become overzealous in assigning grades for every activity. They make, collect, and grade daily assignments. They regularly call upon and grade every student. They give and grade short unscheduled tests. Each preparation and each class session become tense experiences. Students, under such policing, do tend temporarily to learn somewhat more, but this achievement is counterbalanced by their inability to occasionally follow their own bents and by the attitudes engendered toward the course and the discipline. Fear and extreme tension do not constitute good motivation.

Some instructors pride themselves on their psychological approach to grading and occasionally offer success stories to justify their approach. Unmerited A's are given to encourage students; A performances are downgraded because individuals seem indifferent or do not apply themselves; failing students are given C's to permit them to remain in school.

Occasionally instructors hold to an ideal of impossible perfection in grading. I have known professors who pride themselves on never having given an A.

Grades thus are less of a problem than the graders. And the problems of graders arise out of a lack of comprehension of the role of a teacher. Grades can be based on objective appraisal of student performance or can be subject largely to instructor whim. They can be used as rewards to encourage a continuing commitment to learning or to enforce specific requirements. But efforts to correct inadequate instructor grading are often perilous because of the widespread view that such correction constitutes interference with professional judgment and even with academic freedom.

Improving Practices and Policies

Some inequities in grading can be corrected by devices or procedures readily available, but not generally used. I discuss four such procedures here: consistency in grading, pass-fail grading, criterion-referenced grading, and grading from test scores.

A block of common questions in examinations for sections of the same course can be used as a standard to provide *consistency* in adjusting grades across sections. However, that common core of questions must be equally appropriate to the emphases of all instructors, or else a section may be penalized by instructor differences in emphasis or selection of topics.

An examination for all students in a course prepared by

examiners or a committee of instructors can be used as the sole instrument for summative evaluation and grading. Individuals may still suffer because of differences in teaching, but at least a common standard prevails. However, some instructors both fear the possibility of invidious comparison of teaching and dislike the loss of responsibility for grading. Most students dislike risking all on a single examination. Hence, this device is not extensively used.

Controls over grade distributions can be provided by computation of the ability level of classes from aptitude or ability tests given to entering freshmen. Some instructors have used this approach, but most find it tedious and even unfair since it sets limits on grades a priori and may penalize the student who works unusually hard or whose test scores were underestimates of ability. Cumulative average grades to date in all or in related courses can provide expectations of average class performance, but variations in grades from one course to another raise doubts about the validity of the approach. Estimates of class performance made by an instructor prior to key examinations may be of use in preventing unreasonable grades resulting from an unexpectedly easy or difficult examination. Yet, this approach rests upon a subjective judgment and may be inequitable.

Prior interpretation to students of emphases and expectations as to performance helps to avoid situations in which examinations and grades are based upon factors different from the ones students anticipated. Carried to an extreme, this procedure can take the form of a threat, and it may unreasonably narrow the focus of student effort. However, use of one or more of these techniques on occasion, if not regularly, assists the instructor in review of grading practices and in adapting them to those of colleagues and to student expectations.

Hunt (1972) proposes that the grading system be made more consistent by adoption of a confidential multiple grade for feedback to students. He would provide (1) a student grade, which is the instructor's subjective judgment of progress relative to the student's own norms; (2) a grade reflecting the instructor's judgment of student performance independent of the rest of the class; (3) a grade reflecting the instructor's judgment of individual performance in reference to how others in the class are performing; (4) a grade indicating how the individual compares with a large normative sample of students at the same point in their education; and (5) a grade indicating the final status of the student. In effect, these five grades use different standards of reference—the individual, the instructor, the class, a larger reference group, and a final summary judgment. Attractive in theory, the approach is totally unrealistic and impractical, for few instructors would either make the effort or be able to make the distinctions involved. Probably the grade for the reward would overshadow and negate all others for most students. Again, however, the instructor who occasionally engages in such activity gains insight into his or her own standards and practices.

Pass-fail grading merges readily into pass-no record, credit-no credit, and no grade. If every student is passed, the result is the granting of credit to every enrollee in a course. Credit is automatic and the only record is that of courses in which the student was enrolled. If students do not complete requirements in the customary period and no report is made until they do so, pass-fail becomes pass-no record or credit-no credit. Evidence of enrollment without a culminative pass indicates incomplete commitments. Records become messy, and the burden on the instructor may become intolerable. At the graduate level, where grade distributions, even on the five-letter grade scale, are usually reduced to A, B, C, or A, B (reflected in the practice in a few graduate programs of requiring a 3.5 minimum average), professors have been known to give A's to almost all students, using the B only to designate grossly inadequate (essentially failing) performance. Liberal use of deferred grades for those whose efforts are nonexistent or negligible (and A's for all others) can thus transform the five-letter grade system into a credit-no credit pattern.

The theoretical advantages of pass-fail or pass-no record are readily enumerated: (1) Students can pursue their own bents rather than slavishly conforming to instructor requirements or prejudices. (2) Students are encouraged to enroll in courses without fear of low grades resulting from competition with majors. (3) Anxiety over grades is reduced, thereby freeing the individual to pursue knowledge for its own sake. In brief, pass-fail grading has been applauded as a way to motivate exploration and learning. Another factor not usually expressed is that some instructors are pleased to be relieved of the necessity of evaluation and grading. The teaching burden is lessened, while the satisfaction of lecturing before an audience is retained—if the students continue to attend.

With few exceptions, faculties have moved toward pass-fail with great trepidation and have so hampered its utilization that the results are trivial. Restrictions such as the following are common: (1) the privilege is limited to juniors and seniors; (2) courses from the major field are excluded; (3) no more than one pass-fail course is permitted per quarter; (4) the maximum number of pass-fail credits is specified; (5) required courses in mathematics and foreign languages are excluded; (6) the privilege is limited to elective courses. Other practices have arisen to limit the use of pass-fail. Pass may be restricted to C or above. The pass-fail option must be chosen by the student initially and cannot later be altered. Usually the majority of students in a course are taking it on the customary grading basis so that some compulsion for conformity results, especially for the student who fears unfavorable comparison with others. Frequently, those students using the pass-fail option are not indicated to the instructors, who must, therefore, evaluate them on the same basis as others. Only after grades are reported is the pass-fail distinction made in the processing and recording. This practice of anonymity is viewed by some professors and administrators as ensuring that the pass-fail enrollee will neither be discriminated against nor absolved from work.

Many studies have demonstrated that with a pass-fail system students are less motivated, do less work, and earn lower grades (on the initial letter-grade reports) than do students subjected to the full range of grading. Also, at two institutions where pass-fail grading was instituted, students complained that instructors lost all interest in evaluation (Sgan, 1970). Some students use the pass-fail alternative to gain time for more study of other courses. This evidence can be regarded either as negating or demonstrating the expected benefits of pass-fail. It can also be viewed as an inevitable distribution of student effort in a mixed system. Most advisers and professors know that taking a course with frequent examinations or heavy requirements in papers causes students to slight less demanding courses. The evidence of numerous studies also shows that few students take advantage of pass-fail to significantly expand their horizons. The major objection of those who view grading as punitive or as essential motivation in the face of many and pleasurable distractions is that pass-fail encourages sloth.

The success of pass-fail when this is the prevalent practice for all courses has not been adequately assessed and is not likely to be. In professional programs, the necessity of passing external examinations appears to provide adequate incentive, especially since the students may already have been carefully selected and are highly motivated. In undergraduate programs, students' motivation and effort depend greatly on the extent of their association with the faculty and the approval or disapproval evidenced in these encounters. Merited and judicially offered praise or criticism is, for many persons, a more potent motivator than either self-evaluation or grades.

Major opposition to pass-fail grading is found among deans and admissions officers of professional and graduate schools. They argue that a few pass-fail elective courses are of little consequence, but as the number of pass-fail courses expands to include courses in the major and supporting disciplines, the opposition increases. Test scores and recommendations must be weighted more heavily for students presenting pass-fail records, and comparison with other applicants becomes more difficult. In highly selective professional or graduate programs, the student with a complete pass-fail record may be ignored. If admitted, he or she may not receive the same consideration for awards and scholarships as does the individual with a full complement of excellent grades.

Most students (though not all) express approval of the pass-fail option and urge its continuation and expansion. Every survey of student reaction has indicated however that students who plan to continue with graduate study or in professional programs are concerned about the impact of the pass-fail pattern on their prospects. Most of these students recognize that selection is always competitive. Moreover, as students veer from the antiestablishment position of a few years ago and return to the realities of a competitive society, they display less interest in "soft" courses lacking a sound base of knowledge and methodology and turn to those which provide some substance and have vocational significance. Grades suddenly become more palatable because they have more tangible, immediate meaning and ultimate import.

Pass-fail or no grade is certainly not a solution of an educational problem; it is a feeble attempt to alleviate some of the inadequacies of teaching and curriculum organization by manipulating what is only a peripheral aspect of education. Pass-fail may encourage rather than discourage poor teaching, inadequate curriculum planning, and student aversion to scholarly effort.

The *criterion-referenced system of evaluation* (see Chapter Ten) appears to provide a solution for those who desire to retain an objective evaluation for grades but avoid comparative or normal curve grading. If grades are awarded on the basis of previously specified levels of performance, the student can determine the grade by the effort put into the task. This possibility is less realistic than it first appears because the levels are usually defined by the instructor and the differences in student interest and preparation combined with calendar limitations render it unlikely that all students will attain the A or B level. If some students are prepared to settle for lower levels, a contract approach to grading may be effective.

Repeated testing to demonstrate mastery and improve grades poses difficulties in test development. Answers to a single form soon become common property. Equivalence in test forms or tasks is not readily achieved, and few instructors are willing to undertake the task.

Another issue arises with criterion-referenced grading. Time, persistence, and effort may become more important factors than ability. A high-level performance achieved in two weeks is quite different from the same level of performance after eight or ten weeks. Facility in learning is often more important than the learning itself. Thus, A's reported for two different students under this system may conceal more than they reveal. Moreover, criterion-referenced measurement tends to reduce the range of objectives assessed both in number and in difficulty. Nevertheless, attempts to move toward criterion-referenced grading could have a tremendously beneficial effect on teaching and learning by forcing professors to be much more clear and specific about expected outcomes than they now are. The effect on students would also be beneficial. Even though individuals would cover different amounts of material in specified time periods, each would have the satisfaction which can come only from mastering a task.

Test scores, whether derived from summation of points given to each question or subtraction from a perfect score of accumulated error deductions, are usually transformed to grades. Such transformation is highly subjective. In the attempt to justify the resulting grade distinctions (and also to avoid grade changes if the student detects an error), gaps in score distributions are used as grade division points. For example, a four-point gap may be seized upon as a basis for the distinction between A's and B's or between D's and F's. Seldom do such gaps occur between B's and C's or C's and D's because of the accumulation of cases toward the middle of the score distribution. The practice is convenient, but may do an injustice to students if, on a more defensible rationale, scores contiguous to the break would merit the higher or lower grade. The practice demonstrates the arbitrary nature of the grading process.

Alternative procedures include the imposition of a previously determined grade distribution upon the test-score distributions. This grade distribution may be based upon the concept of a normal distribution. Many of the early attempts at systemizing grades involved elementary statistical methodology and adaptation of the normal distribution. This procedure reflected enthusiasm for a mathematical function found to describe the distribution of many characteristics and measurements, particularly those involving random errors. In fact, there is little reason to believe that successive grade distributions based upon a continually more selective group should follow that pattern. One might as well argue that the teaching abilities of the college faculty are distributed normally and then terminate (fail) those making D's and F's.

Scoring is a procedure whereby the papers or tests are arranged in order of quality. Grading is the assignment of grades following scoring. Either or both of these tasks may be performed in a relative or absolute manner as indicated in Table 4.

Table 4. Relations Between Relative and Absolute Scoring and Grading

Relative	*Absolute*
	Scoring
Subjective ordering	Number or percentage correct
Grouping without scoring	Use of natural breaks in score distribution
	Grading
Subjective ranking	Number or percentage right
Fixed percentage grade assignments	Predetermined grade standards

Papers may be ordered subjectively or assigned to groups thought to be composed of those whose performances are roughly equivalent. Grades are then assigned in order or by groups. This is relative scoring-relative grading. If the ordered papers are graded on the basis of previously fixed percentages, the scoring is relative, but the grading is absolute—not of course in terms of performance standards, but in terms of a conviction as to how grades must be distributed. If scoring is by number right or percentage correct, grading may again be relative to the idiosyncracies of the distribution or according to a predetermined conviction as to what level of performance justifies a particular grade. Obviously, the absolute scoring-absolute grading combination is more reliable in the sense of being repeatable than are combinations of relative and of absolute grading and scoring. And only the absolute scoring-absolute grading pattern is applicable if mastery or criterion-related evaluation is desired.

Absolute grading is difficult to achieve unless objectives are stated clearly and tasks reflecting levels of achievement are carefully specified. Attempts at absolute grading by other routes seldom are successful. Occasionally a teacher attempts to evaluate student work on a percentage basis and assigns grades on such a basis as this: 93-100 (A), 85-92 (B), 75-84 (C), 65-74 (D), 0-64 (F). With experience, the teacher may end up with a reasonable distribution, especially if students have already been subjectively appraised. This is not absolute grading, for the totality of possible tasks is not covered and hence even 100 is not perfection.

Another approach is possible with objective examinations. Agreement may be reached in advance as to the number of correct answers required for each grade. Attempts to use this system point up two flaws. The first is that faculty members differ markedly in their expectations. The second is that even a compromise of these expectations may yield so many high or low grades that the results are deemed unacceptable.

These last two approaches demonstrate the difference between evaluation (or scoring) and grades. The initial effort of the teacher produces an evaluation or a score and, if the results do not accord with expectations for a grade distribution, further adjustments are made, sometimes without full realization that this is being done.

Grade Point Average

The averaging of grades is a common practice which has received much less attention than the grades themselves. It might seem that if grades are eliminated or reduced to a pass or no-record pattern, averaging of grades would be impossible. But there are reasons for some form of averaging, even then. In one college which I reviewed, the student record was an accumulation of papers, instructor comments, project reports. After four years, the bulk was formidable. The contents were also variable. Most folders contained an ambiguous and uninterpretable array of vague comments and homilies. A few folders contained relatively few materials. None contained clearly derogatory comments. For the individual with the time and disposition, such folders yielded significant insights into the capabilities and value orientations of the outstanding students—much more than grades would yield. But for the other students, instructor comments were often so noncommittal or guarded as to be meaningless. Here reviewers are on their own; they must read and judge the student work in the folder. Few employers, graduate schools, or professional schools can afford the time required or know how to relate such materials to more traditional transcripts. In recognition of this difficulty, a clerk in the registrar's office was given the assignment of reviewing a student's record and preparing a summary for submission to other institutions. Averaging was taking place, but by an individual of dubious qualifications.

The more common approach to averaging assigns weights or quality points to letter grades and computes a credit-weighted arithmetic mean.

Credits	Grade	Points
4	A	4
5	B	3
3	C	2
3	F	0

$$\text{GPA} = (16 + 15 + 6)/15 = 37/15 = 2.47.$$

Several questions arise. If an F is received, should the credits failed be added into the denominator (as they are here) in computing the average? Since the credits were not earned, it seems at first thought they should not enter into the average, but, if not, the average will be $37/12 = 3.08$. A student under the necessity of maintaining a 3.00 to retain a scholarship should be advised to seek an F rather than a D. Accordingly, most institutions, in computing a point average, use credits carried rather than credits earned and must, therefore, accumulate totals on both.

A further difficulty arises with courses which are repeated in order to raise the grade. If point averages are based on all credits carried, an F must be balanced by an A to achieve the equivalent of a C. In many colleges, when a course is repeated, only the second grade counts. This policy has been hotly contested on some campuses by faculty members who take a punitive view of grades and argue that all grades, including the initial failures, be counted. The deletion of F's from records after replacement by a satisfactory grade is another policy which has aroused concern. Some persons argue that the record should accurately reflect the academic history of the student. Others, and these are many more today than a few years ago, assert that only final status should be revealed. That the issue is still present is indicated in the pass-fail and credit-no record dichotomy; both of these have attained some acceptance in recent years.

Another issue in the computation of grade point averages has to do with the division points or boundaries between grades when points are assigned. If A is assigned 4 points, does that 4 correspond to the top, middle, or lower end of whatever continuum was envisaged as corresponding to the A? Since in equating A to 4 points, all A's are made equivalent, the argument could be made that the minimum A is worth 4 points or that the A corresponds to a range from 4.5 down to 3.5. One university pursuing this line of thought moved to a 4.5, 4.0, 3.5, 3.0 pattern with the intent that the 4.5 would be used only rarely to indicate outstanding excellence. Horrified to learn that point averages of transfers and graduates were being routinely reduced by .5, the faculty quickly discarded the 4.5. The question remains: if the minimum A is worth 4 points, should not some A's be worth more? This question becomes most troublesome when applied to the C level. In some colleges a C average is required for graduation. What is a C average? Is it a 2.00, or is it something less? Since 2 points are assigned to all C's and 1 to all D's, these do correspond to minimums, but perhaps the minimum C average is 1.50.

The insertion of 3.5, 2.5, 1.5, .5 made at Michigan State University significantly raised point averages. It appeared that F's became split between .5s and 0s rather than being all 0s; D's between 1s and 1.5s, and so forth. However, since letter grades were dropped entirely, this raising of averages can be judged only by comparison of grade distributions before and after the change. And the interpretation is uncertain because numerous studies of point averages have shown a marked upward trend in recent years. Indeed, the most potent present argument against grades may well be that, in many institutions, the increase in A's and B's and the concomitant decrease in D's and F's has virtually destroyed their significance as a basis for scholarship awards or differentiation of the most able students from the average. This semblance of mastery grading without the reality threatens to weaken the motivational impact of grades and destroy whatever contributions they might make to standards.

Advice to Instructors

The evaluation practices and grading standards of any teacher are judged by comparison with those of colleagues, and these judgments influence the selection of courses by students. If only A's are given by an instructor, the number and quality of students enrolling will shortly focus attention on that instructor. If a high proportion of F's and D's are given, borderline students will avoid the instructor; hence, average or better students will be receiving F's and D's. Complaints and mass avoidance will shortly bring about a confrontation. The professor thus buffeted by departures from the extant though not well-defined norms may either accept the necessity for alteration or attempt to fight a battle of standards and resort to the ambiguities of the doctrine of academic freedom. Only the well-established professor with tenure can afford to be atypical in his standards and grades. The new instructor or the one whose practices have raised questions does well to adjust grade distributions so that they are close to those of colleagues, and, in so doing, note that these distributions may differ for beginning and advanced courses, for majors and electives, and for core or required courses and service courses.

This view implies that instructors may have to lower standards to those of colleagues and the quality of the students in classes. To some extent this is true, but the relation between standards and grade distributions is not clear. A high percentage of F's does not tell anything about standards; a carefully defined standard could quite justifiably result in 100 percent failure. However, the standard or the instruction probably should be reexamined. Neither do all A's reflect low standards since this could and should be the result if a high degree of selection has been exercised. The instructor who persists in imposing F's on every score distribution may end up by allowing a one-point score difference to divide F's and D's. The division is clearly contrived. Consideration of the possibility of errors in marking and of the reaction of individuals might dictate a different course of action.

Few instructors fully realize that their grading reflects upon themselves as much as upon their students. Excessively high percentages of low grades may be justified under some section-assignment practices, but often such a distribution only indicates poor teaching and unrealistic standards. Excessively high grades on a continuing basis suggest that the instructor offers no great challenge to students. Mastery-learning ventures may well have this result if they are inadequately planned and managed.

Occasionally an instructor avoids the woes of grading while preserving the practice by requiring students to assign their own grades and provide a rationale for them by stating what they learned in the course. This practice appears to be a complete perversion of grading. Individuals who find the course of little value are under a double hazard. To be honest, they must both tell the instructor the course was worthless and give themselves low grades. The result is that students are falsely laudatory of the course, the instructor, and their own accomplishments. The instructor would do much better to give all A's and request separately an evaluation of the teaching and the worth of the course. However, if time permits, a conference with each student in which the student's work is reviewed, the instructor puts forth an appraisal and tentative grade, and the student reacts can have great benefit in clarifying the meaning of a grade, in causing the student to reflect on his or her experience in the course, and in forcing the instructor to provide a firm rationale for the grade.

The instructor should distinguish between feedback (or formative) evaluation and final (or summative) evaluation.

Grades or comparative evaluation can provide motivation, but if every paper, every test, and every recitation receives a grade which is final and not subject to change, regardless of review and improvement, the effect is deadening. Moreover, such a procedure tends to break a course into discrete segments, with successive tests and grades based only upon what has been covered since the last one. Students do not generally attempt to organize and integrate their accumulating knowledge and skills unless they are forced to do so by the evaluation practices.

Instructors must learn how to deal effectively and fairly with students who request reconsideration of a grade, be it on a single test or for the entire course. The instructor who too easily adjusts grades upward faces ever increasing demands and is likely ultimately to be treating unfairly those who do not complain. Student complaints usually focus on the mark given on a particular question, the fairness or ambiguity of the question, or the adequacy of the instructor's reading. The best preparation for these complaints is careful reading, marking, and grade assigning in the first place. Reproduction of the frame of mind and standards used initially is difficult and, except for correction of an obvious error, a review of a grade must involve reconsideration of the entire paper.

Instructors who seem to have no problems in assigning grades to students are often loath to be evaluated by students. If one agrees that one of the goals of education is learning how to evaluate one's experiences and their benefits, evaluation of a course and of the instructor may be an educational experience to the student as well as to the instructor. This issue is discussed at length in Chapter Fifteen.

Summary

Warren (1971, pp. 1, 2) notes:

Of almost two hundred articles, papers, and reports related to grading that appeared from 1965 to 1970, about one-fourth were concerned with the form of grades, usually whether they should be limited to indications of pass and fail in place of the customary four levels of passing grades plus failure. Another one-fourth were concerned with the use of undergraduate grades to predict grades in graduate and professional schools. Half of the papers that have appeared during the recent surge of interest in grading were occupied, therefore, with two limited aspects of grades—their external form and their predictive relationship with later grades. The remaining half of the literature was scattered over a variety of topics, none appearing in as many as 10 percent of the papers. These included variability in grading standards, disadvantages of grades, effects of grades on students, use of grades in predicting occupational success, determinants of grades, and the social effects of grades. Excluded from this count are the large number of articles on the prediction of undergraduate grades.

The accumulated knowledge about grades is not impressive in any scientific sense and is not likely to be. There is too much of affect involved, and interests are too diverse and contradictory. Much recent attention has been focused on two almost diametrically opposite issues—the use of grades to predict future grades and the replacement of grades by pass-fail or credit-no credit, which would destroy the predictive usage. Most studies, too, deal with grades as separate entities seemingly subject to manipulation, alteration, or elimination without the need to significantly change the attitudes or behavior of faculty members. But many of the problems with grades stem from the lack of direction and of control of grading processes. Departments and individual faculty members seldom have well-thought-out policies and thus tend to arrive at individual patterns characterized more by a recurring distribution of grades than by any agreement as to what grades mean.

No doubt, with modern means of information processing, much more elaborate systems of grade reporting could be developed. The cost in processing would surely be increased. The increase in faculty effort directed to clarification and evaluation of a reasonably discrete set of characteristics would be great. But the utility of all this effort is uncertain. Feedback evaluation procedures separate from grades might perform some functions assigned to grades better than grades themselves, while grades carefully defined and restricted in meaning might become more valid, reliable, and useful for a specific range of functions. There is a possibility that, if the grading process becomes overly elaborate, it will usurp time that should be used for effective feedback evaluation aimed at motivating learning and improving instruction and the curriculum.

Much of the reaction against grades—shared by many of those who favor their continuance—is a reaction against the inadequacies and inequities of the grading process. The inadequacies of a single grade as feedback to direct and motivate improvement are amply apparent. Extensive and multidimensional formative evaluation is certainly to be desired, but eliminating grades has not, in any program that I have viewed, resulted in increased learning or improvement in evaluation. Rather, the lack of grades and the elimination of the necessity on the part of both student and teacher to define essential goals or tasks have encouraged either anonymity and a shifting of all evaluation to comprehensive examinations (or to a dissertation) or, as in some innovative colleges, a discounting of knowledge and scholarly effort in favor of continuing warm baths in affect. This latter result is not wholly bad; indeed, it is probably better for most students than an attempt to develop cognitive abilities devoid of affective abilities. But education, to be worthy of that designation, must have a balance. Some portion of the objectives within that balance—mainly those which are cognitive—are gradable in valid and reliable ways. Such grading serves a significant function for the individual, and it serves many useful functions within the higher education establishment. Like democracy, the grading process lacks perfection, but, all things considered, if properly done, it does meet an array of needs not readily met otherwise. (The democratic ballot is itself a form of grading on a pass-fail basis. Competing candidates can be compared on many dimensions, and it is desirable that voters make this comparison for themselves. Ultimately, the decision must be for or against. Abstention from voting or the elimination of the ballot as correctives to the inadequacies of the process offers no solution. Neither does elimination of grades.)

Some uses of grades—as a basis for award of scholarships or honors, for example—appear fully justified. Unless such recognition of merit is in itself deemed undesirable, the unavailability of grades forces the use of other measures such as special tests, faculty judgments, and essays. Use of grades for decisions on financial assistance has come under scrutiny in recent years. Financial aids should not be limited to A students, but there is little justification for loans or grants to students whose grades indicate that they will not long be students. The provision of student point averages to fraternities or student groups for selection of pledges is completely inappropriate.

Grading has been criticized not only because of inequities in the system but also because grades do not predict success in later life. Why should they? Grades appraise learning, not its application. Indeed, it would be disturbing if grades correlated to any extent with salary, advancement, or contributions to society. Education, at best, enhances the chance that an individual will have a satisfying and productive life; it cannot ensure it. Moreover, success in many segments of our society does not depend especially on knowledge and understanding or on academic patterns of ability.

The real difficulties with grading are twofold. First, the expected results of education are not matters of complete accord, and evaluation is therefore unsatisfactory. Grades which can at best summarize only a portion of an evaluation must be deficient in many respects. Second, college faculty members are not, by tradition, prepared for teaching; they know about evaluation and grading only through their own experience. As Feldmesser states (1972, p. 72):

Ultimately, training in evaluation should be the responsibility of the graduate schools that produce college teachers. Meanwhile, each college could well undertake to fill the gap itself. It could, for one thing, publish a clear statement about grading policies and practices; faculty and students should naturally participate in drawing it up—an instructive experience in itself. For another thing, a college could conduct a seminar on evaluation at the opening of each academic year, with all fac-

ulty members expected to attend in their first year and perhaps every third or fourth year thereafter to keep up to date on theories and technologies. It would be highly desirable for students to attend this seminar, too. Exposure to the mundane procedures involved in evaluation would help students appreciate the fallibility of evaluative instruments, would tend to divest grades of their moral overtones, and might thereby lead to a more relaxed attitude. Furthermore, knowledge on the part of faculty that their students were moderately sophisticated in the matter of grades would be an efficacious way to enforce good practices. These steps would help overcome the evil that grades can do, allowing everyone to take full advantage of their positive functions.

Bibliographical Note

Warren's (1971) overview of college grading practices is an excellent start in further reading on this topic. Thorndike (1969) should also be read. The Office of Institutional Research, University of Michigan (1970), provides an extensive critique of credit hours. On pass-fail grading the two publications of the American Association of Collegiate Registrars and Admissions Officers—one (1971) on institutional grading practices and the other by Bailey (1972) on the acceptability of nontraditional grading patterns—indicate both practices and problems.

Chapter 13

Curriculum

The meaning of *curriculum* in higher education differs considerably from the meaning in the public schools. A curriculum in elementary education connotes an integrated system of teaching activities, study materials, and learning experiences based upon a well-defined set of objectives. The expectation in this setting is that the curriculum will provide for both teachers and students a sense of continuity, sequence, and unity over courses and time. The detailed curriculum specifications are also expected to ensure a reasonably high degree of uniformity in teacher behavior and in programs throughout all schools of a system and a minimal level of attainment of the objectives by each student.

In higher education, the meaning of curriculum is far less explicit. In some institutions, it covers all courses offered rather than referring to particular programs. Usually, however, a curriculum refers to a field of study or a course of study. A program (or curriculum) in this sense is made up of required and optional courses. The underlying assumption or rationale for a program or curriculum in this sense is often not clear. The intention may be to specify coverage of distinct disciplines. It may be to assure sufficient enrollment to justify courses reflecting specialized faculty interests. It may be to specify the courses necessary to meet job requirements in vocational or professional fields. Occasionally, but much less commonly than a curriculum theorist or evaluator would desire, the curriculum is planned to provide experiences which will move students toward the achievement of a carefully defined set of behavioral objectives.

Goals

In professional and technical fields, the overall goal of preparing the individual for a definite career has encouraged the faculty to think about the curriculum as a well-planned and organized course of study. Requirements tend to be heavy, and electives are limited. Courses are thoroughly reorganized or supplanted by new courses at intervals in order to maintain currency, but alternative courses are unlikely to proliferate because, without requirement by the program, a significant number of students are not likely to enroll. It may also be that the available faculty members are not prepared for such expansion. But because new developments constantly generate new courses which must be taken, the general education requirements tend to be frozen out, and even greater rigidity is established in the curriculum. Nevertheless, the fact that the students are being educated for a job forces a degree of unity and coherence in the program.

In contrast, the goal of preparing liberally educated students in the basic disciplines of the sciences, the social sciences, or the arts and humanities provides little or no direction for planning a four-year curriculum. Consequently, most courses are taught with minimal attention to what is done in other courses in the same or in different departments. Courses tend to be developed out of specialized faculty interests which have little to do with the essential nature of undergraduate education. But such courses cannot long exist unless faculty advising or forced choices among a limited number of alternatives provide a sufficient enrollment to support their continuation. Distribution and major requirements also ensure this enrollment. The impact on students in their developing roles as persons or as citizens becomes a secondary consideration to the perpetuation of faculty interests. Proponents of the resulting proliferation of courses defend it on the grounds that individualization of student programs is made possible by the rich array of courses offered.

Structuring the Curriculum

Because the goal of liberal education is to prepare students in the basic disciplines, the disciplines have an important role in curriculum development. A discipline is much more than a large collection of data or facts. The specific facts are generally of less value to persons drawing upon the discipline than are other aspects. As a discipline develops, it provides:

1. descriptions of the phenomena (subject matter) with which it deals
2. questions which it is to answer
3. procedures or tactics useful in attacking problems
4. methods of inquiry useful in understanding the field
5. concepts which give order, meaning, and structure to the objects and events studied
6. generalizations expressing relationships among concepts
7. procedures for validating generalizations and conclusions about the phenomena studied
8. organized catalogs of facts, generalizations, concepts, and methods for ready use by scholars

Many introductory courses in the disciplines tend to emphasize an accumulation of knowledge essential for further study of the discipline, but do little in developing the ability of students to use the discipline as a tool for adding knowledge. The subject matter of a discipline (the source of the knowledge often imparted in introductory courses) lies outside the discipline; it is a field or area of concern to which the methods of the discipline are applied. For example, art is the subject matter of many disciplines, such as mathematics, chemistry, and philosophy. The mathematician may examine the extent to which mathematical concepts of similarity, symmetry, and balance are apparent in works of art. The chemist can apply chemical principles to analyze the paint used and to assess deterioration over time as a result of the use of inappropriate materials. The philosopher views art as a product of the aesthetic drives of individuals. The discipline thus is a means to an end rather than an end in itself. Vocationally oriented programs tend to be concerned with the application of relevant disciplines to subject matter peculiar to a particular vocation, while the arts and sciences tend to be preoccupied with the discipline as a body of knowledge and as a methodology, and often deplore any demand for utility. In one form or another, the discipline, either as an end in itself or as a means to other ends, is one of the basic ways of structuring curriculum requirements.

Interdisciplinary, multidisciplinary, and transdisciplinary courses attempt to deal with concepts, ideas, issues, or problems which require insights and analysis from more than one discipline. There are numerous difficulties with these attempts: (1) Faculty members trained in single disciplines have difficulty individually in acquiring proficiency in other disciplines and collectively they may lack even a common language. (2) An interdisciplinary course which attempts to isolate those elements common to several disciplines—the social sciences, for example—is likely to suffer because social science is largely a convenient category for grouping certain disciplines rather than a discipline embracing concepts, principles, and methods used by several subdisciplines, (3) As a result of the difficulties indicated in (1) and (2), what purport to be interdisciplinary courses readily degenerate into a conjunction of segments of disciplines or a loosely coordinated tour of disciplinary differences in terminology, values, and concepts. (4) Unless the focus of a course is on a problem, concept, or concern which transcends the disciplines, it is difficult to achieve a meaningful interdisciplinary stance. Indeed, the only way to be truly independent of disciplinary boundaries is to deal with issues that are supradisciplinary. The disciplines then become—as they should—reservoirs of organized knowledge and modes of search. Structuring programs on this basis in a discipline-based college, using advisers who are themselves discipline oriented, is well nigh impossible unless requirements are minimal and individualization is possible.

If one turns from the discipline to the instructor, the interest of this individual in some aspects of the discipline or in particular applications of the discipline may be a major factor in forming the curriculum. The resulting presentation of a large array of courses representing specialized faculty interests tends to be an expensive way to individualize student programs, and it is a limited approach in that students may still not find among the alternatives any one which treats issues of concern to them. The organization of a discipline as it appeals to a scholar in that discipline may have little relevance to those who view it as a resource.

If one turns from the discipline and the instructor to the student, still other factors may be taken into account. Certain instructional techniques or learning experiences are attractive to some students, perhaps because their own modes of learning are adapted to that particular approach or because their personality and social traits lead them to prefer certain learning situations over others. If the student, in planning a program, is greatly concerned with affective outcomes, values, and ideas, he or she may consciously select professors, disciplines, subject matter, as well as learning or teaching experiences which seem to be particularly relevant to such outcomes. In this approach, it sometimes becomes uncertain whether the discipline or the subject matter to which it is applied is the primary consideration in course organization. The nature of the discipline itself has something to say about this. Certain aspects of the disciplines inevitably deal with affective development in individuals and groups (psychology or sociology). A cognitive approach to such materials may lead to affective outcomes for students, but it is more likely to provide a new level of insight and sophistication which ultimately affects their attitudes and values simply because of increased sensitivity. If a course uses as subject matter some of the major social and economic problems of the day, it may be forced into an interdisciplinary or multidisciplinary pattern to such an extent that the basic concepts, principles, and techniques of the several disciplines are ignored in the profusion of affect created by dealing with a heterogeneous group of students and a number of disturbing problem situations.

Individualization structures programs according to student needs, but it requires faculty commitment. It can take place in many ways. Within a rather highly structured course, different assignments can be made, different topics can be given for papers, and group collaboration can be organized from time to time to deal with different aspects of the discipline or with a problem area. Individualization can be promoted by the development of highly structured learning materials which each individual must work through independently. Workbooks, computer-assisted instruction, programmed learning materials, and even textbook reading followed by the requirement of answering a set of questions or working out a set of problems are examples of individualization.

The discussion thus far has emphasized the numerous ways of structuring the curriculum and the programs within it. The disciplines probably weigh heaviest in curriculum structuring in the typical college or university, frequently supported by recommendations of professional societies in the various disciplines. The interests of the department in specific aspects or applications of the discipline probably supply the next most common emphasis. Selection of various parts of one or more disciplines based on the needs in professional or technical programs is a third approach, but it is so interrelated with the previous one that they are not often distinguishable. The faculty member associated with a professional school or technical college frequently has interests corresponding to those commitments.

Innovative programs have usually made much of affective outcomes, desirable experiences, individualization, personal and social problems, and modes of learning emphasizing interactions and patterns evolved from group therapy. Yet, if one recognizes that not all students are enchanted by these approaches, it is apparent that programs which shift from instructor and disciplinary bases to problem and student bases for structure are just as confining and unsatisfactory to some students as the former. Indeed, there is evidence that this is the case if characteristics of the students are carefully studied. Neither the discipline nor the student can be the sole basis for curriculum planning.

Another way of structuring the curriculum is to specify outcomes. In some sense, all requirements involve a set of outcomes, but these may not be clearly specified. When objectives are not made explicit, the result is almost certainly a preoccupation with specific knowledge. If students are expected to develop a degree of independence in pursuit of learning, reach a satisfactory level of skill in communication, demonstrate sensitivity to their own values and those of their associates, become capable of collaborating with peers in defining and resolving problems, be able to recognize the relevance of their increasing knowledge to the current scene, and seek continually for insightful understanding and organization of their total educational experience, these outcomes must be specifically stated. In addition, they must be made explicit in relation to learning experiences and by providing opportunities for demonstration of the developing behavior and for evaluation of it. Content, subject matter, and behavior are interrelated and must be so construed by teachers, students, and evaluators. This requires an interrelated trinity of conceptual statements defining the objectives of operational statements, indicating how the behavior is to be evoked and appraised, and providing standards for deciding whether progress is evident and whether accomplishment is finally satisfactory. If this approach is fully implemented, the traditional distinctions between majors and distribution (or between depth and breadth) become meaningless.

No matter what the elements involved in planning a curriculum, it must involve content and learning experiences chosen to produce the ultimate capabilities desired in those whose educational experiences it provides. The early undergraduate curriculum was a relatively rigid exposure to the classics because they were the best available source of values and of modes of thought and communication. With the rapid accumulation of knowledge and the development of ever more complex issues, a curriculum or program now is made up of two basic components. Breadth, ideally, provides an overview of accumulated wisdom, of traditions, and of the cultural heritage. Depth, provided through the major, contributes mastery of some modes of thought and the ability to apply knowledge to relevant issues of the day, external to the course and the learner. Mastery of the knowledge accumulated within a discipline does not constitute an adequate education, for knowledge itself is continuously revised and expanded by pure research and by adaptations required as efforts are made to relate that knowledge to external realities. An undergraduate major should be viewed as something more than preparation for specialized and narrow graduate study. It provides equally a systematic way to seek knowledge and insight and to think and make judgments about issues and problems arising in life after completion of formal schooling. Clear communication, accurate inquiry, valid reasoning, wise evaluation, and synoptic understanding should result from study in any major or concentration. Breadth should contribute to these skills by forcing recognition that many issues require capabilities extending well beyond the boundaries of any single discipline. Mastery of any discipline should encourage generalization and transferability of competence to other subject matter and other problems. Study of any discipline appropriately includes topics to which that discipline contributes only partial, marginal, or even dubious insights. If this broad view be adapted, then introductory courses in mathematics, statistics, logic, art, music, literature, and foreign language should be so constructed and taught as to promote communication skills, cognitive abilities, and sensitivity to various humane values and attitudes. The sciences, social sciences, mathematics, and statistics should provide experiences in accurate inquiry. Logic, the sciences, and mathematics should accept responsibility for promoting capability in valid reasoning. Ethics, aesthetics, and literature in their basic offerings should emphasize the development of wisdom in evaluation. History, philosophy, and theology are uniquely appropriate for encouraging synoptic understanding—a goal which lends itself readily to general education. Thus, discipline-based courses may obviously make contributions to general education, but they are unlikely to do so unless planned to. Evaluation within this framework will certainly promote attention to general education outcomes.

Specification of Requirements

The prevalent requirements for a major include a minimum number of courses or credits. A maximum may also be imposed to prevent students or their advisers from undue specialization. In addition, departments usually specify introductory or core requirements which are viewed as providing an essential common base for advanced courses. Occasionally, related courses from other disciplines are included as options or requirements in a major. The array of upper-division courses frequently provides either for several different specializations in an aspect of the discipline or for electives chosen in reference to student interests. Breadth in the discipline results from the required core, and depth from the selection of upper-division courses. Depth can result either from a well-defined sequence emphasizing increasing understanding and ability to use the discipline as a mode of inquiry or from specialization in content or subject matter. Discussion of a particular discipline—history—will clarify these comments. In this discussion, I incorporate some characteristics which, in fact, may be somewhat less true of history than of other disciplines. The intent is not to criticize history specifically but, rather, to present a point of view about the difficulties of presenting any discipline in a manner attractive to a wide range of undergraduates.

History was earlier characterized as a synoptic discipline. It is inevitably, in some sense, chronological, but a course may cover centuries or focus on a few years or days. It may also be political, economic, social, national, local, racial, cultural, linguistic, or military in focus. Specific aspects of human effort or development also form the basis for history courses: the industrial revolution, commercial capitalism, colonialism, the reformation, communism, constitutions and law, foreign policy, international relations. History can be applied to study the development of other disciplines, such as history of mathematics, science, technology, and religion. Alternatively, history can be studied and interpreted by recourse to those disciplines —for example, the impact of technology on society. Charles Beard emphasized an economic interpretation. Frederick Turner, in studying the impact of the western movement in the United States, frequently noted the significance of geographical features. Forms of government and religion, the development of technology, the search for freedom and equality, and the influence of individuals also have affected the course of history. Underlying and binding all these is historiography, which deserves study in its own right.

The prospective history major faced with an array of courses sampling all the various topics, emphases, and periods suggested here is much like an individual undertaking a tour of a foreign country without knowledge of the language and with no prior experience upon which to plan. Travel agents (like professors) have packaged travel plans and tour groups from which they suggest alternatives based upon their own preferences or attempt to elicit preferences from a client who lacks any basis for choice. A map, like a curriculum, may be interesting and intriguing, but it is singularly unhelpful unless approached with some understanding and some sense of where one wishes to go.

The typical offerings in a department are comparable to the offerings of several competing travel agents, each of whom has somewhat different conceptions of what is of the greatest worth, what route to follow, and which people are most helpful along the way. Many different structures could be developed which would assist both faculty and students to perceive the total array of courses in a meaningful way, permit evaluation and modification of that array, provide guidelines for planning a productive tour of the discipline, and assure that students grasp the nature of the discipline as a way to study and understand various other problems and subject matter.

The following structure (or set of recommendations) emerges from my own biases. Although history has been for me only a field of recreation, I believe that many undergraduate history offerings and recommendations for the undergraduate major are determined primarily by the graduate specializations of the faculty rather than by any convictions about the desired experience for the undergraduate. I propose (primarily to offer an example of an approach rather than from deep-seated convictions) that the undergraduate major in history include several elements. The actual mix could vary considerably for individuals and obviously would depend upon the range of courses provided.

One component of the history major would be a continuing depth study of the history of one nation and several closely related ones over several centuries; such study would examine interactions, trends, and the dependence of later events upon earlier ones. This sequence might well extend over three years, total about twenty-four credits, and account for about 50 percent of the major. No single text would be used in any course. Since each student would be expected to complete all six semesters, at least six texts would be required, sampling history as written by six different historians of two or three different nations and at various times. In anticipation of certain segments of the course, students would be encouraged to elect relevant courses from other disciplines and to use an existing foreign-language facility or even to develop one. The emphasis in this sequence would be on viewing history through reading and discussion of multiple and contrasting views and interpretations of what happened.

A second requirement would be a depth study of a particularly significant period in a culture—for example, Florence in the 1500s. Courses covering several such periods would be available, more than one could be offered at a time; and the periods would be regularly changed so as to challenge both teachers and students with a new task. Students would be directed to examining the full range of literature, art, science, mathematics, music, and the interrelationships and the origins of developments in these areas. Students would be encouraged to emphasize those aspects of the culture of special interest (art, literature, music, science, technology, politics) perhaps working in teams based upon a group interest, but ultimately sharing gleanings with all. This experience would involve six to nine credit hours.

A third requirement would be an examination of a period in American history—the colonial period, the Revolution, the Civil War, slavery—as studied and reported by historians with different values and writing from various vantage points in time. This theme would be allotted three to six credits.

A fourth course requirement would be a biographical study of some phase of history which the student has previously studied. This course would be allotted three credits. Psycho-history would be a possible alternative.

A fifth requirement would be a historical study of a field such as science, technology, or art. This course might be offered in a department other than history; but its role in the experience of the student would be to provide insight into another discipline by study of its development, while simultaneously acquainting the student with the task of sorting out one aspect of man's heritage. Such a course would be given no more than three or four credits.

The sixth and last formal course requirement would be a course in historiography—another three credits. Obviously, the earlier courses would have already contributed greatly to a sense of history and to the task of analyzing and synthesizing it.

A final requirement would be an independent effort—a senior thesis on some aspect of history. The student would, without great difficulty or expense, have access to some primary sources as well as secondary materials. This effort would be sufficiently extensive to receive three to six credits.

The total requirement specified ranges from forty-five to fifty-five credits, but at least one of the courses would be in another department so the requirement is not unreasonable. There is flexibility, too, for the requirements specify types of experiences rather than a rigid curriculum for all. Unlike the usual major requirements, the elements of this pattern reflect a concern for a range of experiences with history. It would provide almost as much of general education as of specialization. A rationale for this program could be readily provided for students and faculty alike. Objectives could readily be written; they would relate primarily to a grasp of the nature of history as a discipline and to an understanding of its relevance for relating various aspects of man's heritage and present state. This approach would be highly beneficial to the part-time, nontraditional student, especially because the continuity and coherence of the educational experience are based in the curriculum, not in the residential status of the student. A curriculum developed on such a rationale would be evaluated in reference to the effectiveness of the rationale and the objectives implicit in it, rather than by imposing objectives upon it. Knowledge per se would be less important than understanding the nature of history and developing the ability to analyze, synthesize, and evaluate.

There are impediments to this approach to curriculum development. Obtaining consensus on such a pattern would be difficult—perhaps impossible. The specialized interests of some history professors might have no outlet in such a program. It might be difficult to convince students of its merits—especially if a segment of the faculty continued to oppose the pattern. Even so, the planning of the major for individuals could take such considerations into account, so that the courses selected would have some pattern grasped by the student, even if unknown to many of the teachers.

Table 5 suggests the several elements which in varying ways and to various degrees are involved in planning a curricu-

Table 5. Planning the Curriculum

	Discipline	Professor	Vocation	Student
Knowledge	*		*	*
Cognitive abilities	*	*	*	*
Social goals, needs, and personal obligations			*	*
Psychomotor skills		*	*	*
Affective development		*	*	*

lum, the associated instructional activities, and the learning experiences. To the three bases for curriculum planning mentioned above—disciplines, faculty, and students, a fourth—vocation—should be added. Of these four, either the vocation or the disciplines are traditionally the bases. Both institutional organization and student requirements are structured around the disci-

plines. In the case of the vocation, the nature of the tasks involved requires selection of relevant disciplines, and the institutional organization is characterized by titles designating the
vocation (engineering, business, medicine). The professor becomes a basis for planning in one of two ways. Either the professor teaches an essential specialization in which the student
needs experience, or the professor has personal qualities which
are deemed by students or colleagues as so significant that students should have contact with him or her. The student is seldom the basis for planning except in nontraditional or experimental programs. In the traditional program, adaptations to student interests and needs come only through selection of
electives or of professors.

The vertical categories in the table are objectives (or outcomes)—the second set of elements in curriculum planning.
These range from knowledge and cognitive abilities through
social skills and psychomotor skills to affective qualities.

The asterisks indicate either usual or desired conjunctions
of the two sets of factors. Disciplines are preoccupied almost
solely with organized blocks of knowledge and with student
exposure to and mastery of them. Students should attain understanding of the nature of the discipline and of its structure, concepts, modes of analysis and synthesis, and criteria for seeking
and validating knowledge. Although study of the disciplines can
contribute to social goals, psychomotor skills, and affective
development, they seldom do unless taught by a professor both
concerned with these objectives and sensitive to student concerns and needs.

Professors usually become known and regarded for their
success in stimulating students to think and evaluate in both
affective and cognitive realms and for their capabilities in demonstrating and promoting mastery of psychomotor skills (in
laboratories, surgery courses). Experience as consultants or as
solvers of social problems may also add to the luster of professors. Knowledge, by itself, seldom leads to a professor's being
regarded as an unusually effective teacher.

Vocational programs require attention to the full range of
outcomes. Knowledge is essential, but cognitive abilities in

selecting, gaining, and applying knowledge are even more essential. Every vocation or profession meets certain social needs and therefore involves professional obligations and a code of ethics which must be studied, understood, and accepted by each practitioner. The affective development of the individual is involved in effective relations with clients, and psychomotor development is essential in performance of duties. Thus, sound vocational education rightly conceived must be a complete education.

Certainly a complete education for each student also requires the attainment of objectives in each category. This, however, is an ideal. Not all curriculums based upon concern for the student either seek or successfully attain the full roster of objectives. Some experimental or innovative programs have placed so much emphasis upon affective development and provide so little in the way of either rigor or wise advice that the resulting education becomes little more than individual and group therapy. The too-ready assumption that affective growth leads to social responsibility and to an earnest search for knowledge and the development of cognitive abilities has not been and is unlikely to be validated. It may happen, however, if the individual at some stage develops a vocational goal which makes it evident that knowledge, abilities, and skills are essential for personal success and a responsible role in society. Individualization through advising rather than preoccupation with either knowledge or affect is the key to development of a sound undergraduate experience.

Multidisciplinary Courses

The hallmark of many attempts at general education was the development of broad-gauge offerings in the humanities, social sciences, and sciences. These arose out of a concern that introductory courses in the disciplines failed to provide students with the breadth desired as a balance to the depth incorporated in the major. Many of these efforts quickly degenerated into offerings with little or no focus or continuity—quick and confusing tours in which the student saw much but grasped little.

Integrating such courses around ideas, themes, concepts, principles, scholarly methodologies, or problems was tried with varying degrees of success. That success depended upon inspired teaching, and discipline-based teachers tended in time to drift back to their original disciplines, partly because of the exacting nature of the interdisciplinary effort and partly because the path to career development and reward was much more certain in the discipline.

In the present day, interdisciplinary efforts have taken a somewhat different direction. They are focused more on intercultural concerns, regional policy, or specific problems: nutrition, ecology, urban problems, racial concerns. These efforts arise primarily out of recognition that major problems besetting our society are dealt with in an inadequate fashion within the separate disciplines. As the disciplines have become structured and have narrowed their focus and methods of inquiry, they have become less relevant to understanding the major problems of individuals in complex societies. Thus the problem approach is essentially supradisciplinary. Studying nutritional deficiencies, for example, involves work in agriculture, geography, religion, economics, personal habits, social mores, and family and child-rearing practices.

If the problem approach is taken, development of a course or curriculum becomes much like that of planning a program for a professional field. The questions faced are, essentially: (1) What do we already know that is useful in understanding and solving this problem? (2) How can this knowledge be organized and presented in an integrative manner in respect to the problem? (3) What else do we need to know to deal effectively with the problem? (4) How do we acquire this additional knowledge? (5) What are the possible solutions to the problem and how do we choose among them? (6) How do we gain support for the solution proposed?

The significance of this approach can be seen if we consider three elements as providing the basis for education: disciplines, problems, and students. Traditionally, education has been based upon disciplines. The task of the students has been that of mastering the disciplines (or at least one of them) with the belief that they would then be able to deal with problems in an effective manner. However, individuals do not readily apply their knowledge if they have not learned to do so in the process of acquiring it.

Disenchanted with this emphasis on the disciplines, others have sought to develop education around the needs and concerns of the individual. These attempts attract few faculty members and only a minority of students. On the whole, individual programs are unsuccessful and either expire or drift back toward a more traditional disciplinary emphasis.

Both disciplines and students however are concerned with personal and social problems. Education rightly conceived should help individuals become aware of the problems of humanity and aware of the accumulated knowledge and experience of mankind in attempting to deal with them. Anyone who would undertake to resolve imbalances and inequities without understanding the complications of an issue and the history of various attempts to resolve it is unlikely to make a significant contribution and may, in fact, succeed only in making it more difficult for others to do so.

Viewed in this way, not only multidisciplinary efforts but all education should be evaluated in reference to the extent that it produces understanding of man's present state and commitment to improving it through creating a better social order. Thus the objectives of education extend beyond the disciplines; education is supradisciplinary, incorporating cognitive, affective, and psychomotor outcomes which must be integrated within each individual.

Evaluation

Evaluation of the curriculum can take place in various ways. The approach taken depends upon the people involved and the purposes to be served. The evaluation of the classical curriculum was implicit and based largely upon historical considerations and philosophical presuppositions. The content and the substance of the classics—the cognitive and affective heritage of the Western world—was viewed as incontestably valuable in its own right. And the classical-liberal education had also (in the minds of its proponents) practical utility in the professions. Yet the failure of the classical curriculum to adapt and maintain utility and relevance ultimately led to its demise. Historical and philosophical validation was not in the end adequate. An external and more objective evaluation eventually decreed the irrelevance of the classical curriculum in modern society.

A second approach to curriculum evaluation starts with the rationale—the assumption and principles—upon which the curriculum is based. In professional or technological education, the specification of particular courses may be important. Hours and types of field work, clerkships, and internships become standards for curriculum evaluation in these circumstances. This approach to evaluation thus is through specification of the process and experiences as derived from the original rationale and desired outcomes.

Evaluation of the major curriculum suggested in history could also be process oriented. Are the various types of courses described offered? Do students fulfill these requirements as stated? Is there evidence that students and faculty understand and accept the rationale? Does understanding of the fundamental nature of the discipline emerge from the program? Do students obtain insights into other disciplines and into current social issues? What behaviors or tasks provide evidence of success? The culminating project is intended to afford such evidence, but does it work? Are students in adequate numbers attracted to the program? What happens to the electives which are usually a major source of history enrollments?

Another approach to evaluation of the curriculum might consider its quality—the extent to which it is current in offerings, content, bibliography, and instructional techniques and methodology. Adequacy of faculty preparation in relation to the courses taught is another criterion. The existence and appropriateness of courses for nonmajors is an issue of importance, especially in science, mathematics, and statistics, which frequently provide essential background for students in other fields. The adequacy of classrooms, laboratories, and other facilities is an important consideration in some programs. Library holdings and their usage also require assessment.

In this process of evaluation, the opinions of various groups may be sought. Students completing, entering, or considering a program may have views worthy of collection and consideration. The views of faculty members in other disciplines about the adequacy and quality of courses deserve consideration, especially since these views may be communicated to students in various ways to the detriment of their experience in the courses. Comments or criticisms by external groups such as employers or accrediting agencies are relevant. The recommendations or standards suggested by professional societies or committees should be used in reviewing curricular offerings and requirements. Some of these may ultimately be deemed inappropriate, but this is a decision to be reached by deliberation rather than by omission.

Curriculum review should also consider the number of offerings as well as character and quality. Needless proliferation leads to small classes and to high costs or heavy loads. It may also result in loss of sequential character and a meaningless potpourri of courses. Opportunities for independent study disappear when courses cover every conceivable aspect of a discipline. An undue number of low-credit offerings adds greatly to student load and jeopardizes performance. Duplication of offerings in several departments can also increase costs and lower quality—the latter because of the use of poorly qualified faculty. Such duplication can also permit or encourage students to accumulate credits without adding to their educational stature. Multiplication of courses because of external demands for slight modifications in content or a reduction in credit hours can be costly and may lead to deterioration in the quality of offerings. Unduly heavy requirements or advising which encourages students to pile up courses in their majors can interfere with institutional policies in regard to breadth and lead to undue expansion of a single department. Stated requirements or policies are frequently ignored and remain uncorrected until analysis of student transcripts demonstrates conclusively that this is the case and points out the circumstances or persons responsible.

The ultimate and most difficult task in evaluation of the curriculum is determining the extent to which individuals have become aware of the problems of society, have internalized some values involved in the solution of these problems, and have seen their education as providing resources for coping with these problems. Breadth and depth become interrelated in a manner which transcends the usual distractions between major and general education.

Most of the evaluation emphases suggested are quite different from the traditional approach through definition of objectives and assessment of student progress relative to them. But the emphases suggested, although they focus on processes and rationale, are likely to be more productive in most colleges and universities than is the traditional approach. Unless and until curriculum outcomes are defined in broad terms which transcend individual courses, curriculum evaluation and revision through assessment of student performance are simply not possible.

The procedures or instruments for assessment of curriculum outcomes are plentiful and are discussed elsewhere in this volume. Locally developed comprehensive examinations and nationally available tests are useful. Papers, essays, projects, and student performance in laboratories or studios can be required, observed, and rated. Effective participation in discussions and seminars can be noted. The ability of an individual to read or listen to a formal presentation and thereafter to analyze and critique it can be ascertained. Follow-up of graduates to obtain their suggestions and those of employers is a frequent but rarely productive approach because the replies seldom relate clearly to the course orientation of the faculty.

Curriculum evaluation is sorely needed if unity and sequence are to be restored to the undergraduate curriculum. The lack of effort in this regard is a composite result of professorial preoccupation with courses, a lack of clear objectives transcending courses, and a consequent lack of sequence and cumulative character in disparate courses. The effort, costs, and changes in view required also tend to discourage comprehensive curricular evaluation. It is therefore not surprising that administrators, rather than the faculty, initiate such activity.

Bibliographical Note

As is to be expected, much of the writing about the curriculum in higher education is directed to the disciplines or to professional programs such as nursing, engineering, business, and medicine. I have avoided elaborating these treatments in the bibliography because (1) they are extensive, (2) interested faculty members in these fields are likely to already have access to this literature, (3) much of the literature is analytical, developmental, or descriptive, rather than evaluative, and (4) the focus here is upon the broad concerns of evaluation of curriculum in reference to student development and educational objectives, rather than in reference to specific fields. The following references have this broad focus.

Posner (1974) presents a conceptual scheme for curriculum structure. Hively and Associates (1973) developed a technical handbook for domain-referenced curriculum evaluation. Lindvall and Cox (1970), focusing on individually programmed instruction, consider the role of evaluation in curriculum development. Tyler, Gagné, and Scriven's volume (1967) in the American Educational Research Association monograph series on curriculum evaluation is excellent. The volume on curriculum evaluation edited by Payne (1974) also deserves attention. The volume by Mayhew and Ford (1971) provides an excellent analysis and a provocative final chapter which attempts to propound a theory of curriculum. The volume on curriculum by Dressel (1971) is perhaps the most extensive current discussion of all aspects of the higher education curriculum.

Chapter 14

Graduate Education

Much of the discussion in other chapters of this volume is directly applicable to graduate education. However, two major differences exist between graduate and undergraduate education which make graduate education even more difficult to evaluate than undergraduate education. Whereas most undergraduate programs utilize courses and teachers from several departments, most graduate programs call for specialization in a single department with only a few (and often no) courses from other departments. As a corollary, most graduate programs are based in and (except for general policies established by a graduate dean and graduate council) controlled by the departments. Furthermore, prestigious professors in a department, because of the autonomy accorded them, can operate their own private graduate programs with minimal attention to departmental or institutional policies.

Obviously, these circumstances present problems in evaluation. Except for looking at the role of graduate deans and councils in establishing and enforcing policies and approving and reviewing programs, evaluators must emphasize departmental programs, procedures, and policies. Since the graduate degree is almost entirely a disciplinary or applied specialty planned and supervised by faculty of stature in the specialization, adequacy of coverage and quality of content are evaluated in developing the program. This evaluation may overlook other matters, but external evaluation or even externally devised criteria are not always regarded as necessary or useful. However, the combination of review by graduate deans and councils, accreditation reviews in some cases, the pervasive concern of faculty members for recognition of their programs by other universities, and the concerns about costs and overexpansion of graduate education in some fields have brought recognition of the need for careful and continuing evaluation of graduate programs.

Expansion in particular requires evaluation. Faculty members believe their own status is enhanced by the presence of a graduate program. Administrators, partly to mollify the faculty and partly to enhance their own status, often support the introduction or the continuance of graduate programs which are costly, marginal, and unneeded. And administrators seldom attempt to eliminate a program because of the internal strife and the external recriminations which are aroused by the mere suggestion of such a possibility. Nationally, perhaps twenty universities are widely recognized for quality in at least some of their doctoral programs, as documented by the surveys and evaluations made by Cartter (1966) and by Roose and Andersen (1970). Back of this group of elite institutions is a horde of others which have a special obligation for critical examination of their graduate programs. Some of this group are limited to master's degree programs and many others should be. Degrees also differ markedly in quality among and within departments in an institution, depending upon the capability of the students and the particular faculty members directing their study. Because of these circumstances, continuing evaluation of graduate programs is essential both to maintain quality and to support decisions regarding expansion, contraction, or termination. Appraisal of success in placement and of changing social needs can point to the desirability of introducing new programs by modifying existing ones or to the desirability of gaining resources through the elimination of programs.

In state-supported institutions, because of the increasing power of state coordinating agencies, the range of graduate programs is often prescribed. Some institutions are being forced to phase out existing graduate programs, and others have been barred from starting them. Despite the damage done to faculty morale, these are generally wise decisions dictated by costs, lack of need, and concern for quality.

There are two types of graduate degrees and two or more levels in each. The traditional research degrees are the master of arts or science and the doctor of philosophy. Practitioner degrees include a host of master's degrees, many requiring two years of study, and numerous doctoral programs. The master of social work exemplifies the former, and the latter include such degrees as doctor of business administration, doctor of education, and doctor of arts. Compared with the M.D., however, the D.B.A., Ed.D., and D.A. are much closer to the Ph.D. and are often treated as the equivalent for teaching appointments in colleges and universities. The significance of the master's degree has become clouded in the present day by the ease (credit accumulation alone) with which the degree is acquired in many institutions. Many elementary and secondary school teachers whose undergraduate records would not have gained them admission to a graduate program in earlier years now routinely complete master's degree requirements, often through extension offerings without placing foot on the main campus. Some colleges and universities which offer the master's as their highest degree however maintain standards well above those of more prestigious institutions, which routinely award the master's for credit accumulation, with no pretense that it is either a research degree or a step toward the doctorate. An occasional small institution with a few highly capable faculty members may, in fact, produce a limited number of exceptional master's degrees under a pattern almost collegial and tutorial in nature and at no great cost.

Characteristics of Programs

No institution should launch or maintain any graduate program until detailed analysis by unbiased external consultants has determined the presence of adequate resources in capable faculty members with demonstrated research productivity, in facilities for research, and in satisfactory library holdings for support of the program. A recurrent problem within institutions is that some departments or disciplines meet such reasonable standards while others do not. Yet none are happy about being bypassed when graduate programs are initiated. The alternative of interdisciplinary degrees involving several departments is attractive in some respects, but generally undesirable as an initial graduate program since the successful launching and conduct of these innovative degrees require high capability and prior experience in graduate education.

As just mentioned, a graduate program requires a capable core of faculty members representing the major subdivisions of a discipline and with some history of productive scholarship. The graduate faculty should include younger individuals as well as scholars of established repute to ensure continuity—maintenance of quality and orderly replacement—as senior professors retire. A strong tradition of academic freedom and of faculty participation in governance is necessary to attract and hold such a staff. In addition, unless a faculty has already demonstrated its ability to mount an unusually strong undergraduate program, it is surely not capable of launching advanced-degree programs. And unless the undergraduate majors in a department are numerous, a graduate program (which usually draws first on its own baccalaureate recipients) is unlikely to be of sufficient quality or size to be long viable. Moreover, the recruitment of able graduates of other institutions is necessary to stimulate both the faculty and the students. (To some extent, interaction and friendly competition among graduate students are also essential for quality.)

A review of studies and critiques of graduate education yields an array of desirable or essential characteristics which become criteria for evaluation. Because of the individualized nature of graduate programs, these criteria are often stated as exhortations rather than absolutes. "Should" rather than "must" is part of many of them. They must be applied with judgment.

The individual attention which must be given to graduate students in program planning and in their study and research requires that graduate faculty members have a lesser teaching load than do strictly undergraduate faculty members. The graduate faculty member must engage in extensive reading and some scholarly productivity to keep abreast of the field and maintain the capability of directing research seminars. Advising graduate students on programs and directing several theses or dissertations can readily build a load equivalent to teaching one or two courses. In practitioner programs, the direction of internships and clinical experiences is time-consuming, especially since the practitioner must maintain his or her own capability in such work. These circumstances require that graduate faculty load be carefully evaluated and some criteria developed for load assignments.

Graduate programs, except possibly in the most mature graduate universities, require strong coordination from a graduate dean and graduate council. Some departments tend to be overly lenient in admissions and in standards in order to build up or maintain a sizable program. The close relation between graduate students and professors frequently induces professors to overlook inadequate performance in courses or on examinations. This tendency is reinforced by the liberal grading practices at the graduate level. Only careful and continuing scrutiny of admissions by the graduate dean and rigorous enforcement of regulations and quality standards laid down by the graduate council can ensure sound graduate education. Although these obligations are generally recognized, they may not be met unless periodic, formal, possibly externally initiated evaluation is carried on.

It is sound practice to require that the dean or a member of the graduate council sit in on oral examinations, thereby placing both the student and the faculty on warning that this is more than a social occasion. Practices with regard to program structure and theses or dissertations should be monitored. In the initial stages of a new program, an outside professor from a long-established graduate program in the same discipline may be used on each committee. His or her approval of the dissertation and presence at the final oral guard against laxity in standards. Although these practices have an evaluative implication, they are all too often carried out so perfunctorily as to have no effect.

In the programs of graduate students, like those of undergraduates, some balancing is necessary between breadth and depth. The programs may include undergraduate courses required (without credit) as essential background, particularly for students with undergraduate programs which are not direct preparations for their chosen graduate field; but overuse of undergraduate courses is a signal of deterioration in admissions or program standards. Most programs include supportive or related courses from one or more disciplines other than the major. And, in some departments, a common core of courses is required for everyone, although flexibility in adapting to individual needs is desirable. Depth, whether provided through a sequence of courses in a single discipline, through mastery of certain research methodologies, or through attention to a particular problem requiring knowledge and techniques from several disciplines, is also an essential component of every graduate program. So, too, is a demonstration of independent performance—through original research, review, summary and interpretation of research, or demonstration in field work and internships. Thus a graduate program can frequently be viewed as comprising three parts: a common core for all students, one or two related areas, and a specialization sequence.

The program must also achieve a balance among theory, research, applied research, and practice, with the research degrees emphasizing the first two and the practitioner degrees the latter two, although either may include experiences over the entire range. Programs should also balance formal classes, advanced research seminars, and independent study. The seminars, as well as independent study, should be demonstrations of increasing student competence with minimal faculty direction. When programs require field experiences or internships, the availability of these in adequate numbers should be ascertained, and their quality should be assessed at intervals. This assessment should consider the nature of the work, the on-site supervision, and the character of supervision from the campus.

Mastery of research tools is important for most graduate

programs. These include the research methodologies unique to the field of study, but may also include as appropriate, one or more foreign languages, statistics, mathematics, evaluation techniques, econometrics, sociometrics, and computer utilization. Generally, the initial or elementary use of these tools should not be counted for credit toward degree requirements, but advanced use may appropriately be counted with the approval of the committee and dean's office.

The overall structure of graduate programs should be carefully developed and approved by the dean and graduate council, and individual variations should be permitted only for adequate reason and by approval of the dean. At the same time, a reasonable degree of flexibility should be permitted in adapting to individual needs as long as satisfactory standards are maintained.

Graduate students should have a voice in their own programs and should be able collectively to express concerns about requirements, assistantships, financial aid, living conditions, and recreational facilities. Both graduate teaching and research assistantships should be regarded as significant components of graduate programs, and therefore they should be carefully supervised and evaluated.

Evaluation of Student Progress

A sound program of graduate education engages in a continuing evaluation of the progress of students. This evaluation begins with the admissions process, in which such criteria as degrees, credits and grades, course patterns, recommendations, examinations (Graduate Record Examination, Miller's Analogies), and interviews are used to select those admitted. Probationary, conditioned, or special admissions are appropriate when used with care and when not permitted to become an easy route to bypass admissions standards.

Graduate education is so decentralized in most universities that departmental examination policies carried out through doctoral committees and graduate advisers often deviate significantly from principles enunciated by graduate deans and councils. Accordingly, a summarization of examination practices is a set of generalizations which may not accord with practice in any single situation. Since master's degree programs have become, in many instances, defined solely by credits accrued, I shall look here at examination requirements for the doctorate.

Generally, three to four examinations are required. A *preliminary examination* certifies basic knowledge in the field and establishes that the student is qualified for advanced work. This preliminary examination may be required during the first term or sometime during the first year; if the student follows both master's and doctoral programs in the institution, the preliminary examination may be the final master's examination or simply the completion of the master's degree. This preliminary examination may also be used to provide information on strengths and weaknesses as a basis for individual program planning.

The next examination is designated as either a *qualifying field examination or a comprehensive*, although the terms may have somewhat different meanings. In some disciplines, qualifying examinations may be required in all or a specified number of subfields. The comprehensive examination may be divided into fields or may have a broader base. Generally, it is required at the completion of all course work and tests the student's knowledge and mastery of research. The comprehensive examination may have both written and oral parts, which may be related. The *oral examination* may follow the written and be used to further explore written responses which were not regarded as entirely satisfactory. The oral examination also provides the opportunity to test communication skills, the ability to think under pressure, and the ability to recall and organize ideas on short notice. In some cases this oral also covers a proposed plan for dissertation research. A certification of candidacy may be issued at this point. The *final examination* is usually an oral examination on the dissertation.

When this sequence of examinations works as intended, it moves the individual through a series of steps from certification of a broad base in the discipline through demonstration of detailed knowledge of one or more subfields, mastery of research methodology, development of a research project, and finally completion and defense of that research. The series is pyramidal, sequential, and logical. When the sequence does not work as intended, it may place a heavy burden on the student, who spends excessive time reviewing details, reading widely and without definite purpose to cover all topics that might be included on the examination, and generally finding that forced, excessive attention to courses and content is not adequate preparation for independent research. This examination system also has implications for the faculty. It assures that no graduate adviser or committee ignores the necessity for upholding the intended policies and standards. In fact, the examination requirements are viewed by segments of the faculty as necessary to keep some colleagues in line as much as to assure adequate performance by students. Some faculty members, aware of their tendency to empathize with students, gladly use the policies as reasons for denying special requests. Certainly, continuing evaluation is desirable, but the elaboration of such hurdles can be debilitating to both faculty and students, for they are time consuming and can destroy morale if many students are failed or are forced to repeat at each stage. Quality should certainly be maintained, but excessive examining can be a waste of time, diverting the student from forward movement to spend many hours instead in time-consuming review of inconsequential matters. Effective use of such evaluation for feedback and program planning might significantly increase the completion rate in graduate programs.

Preparation for Teaching

Universities and departments differ markedly in accepting responsibility for preparing doctoral recipients to teach at the undergraduate level. Some departments, regarding the doctorate as a research degree, see the introduction of any courses, seminars, or supervised internships in teaching as an irrelevant distraction, whether offered for credit or as an option. Even the new doctor of arts programs, presumably developed for the special purpose of preparing undergraduate teachers, differ markedly in the extent to which teaching-related courses and experiences are included. The view, widespread among academics, that competence in a discipline and experience in research are the major qualifications for college teaching still exists. However, some departments take the obligation of providing supervised teaching experience quite seriously. Teaching under the supervision of a senior faculty member, seminars on teaching and curriculum, and experiences in making and marking examinations are provided for all doctoral candidates. Since most doctoral students will teach some undergraduates and some will spend their entire careers doing so, I believe that such experiences should be included for all doctoral students. Occasionally, a department asserts that many of their graduates accept positions in business or industry or government and never engage in teaching. Even so, the experience of teaching is also an experience in communicating about the discipline and its significance with naive individuals. Teaching experience can be justified solely upon that basis, for it usually increases insight into the discipline itself. Chapter Fifteen provides extensive discussion of teaching and the evaluation of it.

Evaluation of Programs

The suggestions and cautions already presented relate to matters which require continuing evaluation. In large programs, it may not be possible to review all admissions, rejections, and enrollments each year. In such cases, a rolling review of departments should be scheduled so that each area is appraised in full every three to five years.

Student programs should be analyzed to determine evidence of coherence and flexibility, including use of graduate courses in other departments; use of undergraduate courses (basis for selection, number in a program); balance of courses, research seminars, independent study, and nature of work in each area; completion of language and research-tool requirements; completion of examinations; fulfillment of residency requirements; graduate student load and fee payments; quality of research; degree completion rate and time required.

In addition, the adequacy and the use of office space and of research and training facilities should be reviewed from time to time. The qualifications of faculty members teaching graduate courses, serving on committees, and directing research require regular review since some departments may tend to ignore specifications if the graduate student load becomes unduly heavy. This possibility indicates also the necessity for monitoring the number of students accepted in relation to the qualified faculty. Faculty load deserves annual review for two reasons. First, if the load of the graduate faculty becomes unduly heavy (because of laxity in upholding admission standards, for example), quality will certainly suffer. Second, there is a tendency for the teaching load of all faculty members to be reduced to accord with that of the graduate faculty. This is at once unfair to the graduate faculty and a source of vastly increased costs.

The sources of data on many of these factors are evident. Admissions office records and graduate student records yield much information if carefully scrutinized. Interviews with graduate students or questionnaire surveys reveal many dissatisfactions and problems not otherwise brought forward. Views of the graduate faculty obtained by individual interviews frequently alert interviewers to internal problems and gripes within a department. Placement records and reactions from employers provide some evidence on program quality.

The use of outside examiners or consultants on a periodic review basis is desirable. This examination is most revealing if arranged by the graduate dean rather than by the department, with the requirement that both oral and written reports be made to the dean.

The costs of each graduate program should be regularly computed and studied. This is a somewhat complex task requiring reports on faculty time utilization as well as on other factors. When costs are high, the importance and the need for a program in relation to the availability of similar programs in other institutions should be assessed.

The fact that graduate programs are largely departmentally based and jealously guarded both complicates such assessment and makes it absolutely essential. Departments find it difficult to scrutinize themselves critically, and they are understandably hesitant about condemning lenient practices of members of the faculty. Only relentless review by the graduate dean, supported by the budget powers of the chief academic officer, ensures the maintenance of quality and the elimination of unsound programs.

Bibliographical Note

The rapid expansion of graduate programs and the subsequent overproduction of graduate degrees have resulted in numerous studies and reports of all aspects of graduate education. Mayhew and Ford (1974) provide an excellent review of the problems and deficiencies of both graduate and professional programs. They recommend at least three tracks (research, teaching, practice) in doctoral programs, revision and limitation of the curriculum, revival of the master's degree, review of examination requirements, improvement of graduate teaching, modification of examination processes, inclusion of career-relevant experiences, and assignment of greater power to graduate offices.

Scholarship for Society (Educational Testing Service, 1973) calls for a clarification of institutional mission in graduate education, notes many of the same problems as Mayhew and Ford do, and emphasizes the necessity for new programs related to the current needs of society.

Meeting the Needs of Doctoral Education in New York State (Regents' Commission on Doctoral Education, 1973) recommends that all doctoral programs in the state be regarded as part of an interrelated system, that there be continuing review of quality and need, and that graduate programs be concentrated in a few of the stronger institutions.

Several publications of the Ford-funded Research Program in University Administration at Berkeley deal with many facets of graduate education. Breneman (1970a, 1970b, and 1970c) looks at the production of Ph.D.s and the factions involved. His report on the Ph.D.s at Berkeley (1970b) examines departmental behavior, and, noting the high attrition rates, calls for a decrease in enrollment, elimination of outmoded and irrelevant requirements, increased personal relationships with professors, and provision to applicants of detailed information on the probability of getting a degree and a job.

McCarthy and Deener (1972) analyze the costs and benefits of graduate education and give recommendations. They note that benefits accrue to the individual, the institution, and society.

Chapter 15

Faculty

A college or university is supported by society to enable individuals to fully realize their own potential and aspirations and to become more rational and productive participants in society than they might otherwise have been. This definition recognizes the personal, social, and economic benefits of education. The institution also engages in research and provides an extensive array of public services directed to increasing wisdom and its application for the betterment of society. Each institution and every employee in it share these responsibilities.

Evaluation of institutional performance requires evaluation of personnel performance in an institutional context. Some faculty members insist that the faculty is the university. This erroneous view ignores both social responsibility and accountability, and it presents a major difficulty in developing a faculty-evaluation system; if the faculty is the university, then faculty evaluation must be conducted by the faculty. But professional courtesy, specialization, academic freedom, and dislike and distrust of evaluation combine to seriously limit any formal

331

faculty evaluation of its own efforts. If the social responsibilities of the university require evaluation of the faculty, then evaluation efforts must be so supported by administration and students that the faculty cannot ignore them. This virtual imposition is viewed by segments of the faculty as intolerable, as unprofessional, and even as a violation of academic freedom. The basis for this concern is obvious and real; those who evaluate may ultimately direct and control. Faculty values and priorities differ within and across disciplines and from those of the administration and society. Evaluation, which would expose these differences, does, indeed, constitute a threat. Yet it may now be that only by accepting the necessity for continuing evaluation can the faculty avoid the use of evaluation in destructive ways.

The university itself is surprisingly irrational in its operation, an inevitable result of its assimilation over centuries of distinctive and conflicting roles and modes of operation and of the varied expectations of its constituencies, internal and external. This irrationalism is amply evident in the contradictions between the graduate programs, which presume to train researchers, and the undergraduate teaching responsibilities, which most professors assume.

Professors engage in many activities, for most of which they have no specific preparation. The seven most common activities are instructing undergraduates; instructing graduates; course and curriculum development, preparation of instructional materials, evaluation and grading of student progress; advising students; research, creativity, and scholarly activity of a pure or practical nature; professional service, both internal (for example, advising faculty members in other departments in regard to aspects of one's specialty) and external (for example, belonging to state and national professional organizations, consulting with community groups and individuals); participation in governance at departmental, college, and university levels in order to attain and preserve an environment and morale which are conducive to the fulfillment of the obligations of the university. The range of faculty interest in, capability in, and commitment to these seven sectors varies greatly.

Although discussions of faculty evaluation frequently revolve around teaching, the faculty is not much more receptive to critical evaluation of other activities than of teaching. Highly critical reviews of research or books and the resulting interchanges between author and critic provide firsthand evidence that affect rather than intellect often predominates on both sides. Advising has seldom been evaluated because the contrasting definitions and expectations of students, faculty members, and administrators provide no common ground for evaluation. It is much like teaching in these respects, but with the additional difficulty that disciplinary expertise, sometimes used as an excuse for poor teaching, does not excuse poor advising.

Acceptance of Evaluation

Faculty members find evaluation acceptable if it leads to satisfaction, to suggestions for improvement, or to reward. Each of these results may be purely personal and internalized or may involve the plaudits of others and tangible recognition or economic gain. An analysis of these considerations provides further insight into faculty priorities and reactions to evaluation.

Research productivity is both objective and tangible. Sending a publication to anyone usually yields a note of thanks and a compliment. Lists of one's publications are long-lived and cumulative and bring additional compliments and recognition such as research grants, fellowships, and invitations for participation in national and international seminars and conferences. Public service takes the professor into social, business, governmental, and industrial scenes, where being the expert is a heady experience productive of numerous impressive anecdotes for recounting upon return to the campus. The accompanying travel, honoraria, and absence from the campus bring envy and respect, as well as financial reward. The recognition is more than local and may yield influential contacts which lead to an enhanced academic or entirely different career. Participation in campus governance brings to the faculty member a sense of involvement and power, contact with administrators, and public recognition. There is also the possibility of advancement to an administrative post. And an inflated sense of importance arises out of busyness and possession of the latest information from the top.

Teaching and advising simply do not offer the same measure of satisfaction and reward. Favorable comments by students have, even to the recipient, nowhere near the same level of prestige as those of colleagues and administrators. The reputation of being an excellent teacher is entirely local and, to some extent, depends upon continuing self-glorification with attendant irritation of associates. Both teaching and advising are student oriented, separating the professor who excels in them from colleagues and, in the extreme, making him or her an academic stranger with no strong attachments to research-oriented departmental associates. Thus the returns or satisfactions from good teaching or advising are less well defined and more intangible than are those of other faculty activities and are less likely to receive the plaudits of peers and superiors. Good teaching and good advising also require continuing striving; there is no closure at any time, and no drawing account is established for the future if performance deteriorates.

Since some teaching is expected of almost every professor, whereas involvement in other activities varies greatly, it is more difficult to achieve distinction as a teacher. The research and publication efforts of an individual are unique to that person. In public service and governance professors also play, at any time, a unique role. These achievements can be praised without invidious comparison with others, but recognition of some faculty members as good teachers inevitably carries the connotation that others are less good. Conceptions of good teaching do vary among professors, and efforts which evoke the praise of students may be viewed as coddling by those professors who are convinced that their mastery of the discipline and high standards inhibit student recognition.

Faculty distrust of the evaluation of teaching is also based in part upon the many variables involved: level and type of students taught, attractiveness of discipline to students, difficulty of courses, class size, differences between required and elective courses, room assignments, educational philosophy and objectives, grading standards, techniques by which teaching is assessed, purposes of the evaluation, and accessibility of the evidence to associates, students, and administrators.

In summary, faculty members view their various activities in relation to their preparation, the effort involved, and the material rewards and prestige which ensue. Research, public service, and participation in governance bring greater recognition and opportunity for advancement than does teaching. Those who establish reputations in these areas are less vulnerable to administrative intervention. Evaluation of teaching promises neither great reward nor prestige and may operate against rather than for one's career. Even designation as an outstanding teacher has limited and passing prestige so that improvement may not be worth the effort.

This discussion reveals clearly why evaluation of teaching is so much discussed. To administrators it appears to constitute one necessary and justifiable response to student and public criticism and demands for accountability. But to faculty members, such evaluation and the accompanying demands for improvement require an extra effort or a reallocation of effort which they do not see as especially beneficial or even possibly productive. Meanwhile, evaluation of a type also goes on with other faculty activities. Research, service, and governance activities bring satisfaction to the individuals and enable administrators to speak effusively of research and service activities and of faculty participation in governance.

But the evaluation of all faculty activities is generally quite limited, sporadic, and inadequate. An adequate evaluation of teaching and student learning, for example, would require a major effort with attendant costs, so the relatively easy and inexpensive alternative of some form of student evaluation is adopted. Whether any actions are taken on the basis of these evaluations, a sop has been thrown to students; and both administrators and faculty can join in asserting that instruction is evaluated at Euphoric State University. Though the furor about evaluation of teaching might lead one to believe that other functions are adequately evaluated, they generally are not. In the following sections of this chapter, each type of activity is discussed, and a framework is developed for evaluation of it.

Purposes of Evaluation of Instruction

The purposes served by evaluating instruction are manifold and depend upon who initiates the evaluation and the audience to whom it is addressed. At the most general level, the stated purposes usually include improvement of teaching; improvement of learning in reference to behavioral objectives; provision of bases for selection, recognition, and reward of good teachers; research contribution to understanding teaching and learning; and assurance to students and the public that teaching is regarded as important.

Some *instructors* delight in teaching and are internally motivated to improve. They desire evidence to demonstrate their effectiveness to others. Other instructors may be motivated by evidence of inadequate teaching to engage in improvement, and here a distinction between threat and proffer of assistance is vital. *Administrators* are more broadly concerned with learning transcending course content. They seek evidence to help in selection, reward, assignment, and termination of faculty members. Resources for the improvement of teaching, curriculum, environment, and facilities can be wisely allocated if evidence on present instructional strengths and weaknesses is available. *Students* (and their advisers) desire information for selecting courses and instructors. Information on course requirements, opportunities for personal involvement, evaluation and grading patterns, and learning objectives can be effectively used in planning a student's program. Evaluation of instruction also demonstrates to students a concern for their welfare. It should, in addition, provide a model of evaluation which students may later emulate. The dissatisfactions of the *general public* with higher education can be, to some extent, mitigated by a well-advertised program of evaluation, which can simultaneously be interpreted as an insistence on quality and as an effort toward accountability. The *researcher* on teaching and learning seeks increased knowledge about teaching and learning in relation to a host of other factors, including environmental factors, teacher traits, curriculum, instructional materials, methods, educational technology, disciplines, and objectives.

Obviously this range of necessary evidence is too extensive to be met by any one method. Instructors, interested in improving teaching competence, need to define the learning expected, the stages of student development, and the means of motivation. They require continuing and detailed information to suggest means of improvement. They are likely to seek insights from their students and generally welcome assistance from learning and evaluation services. Clearly, this evaluation is formative. Instructors have little need for or interest in comparative data on other instructors.

Administrators, faced with a variety of personnel and budgeting decisions, want a brief evaluative summary and usually prefer comparative evidence to guide their decisions. Such information is however often not reliable, valid, or adequate.

The student needs systematic descriptive information on courses and instructor characteristics provided in a summary, comparative fashion in time to facilitate enrollment decisions. The public requires little more than assurance that evaluation is taking place, accompanied perhaps by student comment and occasional recognition of outstanding teachers.

The researcher is seldom satisfied with the evaluation methods used by the preceding audiences. He or she desires more elaborate research designs and control of numerous factors, and seeks generalizations which apply across time, space, and people. The existence, nature, and applicability of such generalizations are not yet demonstrated, and some (including myself) doubt they will emerge. Yet researchers remain optimistic and apparently are convinced that only lack of funding delays a breakthrough.

Approaches to Evaluation of Instruction

Although teaching and instruction are, in common usage, virtually interchangeable, there are possible distinctions. Teaching refers to situations in which teachers and students face or interact with each other. This definition is evident in teacher or course rating forms developed for use by students, for these forms concentrate on the classroom. The instructional role is much broader, including all tasks related to teaching. These tasks extend to selection of text, additional reading, preparation of instructional materials, preparation of bibliography, preparation and grading of tests, interactions with other faculty members teaching the same course or with those in other departments whose majors take the course. Like the tip of an iceberg, classroom teaching is the most visible part of instruction, and concentration solely on that visible portion can result in tragedy. Yet, student evaluation of classroom teaching behavior (and a few closely related factors, such as scholarship and accessibility) is the most prominent and most discussed means of evaluating teaching. Ease of administration to students in classes, the resulting quantity of data quickly processed by electronic equipment, and the pseudoobjectivity of responses, buttressed by much talk about the reliability and validity of the results, yield a false sense that the evaluation is constructive and is contributing to progress.

In reality, there is but one significant reason for evaluating instruction—to improve the quality of learning and increase the percentage of students who attain the important and agreed-upon goals of learning. All else flows out of and is secondary to that central goal.

Reward of good teaching is one way to accomplish this goal. The existence of rewards may motivate some teachers to improve. Those poor teachers who cannot or will not improve should not be rewarded—at least not for teaching—and those who are especially bad should be terminated. Even so, student learning will not thereby be improved unless there is previous agreement on educational objectives and an evaluation program based upon evidence of student accomplishment in respect to those objectives.

Effective evaluation of instruction must be based upon certain principles:

1. Because evaluation is a complex process, no one method by itself is adequate. In fact, overemphasis on one method may do more harm than good. Various facets of the process can be examined by different and appropriate means of assessment: student rating scales; instructor self-appraisal; peer appraisal;

review of tests, syllabuses, and other materials; evaluation of student attainment of objectives; videotapes; and classroom visits.

2. Evaluation must employ the best possible procedures, and it must be an integral part of the teaching/learning process— not simply a distracting add-on which interferes with learning rather than reinforcing it.

3. Evaluation of an individual instructor must be based upon observations and collection of data on well-defined behavior accepted as desirable by both students and teachers.

4. The evaluation procedures must encourage students to recognize and accept personal responsibility for assessing the extent and adequacy of their own learning.

Based on these principles, evaluation processes should take into account a number of criteria.

1. Environmental factors (already discussed in Chapter Eight) condition the character and quality of learning. The physical environment, including heating, lighting, acoustics, seating, and appropriate equipment, should be appraised. The climate of the classroom as determined by mutual respect of students for each other and for their instructor creates ease or dis-ease. The expectations and motivations of students (for which the instructor must assume some obligation) also bear on the effectiveness of any instructional procedure. Students must have confidence in the worth of their classes and must experience success within the classroom to stimulate continuing learning outside the classroom.

2. Instructors must be confident of their own understanding of the topics or problems discussed and must convey this understanding to students without dominating every phase of classroom activity. Instructors must be thoroughly prepared with a definite plan in mind, yet sufficiently flexible to adapt to relevant student needs or questions. Instructors' convictions of the worth of course substance, not only for themselves but for the students, should be evident. They must be convinced and make it evident to students that their worth as teachers depends upon their communication with and impact upon the students. Their concern that the class experience be productive for each

student should be constantly in evidence. They must also identify and eliminate personal mannerisms, speech peculiarities, evidences of bias, and undue sarcasm directed to students; these characteristics annoy students, antagonize them, or divert their attention from course objectives.

3. The obligations of the instructor are interwoven with the content and the instructional methods. Every student permitted to enroll in a course has a legitimate claim upon the attention of the instructor. Students who are unprepared for or who have misunderstood the objectives of a course should be identified and encouraged to withdraw quickly. Such changes can be made only if prerequisite learnings and skills are made clear and if the course objectives, requirements, and standards are specified in the first or second class session. Methods, materials, and assignments should be clearly related to objectives and appropriate to the students enrolled. Recognition of individual differences in backgrounds, interests, and goals should lead to individual adaptations or options which promote motivation and learning.

4. To assist students in organizing their learning, the instructor should schedule occasional reviews and relate new topics both to previous and to forthcoming topics and tasks. Adequate testing or feedback should be planned so that the instructor and each student are mutually informed as to progress. Opportunities should be available for individuals or for the entire group to revert to earlier tasks when this seems necessary for adequate mastery. Tests should obviously involve the stated objectives, and they should be corrected, adequately critiqued, and promptly returned. Even if formal tests are not used, students should be periodically apprised of their progress.

5. The instructor should emphasize the relationships of facts, concepts, principles, methods, and skills to other courses, disciplines, and issues or problems in daily life or society.

These criteria describe one conception of good teaching, though not one acceptable to professors who see their task as that of dispensing knowledge of their disciplines in the purest possible form. Neither will it be acceptable to professors who view their task as primarily that of assisting in the character development of the individual through therapy, introspection, and group interaction. For those who wish only to dispense knowledge of their disciplines, improvement indeed comes primarily through alteration of classroom behavior. The poorly prepared, disorganized, mumbling professor who is scarcely aware of students can improve by overcoming these weaknesses. For those concerned with character development, recording or videotapes may be helpful in analyzing the instructor's role and the group interaction, but the ultimate evidence of success may well be the student appraisal of the benefits of the experience.

Responsibilities of Instructors in Promoting Learning

There is no agreement among faculty members as to what constitutes good teaching. College and university teachers tend to overemphasize the importance of teaching to the point of ignoring learning as an individual accomplishment. In effect, they see learning as what takes place in students as teachers teach. Teachers perform as they prefer, secure in the belief that any serious, intelligent student will learn. No changes in structure, class size, calendar, materials will change the instructional patterns of such teachers. Only when they are willing to turn their attention from themselves and their disciplines to their responsibilities as facilitators of learning can they begin to consider the full range of educational adjustments.

The first responsibility of instruction is to motivate the student. Most students have some motivation for self-improvement, but this motivation seldom extends to every course and requirement. Mathematics is essential for engineering students, but it does not so appear to engineering students taught by a mathematics instructor who has no knowledge of the role of mathematics in engineering and no willingness to acquire such knowledge. A student must usually be shown the relevance of a course to ultimate goals or at least to issues of interest. The student should understand the importance of the objectives of a course and their significance for a career. Unless the student recognizes the relevance of the experience, he or she will do little to effect the desired changes. Instructors who are unable to provide these connections either should undertake to extend their own learning or should be relieved of the responsibility for teaching.

The second obligation of instruction is to guide the student toward the new knowledge, behavior, and capabilities expected. This obligation requires supervision of the student's efforts to acquire these abilities. Laboratory instruction is a good example. The students, perhaps as a group, are shown how to use certain equipment. For some this demonstration will be adequate; others must be observed, helped, and even guided through an operation once or twice. A demonstration of a solution to a mathematical problem can be followed by observation and assistance of student attempts at their seats or at a blackboard. The instructor can aid those having difficulty until they complete the procedure at least once. Programmed materials, computer-assisted instruction, or other techniques can fulfill this obligation. But lectures, reading assignments, and even discussions often fail to provide concrete guidance for students.

The third responsibility of instruction is to provide extensive and meaningful materials and experiences for students. A demonstration or even careful guidance of an individual through a task ensures neither understanding nor a sense of accomplishment or mastery. Whatever is done in the classroom is an introduction, a prelude to the learning which usually results only when students repeatedly engage in a behavior until they understand both what they are doing and why it is worth doing. Educational technology can supply improved and self-correcting materials for this purpose, but these are only crutches to be used until independent performance is acquired. All too much of learning is motivated only by repeated, frustrated, and often futile conjecture as to what the teacher expects or wants. Thus the efforts of students are directed to satisfying what they view as the whims of the instructor rather than to satisfying themselves. And they memorize those portions of what the text or teacher says which seem likely to be demanded. They are not learning how to deal effectively with materials on their own initiative. They learn facts, but not how to appraise or use them. When many students in a course so proceed, the failure of the teacher is apparent.

A fourth responsibility of instruction is to provide the student with satisfaction through a sense of progress. This responsibility requires pointing out to the student both successes and deficiencies, with the attention to deficiencies being directed to the reasons for failure and the adjustments required. Unfortunately, grading practices usually emphasize inadequate performance and record it, allowing no opportunity for improvement and, indeed, discouraging it by insisting that a grade once recorded cannot be altered. Moreover, teachers make it clear that an A (and perhaps a B) is the only creditable grade, with anything less being evidence of poor performance and sloth. Those who criticize grading as interfering with learning are quite right, but the criticism should be directed to grading practices rather than to grades per se. (For an extensive discussion of grades, see Chapter Twelve.) Evaluation for feedback and motivation to improve is an essential component of good teaching. Study and learning materials with built-in evidence of progress are useful, but they cannot replace the personal commendation of an admired teacher. Praise or the regard of others is a potent motivator.

Moreover, tasks that are sufficiently complex to demonstrate progress are seldom completed perfectly upon first effort. They require repeated comment and critical review. Some psychologists propose that learning tasks be divided into such small steps that the learner succeeds at each step. I am convinced that this is both impossible and undesirable. An indispensable aspect of learning is the recognition and admission of error, combined with the ability to profit from error. Failure must come to be regarded as a challenge, not as a disabling and uncorrectable event which impedes further progress. And, if so regarded, failure is no more than evaluation preliminary to a new effort. The professor who treats failure otherwise is not teaching but rewarding those who are capable of progressing without assistance.

The fifth responsibility of instruction is to organize learning experiences so that their sequential, cumulative aspect is apparent to the student. This responsibility requires that current learning be seen by the student as related to past and future learning. The learning of isolated facts or skills must be reinforced by activities and discussions which demonstrate how they fit together. No tennis instructor would get sustained endeavor by students if he or she required, for weeks or months, the continued practice of serves and strokes without putting these together into a game. Playing tennis requires putting serves and strokes together and provides the first evidence that the individual is capable of so doing. Repetitive practice of particular skills bores the student, and loss of incentive interferes with progress. Course work must be organized to provide both novelty and increasing complexity in order to maintain interest. General education requirements, as compared with professional or major sequences, pose special problems for teachers. The major or professional ordinarily has a sense of how a course fits long-term goals, whereas single electives or general education courses take on meaning only if they relate to issues or problems of general interest or if they develop abilities (communication skills, sensitivity to values, understanding of current events) which are readily seen by students as having pervasive significance. The organization of courses, course sequences, and curriculum is a vital aspect of good teaching because such activity fosters the progress of individuals toward educational objectives of long-term significance.

The sixth obligation of instruction is to assist students in defining acceptable standards of performance and to provide them with means for judging performance in relation to these standards. This obligation requires that students understand and accept the rationale for these standards. If the individual is to acquire an incentive for continued learning and increased mastery, the standards must be more fundamental than those on which classroom tests and grades or normed or standardized tests are based. Indeed, norms are irrelevant or even inimical to the attainment by each individual of a defined level of mastery. Individuals cannot plan their own learning until they have acquired standards and techniques for evaluating their efforts.

A final responsibility of instruction is to encourage each student to expect and seek for relationships among courses and life experiences external to courses. Each educational experience must promote progress toward capabilities which characterize the college-educated individual. The student alone can seldom find these relationships and is unlikely to do so or to cultivate the habit of doing so unless the instructor encourages it.

This statement of responsibilities, in various ways, reiterates the point that improvement in the quality and impact of educational experiences requires an overt acknowledgment by the instructor that he or she is not simply an expert dispenser of organized knowledge in a discipline but, rather, the planner and evaluator of part of an educational process which, if thoughtfully directed and adapted to individuals, assists them in becoming educated individuals. In this context, the various facilitating devices of calendar, methodology, special materials can take on profound educational significance. Otherwise, they amount to little more than fiddling with inconsequentials while the student burns without being enlightened.

Student Evaluation

What aspect of faculty performance should students evaluate? Faculty members usually wish the items in any evaluation form to be appropriate or even specific to the discipline, the content of the course, and their personal conception of the teaching act. Student reactions based on the broad behavioral objectives of a liberal education are generally rejected by the faculty and are generally meaningless unless these objectives have been highlighted. Likewise, many faculty members reject the idea that students can evaluate the quality and fairness of an examination or the justification of specific course requirements. Administrators, accustomed to hearing students complain about unreasonable assignments, poor examinations, inability to hear the professor, professorial absenteeism, and the like, generally take a broader view than does the faculty of what might be evaluated by students.

Students themselves generally have a rather narrow conception. They are concerned that professors express themselves clearly, that their statements be audible, that their assignments be clear and not too demanding, that their examinations be directly related to classroom coverage, and that they require neither unreasonable memorization nor extensive thought. Students like clarification of objectives, but are readily satisfied with a statement of the content to be covered and the requirements to be met—examinations, papers, and the like. They are seldom encouraged to think about a course or the instruction as relevant to their personal interests or their other courses. They are not urged to view the course as a contribution to a liberal or general education. Students do not expect that, as a result of a particular course, they will be increasingly capable of independent effort in the field.

In short, we impose such limits on what students evaluate that the student sees each course and each instructor in isolation rather than as a part of a much broader and more significant cumulative educational experience. Generally, students are asked to evaluate petty details which have little significance to them and often no significance to the instructor who might wish to use student reactions to improve teaching. For example, when students in large numbers assert that "objectives are not clear" instructors obtain little assistance in improving the situation. When many students say that "not much was gained by taking this course," most instructors assume that this response is characteristic of students who get low grades (although it may as well be the view of those who get A's). It is singularly unhelpful to learn that a group of students believes an instructor is (or is not) friendly; good teachers are not necessarily overly friendly to students. When students indicate that much outside reading is required, one can scarcely judge whether this is a commendation or a criticism. Students are frequently asked to respond to such an item as "the laboratory was a worthwhile experience." Much of the laboratory experience in freshman science courses is a waste of time and money (although this need not be the case); it typically does not provide any vision of what scientific experimentation is all about. But most students lack the experience to reach this judgment, and those who do would hesitate to record it in the face of the teacher's commitment to the laboratory.

Students are capable of evaluating much more than we permit. On the whole, they evaluate what we let them evaluate, and faculty members tend to eliminate from student evaluations any aspects that might require a change in their conception of teaching.

In some institutions, students carry out their own teacher evaluation, motivated largely by two considerations: (1) they have had (or have heard of) some unfortunate experiences, and they want to record dissatisfaction and have it recognized; (2) they hope by this means to warn other students to avoid certain courses or instructors. Some students would also like a say in promotions, tenure decisions, and possibly salary increases or other forms of recognition to faculty members. Students hope that, by the publication of reports which reveal the poor quality of teaching, professors, through the reward system, will be forced to improve or to leave.

The impact of student-conducted evaluation and reporting is unknown but is probably minimal. Some statements in these published reports, particularly about young faculty members or teaching assistants, are distressing. Faculty members are antagonized by them, although, on the whole, students tend to be charitable in their criticisms. The sheer inexperience of students in evaluation and their lack of understanding and lack of sensitivity as exhibited by their selection and editing of comments cast doubts on the worth of such enterprises. Evaluation of teaching is a complex and difficult task. Students are not likely to carry off effectively what faculty and administrators have thus far failed to accomplish.

Without relying on student- or institution-initiated surveys, any instructor can still learn much about teaching by careful observation of students, by interviews with individuals, and by classroom discussions. Some professors who reject checklists and other objective formats are willing to use open-ended essay responses to questions or to a suggested list of course factors or characteristics. The critical-incident approach, which calls for identification and comment on the best and the worst aspects of a course, can be useful in revealing both common and individual student perceptions.

Students are reluctant to express some concerns directly to the instructor, but this reluctance in itself is a judgment of great significance. Instructors who cannot convince students of their ability to separate their evaluation of student performance from student evaluation of the course or of the teaching have thereby revealed a major deficiency. Until and unless such instructors can tolerate frank discussion and criticism, they are unlikely to improve.

Yet students still may be unwilling to express their most critical concerns directly to an instructor. They may be even less willing to do so to department chairmen, the instructors' colleagues, or deans. An outside interviewer, evaluator, or observer can bring out views not readily expressed and can call to the instructor's attention characteristics that are not readily apparent. Personal experiences in classroom observation have convinced me that few professors can appraise the quality of a discussion or are even aware, for example, that, in what passes for a discussion, they may talk for forty to forty-five minutes out of fifty, as verified by use of a stopwatch.

I have visited campuses in which students are encouraged to write letters, fill out forms, visit the dean, or in other ways present their complaints (or commendations) about teachers. The sampling in these cases may be of concern to some, and the motivation of those using this approach may be suspect. But the extent to which such letters are written and the nature of the complaints registered at least indicate student involvement beyond the quiescent response to a form passed out in the classroom.

Another approach to evaluation by students is the investigation of changes in student behavior outside the class and in following years. Some instructors, in an overt effort to encourage such transfer, encourage questions or discussions which reach into other disciplines or current problems and events. Others view this attempt as irrelevant and disruptive, perhaps without realizing the narrow conception of learning to which they thereby subscribe.

Some years ago I found on a college campus several groups of students in their senior year who were meeting biweekly to talk about developments in the natural sciences. These sessions had started spontaneously in the freshman year as a result of a general education core course required of all students. The course dealt in part with current developments in the sciences, and students were made aware of and led to read magazines reporting on research and its implications. After completing the course, students organized spontaneously to continue reading and discussing. Several of these groups were continuing three years later. I can think of no more potent evidence of the effectiveness of a professor than that his or her students continue an activity that was originally part of a freshman requirement. If from taking a course an individual does not acquire some ideas and some techniques and insights for continuing activity in that area, and some motivation and ability to do so, he or she has not acquired anything of significance. The failure to deal with these broad outcomes is one of the gravest weaknesses of the usual practices in student evaluation, and that failure perhaps reveals that neither student nor teacher expects such results.

Some institutions have undertaken alumni evaluation of teaching. This approach has a serious weakness: Within a few years of leaving college students have had such a variety of experiences that their recollection of specific instructors and courses is unlikely to be accurate. Furthermore, one tends in retrospect to see one's experiences through rose-colored glasses and perhaps to become charitable toward professorial weaknesses simply because of one's increased awareness that people generally perform less effectively than expected. Furthermore, the showman rather than the truly excellent teacher may be remembered.

The use of student rating scales is frequently accompanied by the preparation of instructor norms. This emphasis greatly limits the nature of the items in the scale and forces students to react to a series of statements selected to apply across courses. Inevitably, such statements are ambiguous to some respondents and inapplicable in some courses. Moreover, the instructor rating low on such norms is naturally inclined to criticize the instrument and the procedure rather than to improve. A high rating denies the need for improvement. In an era in which there is great interest in and some movement toward criterion-referenced testing and mastery testing for students, should not similar consideration be extended to evaluating teaching? Do we want to rate teachers or help them improve? If the latter, norms are not only irrelevant, they may be harmful.

Other aspects of student performance are relevant to the evaluation of teaching. The extent to which students elect a course or a particular faculty member, for example, surely indicates the worth of that experience. If common examinations of any kind are used, either for a course or a group of courses taught by the same individual, the examination performance of the students is certainly an evaluation of the teaching, although one must hasten to add that performance has to be weighted by the nature of the examination. I should not necessarily regard as an excellent teacher a professor whose students all made high grades on a highly factual examination, although some faculty members would be satisfied with that evidence.

If students of one instructor do better than those of another on a common examination (whether locally constructed or standardized), the conclusion that the higher performing group received better instruction is not necessarily valid for many reasons. One reason is that this experiment would require either careful matching of students in ability and preparation or adjustment for possible differences. Times and places of class meeting can also affect performance. Furthermore, many persons argue that some, perhaps the most important, aspects of teaching are ignored or inadequately sampled by examinations. The instructor who drives students unreasonably hard may report high scores on an examination but cause students to avoid the discipline thereafter. Yet it would be inappropriate to regard attitudinal and value outcomes as more important than cognitive goals. Satisfaction and substance must both be achieved in a coordinate manner.

Peer Ratings and Self-Evaluation

There have been a few studies of peer ratings of college teachers, but the practice has not been used either with the care or to the extent required to evaluate it. Faculty members commonly have some views about the teaching competence of their associates in the same department, but seldom are these views based on direct observation. Rather, casual conversations, student remarks, student performance in later courses, research, and colloquium presentations are the bases for the appraisal. Classroom visiting by peers is seldom practiced. Visits by department chairmen and deans add a somewhat threatening element in that these people can and must make decisions affecting the teacher's career. Such visits imply that the teacher is under rigorous review. Both peer and administrative visits are time-consuming; an isolated observation is essentially a wasted effort, for the presence of an outsider can so disrupt the usual classroom tempo as to destroy validity. Moreover, peers and administrators are not necessarily either good teachers or competent observers and critics of teaching.

If such visits are used, they should be regular. Scheduling, behavior of the visitor, items to be included in observations, and subsequent discussion should be known in advance. Observers who compulsively intervene to demonstrate their own superiority make a travesty of such visits. Moreover, reasonable correspondence in educational philosophies is desirable. Professors who pride themselves on scholarly, meticulously planned and timed formal lectures are not appropriate observers for a teacher who seeks an informal, student-participatory classroom.

Visitation among colleagues and subsequent discussion in staff meeting of classroom procedures and teaching techniques can be used effectively in involving a total department in review of its teaching practices. External consultants should also be brought in to raise departmental sights above traditional practices.

An effective device which instructors can use to evaluate their own performance is audiotape or videotape recordings. Many campuses now provide one or more classrooms so equipped that audiotapes or videotapes of complete class sessions can be made. Replay of these tapes by the teacher is both a painful and an illuminating experience; it clearly points up weaknesses in delivery, in expression, in emphasis, and in attention to students—all of which can be improved. A friendly critic with experience in study and improvement of instruction can add to the teacher's own analysis. The students, too, can add insights and reflect on their own roles if the instructor has the courage to exhibit all or parts of the recordings to them and undergo their critical scrutiny. In using tapes, there is a tendency to concentrate on what the teacher says and does. But a videotape of students in class or of the interaction between students and teacher is much more revealing of classroom dynamics and input than a videotape focused solely on the instructor.

Evaluating Instruction in a Broad Context

Ericksen and Kulik (1974, p. 1) comment: "Judging the quality of instruction is a far too complicated process to be based solely on an administrator's personal assessment or on the consensus judgment of peers or on the filling out of rating forms by students or on an examination of the course syllabus, tests, and other instructional materials prepared by the teacher. Each of these is useful, but none is sufficient. Teaching is an omnibus profession, but each teacher is an idiosyncratic person, and many yardsticks are needed to measure competence in this role. Care must be taken to establish the criteria appropriate for each instructional setting and to judge the teacher within this context."

Attempts to evaluate teaching by focusing upon the classroom behavior of the teacher tend likewise to focus upon single courses. Any one course can scarcely have sufficient effect upon students to materially and permanently change attitudes, values, or thought processes. A single course offered for three credits for a semester affords no more than forty-five hours of student-faculty contact—20 percent or less of a full semester load, and 2.5 percent or less of the degree requirement. On the basis of two hours of preparation outside class for each hour in class, a three-credit course requires nine hours per week, which is less than 6 percent of the student's time. Or, by relating that three-credit course to the student's total prior life, we can readily determine that the course is less than one-tenth of one percent of that total. It will be a rare course and a rare professor indeed that will greatly affect the attitudes, values, creativity, and critical thinking of students. Research on and evaluation of significant learning must surely be based upon longer time spans than a quarter, a course, or a few contacts with a teacher. Even if we believe that revival meetings lasting perhaps a few hours cause permanent conversions, a course is not a revival meeting.

Research on Teaching

Thus far, I have said little about research on teaching. This research is extensive, and attempts to summarize the implications are numerous. Unfortunately, the results have little to say to one undertaking the improvement of teaching. A brief venture into the literature indicates why this is so. Peters (1974) remarks that some researchers hope to improve teaching by evaluation, by alteration and improvement of teaching methods, or by changing educational programs. Other researchers report that teachers differ significantly in many ways—and that what a faculty member teaches apparently has a bearing on how he or she teaches. Other researchers point to vast differences among teachers in acceptable learning objectives, varying from sole emphasis on learning facts to demands for facility in analysis and application of concepts and principles, for creativity or originality, and for ability in problem solving.

There is research evidence to support the following statements: (1) Teaching effectiveness and scholarly publication records are unrelated to each other. (2) Ratings of a teacher by college administrators are virtually interchangeable with ratings by the teacher's colleagues. (3) Ratings by faculty colleagues agree fairly well with student ratings. (4) There is negligible correlation between self-evaluations and evaluations by administrators and students (Blackburn and Clark, 1975). (5) Ratings by students, peers, or administrators are not good measures of teaching ability because they are contaminated with inference, do not assess learner growth, and are collected in highly variable, nonuniform situations (McNeil and Popham, 1973). (6) There is little evidence that student ratings are effective aids for the improvement of teaching. (7) Other things being equal, small classes are probably more effective than large, discussions more than lectures, and student-centered discussions than instructor-centered discussions in promoting retention, application, problem solving, attitude change, and motivation for further study. (8) There is little evidence that performance measures (course examinations) are useful as indices of teacher effectiveness (Peters, 1974).

As this sample of research-based conclusions indicates, the present state of information about teaching methods, cognitive styles of learning, and educational objectives is something of a morass of contradictions, overgeneralizations, and basic disagreements. But such problems are of primary concern to the researcher. Most professors are unaware of and indifferent to the findings. If it be true that anxious, sensitive, impulsive, and socially inclined students make optimal progress by nondirective methods (as some research suggests), lecture-oriented professors are unlikely to change their teaching styles. If it be true that small classes and student-centered discussions are educationally more potent for some students than for others, small classes are a luxury not to be offered to any significant number of freshmen or sophomores in most universities. Small classes, in any case, are still largely professor dominated and lecture oriented. Incidentally, if one hypothesizes that those teachers who effectively use small classes for attainment of objectives other than knowledge do so because of their concern for such objectives, whereas those who lecture ignore them, the research findings supporting the advantages of small classes become meaningless. It is not the size of the class, but what happens in the class that counts. In brief, much of the research on class size is unrelated to the reality of costs, of lecture traditions, or of the educational objectives accepted by most professors. Something much more fundamental than such research findings or student opinions is required to alter existing patterns.

Careful analysis of some of the research which suggests that administrative, peer, and student evaluation of teaching agree indicates that researchers emphasize inadequate agreement based on covering a full range of teaching capabilities. The typical test given to a candidate for a teaching position—preparing and delivering a lecture—suggests that scholarly competence and fluency may well be the major factors considered by administrators and peers. These characteristics are also prominent in student ratings, which suggests some agreement in these approaches. It is of some interest that self-ratings by teachers and student ratings do not always agree. Centra (1973b) reports that usually only when this discrepancy occurs do student ratings effect change.

But the basic trouble with all these appraisals, as McNeil and Popham (1973), as well as many others, point out, is that they have nothing to do with learner growth or with the nature of the objectives sought. Even if instructors modify their behavior to improve their ratings, they might not improve their teaching.

Numerous researchers or synthesizers of research have attempted to define individual cognitive styles and to suggest that certain patterns of teaching may be more appropriate for one learning style than for another. The following generalizations are used to support this view: (1) Some students are predisposed to learn facts; others, to apply and synthesize facts. (2) The student who is independent, flexible, or has a high achievement level likes and achieves well in classes which give opportunity for self-direction. (3) Students and professors inclined toward certain disciplines prefer certain methods and appear to learn more effectively by them than do students and professors in other disciplines. (Mathematics and the sciences are commonly contrasted with the social sciences and humanities.)

There may be validity in the studies which report distinctive cognitive styles, but there is still a question as to how far such findings should be used in adapting courses or classes to the preferred learning style of students. Several questions are pertinent. Are these learning styles artifacts of past experiences or are they personal preferences? Are they truly indicative of basic differences in the learning capabilities of students? If students have difficulty with typical instructional patterns in certain disciplines, should they be excused from any requirements in those fields? Or, alternatively, should mathematics and physics, for example, be offered in small, student-centered discussion classes for those who have difficulty with lectures and textbooks?

Is a college education an experience in learning by the method easiest for each individual, or is it primarily an experience which develops the broadest possible learning capabilities? If the latter, can we justify narrowing the learning experiences to a single type? Too much of the discussion of research on cognitive styles focuses on existing deficiencies in learning, whereas the ultimate aim should be to broaden the individual's capabilities to include all approaches to mastery and use of learning.

Evaluation of Nonteaching Aspects of Instruction

The *planning of instruction* takes many forms. Formulating objectives for a course, relating them to the broad objectives of the total educational program, and communicating them to students are important instructional functions. Another significant function is the selection of educational experiences which promote student achievement of the stated objectives. The selection of textbooks, readings, laboratory activities, classroom activities, methods of presentation, appropriate assignments and tests should not be based on content or on subject matter alone. The professor should consider what each activity requires and how it contributes to course objectives. Most professors are more concerned with their own activities than with those of the students, with the result that their courses are seldom organized in relation to student interests, capabilities, and learning patterns. Conscious variation of learning patterns from day to day emphasizing such principles as the following helps. Learning experiences may move from the simple to the complex or the reverse. In some circumstances, it is preferable to introduce a general idea first and then talk about specifics. In others, it is better to start with specifics and let the students construct their own generalizations.

Another major element in good teaching is the *evaluation of student progress*. The examinations given by instructors are the best evidence for judging the effectiveness of their instruction as they perceive it. The objectives implicit in testing practices determine student learning much more effectively than the objectives stated to impress colleagues.

Evaluation plays many roles in teaching but an even more important role in learning. Ultimately, students must assume responsibility for evaluating and improving their own activities. If every aspect of student performance is graded, self-evaluation is discouraged; students should instead be encouraged to view evaluation as a means of improving their performance. Students should not be evaluated in reference to some instructor objectives. If an instructor's objective is to arouse student interest in the discipline, he or she expresses a reasonable hope but has no right to fail the student who performs well but dislikes the field and the course and says so. The evaluation of a course or an instructor may be based on overall student interest, but the individual student who is not interested should not be downgraded.

The final and perhaps least significant role of evaluation is determining a grade for a student. The ideal—total elimination of grades—is possible in only a few small, experimental institutions. Grading evaluates only a limited number of objectives, but it should be done as honestly and fairly as possible, and the student must recognize that grades cannot cover some of the most important outcomes of education. Grading and related evaluation problems are extensively discussed in Chapters Ten, Eleven, and Twelve.

Good classroom teaching depends also upon *effective communication*. The instructor's use of the English language should be fluent and exemplary. Incomplete or poorly constructed sentences, mispronounced words, and misused words should not be tolerated in any college classroom, and the teacher who fails to improve in this respect should be released. Too many colleges and universities employ foreign-born and foreign-educated faculty members and graduate teaching assistants whose mastery of English is extremely rudimentary.

Good classroom teaching also requires the ability to give clear direction to students for study and performance. Professors must specify in detail what they expect. Some students demand more specificity in instruction than is consistent with

the goal of making them responsible for their own learning, but
the teacher should explain the inconsistency rather than using it
as an excuse for vagueness and ambiguity in assignments.

Effective communication is facilitated by careful assessment of student ability, interest, and background. Teachers
should specify the background they expect and should verify
that the students possess it. Some rapport with students is
thereby established for effective communication.

Clear and repeated interpretation of course objectives,
summarization of major points, well-structured presentations,
encouragement of discussion and criticism are vital to communication. And underlying all is a concern for and sensitivity to the
student audience and the responsibility of advancing the education of each individual.

Evaluation of Noninstructional Activities

Faculty *advising* receives far less attention than instruction, but is generally even less effective. Graduate students in
major universities complain that advisers are unavailable or have
so many appointments and research demands that the student is
dealt with brusquely. Only when graduate students are doing
research that requires close contact with their major professors
do they have opportunities for informal contacts and discussions of problems, courses, and careers. Undergraduates suffer
even more because few faculty members have a unified conception of undergraduate education or of the needs and objectives
of undergraduate students. Faculty members' perceptions are
directed by their own commitment to a discipline and a department and are limited by their lack of familiarity with educational opportunities outside their disciplines. The proliferation
of courses within disciplines also impedes understanding of their
structure and educational significance, as I point out in Chapter
Thirteen. Many institutions still assert, by their requirement
that the adviser be from the student's major field, that the
undergraduate major is the most significant part of the program,
although the major may account for only a fourth or a third of
the total credits. In fact, the problems of the undergraduate stu-

dent relate less to the major than to the choice of major and the selection of other courses which satisfy general education or distribution requirements and cultivate other interests.

Thus, faculty advisers should regard students not as department majors but as individuals whose programs should be adapted to their particular needs, aspirations, and interests. Advisers should acquire adequate up-to-date knowledge of the university, its course offerings, and regulations so that they can provide accurate and useful information. Advisers should also know enough about vocational prospects in relation to various programs to provide advice and direction in seeking further information. They ought also to acquire knowledge about the learning process so that helpful suggestions can be given about study habits and the selection of courses, teachers, and experiences in relation to student strengths and weaknesses.

If faculty members are to accept advising as an important function, they must have time to prepare for it and to do it, and they must be rewarded for it. Certainly, academic advising is not a task to be required of every faculty member. If faculty advisers are not interested in advising or feel that their time is too valuable to be allotted to this activity, the student suffers. Advising could be improved if a special corps of advisers was carefully selected, trained for the task, and given sufficient time, responsibility, and freedom from regulations to plan with each student a program unhampered by self-serving departmental and college policies.

Whatever the pattern of advising selected, the following criteria should be utilized in evaluating its effectiveness: Are students satisfied with advising, including help received with course selection in reference to a vocation? Are degree requirements being systematically met without loss of time? Do placement officers think student programs are adequate for job placement? Are individual adaptations—including enrollment in interdisciplinary programs, waiver of requirements, and variation in program when justified by sound educational principles —allowed? How frequently do advisers refer students to other appropriate services, such as personal and vocational counseling, psychiatric counseling, and study habits or learning centers? Are advisers satisfied with their efforts and are they appropriately recognized and rewarded? These criteria are quite different from those which have frequently been used, such as whether requirements have been fulfilled, proper sequences have been followed, and marginal performance has been monitored.

The meaning of research is often restricted to the pursuit of new knowledge and to the publication of works which extend the frontiers of knowledge. Not all faculty members engage in such research nor should they. But evidence of *continuing scholarship* is essential for all in order to maintain alertness and to ensure that the implications of increasing knowledge for revision of undergraduate offerings are explored. Much of this study can be done informally through reading books and journals, but fellowship programs, institutes, workshops, and sabbatical leaves provide structured opportunities for increasing one's knowledge of the discipline, instructional and evaluation techniques, course development, use of educational technology, related fields (important for planning problems courses or interdisciplinary efforts), and computer utilization (which is becoming important in many disciplines). Scholarship can, to a considerable extent, be evaluated by how often an individual uses these opportunities. It can also be assessed by examining the textbooks and materials used and the recency of items listed in course bibliographies. It is readily appraised in talks with colleagues. And, to a considerable extent, it is evident in the enthusiasm of the instructor and in his or her allusions or examples in the classroom. In teaching, scholarship is evident in one's knowledge of the literature and research in the field and one's analytic, synthesizing, and evaluative ability in its use; awareness of views other than one's own; familiarity with facts and concepts from related fields; awareness of the implications of various views; ability to discuss recent developments and theories in one's field; ability to apply knowledge in one's field to other fields and to personal and social problems.

At least four purposes guide *research* and other creative and scholarly efforts in colleges and universities. First, faculty research has as a purpose the enhancement of teaching programs. In this sense, research must contribute to the accomplishment of objectives of instructional programs. Several more or less generally accepted assumptions provide the basis for this fundamental purpose of research: faculty research creates an environment of inquiry which is conducive to learning; students learn by participating in research; research activities provide stimulation to faculty members, and their enthusiasm carries over into classroom teaching; and research produces knowledge to be taught.

Second, faculty research may be directed to the improvement of the curriculum and to the improvement of teaching and learning. Such research, in methodology and purpose, takes the professor somewhat outside the discipline. This purpose has relatively lower prestige than the other three purposes.

A third purpose of research is the production of knowledge which enhances or expands the basic disciplines. While the production of knowledge through research is carried on elsewhere than in colleges and universities, a major portion of this responsibility has been assigned to and accepted by higher education in our society. Through funding of research in colleges and universities, the federal government has been principally responsible for this development and for the fact that, at some institutions, research has higher priority than instruction.

Fourth, some research efforts in colleges and universities have the specific purpose of solving industrial, community, and social problems; these efforts are tied to the external service function of the institution. The agricultural experiment stations of the land-grant universities are illustrations; in them research is directed toward the solution of specific problems more than toward the production of knowledge per se. Colleges of education provide staff to conduct school system surveys to solve local educational problems. In recent years, colleges and universities have assisted, through such mission-oriented research, in solving problems created by urbanization and by environmental pollution.

No graduate program can be regarded as acceptable unless the faculty engages in extensive research or scholarly activity. A master's program may not require a thesis of the student and it may not require research in depth on the part of faculty members; even so, faculty members would be ill-prepared were they not engaged in scholarly activity which keeps them in the forefront of the thinking in their fields. To some extent, research is also requisite for faculty members who teach in undergraduate programs. While overinvolvement has its obvious difficulties, the faculty member who is not involved in scholarly activity is shortly outdated, and several generations of students may suffer as a result. Direction of independent study also requires that the faculty member be capable of independent scholarship.

It is often assumed that the appraisal of research output is simpler than the appraisal of teaching. There is little to justify this view. One can note the amounts of staff time assigned to research (input). One can look at the number of publications produced (quantity of output). To a limited extent, the journals in which articles are published suggest the quality. But this evidence does not indicate the extent to which that research is related to instructional activities of the faculty member. Research which is done primarily to develop a list of publications or to satisfy idiosyncratic interests of a faculty member may contribute little to knowledge and even less to the quality of instruction. At the undergraduate level, the impact of research on teaching can be favorable or unfavorable, depending on the degree of immersion of faculty members in research and on the extent of their interest in undergraduate teaching. Undergraduates can and do get a thrill out of contact with a productive scholar who is able to interpret his or her research with enthusiasm and clarity.

There have been relatively few successful attempts to demonstrate the economic value of research. But, in much of this research, the gains transcend any dollar evaluation. A new drug or antibiotic resulting from medical research may reduce the discomfort of many individuals or save many lives. A new insecticide may increase productivity or successfully keep mosquitoes from bothering people. Thus a product may have significant impact which transcends economic benefits. It may also have devastating environmental impacts not immediately realized.

As with instruction, observers of research activity can

make judgments about how well it is organized and designed and how effectively it is administered. The adequacy of the equipment and the extent and effectiveness of its use reflect not only the availability of resources to purchase equipment, but also the amount of care exercised in planning research. In some ways, the research process can be evaluated by the quality and the extent of the support services provided. A chemistry department without a glass-blowing specialist has limited capacity for research. Special facilities are required for the care of animals used in research programs. Lack of separate research laboratories for various types of research does not necessarily mean that quality research is not being done, but it does suggest that whatever is being accomplished is being done under serious handicaps and that the research activities engaged in are severely limited by the inadequate physical facilities.

In assessing the research productivity of an individual faculty member, the following criteria are appropriate:

1. To what extent does the individual engage in each of the four types of research: directly related to both discipline and courses, educational, pure, applied?

2. How important is each type, and to what extent do departmental appraisals ignore or downgrade educational research and research directly related to both discipline and courses?

3. How effective is the individual with graduate students and independent study students, and how original is the work done by these students?

4. What is the quality of the journals in which articles are published?

5. Has the individual published scholarly reviews of articles and books?

6. How do both local and national figures in the same general field assess the individual's research?

7. What is the chronology or spread of research and publication (increasing, decreasing, recent)?

8. Can the individual attract funds, graduate students, postdoctoral students?

Professional activity includes participation in professional organizations and dissemination of the results of scholarship to the profession and the community through publications, speeches, and consultations. Participation in professional associations does not require research productivity, but election to an office or appointment to a major committee usually does require previous appearances on programs and panels. Faculty members require little encouragement to engage themselves with their professional associations, especially if travel expenses are provided by the institution. Consultation is also a desired role, particularly when sizable honorariums are available. Reimbursed consultation requires monitoring and limitation since it amounts to a second job and detracts from university obligations. In some fields, however, research findings have direct relevance to the problems of communities, government, business, and industry so that professional activity and responsibility overlap with the external service role of the university.

Internal service programs support the achievement of the basic purposes of instruction, research, and external service, and the contributions of each supportive program can be evaluated on this basis. Faculty members may be in charge of these programs, may occasionally make significant contributions to these areas, or may serve on committees which deal with these functions. The number and variety of types of support programs prohibit a thorough treatment of them here, but brief references to a few reveal how their objectives interact with the primary purposes of the institution.

Educational service programs provide direct support to the primary programs. The library, in keeping its holdings properly cataloged and shelved, contributes to learning, research, and external services. Related educational service programs with similar purposes and objectives include audiovisual and computer services. Student service programs provide conditions and activities which contribute to an environment conducive to learning. Activities have unique purposes related to student development; the accomplishment of each activity can be evaluated on the basis of its special purposes. Admissions and registration services are also facilitative. Their purposes are perhaps best accomplished when the activities are carried out with maximum convenience and satisfaction to the student.

The list of internal service functions could be extended to include general administration, financial affairs, development, operation and maintenance of the physical plant, and other processes and operations. All have purposes involving the instruction of students, the conduct of research, or the extension of the expertise of the institution to the public, but recurrent review and evaluation are required to remind these offices and operations of that service role.

Faculty members also frequently provide services to other faculty members, students, and administrators. Individuals with competence in statistics, in the planning and conduct of research involving computers, in research design, in language, in evaluation, and in test construction may be extensively used by their associates and thereby make a research contribution which is not always formally acknowledged by the researchers themselves. Members of professional school faculties are frequently sought for advice on university or personal problems by their colleagues. These services should be recognized in making promotions, salary increases, and service awards. An evaluation of a faculty member in this area should undertake to determine the extent of such effort and the overall importance of that contribution to the university.

The *external service* of faculty members includes involvement with cooperative extension; continuing education; and institutes, centers, or other units which carry on consultation and research with various groups and organizations outside the university. Specifically, external services include off-campus credit and noncredit courses, on-campus noncredit courses (usually in the evening), workshops and conference sessions, and research or consultation on a variety of social and community problems. (The usual attitude toward external service programs is that they should be self-supporting, although, in fact, the salaries, facilities, and other support for most of these programs are provided through the same funds that support on-campus activity.)

College and university public service programs, which, in general, carry the expertise and competence of the college or university to the public, are guided by purposes and objectives, and the accomplishments of these programs may be evaluated in reference to them. There are at least three kinds of public service programs and associated purposes.

The first type is national missions. Land-grant universities have been assigned the cooperative-extension function by law. Various federal departments experimenting with adaptation of this agricultural model to other areas of national concern have involved higher education in these efforts; industrial-extension programs, for example, apply the agricultural model to problems of business and industry. Title I of the Higher Education Act of 1965 is directed toward establishing community services and solving urban problems with college and university involvement. Additional legislation is almost certain to expand the range of extension programs related to national life.

A second type of public service program comprises courses, workshops, seminars, and other instructional experiences for professionals and other adults. The purposes of continuing education are similar to those of traditional instruction except for the acquisition of academic credits and degrees. Regular college courses offered for academic credit away from the college campus, as in evening programs, share certain of the purposes of continuing education, but they are perhaps better viewed as extensions of the degree-granting function of instruction to special populations of part-time students.

A third type of public service program is assistance to community groups. Appropriate discipline-based knowledge can be selected and organized after analysis of the specific problems of such groups.

The evaluation of an external service program could be made quite simply by determining whether it accomplishes its intent; however, the objectives of many of these programs are quite unclear. Workshops and conferences usually originate in response to a request from an external organization. The substance of these sessions is often ill-defined, and behavioral objectives are often totally neglected. Therefore, such conferences and workshops are evaluated largely through the number of conferences held, number of people in attendance, and relatively crude indices of satisfaction on the part of those who attend. Success tends to be measured by growing demand rather than by product evaluation. However, such process evaluation does have some significance. If activities are well organized, if the programs move along efficiently, if people find the content of sufficient interest to merit remaining in the sessions, and if, on the whole, those who attend are satisfied and even excited with the experience, the programs are clearly not failures. Noncredit course offerings can also be evaluated on the basis of process evaluation. The facts that people come, pay their fees, continue to attend, and express satisfaction seem to be evaluation enough for those charged with operating public service programs. Yet a deeper evaluation is required, for there may be alternative programs with greater benefits.

The professor should be willing to participate in public service, with or without pay. The professor gains insight from the experience, the public benefits, and instruction becomes increasingly relevant. Public service is a professional responsibility; time should be assigned to it, and the service should be evaluated. It is at times difficult for professors to distinguish between personal participation as an individual and participation as a representative of the university. One conflict in land-grant institutions is among faculty members who engage in public service as a part of their job, those who do so in addition to their job but with pay, and those who spend much time away from the campus for extra compensation. Some institutions ignore excessive absence, its impact on students, and the imposition of an extra, unjust burden on other members of the faculty. Clarification of this public service role is especially important in institutions that recommend or require off-campus service experiences for students. Faculty members cannot effectively supervise or integrate such experiences if they are campus-bound.

When the efforts of individual faculty members are being assessed, external services are sometimes ignored or assigned an inferior role unless the individual is primarily employed for that task. Certainly the mere extent of involvement is not an adequate evaluation, although it suggests whether detailed assessment is required. Such data as number of persons attracted to the programs, requests for an individual's services in developing similar programs elsewhere, evaluation reports of those involved, comments by agencies or firms which request the services, grants or contracts for extension or expansion of services are all useful in assessing the contribution of a faculty member to external service programs.

Professors as Professionals

Despite the recognized existence of these several roles and functions of faculty members, little systematic evaluation of them is evident in most institutions. The current focus is limited to teaching. It tends further, as already remarked, to be limited to what goes on in the classroom as perceived by students. Why is this so? In part, it is simple expediency, but a second basis for focusing on student reactions is the concept that professors are autonomous professionals whose performances can be judged only by themselves.

Yet, it is not obvious that professors are professionals. If they are, it must surely be in reference to training rather than to function. The typical Ph.D. in economics is a professional as an economist and as a researcher in economics. With few exceptions, the Ph.D. does not prepare for college teaching, for advising, or for any of the other tasks (other than research) to which large sectors of faculty time are committed. For most of what they do, professors are amateurs and novices, not professionals. If this view be accepted, there are several consequences:

1. Academic freedom applies to the professional scholarly role and should not be used to ward off performance reviews and evaluation necessary to assess the effectiveness of teaching or of any other activity or function. Even performance of the professional or research role must be checked from time to time.

2. The institution which employs an individual to do chores for which he or she is not specifically and verifiably prepared has an obligation to provide training and has a responsibility to its students and supporting clientele to finally vali-

date a minimally satisfactory level of performance in that area. This right of validation should be made clear at the time of appointment. In fact, contracts with new faculty members might well spell out their functions, the expectation of the need for in-service training, and the requirement of evaluation of performance as a basis for reappointment or tenure. Unless such contracts are signed, the spread of unionization may well void all evaluation and move all promotion, tenure, and salary decisions to a seniority basis.

3. The common expectation that every professor should engage in classroom teaching, teach undergraduates as well as graduates, do research, advise, and serve on committees should be discarded. Professors, like everyone else, vary in interests and abilities. To retain their positions, they should be asked to demonstrate effective performance in at least two of the major faculty functions, and their assignments should take these individual differences into account. For example, to require all professors to engage in undergraduate advising is surely to subject some students to bad advising, a practice which no educational institution should countenance.

4. The university is run to meet societal needs. Hence, professors must be subject to management and to accountability. If we inside the university cannot or will not accept this responsibility, individuals and agencies outside will attempt to do the task—and will generally do it badly because they lack understanding of the nature of the university. External attempts at evaluation usually cause confusion, arouse irritation, waste resources, and ultimately substitute the rigidity of regulations for informed judgment, thus regimenting faculty and destroying the quality of the educational program.

The university has an obligation to its students and its supporting clientele to evaluate every aspect of the performance of academic staff. Only by so doing can the university maintain respect, support, and autonomy. And the evaluation practices of the university in scope and character should provide a model worthy of emulation by students, by other social agencies, by business, and by government.

Costs and Benefits

The evaluation of faculty activities, whether done well or poorly, already involves many hours on every campus. The costs in time spent filling out forms in multiple copies and in reviewing those in numerous committees and levels of administration are heavy.

The benefits of the present system are unknown in any objective way, but institutions point to percentage of Ph.D.s on the faculty, publications, and awards as evidence of quality. As it becomes increasingly difficult to terminate any professor, more attention will need to be given to using evaluation for improvement rather than for selection.

The cost of not evaluating faculty members is reasonably clear—a decrease in faculty quality—but whether added costs will bring added benefits is uncertain. One might hypothesize that a certain number of hours are going to be spent on faculty evaluation simply because it is an important and sensitive matter, and there must be an indication that care has been exercised in these judgments. Since so much of the evidence now used is highly subjective, one might be tempted to hypothesize that more objective evidence would permit wiser decisions with less time involvement. Only if decisions are more or less automatically based on objective criteria specified in advance is a reduction in time likely. But automatic decisions on complex and sensitive personnel matters are neither likely nor justifiable in the university milieu. We can expect that more and better data will require increased time and costs to collect and process and will require no less time and possibly more to assimilate and use as the basis for decisions. And, with more data available in the several areas of faculty activity, decisions will likely become more difficult. The real payoff then will most likely be in using the data to encourage improvement rather than to reach personnel decisions.

The survey of student opinions is the one area of faculty evaluation in which evidence on costs is available. Rating scales given to students are either filled out in class and immediately returned or taken home and returned later. If completed in class, the expected ten to fifteen minutes may extend to thirty or forty minutes. Furthermore, the tone of the class will be altered. These costs are beyond estimation.

Generally speaking, the major costs are probably involved in the committee, administrative, and individual time involved in developing, editing, and altering forms. An externally available form still must be extensively reviewed by local committees and perhaps given one or more trial runs before acceptance. Even so, this procedure is likely to be less expensive in hard dollars than the local development of forms, which requires collection of possible statements and many hours of editorial work, tryouts, and revision before printing. Explanations and manuals require more time. And no sooner is a form out than faculty objections accumulate.

In addition to the costs in time and frustration, there are cash outlays for printing, scoring, and compiling norms. At Michigan State University, for example, the estimated cash outlay is ten thousand dollars per year, and when new forms are being developed (every two or three years), the total cost is more nearly fifty thousand dollars. Are the benefits worth the costs? The benefits are at least four in number.

First, the involvement of students in the rating process displays a concern for their opinion and their welfare.

Second, the administrative and financial support favorably impresses the student and perhaps, to a limited extent, the public.

Third, the extensive discussions on any campus when student rating of teaching is under consideration probably have educational value. Members of the committees and others who become involved are led to think about the characteristics of good teaching, and this process may have an influence on some of them which transcends any direct benefits from the use of the forms. It would be difficult to assess each of these educational benefits. My own observation leads me to believe that the discussions at the formative stage of such a program may be the most valuable result of the whole venture. If this belief is accurate, use of published evaluation forms may be unwise.

Fourth, student ratings may affect hiring and reward criteria. In those situations I have had a chance to observe, however, the lapse in time and the almost complete separation of student ratings and procedures for selecting new faculty make it unlikely that anything more than the most general consciousness about teaching carries over from the evaluation program. It has probably happened, but I have yet to learn of a faculty member who was asked to present student ratings on his or her teaching in applying for a position elsewhere.

Whether these benefits justify the costs is a matter of opinion. Complete elimination of such forms however would not release sufficient dollars for significant development of any other evaluation procedure and would be regarded by many (faculty members, students, the public) as a backward step. The tangible evidence of concern may well be the most significant benefit and one which fully justifies the cost. Having taken this position, I should state that student evaluations do not provide an adequate appraisal of instruction for these reasons.

1. The usual faculty and student conceptions of the nature, objectives, and obligations of teaching and learning are too restricted, being bound by traditions, limited experience, and bias.

2. Unless based upon objectives and teacher obligations beyond the traditional classroom, the impact of student evaluation is limited. It may indeed be more of a distraction than a benefit.

3. Student evaluation alone, whether by structured inventory or other means, is obviously not an adequate basis for judging total faculty effectiveness. It is even inadequate for assessing teaching effectiveness. Hence, unless balanced by other evidence, student evaluation may be both inequitable and dangerous.

4. Published student evaluations are not useful to faculty members, are probably used by a minority of students, and may be grossly unfair to junior members of a faculty whose careers are still in a formative stage and who should be receiving concrete positive help in improving their teaching rather than published criticisms made by naive individuals whose own conception of teaching, formed as it has been by their limited college experience, is grossly inadequate.

Summary

Efforts in evaluation of faculty performance have been sporadic, limited in perspective, and largely ineffective. The widespread assumption seems to be that faculty research is adequately evaluated, but except possibly in a few elite institutions and departments, even this is not true. Publication rather than quality is the criterion in most institutions. Advising and the various forms of internal and external service are seldom carefully evaluated except when these functions are a person's primary obligation. Although evaluation of teaching recurrently becomes the focus of attention, there is virtually no evidence that the effort, carried out largely through student evaluation forms or checklists, has had significant impact on the improvement of teaching. Those who develop forms, collect data, write articles, and react almost vindictively when anyone reports research which suggests that student ratings may not even be positively related to good teaching talk mainly to each other and have virtually no audience among or impact on the faculty.

Other forms of faculty activity have much more tangible and more widely recognized rewards than does teaching. Moreover, faculty members who criticize the inadequacies of the present efforts at evaluation of teaching are quite right, although generally for the wrong reasons. Teaching cannot be adequately evaluated until its nature in relation to stated learning outcomes is considered.

Despite the current resurgence of interest, the immediate future is not likely to bring much improvement. Graduate programs supply no training for most faculty tasks, and even the new doctor of arts programs are but halting steps in this direction. Those professors who believe that research and scholarly activity are the essential elements in their careers resist evaluation other than by their peers. An across-the-board attempt to evaluate faculty services requires extensive resources and an unbending stance on the part of administrators, students, the public, and those faculty members who also support the idea. Any strong push in that direction could reinforce the present trend toward unionization. And then seniority rather than evaluation may become the primary basis for reward.

Only if our efforts in faculty evaluation are turned to analyzing the strengths and weaknesses in the performance of all faculty activities and to providing assistance for improvement of performance and changes in assignments, capitalizing on strengths, is faculty evaluation likely to be productive. For such efforts, standardized forms and norms are not only inconsequential, they may be counterproductive. Forms, norms, or procedures cannot be imposed upon a faculty until after extensive discussion and agreement on what is being evaluated and the criteria for so doing. This procedure is time-consuming, but it may have a most significant role in cultivating acceptance of the ideas and enthusiasm for the task.

These beliefs lead to two general principles for directing faculty evaluation.

1. Because there is not and will never be a perfect evaluation system for instruction and because there is not and will never be consensus on good teaching, advising, research, or faculty performance in any other area, assessment activity must be broadly conceived as a basis for improvement, not for the making of personnel decisions. Evaluation can be linked to the reward structure for faculty, for administrators, and for students, but with recognition that improvement and development are the first concerns.

2. The evaluation system should be viewed as one of the major aspects of the educational program, and because it is a model, students should be involved whenever possible. Evaluation is also the major objective of education. Evaluation is both a process and a result—a means of determining goals, of appraising the processes or paths for reaching them, and of assessing the extent to which they have been met. The development of the capability for evaluation is what education is all about. Anyone who engages in evaluation without recognition of this objective may do more harm than good.

Bibliographical Note

The amount of literature on faculty evaluation is astounding, especially in contrast with its apparently limited impact. Centra (1973a, 1973b, 1974; Centra and Linn, 1973), in studying various aspects of evaluation of teaching, tends to confirm this lack of impact. Miller has produced two useful books, one on evaluating faculty performance (1972) and another on programs of evaluation (1974). Miller takes the broad view of total faculty performance and provides copious specific examples. Doyle's (1975) book is perhaps the most extensive treatment of student evaluation of instruction; he provides numerous references. Manning and Romney (1973) developed a procedures manual for faculty-activities analysis which is helpful in applying the broad approach developed in this chapter. Doi (1974) edited a sourcebook on assessing faculty effort. For those who like theory, Hind, Dornbusch, and Scott (1974) have attempted to develop a theory of faculty evaluation.

Chapter 16

Administration

Although much has been written about administration in higher education, relatively little of this material is directed specifically to evaluation of individual administrative performance. Extensive reminiscing by presidents is somewhat enlightening, often entertaining, and revealing of the problems involved, but it provides no contribution to understanding administration as either a science or an art. The extensive studies of administration in business, industry, government, and the public schools are, in my judgment, irrelevant. The few analytical studies of higher education administration have been directed to understanding the peculiar nature of governance and the varieties of existing patterns rather than to evaluation.

Problems

A primary problem in evaluating administration in higher education is defining exactly what administration is. The related terms *leadership* and *management* provide some clues. Leader-

376

ship is more nearly equated to administration than to management. It has been characterized as knowing where to go, and management has been characterized as knowing how to get there. (This definition leaves unsettled the crucial issue of who decides where to go.) Leadership involves knowing and possibly setting the goals; it tends to be idealistic, qualitative, and charismatic in nature. Leadership also tends to be unique in that only one person at a time exercises the primary leadership in any particular activity. In contrast to leadership, management is directed to the achievement of goals, using analytical, quantitative, and pragmatic approaches. Generally, it seems to be assumed that management is better defined than administration; that an effective manager can be produced and can be exported; and that management, being more objective and quantitative in nature, is more readily evaluated and its efficiency and effectiveness more easily demonstrated. But these distinctions are not useful in higher education, for it is not clear whether administration is leadership, management, or both.

Richman and Farmer (1974, pp. 13-16) assign to management such functions as decision making, creative problem solving, formulation of goals and priorities, reallocation of resources, negotiating, resolving conflicts, dynamic or active leadership, diplomacy, statesmanship, and external relations. Administration, in contrast, is (by them) associated with routine decision making; with implementing goals, priorities, and strategies devised by others; and with monitoring, directing, and controlling internal operations. Administration is viewed as more adaptive, passive, and reactive than management.

These distinctions and the inferior, passive roles assigned to administration certainly coincide with the stereotypes and preferences of faculty members. But they also point directly to much of what is wrong with higher education. Both effective leadership and management are lacking within institutions, partly because of faculty independence and partly because boards and external coordinating or control agencies are making decisions, in the guise of policy statements, which gradually become so detailed that they allow no room for local interpretation or variance.

The definition of administration in higher education cannot be equated with the definition and terms used in business. In many large business enterprises in the United States, for example, the chairman of the board is the top executive officer of the organization, with the president second in line. In many businesses, too, most of the board members are executives associated with the business. The route of advancement goes through several echelons of associated or owned companies and ranks, with the culminating position being the board chairmanship. The chairman attends primarily to large policy issues, and the president is chief of operations. In contrast, the chairman of the board in higher education, unless he or she has unusual personal qualities and wields power and influence by virtue of other responsibilities, has only a symbolic role. Indeed, he or she may not even preside over board meetings, this task being reserved in some cases for the president as the chief executive officer of the institution. The president is appointed by the board and serves at the pleasure of the board. The president's powers and authority are delegated by the board, and other powers and authority exercised by others within the university are extended from the board through the president to those individuals. Yet, the major chores of higher education institutions are performed by faculty members, who, to a much greater extent than the workers in a business, are autonomous both in what they do and how they do it. The faculty expects and even believes that it delegates certain prerogatives to the administrator largely to save faculty time for more important matters.

A second problem in evaluating administration is that numerous complications are involved in delineating the power of administrators. In most states, there are local boards for single institutions, a board for each of several groups of institutions (systems), and possibly another statewide coordinating or control board across all systems. Obviously, the role of an administrator is complicated by the nature of this hierarchy. There are chief executives on campus, executives of one sort or another at each of the system levels, and executives at the top of the system. In Wisconsin (as in several other states), which has a single, comprehensive state system of higher education with one board over all institutions, a chief executive officer is designated as president, and a staff consists of vice-presidents and other aides in a central office. Chancellor, a title used in some states for the chief executive of the state system, designates the chief officer on campus.

Assigned responsibilities and power differ from one system to another. Campus executives have somewhat different amounts and kinds of authority, depending upon the nature of the institution and system in which they operate. System boards and local boards (which may be wholly advisory) have varying relationships to system and campus officers. On a campus one finds beyond the presidents (or chancellors), vice-presidents, provosts, deans, directors, department chairmen (or heads), and sundry other titled associates and assistants for each of these, including assistant to the assistant vice-president.

Some of these administrators have line relationships: president, vice-president for academic affairs, deans, and chairmen. Others, such as graduate deans, vice-presidents for research, and deans of undergraduate instruction, have functional responsibilities which cut horizontally across the line relationships. In a single state system in which the central office has second-line administrators charged with academic programs, with research, and with graduate education, administrators on each campus assigned to these areas operate under policies determined by the central office rather than by the chancellor. The life of a chief administrator on a campus when there are one or more levels of administration above is sometimes devoted to seeking those points at which he or she has authority or influence. Obviously, the evaluation of an administrative organization presents problems different from those associated with the evaluation of a specific administrator, but the evaluation of the administrator must relate to the particular functions assigned to him or her and the authority delegated to fulfill them.

The power of administrators is thus limited by the many constituencies they have to satisfy. Not only the president, but a dean of a college (agriculture or engineering, for example) or even a department chairman may find that administrators at higher levels have to be satisfied and that other constituencies including legislators and administrators of state and federal units have an interest in what they do. Direct contacts with foundations and the federal government by administrators and faculty members of various units may be important. With these various constituencies, many decisions in an institution, including adding programs, eliminating programs, putting a ceiling on enrollment in a major, or even hiring or firing a faculty member, can become issues of major proportions.

Clearly in these circumstances the sources of authority, power, and influence are multiple, and they exist both within and outside the institution. In the institution the internal and external contacts of some professors may be so potent that any action or decision which they find unacceptable is reviewed and possibly negated or altered. Increasingly, students take an active interest in decisions made within an institution, and frequently they make major attempts to influence policy on what would usually be minor matters, such as where certain supplies are purchased or in what companies the funds of the institution are invested. In almost all institutions power and authority are vested in a board of trustees, but influential legislators can exert more power than members of the board through their influence on appropriations. Thus, power and authority on a university campus, no matter how clearly delegated, ultimately are effective only when acceptable to those to whom they are directed.

Every educational institution has a statement of purposes; it may have a self-devised or an assigned institutional role in the region or area. Each institution also probably has one or more statements of objectives which purport to describe the expected results of the activities in the educational programs. But within a university many programs exist, varying from liberal education to technical and semiprofessional programs at the undergraduate level; from discipline based to highly practically oriented graduate professional degrees; from research, both pure and applied, to a variety of service programs. Academics do not particularly prize agreement. Indeed, they thrive on differences and sometimes on distinctions which make no difference; they are inclined to analyze and to engage in dialogue to gain even a slight modification of policies. Administrators with definitive educational philosophies find that attempts to promote their views arouse strong opposition from sectors of the campus holding contrasting points of view, especially if they appear to be intervening in matters regarded as faculty prerogatives.

A third problem with evaluating higher education administration and management is that there are no clear and generally accepted criteria of success. Every administrator and faculty member talks about quality. Every institution according to its own descriptions provides high-quality programs. Lacking either locally or generally acceptable criteria of success, each institution and program lays claim to excellence, and the great rallying cry in opposing a reduction in financial support is that such reduction will erode quality. Quality is always threatened, but never undermined by financial reductions—at least in official publications. It is also true (though never publicly admitted) that the quality of undergraduate programs has at times been undermined by financial increments which have permitted institutions to embark upon graduate and research programs. The inability to measure quality seldom bothers faculty members who are convinced that they know what it is and that they are engaged in producing it. And the administrator who would propose changes to improve quality is venturing at once on sacred ground and into quicksand, for the suggestion of the need for improvement implies less than desirable quality.

A fourth major problem for evaluators of higher education administration and management is that administrators often purposely communicate in ambiguous ways. Administrators at every level deal with several different constituencies, and the communications addressed to one are often carefully contrived to appeal to that particular group. In higher education, as elsewhere, the tendency is to tell people what someone thinks they want to hear or ought to believe rather than the truth. And, of course, some events and conditions in any university cannot and should not be publicized. It is also a curious characteristic of the university, which contains a collection of more highly educated people than any other social institution, that the problems of communication are complicated by the tendency of some individuals to withhold information as a means to power, while an excessive stream of communication by others clogs the channels and is ignored. Communications also tend to be misinterpreted and overinterpreted because of ambiguity in the original phrasing or because the academic mind is always looking for undercurrents, hidden motivations, and implications. Professors who avoid involvement in committee work want to know what problems are being discussed and what points of view are being promoted along with the associated rationale before decisions are made. When they hear only of the decisions, they feel put upon. But if students and faculty are to be informed of all the discussions and invited to assist in policy formulation, communication breaks down, discussions proceed without conclusions, and decisions which ultimately emerge are so long delayed that their significance is buried under the preceding torrent of words and papers. Even then, some individualistic professors do not feel bound by the actions of their colleagues. The democratically inclined administrator can reap a harvest of ill will by attempting to enforce policies developed by faculty committees and approved by a majority of those appearing at a senate or faculty meeting.

Organizational Patterns

The evaluation of administrative effectiveness must be based, to some extent, upon some model which characterizes a particular institution. Several models have been developed or applied to institutions of higher education; none fully applies to any one institution.

The Weberian, bureaucratic model involves a hierarchical or ladderlike structure in which commands or orders move from top to bottom and are carried out at each level by individuals with delegated authority operating in well-defined jurisdictions or areas of responsibility. In this ladderlike (or scalar) structure, each individual is ranked or graded with respect to every other individual. The importance of the functions and of the responsibilities assigned to individuals presumably corresponds to their authority. The activities of individuals at various levels in the bureaucracy are both prescribed and limited by the authority delegated. The decentralization of authority within defined limits would seem to promote both efficiency and effectiveness.

However, many issues or problems requiring action do not fit neatly within a level or even fall in a single one of the parallel vertical hierarchies which arise out of specialization of function. The bureaucratic structure often handles such matters ineffectively because no one person dares assume the authority for a decision and does not wish to compromise or denigrate his or her own authority by negotiation with others. Such items rest long on desks, occasionally being shunted from one to another with no noticeable progress.

Functional operations also cut across the several hierarchies at various levels. A graduate school dean, for example, without either faculty or budget, must attempt to coordinate, monitor, or review graduate programs across academic units, research programs, perhaps residence halls, and other units where graduate students may be employed. Research coordinators have similar problems, although separately identifiable research funds may enhance their authority. Coordinating groups collected around offices at various levels may become large and develop specializations which further obscure the hierarchic bureaucratic structure.

Viewed from a psychological or social psychological perspective, the bureaucratic structure tends to be ineffective because of its negative impacts upon individuals and their attempts to passively resist or actively retaliate. In a university, where what should be the lowest echelon in the bureaucracy—the faculty—is made up of highly self-directed individuals engaging in a wide range of specialized functions, the negative impact of the bureaucratic model on individuals is its greatest defect.

From a human relations perspective, the needs of each individual for self-actualization and a measure of success are not met by a bureaucracy. Personal values and aspirations are sacrificed. Interpersonal relations and group interactions arouse tensions which destroy morale and decrease productivity. Conflict, whether caused by personalities or principles, tends to become accentuated by jealousies bred by concern about preservation of bureaucratic prerogatives. The human relations approach to alleviation of these difficulties is to give primary consideration to "human values." Conflict should be reduced or eliminated, mutual trust and confidence should be created, and the needs of individuals should be integrated with those of the organization. Authority and responsibility should be shared. Thus tensions are reduced, each individual experiences satisfaction and psychological success, morale is raised, and productivity is increased. The preferred means for the achievement of this utopia are the removal of social and personal blocks to effective communication and the improvement of interpersonal relationships through sensitivity training, counseling, group therapy, use of expert consultants, and information feedback.

The importance of human relations cannot be questioned. Unfortunately, there is virtually no evidence that this approach is effective in increasing overall productivity—a fact which does not seem to have concerned those who enthusiastically support the human relations approach. It is not even certain that human relations will be improved, for some people cannot tolerate the approach and some react adversely to it. Furthermore, universities are not supported by society so that each person employed within the institution finds fulfillment. The institutions have responsibilities to meet, and, without proposing that self-sacrifice for the good of the university and of society is the ideal, I think it still conceivable that many individual needs would be met and group conflicts would be lessened were the common social goals and obligations enumerated and a unified effort made to achieve them.

Thus, neither the bureaucratic nor the human relations model applies to colleges and universities, although each contributes insights into some of the problems of governance. In essence, neither of these models applies because the major work of the institution is performed by faculty members, who, individually and in departments and colleges, have capabilities for particular tasks which greatly exceed the capabilities of persons in administrative positions. And whereas in industry, the research, development, production, sales, and service functions are clearly separate, departments and colleges and even individual professors carry out the equivalent of all of these. In addition, they have external professional careers and a role in institutional governance which is unparalleled in any other enterprise. Given this situation, there is and will be a diversity of goals and values. In many situations, the primary issue is not how to achieve goals, but how to select among them or to order them in a reasonable way in reference to available resources. This ordering must be accomplished in such manner as to achieve acceptance by those responsible for accomplishment.

The collegiality model, in its ideal sense, engages faculty and administration (though seldom students, board members, nonacademic staff, the public) in rational dialogue to specify and clarify goals and means of achieving them. This model has long been attractive, although it is no longer realistic in large institutions (and, in fact, was seldom found even in the smaller but less heterogeneous institutions of an earlier era). The educational institution is both an instrument and a victim of social change. External pressures from various publics and internal pressures from students and special interest groups have destroyed the applicability of the collegiality model. Were resources ample, as they have been in a few institutions, or were the various subunits financially self-sufficient, as a few are in some private institutions, then the benevolent-anarchy concept, in which each sector of the university pursues its own interests almost divorced from other sectors or central administrators, might apply. In either the collegiality or anarchical model, the faculty plays a dominant role, and administrators are viewed more as facilitators or perhaps as managers assisting in carrying out policies and attaining specified goals agreed upon by the several faculties of the discrete colleges and departments. This view tends, when carefully analyzed, to end up close to the human relations emphasis—maximizing the satisfactions of the work force with no assurance, and with justified doubts as demonstrated by past history, that the faculty will fully recognize the social responsibilities of the institution.

If we turn from maximizing human values for those who serve an institution to maximizing values for those served by the institution, then we must place primary concern on goal achievement by an institution rather than solely on its internal processes. In focusing on goal achievement we recognize that, both internally and externally, the university has been heavily and rightfully criticized for placing its own development and that of its faculty ahead of its responsibilities to its students and to society. Accordingly, the institution itself requires at least alteration and renovation or innovation, if not a complete restructuring and revitalization. The erratic, competitive, and opportunistic development of institutions, based upon conceptions of excellence in graduate programs and research, demonstrates that change governed by social responsibility must come from careful planning in which all views and needs (external as well as internal) are expressed and reconciled. Change is thus a political process in which conflicting views are to be expected. Power blocks and special-interest groups seek to advance their own values and goals, arguing either that these are best for everyone or that the fullest development of the institution requires that each unit be encouraged and supported to achieve its own goals. The latter is obviously not valid when resources are limited.

In this context, administrative authority is hampered by political pressures, bargaining, delaying tactics, and appeals to power sources outside the institution. External groups are invoked as a means of influencing internal policies and decisions. Decisions become negotiated compromises which fully satisfy no one and may even be inconsistent with announced institutional goals. Policy formulation rather than policy execution becomes the critical concern and therefore the focus of debate and conflict. The resulting compromises may also be so loaded with ambiguity as to be unenforceable. Moreover, those sectors of the faculty who lose in a compromise may not feel obligated to conform. Even though budget allocations are manipulated to enforce conformance, the impact may be negated by indifferent performance. In this circumstance, leaders who seek to define and implement large-scale organizational change consistent with stated values and goals must seek strategies and utilize persuasive powers to gain acceptance of new policies rather than simply exercise authority.

Thus, administration can no longer be an exercise of power for several reasons. Within the university many diverse groups, units, and individuals have access to board members, the legislature, and the public; the usual trappings of power in the form of coercion, penalties, rewards, and incentives are thus weakened. Furthermore, exercise of such powers is discouraged by the character of the university personnel who stand on principle even when to others the principle seems self-serving. Status and assigned authority go for naught if orders are neither acceptable nor accepted by those to whom they are given. Prestige based on admiration, esteem, and respect or influence resulting from personal qualities, recognized expertise, or example becomes potent if possessed and wisely used by an administrator.

Even so, compromise (distasteful though it is to some) becomes the route to change. Compromise appears in various forms. One form gives to each of the contending elements something it dearly prizes. There is no consensus, no attempt to reach agreement. There is only recognition that every group gained something though not all it sought. In rapidly developing institutions during the 1950s and 1960s, many presidents were able to introduce innovations disliked by most of the faculty simply because the president, by increasing the stature of the institution, raising the salary scale, and bringing in graduate and research programs, provided so much that faculty members wanted that they were disinclined to oppose other changes which the president proposed. In a second form of compromise sweeping changes are proposed that affect all and are bitterly opposed by many. Here the changes may be whittled down to a minimum acceptable to a majority, and consensus may be achieved only because some support the compromise to eliminate the controversy. Seldom does such compromise result in any major change. In a third form of compromise protracted negotiations result in a give-and-take process of redefinition and refinement. This process may, in fact, end in a stronger and more rational alteration than was originally contemplated. Subtle continued pressure for change and further negotiation may move the initial compromise even further in a desirable direction.

The preceding discussion of governance patterns, policy formulation, and change is brief and therefore faulty in many respects. Nonetheless, it serves the present purpose, which is simply to indicate that effective administration in an educational institution is a complex task unlike administration in business or the military. The evaluation of administrators must, therefore, take into account the peculiar character of higher education governance, the specific nature of the particular institution, and the external pressures bearing on it.

Criteria of Administrative Performance

As Cohen and March (1974, Chap. 4) suggest, not long ago the criteria for presidential (and institutional) success were relatively few, although not all were readily attainable. Primary among these criteria were continuing growth in programs, resources, students, faculty, salaries, and facilities; recognized high quality in students, faculty, and programs; balanced budget; and respect exhibited for the president by the students, the faculty, the board, and the community. If to this list could be added small teaching load, relatively fast promotions, early tenure, and strong support of research, both president and the institution were clearly successful and so regarded by almost all the various university clienteles. In brief, if the goals and priorities of the university were achieved to an adequate degree and if the institution continued to grow in programs and resources, both internal and external clienteles tended to be satisfied. Success was obvious to all.

Upon closer examination, it is apparent that many of these criteria of success were much more the results of a particular period and the general American commitment to growth than of the qualities of presidential leadership. To be sure, the opportunities for growth and for funding had to be seized by an administrator, but they were there to be seized. The present and foreseeable future appears to require other criteria. Under current circumstances, job security (with or without tenure) has become one of the major criteria affecting morale and the faculty appraisal of administrative performance.

Criteria indicative of unsatisfactory administrative performance today are of two types: unfortunate attitudes or sheer incompetence on the part of the administrator and a tendency to bypass him or her. The first category includes such attitudes as: expects strong personal loyalty and support; cannot or will not tolerate lengthy discussion or dissent regarding one's own ideas or extended controversy over any issue; ignores or bypasses others without clearance or explanation; depends overly much on the advice of a few immediate associates; basks in praise and does not differentiate between the university and one's self in accepting it; blames others for errors or weaknesses; does not encourage or assist able individuals to advance themselves either within the institution or by moving to another one. Such traits reflect a highly self-oriented approach to administration which arouses distrust and opposition.

The following are also signals of ineffective administration: the president is bypassed by individuals (internally and externally) who go directly to board members; the board receives inadequate or incorrect information; dissent and opposition are evident in the institution; numerous complaints and criticisms are made from external sources; frequent and serious crises arise regarding both important and inconsequential issues; ambiguity, uncertainty, and confusion about rules, policies, and needed actions or decisions are apparent; conflicting statements or views are given to various persons or are issued to the press. These events and situations tend to characterize an administrator who avoids and attempts to cover up differences and controversies rather than face and resolve them.

However, good administration is much more than an absence of negatives, and, therefore, a more constructive positive approach is required. The concerns of presidents of universities extend to every aspect of operations, for they are ultimately responsible to the board for all of them. Moreover, their administrative staffs, the faculty, students, and the public, when contacting them regarding important issues, expect them to be knowledgeable and responsive. Yet the total range of operations certainly exceeds any one individual's cognizance or expertise, including, as it does, students, nonacademic employees, faculty

members, board members, alumni, legislators, those in federal
agencies, influential public figures; athletics, academic policies,
programs and standards; graduate and undergraduate education,
professional schools, extension, adult education; building and
plant construction, and maintenance; budget, management of
financial resources, investment policy, and fund raising. Trust in
and dependence upon associates are therefore essential characteristics of the administrator.

The desirable characteristics which have been listed as
essential for a president, if seriously applied, would eliminate
the species. These include approachable, articulate, attractive
(in appearance and personality), charismatic, confident, considerate, decisive, deliberate, empathetic, fair, firm, flexible, imaginative, persuasive, rational, reliable, sensitive, self-assured,
sympathetic, tactful, and tolerant. In addition to this profusion
of adjectives, such phrases as sense of humility, concern for
quality, awareness and acknowledgement of personal and institutional weaknesses, inspires confidence, listens attentively, and
morale builder appear repeatedly.

An equally extensive list of roles and functions includes
such diverse items as mediator, buffer, catalyst, unifier,
synchronizer, synthesizer, and ameliorator of human conflicts.
Designations involving a more active developmental role include
educational leader, both within and without the institution;
promoter of change and adaptation; interpreter and spokesman
for the institution; policy and goal formulator; enforcer of
rules, standards, and policies; coordinator; organizer; and manager. And any list will note the importance attached to the
effectiveness and impressiveness of the manner in which the
president presides over meetings.

To overcome the tendency of the faculty to regard administration as a task too mean or routine to be undertaken by a
scholar, the requirements of an earned doctorate, service as a
faculty member, and evidence of creative and published scholarship are usually added by faculty search committees.

Former presidents and observers of administrators are also
effusive in offering advice or providing specific injunctions to
administrators. These, too, are diverse and easier to state than

to emulate: develop and use the administrative and managerial talents of subordinates; delegate, support and praise subordinates; avoid overreliance on immediate staff or associates who usually reflect presidential preconceptions; avoid favoritism, intimacies, and obligations or covert agreements; maintain distance, objectivity, and perspective on problems and controversies unless intervention is necessary; avoid confusion of office with self and personal goals with institutional goals; listen to and accept advice and criticism from both supporters and antagonists; admit error and subsequently alter decisions and policies; operate by principle rather than by personality and assume that the opposition operates on that principle also (at least until otherwise demonstrated); maintain balance in attention to finance, public, alumni, facilities, general administration, academic programs; work to develop and maintain effective two-way communication internally and externally.

A broad inclusive definition of the president's role would run about as follows: The president exercises overall leadership and direction, combining the interests, capabilities, and efforts of a diverse and sometimes discordant constituency and achieving a commitment by all individuals and groups to a set of general objectives for the institution without stifling individual or group fulfillment. This role requires defining, articulating, putting into operation, and coordinating goals and priorities that are acceptable, relevant, realistic, and attainable.

This statement reads reasonably well but hides or obscures the points or areas of difficulty and conflict which have been pointed out by many writers on administration. A new president or administrator at any level has the choice of accepting and adapting to existing patterns and people or undertaking to alter one or both. Since a new administrator cannot quickly make a name by adapting the habits, goals, policies, and prejudices of predecessors, he or she usually undertakes to change. Some changes which alter patterns set by a predecessor and which are palatable to the faculty may be welcomed, but changes which tend to remake an institution in the new administrator's image come up against faculty which is generally conservative and resists change. Past practices have come to have moral legitimacy, and frequently procedural and instrumental values have displaced or replaced goals which embody the ultimate values to which the institution is committed. Deeply imbedded contradictions and conflicts become sanctified by time, so that there is often a community consensus based upon a seeming, though misleading, unity of commitment to a set of goals and objectives which are variously ignored or interpreted in practice to justify whatever each individual and unit desires to do. Even when faculty members are receptive to discussion of change, the diversity of interests and the uncertainties and threats implied by change, combined with a faculty tendency to debate endlessly, edit and reedit in detail, and leave sufficient ambiguity for exercise of personal judgment, do not augur well for the speedy change required if an administrator is to receive credit.

The administrator must not be deterred from making needed changes simply because of faculty conservatism or recalcitrance. The administrator may have accepted an obligation to make changes in the negotiations leading to appointment or may have become convinced the change is essential to institutional survival. It is also possible however that the personal goals of administrators—survival, income, prestige, reputation, power, advancement—may have more to do with their proposals for change than with the good of the institution. Faculty members frequently and with good reason so suspect. Many individuals and groups, including the president and board members, tend, overtly or covertly, consciously or unconsciously, to divert the institution toward social revolution or to the support of personal or group ends however disparate or inappropriate these may be. Even the revitalization and adaptation of an institution which may involve less of radical change and more of recommitment to its traditional goals and program revision consistent with the current scene evoke opposition because these moves question the worth of some practices and programs by suggesting the need for alteration or replacement.

Definition of an institutional identity can also evoke storms. Usually, such definition requires reexamination of a statement which has long existed and long been ignored but is assumed to sanctify the status quo. Suggested changes are minutely scrutinized to read implications not intended and to arouse opposition based upon such implications.

Finally, administrators must be able to handle publicity. In approving publicity releases, in making personal statements, and in responding to questions, administrators must be aware that both friends and adversaries read or listen for words or phrases which challenge or which can be interpreted as challenging the values or interests of some group. In addition, administrators who continually seek publicity for themselves rather than for their universities and colleagues soon evoke distrust and suspicion. But sensitive use of publicity can rally both internal and external support for needed change.

Approach to Evaluation

Evaluation of the effectiveness of individual administrators must take into account numerous factors idiosyncratic to the institution (its traditions, its goals and priorities), the defined responsibilities and obligations of the office, the circumstances and conditions under which the administrator was hired, the expectations and views of the several constituencies which the institution depends upon or serves, the administrator's perceptions of his or her tasks and responsibilities and of the goals of the institution. The focus of analysis here is on the office of a campus chief executive, but can be readily adjusted to other administrators by taking into account factors unique to each level.

The goals and priorities of the administrator and of various constituencies do not necessarily coincide. Student demands only occasionally deal with basic educational issues or with fundamental policy matters. Faculty members give priority to their own welfare, security, and benefits, and, beyond that, to research, graduate instruction, and undergraduate instruction in that order. The federal government holds professional and graduate education and research as its primary concerns, while state government is more concerned with undergraduate education and the job market, except in such high-priority fields as medicine and law. Business and industry seek graduates in applied fields and also have some interest in practical research and in public service. Thus the administrator is caught in a difficult situation. Only in a period of rapid growth when demands for new programs are met or deferred temporarily on the grounds of priorities is there any prospect of receiving approbation from everyone. And only under these conditions do the administrator's goals and those of the various constituencies fully coincide.

When enrollment and resources are stable or decreasing, new programs and even continued employment of all personnel must be bought by eliminating or cutting back existing activities which are surely cherished by some faculty members, alumni, board members, and others. At this point, voices never heard and never in accord before rise in righteous wrath and cast aspersions on the intelligence, motivations, and social responsibility of the decision maker. Even legislators or board members calling for reductions in spending join the cause. Administrators find that not only what they do (or attempt to do) but also how they approach the task is important. Moreover, those who insist upon participating in decisions when increments are available seldom participate or accept responsibility for cutbacks or eliminations. The faculty ideal of administrators as facilitators of their efforts no longer applies. In fact, administrators who undertake program elimination rather than a general across-the-board cut may destroy themselves whether they succeed or fail in this intent.

A policy of evaluation of administrators at stated intervals for feedback and improvement is therefore essential; such a policy avoids the association of a demand for evaluation with crisis situations. This evaluation should be a joint review in which the administrator is deciding whether he or she desires to continue and others are deciding whether the administrator should do so. Once such a policy is instituted, each evaluation must cover the following points: (1) goal achievement—how the administrator's goals are developed and expressed, the affective and procedural aspects of his or her attempts to acquire support for or to achieve these goals, the extent of success in acquiring support for and achieving goals, the appropriateness of the goals; (2) personal characteristics as perceived by various individuals and groups (both above and below in the administrative hierarchy); (3) the charge or the assigned tasks when the administrator assumed the position (some situations such as "sick" departments may require extreme measures and a high-handed approach); (4) the administrator's own perceptions and personal evaluation of the success of his or her efforts; (5) the approach of the administrator to decision making; (6) the extent to which the options and procedures of the administrator are limited by traditions, regulations, or lack of support from superiors in the hierarchy; (7) recognition that vastly different views of administration exist: some administrators do things efficiently, some simply get things done, some enable others to get things done, and some do what others say to do.

Evaluators must recognize that their judgments may be based on erroneous assumptions, faulty or limited information, inappropriate goals or values, and emotion more than wisdom. Reliably assessed perceptions of people are still perceptions; they are not reality. Both the evaluator and the evaluated must be cognizant of this possibility and weigh it in recommending action or alteration. Accordingly, an evaluation of an administrator may lead to the conclusion that, because of faulty communication, otherwise effective administration is generally misunderstood. Correction may involve an evaluation of the evaluators and the development of an improved public relations and communication system.

The evaluation of an administrator can involve several kinds of evidence. The development and use of objective and descriptive rating scales to which individuals react by checking an appropriate characterization are attractive to those who are oriented to statistics and norms. But norms here are virtually meaningless. An administrator, whatever the assignment, is unique and his or her effectiveness or ineffectiveness depends on personal traits and capabilities and institutional characteristics. Unless reports of typical incidents which have given rise to a rater's reaction are included, the ratings are of no use in suggesting improvement.

Those who serve under an administrator are reasonably concerned that criticism can bring retribution if confidentiality is not assured, so the manner in which appraisals are collected and handled is critical. Interviews conducted by outside, unbiased evaluators or by senior professors or professors emeriti of unimpeachable integrity will evoke comments and specifics never obtained through checklists or written communications. The interviewers, in turn, should convey the substance of their findings informally to the administrator in oral form and later in written form. Following the initial oral statement and discussion with the individual, a discussion with the administrator's superior is desirable, with both the administrator and the evaluator present and actively involved. Copies of the final report should be given to the administrator and to his or her superior. A brief feedback report to those participating in the evaluation is desirable so that they do not feel their comments have been ignored or covered up.

Evaluation of the president of an institution must be conducted by the board annually and quietly, with a senior member of the board interviewing each board member. The senior member can then summarize and present the views expressed to an executive session of the board, including the president but no other officers of the institution. At intervals of two or three years, a more penetrating evaluation should be made in which the views of other administrators, alumni, faculty members, students, and representatives of the general public are sought. This elaborate review of the president is more complicated than reviews of other administrators simply because of the extended constituency to which the president is visible. The president, with board support, will do well to initiate and sponsor the internal review through the checklist or interview format so that it is evident that his or her performance and judgments are not being secretly undermined by board probing. External reactions should probably be sought only from a few persons of integrity who have broad perceptions of the administrator's activities. These interviews can best be arranged by the board chairman and conducted by a board member or a designated individual assigned to conduct the evaluation. Such reviews can and usually should be constructive experiences. More important, they can avoid the distasteful and disruptive confrontations which ensue when a crisis has arisen and differences have become deeply emotional and irresolvable.

Evaluation of the Board

A board which engages in evaluation of the president should also be willing to undergo evaluation. A president may engage in such evaluation in general terms by pointing to instances in which board actions or statements by individual board members have interfered with the president's own effectiveness. A board, however, should consider employment of an outside consultant of stature to sit in on a sequence of board meetings as an observer; talk privately with individual board members, with administrative officers, and others as desirable; and ultimately present to the board in executive session an appraisal of effectiveness and of the perceptions of others as to how they carry out their responsibilities.

The responsibilities of boards include the following: (1) selection, recurrent evaluation, and retention or termination of the president, (2) financial support and management, (3) public relations, (4) clarification of institutional purposes and goals, and evaluation of success in achieving them, (5) awareness of conflicting views and probable consequence of action, (6) evaluation of board performance.

The following are criteria for evaluators of boards: (1) existence and quality of statements regarding the legal, social, moral, and educational responsibilities of the institution; (2) effective board membership and individual performance: selection of new members, attendance (individually and collectively), board size and frequency of meeting, participation and preparation of individuals, diversity in background and outlook and utilization of such diversity in discussions and assignments, levels of trustee knowledge (institution, higher education trends, social changes and needs), committee system (appropriateness and functioning), continuity and change; (3) recurrent delineation of major tasks to be accomplished: agenda and adherence to it, reasons for delays, maintenance of distinction between policies and specifics; (4) dynamics of discussions and decision making: leadership by chairman, participation and roles of members, adequacy of background materials and analysis, participation of president and other administrators, extent of consensus in decisions, use of open meetings and closed briefing or discussion sessions, morale and achievement; (5) relations of board and of individual board members with various groups: president, faculty, students, special interest groups, specific units (colleges, departments), external groups; (6) acceptability of board actions: to dissenting members, to internal institutional groups, to external groups.

Institutions differ markedly in the makeup and functioning of their boards so that the preceding list and the particular procedures used need to be adapted to the local scene.

Summary

Administrators may be effective in a quiet, unobtrusive way which is neither obvious nor reportable. But they cannot expect to receive credit for that which is unknown. They can adopt a posture of austere, dignified noninvolvement, but when the institution is faced with serious problems this posture cannot last. The alternative is active involvement in defining problems, goals, alternatives; in seeking support for sound solutions; and in delineating and enforcing them. Administrators who are actively involved need to know how others are reacting to their efforts and how others perceive their accomplishments.

Many universities have caretakers and paper shufflers in the positions of deans and department chairmen, for, under a rotation scheme, the wise chairman or dean does not alienate those with whom he or she must shortly bed down again. This trend and the narrowing range of presidential influence require that the top level of administration in higher education be evaluated regularly and thoroughly. If effective performance and assumption of responsibility can be demonstrated, the tendency to reduce institutional autonomy may be stayed, and administration at all levels may be restored to an acknowledged stature which will again make possible innovation and leadership.

I have not undertaken in this chapter to specify any forms, checklists, or items for evaluation of an administrator. I have, however, presented an extensive range of traits, characteristics, and procedures which enter into such an evaluation. The criteria for board evaluation include numerous items which apply also in the evaluation of administration. It is my conviction that effective evaluation must start with a sensitive definition of what is to be evaluated relative to the scene of operation and the persons involved. And the administrator should have some input at this stage, for an evaluation which does not deal directly with his or her concerns will not be as well accepted or as helpful as it could be.

Bibliographical Note

The following selections are chosen to direct the reader's attention to issues of academic administration.

Hodgkinson and Meeth's (1971) book is worth attention in that it illustrates how much change has occurred in academe in an extremely short time. Much of the volume is devoted to questioning the proper configuration of university governance. Other excellent essays in a historical or comparative vein are included.

Richman and Farmer (1974) present what could be classified as a typical 1970s approach to administration—an approach characterized by the recognition and incorporation of power groups in academic governance. The book presents numerous case studies, which are helpful to the administrative neophyte and reduce the usual level of abstraction for all readers. This volume concludes with a helpful bibliographic essay.

Kauffman (1974) presents an intensive, descriptive analysis of the procedure of searching for a college president. This selection would be an excellent handbook for a presidential-search committee. Many will be surprised at the author's insistence upon constant vigilance against unwitting exclusionary search processes, as well as his direct attention to the expected role of the president's spouse.

For a fresh view of administration and the effectiveness of administrators, see "Women in Administration," Parts I and II,

Journal of the National Association for Women Deans, Administrators, and Counselors, spring and summer 1975. These issues point out many of the realities and myths surrounding the roles of women administrators and make creative and intelligent suggestions for bringing order out of a too often irrational situation.

Chapter 17

Institutional
Self-Study

Institutional self-study is a planned and organized inquiry by the staff of an institution into the total effectiveness of institutional operations. In a complete self-study, all sectors of the institutional community become involved in a review and evaluation of purposes and goals, selection and utilization of personnel, modes of operation, past and present activities and accomplishments, and future role in relation to societal needs. The first purpose of the self-study is to achieve an understanding of the institution, to determine its strengths and weaknesses relative to institutional purposes and social responsibilities. The second purpose is to revitalize and update goals and operations in order to improve the performance and the quality of output of the institution.

Institutional self-study characterizes an approach to institutional analysis and renewal which may take many forms, have

401

wide or narrow focus, and employ techniques and methods ranging from free-ranging discussion and emotional interaction to extensive data collection and analysis, evaluation, and research. Since institutional self-study has become the preferred preparation for accreditation review and thereby has become something of a fad, clarification of the nature, purposes, and processes of self-study is necessary to separate it from other approaches to study of an institution.

Nature of Self-Study

Institutional self-study obviously indicates a study by those associated with and those who identify themselves with the institution, including board members, administrators, faculty members, clerical and managerial staff, and students. It also includes alumni, donors, employers of graduates, the general public, and, for publicly supported institutions, members of the legislature, executive officers, and possibly coordinating board and staff members at one or more levels. The first step in a self-study is thus to identify the institutional clientele and select from it individuals who are influential, prestigious, and sufficiently interested to give some of their time to an analysis of institutional problems.

The second step is to engage these individuals in identifying the problems of the institution. Even though the problems may be reasonably obvious to persons closely associated with the institution, perceptions of how serious these problems are and how they are interrelated will be quite different. And since administrators are loath to publicize weaknesses and difficulties, a large segment of the institutional clientele may be entirely ignorant of the problems. More than one college has met with serious reverses or closed without foreknowledge by large segments of its various interested publics—not excluding students and faculty members. Thus this second phase is vital in alerting these publics to the full range of problems and enabling them to see these problems in perspective.

The third step in the self-study is to bring together representatives of various sectors of the institution for study in depth of the problems defined. This selection, organization, and staffing phase is critical. The tendency to categorize problems by the existing structure of the institution and to assign the analysis and resolution of problems to those individuals and officials who have already demonstrated inadequacy—either because of personal deficiencies or because of structural weaknesses in organization and in assignment of responsibilities—must be resisted even at the expense of some unrest. The point must be continually made and emphasized in various ways that personal prestige and prerogatives must be set to one side—overridden if necessary—to achieve a new and critical institutional scrutiny unaffected by past commitments. For example, the review and reconstruction of a curriculum which no longer attracts students cannot be left solely to the faculty, which has already demonstrated its inability to adjust the curriculum to the changing interests and needs of students. But it is also obvious that no reconstruction of the curriculum which is not understood and accepted by that faculty can be successful.

Thus the fourth step in institutional self-study must be to document for all concerned the need for change and the appropriateness of the particular changes proposed. A successful self-study must attain a large measure of unanimity and commitment to the changes proposed while simultaneously avoiding a doctrinaire commitment to those changes—a commitment which only sanctifies a new rigidity. A successful self-study inculcates a mood for continuing self-study and for further change as initial recommendations are demonstrated to be inadequate (because of faulty analysis or changing circumstances) or to be attended by unforeseen and undesirable consequences. Institutional change, too, may attract a new clientele, which imposes new needs and new demands not entirely foreseen in the self-study. Either publicity or program then requires further alteration.

If institutional self-study is to achieve these purposes of involvement, insight, and commitment on the part of all or a major segment of the clientele, it must be differentiated from other approaches to institutional change which cannot be regarded as self-study. What sometimes passes for self-study or masquerades under that designation is frequently only an administrator-initiated and -dominated project in which one or more committees or task forces consider the administrator's agenda and endorse the administrator's program. In rejecting this approach, one need not deny the value of dynamic leadership or the potency of charismatic leaders in effecting change. The risks are that some sectors of the clientele will be alienated or antagonized, that the intended impact of the changes will be reduced by lack of enthusiasm or understanding on the part of those who must carry them out, and that centers of discontent and subdued resistance will remain to undermine and ultimately destroy the changes after the initiating leader turns to other matters or departs.

Importation of consultants by administrators is another approach to change. Consultants can and usually should be used in the self-study process, but this role is quite different from one in which consultants analyze an institution and prescribe its future. If a consultant's recommendation is only a thinly veiled endorsement of administrative desires, it is unlikely to be successful even if adopted. But sensitive consultants who have spent sufficient time at an institution visiting with faculty members, students, and board members as well as top administrators can develop and propose plans for change which are enthusiastically received. In effect, such consultants serve as catalytic agents; they are a means of achieving consensus rather than outsiders imposing their own ideas.

A third route to change is, superficially, only a variant of the second—the employment, usually by the president with approval of the governing board, of a firm of outside consultants. This use of a consulting firm ordinarily takes on a character different from the use of one or more consultants who are faculty members or administrators in another institution of higher education. The costs are usually much higher, and the report tends to be addressed to the administration and board rather than to the faculty. A firm of consultants has a reputation to make and maintain, but it also has to satisfy its clients. Since presidents and boards play the major role in selecting a firm, their satisfaction with the report is more to be sought than that of the faculty. Seldom does such an effort involve the faculty sufficiently to achieve widespread acceptance of recommendations. Immediate acceptance and activation of the recommendations may lower morale or even invoke animosity. The alternatives are either ignoring the report (with consequent concern for misspent funds) or having it extensively reviewed by faculty members who can accept, modify, or reject the recommendations. This approach is quite different from the formulation of recommendations through the self-education of all concerned and the consensus achieved by their initial involvement.

Accreditation

As mentioned above, much of the current interest in institutional self-study is motivated by the self-study requirement of accrediting associations. Voluntary accreditation, as practiced by institutions of higher education in the United States, is without parallel elsewhere in the world. Colleges and universities have banded together in six regional accrediting associations to establish procedures which (1) certify to the general public, to government, and to other institutions the minimal qualifications of the institutions accredited; (2) provide limited protection against degree mills and disreputable educational practices; (3) provide counsel and assistance to new and developing institutions moving toward accreditation; (4) encourage improvement in institutions by a review of activities, by development of recommendations regarding program quality, and by preparation of guidelines for assessing educational effectiveness; (5) encourage continuous self-study and evaluation; (6) provide a basis for assuring that institutions are worthy of assistance from various federal programs; and (7) provide some protection to institutions against threatened encroachments on their autonomy, which might also destroy educational quality.

Accrediting practices have not always included such a wide range of purposes. The specification and application of standards such as percentage of doctorates, number of library holdings, and amount of salaries made earlier accreditation practices rather mechanical and inflexible. And enforcement of such stan-

dards only ensured that institutions strove to achieve or maintain them and did not provide any assurance of quality. But
having abandoned specific standards and the application of
them as the major thrust, accrediting associations have not yet
found an entirely satisfactory means of promoting their broader
standards: the quality of educational processes and of the environment. These are difficult to appraise since their relationship
to excellence is unknown.

Since accreditation is primarily a vote of confidence in the
future of an institution and must, therefore, take that future
into account, it becomes evident why self-study has become a
requirement for accreditation. The accreditation of an
institution must take into account its present resources, future
prospects, and their relationship to purposes, goals, aspirations,
and programs. And since the maintenance of the proper
relationships depends upon how decisions are made, the dynamics of the decision-making process must be carefully scrutinized. The expected result of self-study is that it will encourage the institution to move toward a valid and reliable procedure of continuing assessment which will support improvement
rather than stasis or decline.

Patterns

A self-study can take several different forms, which do not
necessarily involve planning for the future. For purposes of
analysis, it is possible to employ a dimensional model of the
self-study process. On one dimension, a self-study may be a
comprehensive institutional process; it may be conducted in one
department or unit or in all (and then combined to give an institutional total); or it may focus on a specific problem, such as
general education or admissions. On a second dimension, a self-
study may be largely historical; it may be a current-status study;
or it may be both of these and project goals for the future and
plans for attaining them. The nine possible patterns indicated in
Table 6 emerge from the conjunction of these two dimensions.

Perhaps most self-studies are of type A—they are comprehensive, designed and carried out at the institutional level with

Table 6. Types of Self-Study

	Comprehensive Institutional	By Unit	Specific Problem
Historical	A	B	C
Current status	D	E	F
Long-term plan	G	H	I

input from all other levels, but they are historical and static rather than intentional and dynamic. By the time the final report is prepared, the study is out of date. Type B covers self-studies which require extensive input by the departments or other units in an institution—input which is then simply combined into an institutional summary. These studies include much laudatory comment and analysis of resource deficiencies, but are not informative about the development and operation of the institution as a whole. Moreover, they abet rather than alleviate the compartmentalization which is at the center of many problems of the university.

Self-studies which are limited to current status (D, E, and F) hardly deserve to be designated as self-studies. However, the profile prepared by institutions for budget requests or accreditation review frequently has this character. Such a profile gives current enrollment and budget, describes the faculty, and indicates deficiencies and problems. It may also include quite unrealistic aspirations in reference to new staff, courses, and programs without any attention to the feasibility or need for them. The basic data for such status studies could be easily and regularly collected to provide a picture of long-term trends, but, generally, these current-status studies are wasted effort because there is no follow-up.

Despite the difficulties of studying one out of many interrelated issues, the majority of self-studies are narrowly conceived and aimed primarily at evaluating a particular program or finding a solution to a specific problem. If particular problems (C, F, and I) are the focus of self-study, the historical and current-status phases are almost certain to be followed by an attempt to establish new policies. The attempt is not always successful, for groups charged with the study of such relatively specific issues as general education requirements, grading practices, and admissions find that the issues are much more complicated and far reaching than anticipated. A change in general education requirements usually affects the load and staff of several departments. The development of new general education courses calls for immediate extra expenditures and may involve long-term budget commitments. Admissions policies go far to determine the character of an institution, and changes may create problems far beyond the campus.

Evaluation of an existing unit (B, E, and H) is always a threat to those involved in it and may even be perceived as a threat to academic freedom and professional integrity by others who rally to the support of the threatened unit. An attempt to solve a specific problem such as too many small classes or too little space usually raises other issues. Self-studies of units conducted in the face of steady-state or declining funds and enrollments pose more difficult problems than those focused on growth and the addition of new units.

Self-studies conducted in support of special funding requests (such as the improvement grants of the Ford Foundation or the Centers of Excellence grants of the National Science Foundation) have tended to place great emphasis on new units, projections of financial need, and the possible assumption of financial responsibility by the institutions. These self-studies, of necessity, have focused on planning as much as or more than on current status.

Ladd (1970), in his review of self-studies for the Carnegie Commission on Higher Education, notes that as significant recommendations emerging from self-study committees proceed through various levels of decision making, their innovative character is eroded or destroyed. Nevertheless, the focus of self-study on a particular problem makes incumbent upon the self-study group the preparation of proposals for resolution of that problem, whereas broad self-studies, undertaken as a presidential gesture toward faculty involvement, a possible prelude to innovation, a thrust toward greatness, or simply as a hoped-for cure of general malaise, may well only end in vague generalities.

There are other difficulties with this limited approach. The problem studied may be contrived to divert attention or may be an unfortunate result of other commitments rather than one of real concern which justifies far-ranging changes. An institution may focus on a problem which has limited implications for revitalization. Thus a faculty-dominated study of faculty promotion and tenure policies is useful, but it can be completed without attention to the major functions, objectives, and fiscal problems of the institution. It may, therefore, lead to recommendations which are unrealistic and unrealizable. Morale is undermined, and the results are diametrically opposite those intended.

Self-study is not likely to be productive unless it is part of a periodic or continuous effort. A spasmodic effort at self-study in response to an internal crisis or external pressure may seek to alleviate the immediate distress rather than to alter the institution in a fundamental way. When the only goal of self-study is the alleviation of pressure, the preservation of accreditation, or the attainment of a foundation grant, success or failure in attaining the goal often ends the self-study.

Characteristics of Comprehensive Self-Study

Of the various combinations of the two dimensions, only the comprehensive, total self-study conducted as a basis for long-term planning (G) adequately provides for institutional evaluation. The adjective *comprehensive* joined with *self-study* indicates an all-inclusive examination of the total operations, problems, and goals of an institution. Such an effort may be a prelude to planning or may be synonymous with it. It is a concerted effort at institutional revitalization.

A successful comprehensive self-study is a major effort in data collection, assessment of strengths and weaknesses, reexamination of goals, and detailed analysis of present and needed resources. Briefly, the points to be considered include (1) purposes and goals, (2) adequacy of physical and financial resources, (3) effectiveness of the governance and decision-making process, including the roles of various groups involved (boards, administrators, faculty, students), (4) educational philosophy, quality, morale, and activities of faculty, (5) strengths and weaknesses of current curriculum organization and instructional methods; (6) campus climate and environment —the role of students, their dissatisfactions or satisfactions with programs and services, (7) effectiveness of the educational program and the educational processes in fostering student development, and (8) effectiveness of research and public service programs and the satisfactions and concerns of those who support and those who presumably benefit from these programs.

It is widely accepted that the first step in evaluation is the specification of objectives. Who determines objectives and their acceptability? At times accrediting groups have suggested that educational institutions are free to define their objectives idiosyncratically and that accreditation should be based on the accomplishment of these objectives. This view is nonsense since it would require that a school for thieves, none of whose practicing graduates were ever apprehended by the police, be accredited. The school is apparently effective, but is obviously not acceptable; its objectives are bad. It is also possible for the stated objectives to be satisfactory, but for a school to be run by thieves. Degree mills partake of this character. The plain truth is that some objectives are more acceptable than others, and self-study must recognize the differences. But even with an acceptable set of objectives, evidence of accomplishment may be difficult to acquire, and evidence is seldom present in sufficient quantity to base the entire institutional evaluation upon it. The search for evidence of quality becomes much more complicated than simply seeking evidence of success in achieving objectives.

If quality cannot be determined solely by recourse to evidence of accomplishment of objectives, what other evidence is relevant? We may conclude, as have many others, that we should look at the environment in which learning takes place, at the processes or programs carried on in this environment, as well as at the results. The environment is composed of people, facilities, equipment, and, less tangibly, of organizational structures, governance patterns, priorities, and morale. The processes in an institution involve various interactions of the human and other environmental factors. Presumably, these interactions are planned to attain educational objectives, but many are, in fact, fortuitous or are based on tradition and enforced accommodation to faculty and administrative preference. These processes, subtly if not obviously, affect students, faculty, and the character and reputation of the institution itself. The processes and interactions must be scrutinized and restructured in a manner consonant with the objectives or else they tend to negate them.

To obtain evidence on all phases of the environment, processes, structures, and results is a complex and time-consuming task. And it may be almost entirely retrospective, giving a static picture of what the institution has been rather than a dynamic one of what it is becoming. The catalog and other publications; the minutes of board, faculty, and committee meetings; the record of changes and additions—all tell much about the history and the present status of an institution, but they may tell little of where it is tending unless they record the existence of long-term planning and of deliberations and actions to put this plan into effect. Changing what is happening to what should happen is the central task of self-study.

A high level of motivation for a self-study must be generated or else adequate time and effort will not be expended to make the study successful. Most faculty members and administrators are relatively conservative, traditional, and protective of their prerogatives and the status quo. Though they may not find these entirely satisfactory, they would prefer incremental improvement to major change. An extensive study is expensive in time and, if well supported, also in money. The time involved is measured not just in the hours spent in collecting data, in committee deliberations, and in projecting plans, but also in the months and even years required to put the plans into effect and to adjust them as circumstances change. In addition, there are extensive costs in diversion of time and attention from other activities.

Determining the Need

Universities should answer a number of questions before deciding to launch a self-study and especially before designating the personnel involved and phrasing the charge to them.

1. Is the problem one requiring restudy of goals or operating policies, or is it primarily a failure in supervision, management, or administrative performance—performance of administrators, academic or nonacademic personnel?

A self-study usually avoids pinpointing individual weaknesses and is not likely to correct problems created by poor administration. A self-study is no substitute for lack of administrative willingness to deal forthrightly with a well-defined issue. Examples of this type of issue are (1) an undue number of small classes when policies already call for elimination of such classes or of courses which regularly produce them; (2) a light instructional load, especially when the difficulty is a flight from teaching to research; (3) undesirable budget priorities in the development of various disciplines. With such problems, administrators may gain assistance from existing faculty committees or invited advisory committees by stating the problem and some proposed courses of action. In this way, individuals or committees can give tacit support to an obviously needed action without having to originate it or actively support it. With such support (even if contrived) administrators can act with less fear of being seen as dictatorial.

2. Is the problem one which should be considered and resolved through existing committees or other agencies?

Committees are of several different types. Some are set up for a particular purpose and terminate when that purpose has been met. Standing committees, by contrast, have assigned areas of continuing responsibility, such as curriculum, retirement and fringe benefits, promotion and tenure. Standing committees may take on any of several roles. The executive type attempts to administer an activity. An example is an admissions committee which insists on meeting to review every application and decide by vote whether to accept or reject. A policy committee attempts to write general policies; application (and perhaps even interpretation) is left to an administrator who may be the chairman or secretary of the committee. An advisory committee provides a sounding board for discussion of ideas and policies and perhaps for collecting and reporting reactions, but remains advisory to an administrator who may accept, reject, or simply ignore committee recommendations.

Executive and policy committees are seldom effective in self-study roles. They are involved in current operations, and, in some sense, they are a part of the status quo. They have neither the time nor the disposition to study a situation or a set of problems which might alter or eliminate their own role. In fact, they may be a significant part of the problem.

Advisory committees can play a continuing self-study role. As proposals or problems are identified, they may be referred (by another faculty member or by an administrator) to advisory committees for study and recommendation—but not for final disposition. The recommendations must still be processed through normal channels.

Although standing committees are not usually appropriate vehicles for self-study, no item that properly can be referred to such committees requires a special self-study. The distinction for the choice is that between minor changes in current practices or policies and possible major changes or innovations which call for alteration in priorities or structure or redirection of the institution. Time and intensity of effort required are also factors; ad hoc self-study groups can be released from other duties and given special assistance.

3. Is the problem of sufficient significance that resources can be allocated to support in-depth study over a period of weeks or months? Will the faculty generally recognize the importance of the task so that some will be willing to absorb part of the ordinary work load of those assigned to the self-study task? Can staff be provided for the study committee to assist in collecting materials and data and in making such studies as may be requested? Can funds be allotted so that consultants can be brought to the campus or can visits of members of the committee to other campuses be supported?

Unless the answers to several if not all of these questions are positive, the problem is not of sufficient importance to justify a self-study. The use of consultants is especially important in opening up a wide range of views which might not otherwise occur. The objective reaction of external authorities who cannot possibly benefit from the changes they suggest is also beneficial.

4. Are the incentives or pressures which appear to require

the self-study of sufficient gravity to cause general acceptance of the need for the study, willingness to contribute to it, and readiness to attend to the results?

A self-study required for initial accreditation or for a grant almost automatically creates acceptance of the need for it, but does not ensure more than perfunctory compliance. Accreditation reviews in well-established institutions create even less pressure. Unless most of those in the institution recognize the existence of a problem, they will believe that the self-study (unless enforced by an external agency) is being generated by administrative officers to achieve certain changes which they could not attain through ordinary channels. To overcome this belief, the prelude to a self-study may be a series of studies which point up certain problems, the publicizing of cases in which present rules or policies have caused an injustice to students or faculty, or reports by one or more consultants which highlight a number of problems and the need for careful consideration of a change in practices, policies, or goals. Institutional research studies of certain problem areas are useful in arousing and focusing attention. Several studies over a period of time emphasizing various aspects of a problem often help to arouse concern when a single study causes only momentary irritation.

5. Are administrative officers willing to make available to a self-study group all the information required to fully understand a problem and the implications of various solutions? Are they willing to entertain exploration of all possible ramifications and consider well-reasoned and documented analyses and recommendations?

In some institutions, presidents regard certain information, such as that on the budget, on salaries, on the rationale and application of certain policies, as highly confidential and refuse to permit access to such information even when it is clearly relevant to the charge given to a committee. A group of individuals should not be asked to undertake study of a problem unless full cooperation is assured in providing any information needed, although some requests from members of a self-study committee can be rejected as irrelevant. A study of general education requirements hardly provides a member of the committee with justification for requesting access to the salary of every member of the faculty. A study of promotion and salary policies may require exactly that information, although not every member of a committee requires all details. Most such needs can be satisfied by salary summaries, which take into account years of service, rank, specialty, and so on.

The general principle remains clear: individuals or committees should not be asked to resolve problems unless they are provided access to all relevant information and are permitted to ask questions which under other circumstances might be regarded as impertinent. An office of institutional research or committee aides should be available to meet such requests. It is unreasonable to expect that the committee members do this themselves.

Operation and Strategy

Assuming that the need for a self-study has been demonstrated to the satisfaction of all concerned, the first bit of strategy in setting up the self-study group involves the selection of the committee members. The breadth of representation depends, in part, upon the scope of the study. A study initiated within a department of mathematics to look at departmental curriculum problems hardly calls for representation from the board of trustees or the college of fine arts, but the group should certainly include representatives from the office of the dean or of central administration and should have contacts with or representation from other units which utilize mathematics, such as engineering, physics, business, and social sciences. It should also use one or more outside consultants. Without such external involvement, the department will usually only reconfirm its traditional stance or end up with unrealistic plans for which it cannot obtain the necessary support and resources. Departments must continually be reminded of their obligations to the institution and of the impact of their decisions on others (both students and faculty) in the institution.

Self-studies of all-institutional problems require that careful consideration be given to the selection of the study group.

Two questions which are regularly raised and some largely personal answers follow.

First, how should study group members be selected? The alternatives are numerous and include: election by academic units (usually colleges in a university since departments are too numerous); selection by deans and advisory committees of colleges; appointment by the president after nomination by a committee on committees; appointment by the president; and some combination of election and appointment.

Although many faculty members and students argue for an election, the individuals elected are too often highly visible and popular largely by virtue of vociferously vented views. In addition, they are unlikely to be persons with any special competence in the area to be studied. Election by units also tends to create the expectation that those elected will represent the interests of their units rather than attempt to find a solution in the best interests of the institution—a commonly noted weakness of standing committees. Appointment of a committee, acceptable in some institutions, is not acceptable in many and by no means ensures an able group. A combination of election and appointment is often an acceptable compromise. Another alternative is to have nominations in excess of the number required from which an administrator selects the committee. Some administrators, such as a director of institutional research or registrar, may serve as consultants, study directors, or ex-officio members.

President, vice-president, and deans should attend committee meetings only on request. Regardless of faculty attitudes toward administrators and regardless of an administrator's deference to faculty views, the opinions of presidents, vice-presidents, and deans tend to be so weighted that they prejudice the report—especially if an administrator who participates in a self-study committee is one to whom the report is ultimately delivered. Faculty members who dissent from the committee recommendations may readily suspect that some of these recommendations were dictated by administrative preferences rather than collective committee wisdom.

Second, what criteria should be considered in choosing

members of a self-study committee? Individuals who already have strong and announced convictions on the issues to be studied are seldom good committee members. Individuals respected by their associates are essential, but overattention to this criterion can result in a group with little knowledge and perhaps with no great interest in the problems. Individuals who might hope to advance themselves through committee recommendations are questionable choices, but this possibility is not easily foreseen. In particular, the chairman should be a person of recognized stature with an already well-established career, especially when a new unit or administrative office is a likely recommendation. More than one self-study chairman (or committee member) has been disillusioned when a committee recommendation which he or she strongly espoused did not lead to his or her own advancement.

Typically, members of a self-study committee receive letters of appointment which contain a brief statement of the task. The committee may meet first with the president or a vice-president and have the charge repeated or enlarged upon with some opportunity for questions and discussion. If the committee elects its own chairman (generally a quite unsatisfactory procedure), it may be done at this time.

The interpretation of the charge is likely to consume many hours. What seemed crystal clear becomes clouded by questions.

1. Does our charge include looking at X as well as Y?
2. To whom should our recommendations be addressed— the president or the faculty?
3. Is our job over when we have prepared recommendations or are we expected to promote action on the recommendations?
4. Are we expected to continue as a committee to monitor and evaluate the results of the recommendations? (This question often indicates a desire for this role or at least a continuation of the prestige of committee membership.)
5. Should our sessions be regarded as confidential, or are we free to discuss our deliberations with others?

6. Are we to submit progress reports to the president (or the faculty) or only a final report?

7. What does the president want? Should we meet with him or her again to gain a more explicit idea of expectations?

8. Must we agree on a single report or can there be minority reports?

9. Should we seek for the best possible solution or for one which is likely to be acceptable? To whom?

10. What is the deadline for our report?

11. Who writes the report?

12. Should we prepare a questionnaire to ascertain student or faculty views?

13. Can we get funds to visit other institutions and see what they are doing?

14. How much secretarial and research assistance can we have?

15. How did we get into this mess anyway (referring both to the self-study committee and the problem which gave rise to it)?

The first question will recur periodically and likely will be the subject of a lengthy section in the final report. Many of the other questions are premature and can be decided only as the study progresses. Some, such as the completion date, the assistance and funds available, the disposition of the report, and the future role of the committee should be clarified as a part of or as addenda to the charge. Some answers are reasonably obvious. The committee should be privileged to look at anything and have any data relevant to pursuing its charge. If appointed by the president, it should report to him or her unless otherwise directed. If elected or appointed by the faculty, it reports to the faculty. The committee task is over when the report is prepared, although the chairman and individual members can be influential in interpreting the report, in gaining support, and later in informally evaluating the results. In fact, committee deliberations probably should include consideration of the steps and the strategy for placing recommendations into operation. It is occasionally useful to informally convene the original committee for one or two sessions after a time lapse to determine the committee's own perception of its success or failure.

The work of the self-study committee can now begin. The points suggested in the section on comprehensive self-study earlier in this chapter offer some direction, but the following detailed outline is likely to be more useful. Moreover, it may suggest ways to assign responsibilities to subcommittees. The particular virtue of this outline is that it immediately focuses attention on outcomes.

A. Determining institution purposes, goals, and educational objectives
   1. Review charter, catalogs, board minutes, presidential statements, published documents.
   2. Determine their significance in specifying the role and philosophical stance of the institution.
   3. Evaluate their consistency with each other and constancy over time.
   4. Determine whether institutional and subunit goals are consistent and mutually supportive.
   5. Ascertain the views of various groups as to the acceptability of the purposes, goals, and objectives.
   6. Determine whether resources are adequate to achieve the purposes.
   7. Determine whether all purposes, goals, and objectives are presently recognized in existing programs.
   8. Review the means regularly used to alert faculty, students, and others to institutional purposes, goals, and objectives.
B. Measuring educational and other outcomes
   1. What are the expected educational outcomes and how far do those involved in planning educational experiences diverge in substance or priorities from those expectations? Evidence may include official statements, inventories, questionnaires, interviews, conferences, and critical review of requirements, actual student programs, and range of experiences offered.

2. Are expected educational outcomes appropriate to the clientele? Characteristics of entering students: ability level as determined by tests, previous academic performance, anecdotal records, recommendations; age, interests, aptitudes, and objectives as determined by appropriate inventories, interviews, or otherwise; attitudes and values as determined by appropriate means; work and other relevant experiences as determined by records, questionnaires, interviews, and other means. Expectations of faculty and others regarding student performance on specific objectives as determined by questionnaires, interviews, group discussions, other means. Student opinions as to appropriateness of goals as determined by questionnaires, interviews, group discussions, other means.

3. How is student achievement evaluated? Evaluation must be in terms of institutional purposes, faculty interpretation of them, social needs, and student expectations regarding intellectual growth, nonintellectual changes, acquisition of occupational or professional skills. Evaluation may be in terms of minimum or mastery level of performance, comparative measures, value added, student-developed (and faculty-approved) goals. Evidence may be standardized tests, attitude scales, written and oral examinations given by institutional personnel or others, anecdotal records, portfolios of student work, evaluation reports from supervisors of off-campus activities or adjunct faculty, student self-evaluation, and peer evaluation.

4. How is institutional effectiveness in achieving other institutional goals evaluated? Community service—evidence may be community reaction as secured through questionnaires, group and individual conferences, other means; institutional personnel opinion as secured through questionnaires, interviews, other means. Other services—checklists of services considered desirable and lists of services provided, clientele

served, and results. Published research, reviews, and so forth—lists.

C. Evaluating learning experiences in terms of desired outcomes

   1. Types of experiences provided and indication of extent to which students are involved in them: formal class and laboratory instruction; tutorial and other institutional interviews, group discussions; statistics; expenditures; use of external activities, fine arts exhibits, musical and dramatic events, visiting lecturers, athletics, residence living; formally organized or informal educational opportunities off campus, including educational experiences in other institutions and agencies (business and industry, service organizations, government, foreign study).

   2. Evidence may include judgments of faculty, administrators, supervisors, students, and others involved in the activities as determined through questionnaires, interviews, group discussions, tests, written reports, lists of accomplishments or tasks completed.

   3. Assessment of institutional climate. Evidence may include environment scales, interviews, group discussions, use of visiting evaluators.

D. Evaluating the adequacy and utilization of resources in terms of desired outcomes—types of resources

   1. Instructional staff including counselors: traditional institutional staff—academic, professional, occupational; adjunct faculty from other institutions and agencies. Evidence may include judgments of administrators, faculty members, supervisory personnel, students; statistics; course requirements.

   2. Library and other on-campus and off-campus learning resources. Evidence may include judgments of administrators, faculty members, supervisory personnel, students; statistics.

   3. Financial resources. Evaluation by administrators, instructional staff, other institutional personnel. Evidence of adequacy or inadequacy of resources to be

based on observations of institutional activities; possibly of costs or expenditures or use of external evaluators.

4. Physical plant and equipment, on campus and at off-campus locations where educational activities are carried on. Evidence may include judgments of administrators, faculty, students, other personnel as secured through questionnaires, interviews, group discussion; statistics; expenditures; use of external evaluators.

E. Evaluating the planning and decision-making processes in terms of desired outcomes

1. What persons and groups within the institution—institutional governing board, administrative officers, faculty groups, student groups—are involved in planning and decision making? What are the actual and desirable roles of each?

2. What agencies, groups, and persons outside the institution—coordinating boards; other organized boards, offices, agencies; alumni, press, community forces and pressures—are involved in planning and decision making? What are the actual and desirable roles of each?

3. How are students involved in (and assisted by faculty) decisions regarding their own programs in relation to desired outcomes?

4. Evidence may include interviews, conferences, questionnaires directed to persons involved in or knowledgeable about the mechanisms and processes.

F. Interpreting objectives, means of attainment, and evidence of accomplishment to new faculty, to students, and to the public

1. Who or what office is responsible?

2. How is the material organized and communicated?

3. What is the reaction of these groups?

In the process of defining the task and simultaneously of getting acquainted, each individual should have an opportunity to state concerns, raise questions, suggest relevant data, indicate sources of help for the committee, and suggest procedures.

If some requested data are already available, these should be prepared for distribution and explained by those responsible for the collection. Usually several resource persons should be invited to make presentations to the entire committee. If a number of studies are necessary, the office of institutional research, other appropriate agencies or individuals, or committee staff should be asked to initiate the studies.

In the remainder of this section I present some advice on the general operation of the committee. It is rarely profitable to record all statements and discussions in detail, but a member of the committee or a study director (possibly the chairman), with stenographic assistance, should keep minutes and process these for distribution at or before the next meeting. Thus agreements and commitments are on record, areas of disagreement are acknowledged, misunderstandings are quickly revealed, progress is facilitated, and repetition of earlier discussions is avoided. Invited statements by resource persons or consultants and research reports should be reproduced and distributed for later use and to ensure that absent members have the benefit of this information.

For comprehensive self-studies, separate committees or subcommittees may have been designated at the initial stage. If so, an overall coordinating committee or council is essential, and the suggestions thus far would be appropriately applied to it or to a combined session of all committees. If subcommittees have not been identified previously, early discussions usually define reasonably discrete aspects of the task, and subcommittees can then be identified on the basis of interest and assigned to these topics. In forming subcommittees it is usually wise to add individuals to each subcommittee who do not serve on the main committee. Such individuals are usually readily identified by interest and competence in the topic. If resources permit, each subcommittee should have a staff person to follow up on its requests and assist the subcommittee chairman in maintaining records of its deliberations. In large institutions, it has sometimes been helpful to identify in each college a liaison person or a subcommittee to discuss and report on the particular issues and problems of that unit. This pattern can become cumbersome, and the same ends can usually be achieved by scheduled hearings at which individuals or groups can, by prior appointment, present their concerns to the subcommittees or to the total committee.

The entire campus should be kept apprised of progress, but early reports should avoid any implication that final recommendations have already been reached. Rather, the emphasis should be on the analysis of the issues, the range of factors considered, and the alternative solutions which have been suggested. Education rather than resolution is the initial goal.

As individuals or groups (committee or subcommittee members or others) develop strong views and begin to argue persuasively for them, they should be asked to put these into position papers with their names attached. These papers can be circulated and the suggested alternatives discussed at an appropriate time. Emphasis should be placed on inclusion of relevant data, rather than simply on expression of opinion.

As such position papers accumulate and as subcommittees come up with tentative recommendations, these can be circulated widely. Open hearings may be scheduled at which individuals express their reactions and rebut the views expressed. As commissioned studies are completed, the evidence may effectively invalidate certain courses of action which have been suggested.

Individuals and committees should take into account the financial implications of their recommendations. These implications, when related to available resources, usually point to the necessity of establishing priorities or of tailoring recommendations to reality. They may completely rule out some recommendations, such as giving all advisers a 50 percent reduction in teaching load.

Subcommittee reports are likely to be overlapping and contradictory. Joint sessions may resolve some of these contradictions, but others may have to be resolved by compromise or by majority vote in the total committee. The issue of minority reports must be resolved. Although minority reports ease the conscience of those who dissent from the majority, they do cast a shadow over acceptance and implementation of the report by tossing the issues they raise into a broad forum. If these debated issues are not central to the problems studied and are reasonably independent of other recommendations, they can be omitted or relegated to a section of the report containing unresolved issues.

A good self-study report is not written by a committee; rather, it is written by one or more individuals who are sensitive to the feelings and insights of the individuals who make up the total committee and who are well acquainted with the rationale and the data supporting the recommendations. The chairman, secretary, study director, and no more than one other individual selected by the committee constitute a maximum-size writing group. After committee deliberations have been completed, an interval of several weeks should be scheduled in which a draft of a final report is prepared and circulated to the entire committee. It may not seem wise to distribute this tentative report widely, for it may arouse such intense reactions as to influence individuals or the committee to reopen old and already resolved issues. Yet, it would be equally unwise to maintain complete secrecy, which is patently impossible anyway. Tentativeness must be emphasized, and openness is to be encouraged. The entire committee should be brought back together for a page-by-page review of the report. Purely editorial suggestions should be made individually, but the committee should be permitted to question phrasing which is ambiguous or statements which appear to violate earlier agreements.

If the self-study was commissioned by an administrator, he or she should decide the extent of its distribution. It would be unwise not to distribute it to all the faculty and to the board. Students should have access to it, but it may be overly expensive to distribute it to all students, most of whom are likely to be indifferent. If the report is voluminous, a digest of the recommendations or a brief version may be prepared. This version is far more likely to be read than the unabridged version. Or, in a large report, background data, studies, and major position papers can be assigned to appendices or to a supplemental volume available in limited quantity.

The order in which recommendations are presented may

seem to be a minor matter, but it is often a major factor in their acceptance. Recommendations are usually interrelated, and some may be corollaries of others. Juxtaposing these interrelated or dependent recommendations may avoid hasty judgments that certain factors have been ignored or downgraded in making a particular recommendation. When this organization is not possible, parenthetical notes appended to each recommendation should indicate related recommendations and perhaps provide a comment on the implications. Since neither the order nor the content of recommendations necessarily indicates to whom recommendations are addressed, consideration should be given to the inclusion of a section in which recommendations are grouped according to the administrative officer or unit which must authorize or approve the change. By this device, many changes can be effected without formal processing through the committee structure and the hierarchy of administrative officers. Recommendations regarding changes in certain courses, if addressed to the departments involved, may be made immediately. If the departments refuse the recommendations, they may then be processed through other channels. A recommendation regarding a new central administrative office should naturally be addressed to the president, who can act at once if funds are available and the recommendation is widely accepted. Thus, action on a self-study report can be expedited by spreading the recommendations over many persons and offices rather than having them remain a monolithic item to be processed somehow through ordinary channels, with parts referred to appropriate committees and individuals. Seldom can an administrative officer put a set of self-study recommendations into effect by fiat, and the impact of the study is lost (and so may be most of the recommendations) if the whole report must be fed from the self-study group to the slow, nit-picking process of standing committees. But if the conduct of the study has created an attitude of receptivity and if each of the recommendations is strongly supported by a majority of the self-study group, a large segment of the faculty, and the individuals or offices most directly concerned, many recommendations may be accepted and put into effect before the final report is ready for distribution.

Maximizing the Impact

No self-study can be regarded as effective if it does not produce change. Sometimes the change is reflected only in a strengthened conviction that everything is well with the institution, although it is difficult to believe that institutions exist which are so good they cannot be improved.

Obviously, the extent to which the study has impact depends upon the extent to which a state of readiness has developed for the study; the clarity of the charge given to the committee; the membership of the committee; the tact and leadership of the chairman; the availability and quality of staff assistance; the cooperation extended throughout the institution in providing relevant information; the effectiveness of consultants, resource persons, and so on; and the quality of the report in substance, logic, and format.

In addition, continuing communication among committee members, administrators, faculty, and students throughout the study is critical. There is no such thing as secrecy on a campus; partial, confused, and erroneous revelation and rumor are the result of any attempt to maintain it. If the committee takes the view (as some individuals on it will) that they have been asked to resolve the future of the institution and that, in due course, they will reveal all, the study is well along toward failure. If the committee views its job partly as education, it must regularly communicate its concerns, studies, and developing points of view to the entire institution. If the committee also views itself as a unifying agent and a synthesizer of ideas, it must solicit opinions, proposals, and reactions so that everyone may feel that his or her view has been heard and understood, even though it did not finally prevail. In this process of communication, opinions are changed, and the views of committee members and those not on the committee may eventually coincide. When this happens, the self-study has been eminently successful.

Achieving implementation of the recommendations is relatively simple if the educative functions of the self-study have been effectively performed and if opinions have been crystalized which are congruent with the recommendations. The duration of the self-study can be adjusted to accommodate this desired goal. If it is apparent that widely diverse opinions exist on some issues, extension of the study period to provide for further analysis, collection of data, and exploration of contrasting views may be desirable. Anyone who observes legislative operations is aware of the fact that some good and badly needed pieces of legislation are the results of months and even years of embryonic attempts. There are meritorious ideas for which the time has not yet come. Individuals have to be introduced to them and meet them several times before they agree to live with them.

Thus it is that any appraisal of the effectiveness of a self-study based upon how many of its recommendations were immediately adopted is unfair. A more sensitive evaluation seeks to determine two or three years later whether practices have been gradually modified to accord with recommendations, even though the recommendations were never formally accepted; whether recommendations, perhaps somewhat modified, have been adopted at a later date with or without reference to the self-study report; and whether changes in policy and in practice have been made which differ from the self-study recommendations, but which emerged as a result of the continuing ferment induced by the study.

In all these circumstances, it is appropriate to trace the role of the self-study group. As individuals, they frequently continue to promote ideas which are not at first accepted. Not infrequently, some of them become administrators and, in this role, accomplish what the self-study did not immediately accomplish. A self-study may solve immediate problems, but it may also be an investment in the education of people who, in the long run, influence the course of the institution.

Role of Institutional Research

In the preceding discussion of self-study activity, I make incidental reference to the roles of institutional researchers. An institutional self-study is unlikely to be effective unless adequate groundwork for it has been laid. Institutional research reports can provide much of the necessary background. Analysis of such diverse problems as student difficulties in fulfilling general education requirements, high numbers of waivers of requirements, and patterns in changes of majors may enable researchers to document the existence of larger issues—such as the necessity of changing not only curriculum requirements but the courses used to fulfill them.

Institutional researchers can assist self-study by collecting or grouping available local, regional, or national data; by making surveys of opinion; or by conducting requested studies. Such research may be carried out even when an office of institutional research does not exist; those who do it are at that time engaged in institutional research.

Although the term *self-study* as ordinarily used implies a committee, task force, or research group with membership on a representative basis, an office of institutional research can define a needed study, select a committee, and give direction to the deliberations of the committee. However, the nature of the problem must be considered before study is undertaken by an office of research. Study of a problem which faculty members or students consider to be in their domain probably cannot be so initiated even if institutional research investigations have pointed out the problem. An effort to improve the statistics available on departmental operations for use in the budgeting process may be so developed because of general recognition that the office of institutional research has special concerns and competences appropriate to the task. The acceptability of recommendations in this case comes from recognition by the departments that the new data systems developed are valid and useful.

The distinctions between institutional research and self-study are essentially these: an office of institutional research is a continuing operation with permanent personnel, whereas a self-study is limited in time and carried out on an ad hoc basis; an office of institutional research is typically charged with continuing study of a wide range of problems, whereas a self-study is focused on a particular set of problems; and an office of institutional research is concerned primarily with pointing up and analyzing problems through data collections and studies, whereas a self-study is initiated to resolve these problems through proposing new policies or structures.

Thus an office of institutional research and a self-study task force can be viewed as interacting and mutually supportive groups. Each becomes effective through the presence and judicious activity of the other. However, many of the problems pointed up by the office of institutional research can be resolved through existing channels. Self-study activities should be occasional in nature, initiated only when the complications of the task require that study be conducted outside normal activities, that widespread representation be involved for educational purposes, and that a synthesis of views be attained to assure the feasibility and acceptability of the recommendations.

Rolling Review

An alternative to the arduous complete institutional self-study and its limited time span is a rolling-review process, in which several topics or areas of study are regularly studied at intervals. For example, a five-year rotation might use the following emphases: undergraduate curriculum—offerings and requirements, general and liberal education; instruction and faculty advising; admissions, student personnel services, instructional services, library, physical facilities; research, graduate education, community service, extension; purposes, role, governance, organization, budget.

Particular emphases might be appropriate in a given year depending on past study. The rolling review would, over a five-year span, cover all activities in a related manner, but limit the amount of energy required in any one year. A major issue or theme might displace or be superimposed upon a planned topic. For example, such topics as health programs, continuing education, or external degree programs might be regarded as sufficiently important for such special treatment.

By arrangement with an office of institutional research, data collections and studies can be related to this process so that materials are available to facilitate study of a particular topic. Questions and relevant data can be provided a committee as it undertakes its task for the year along with digests or copies of previous self-study reports related to the current emphases.

Summary

The self-study procedure as developed in this chapter should provide a basis for review and possible alteration of purposes, goals, and objectives, and for improvement in the means of evaluating student learning and accomplishment of other goals. The success of the endeavor depends upon imbedding review, evaluation, and renewal into the institution and upon the development of ways of both involving the students, faculty, and general public and communicating to them the nature of the commitment and its results.

Once the process of self-study is in operation, it may be efficiently conducted on a regular rolling-review basis rather than as a major task conducted at intervals. Sectors of the institution such as undergraduate education, graduate education, research, and decision-making processes could be designated focuses of a rolling review in which each in turn would be studied carefully at five- to eight-year intervals.

Bibliographical Note

Institutional self-study, in its fullest sense, can treat every facet of institutional operations. Hence almost any reference in the Bibliography has relevance to some phase of institutional self-study. Every accrediting agency has materials on the nature of self-study and the data required for accreditation. The 1971 *Institutional Self-Study Handbook* of the Commission on Higher Education of the Middle States Association of Colleges and Secondary Schools is a good example. Harcleroad and Dickey (1975) relate educational auditing and accreditation. Ernst and Ernst (1969) provide guidelines for study of management practices. The Dressel and Associates (1972) volume on institutional research includes a chapter (Chap. 11) on the conduct of self-study which corresponds closely to the treatment in this chapter. Other chapters of this volume are also instructive for those undertaking self-study.

The Jenkins (1971) volume is specifically aimed at self-study of involvement in urban affairs. Kells (1972) deals with new forms of self-study in the context of accreditation. Ladd's (1970) treatment of selected self-studies and their impact in bringing about changes in educational policy is particularly instructive and somewhat disconcerting in pointing up the lack of success in some cases. Chickering (1974a) suggests some new ideas for making student-aid-program assessments helpful.

Chapter 18

State Coordination
and Planning

State coordination of higher education has existed in various forms for many years, but the recent and rapid development of formal patterns of state coordination and of the unified (or single) system is a reaction to increases in the number of institutions of higher education, in enrollments, and in the financial requirements of these institutions. The tendency of all state-supported four-year institutions to develop graduate programs, obtain research funds, and generally to emulate the one or two preeminent publicly supported universities also encouraged both the extension and the strengthening of state coordination.

There are various forms and degrees of state coordination and control of higher education. In a coordination situation, institutions have their own governing boards, but another agency or coordinating board is assigned certain responsibilities for planning, new program approval, and perhaps institutional

433

budget determination or review prior to submission to state fiscal agencies. In some cases, there are single boards for each of various groups of institutions as well as a statewide coordinating board. In other states, there is a single statewide university, a single board, and a president or chancellor for the entire system. The influence, authority, powers, and responsibilities of coordinating and governing boards and their staffs depend upon the enabling legislation and also upon the political structures and the personalities operating within the system.

A chapter on evaluation of state coordination may seem irrelevant in a book that is devoted primarily to evaluation within an institution, but so many institutions are now affected by policies, rules, regulations, and data requirements generated outside that failure to consider the impact of these policies on evaluations conducted within such institutions would be a significant omission. Formal evaluation can be both useless and dangerous when decisions are made elsewhere. Furthermore, evaluation of coordinating boards and single state systems may be a necessity. These agencies are regularly engaged, without fully recognizing it, in continuing evaluation of the various colleges and programs which operate under them. But evaluators are not notably inclined to evaluate either themselves or their evaluations. Unless coordinating boards recognize the need for self-evaluation, they may become a drag on the development of state higher education rather than an impetus for improvement. Governors or legislatures or both may conclude that the formal evaluation of a coordinating or state governing board is a task which they should undertake. This could be a healthy development were it separable from political considerations, which it is not. To prevent a purely political evaluation, the board and its staff should arrange for an objective external evaluation to assess the success of centralization and to determine the views and concerns of the institutions and their clients.

Purposes

The major purpose of coordination (or a single board system) is that of statewide *planning*. This emphasis arose when increasing enrollments made it necessary to add new institutions and new programs. Political pressures from various communities and segments of the state vying with each other for a new institution or new programs were strong. The task of locating new institutions and new programs was, therefore, extremely sensitive, and occasionally location was determined more by political power than by good sense. Statewide planning now is more likely to be directed to the elimination of some institutions and to the containment of others; but boards still must recurrently survey higher education needs and engage in role and scope studies designed to determine the range of programs and responsibilities assigned to specific institutions. As part of this survey task, for budget review and decisions in central offices and on campuses, state systems have developed elaborate information systems. Considering the previous lack of information on many campuses, this has been a significant and useful advance, but it raises problems in those institutions with unique information systems which may not fit the statewide system. An alternative information system which comes from a higher echelon presents subtle pressures to alter institutional structures and programs to conform to the data system.

The elimination of duplicate programs among institutions is another part of the planning function of state coordination. The record on program elimination is not generally good because program elimination runs into counterpressures and criticisms within institutions and within the community served. Officers of coordinating or control boards are not immune from these criticisms. Repercussions and retributions from regional legislators are also possible. As central officers in state coordinating systems have found, elimination of a program can be an even more sensitive issue than adding a new one. In addition, the immediate gains from program elimination are limited because of the necessity of phasing out the program to accommodate presently enrolled students and because tenured faculty cannot readily be assigned to other activities or terminated.

Another purpose of state coordination, still in the planning domain, is that of encouraging collaboration among institutions. Competition among institutions in services and extension centers has long been a recognized fact, but collaboration does not come readily until a central authority actively promotes it through committees, institutes, or other structures administered from the central office. In fact, any extensive cooperation among state universities usually has to be imposed. One goal in encouraging collaboration has been that of inaugurating multiple-delivery systems. External degree programs and new patterns of adult education can be readily accommodated by such coordination. Desirable as these are from a statewide point of view, such collaboration does not set well on independent campuses because the identity of the institution is lost. Furthermore, new delivery systems require coordination from a central office, which ultimately results in increasing resources in the central office.

Another major purpose of statewide planning is the assignment of the mission and purpose of each institution, which can be enforced by withdrawing funds. This assignment of mission is critical in undergraduate programs and is even more critical in graduate education and professional schools. Such assignment generally places a ceiling on the range of activities, which is not welcomed except by those institutions which already have a complete roster of graduate and professional programs. One of the joys of administrators and the faculty, too, on autonomous campuses has been that of initiating new programs which increase the prominence of the institution and ultimately bring new funds.

A second major purpose of coordination is *management and governance.* Although there is ordinarily considerable difference between the role and powers of a coordinating board and a single governing board, this is not of great significance for this analysis. Both review budget requests from separate campuses and in some cases can reduce them or combine them into a single request. In reviewing this request, the state budget office and the legislature may, depending upon the legislation and practice, review requests of individual institutions or deal with the total request as it comes from the state board. If they deal with a total request, an allocation below the request (the usual situation) gives the board the task of determining how to spread the reduced funds. This reduction is not necessarily made on a proportional basis. Indeed, to do so would indicate that the central coordinating or control agency is not adequately performing its function. The allocation is instead based upon an assessment of efficiency and productivity in the various institutions and upon statewide priorities. This process is essentially a form of evaluation. It involves accountability—using funds as specified in the original request and the board allocation and also ascertaining that the funds are used efficiently and effectively in the production of degrees or other outputs of importance to the state. In performing this function, central agencies may exert detailed control over educational expenditures, even to the point in some systems of specifying salary for each position on the staff, with the result that when an appointment is made at a lower salary or when a position is unfilled, these dollars revert to the central office.

As has already been mentioned, central offices are also involved in the management of multiple-delivery systems within a state. Institutions have generally been competitive in their extension programs, in their service programs, and even, to a considerable extent, in their research and graduate programs. Under a single board or strong coordinating system, duplication of offerings in a particular community is likely to be regarded with suspicion, and strong central coordination may be regarded as the only solution, although it may seem, in some cases, that competition among institutions has only been replaced by competition between the central offices and all the campuses.

Another purpose of state coordination and management is that of coordination with other systems including private colleges within or outside the state and public systems in other states. This coordination can be particularly useful in promoting agreements for exchange of students between states or in developing educational programs on state borders which serve needs in both areas. In some circumstances agreements can also be developed for certain numbers of students in specific programs to be absorbed by a university in another state. It is much easier for two states to develop agreements when they have strong central coordination than when each has a set of independent institutions.

The preservation of diversity is another major goal of state systems. Without coordination or central control all institutions have striven to attain the comprehensive model—full-fledged university status with a complete range of research and service activities. While institutions with this full university character usually regard themselves as unique in contributing to diversity in the education provided, a trend to this model has tended to eliminate diversity rather than to encourage it. At the same time, the preservation of diversity in the sense that it freezes institutional roles by limiting them to their present scope of programs is not viewed as an advantage by the institutions themselves. Diversity is precious when there are no limits on institutional development, but diversity is not so regarded when enforced by someone else.

Another oft-stated purpose is assurance of social responsibility. Institutions, following the desires of their faculty and administrators, tended to proliferate programs and increase costs without much regard for the real needs of the state. New programs were invariably interpreted as meeting an existing social need, but the interpretations were based solely on institutional aspirations and a highly dubious interpretation of hastily gathered evidence. A central coordinating office can resist local pressures which lead to such proliferation and can assure that total state needs are met.

Another stated purpose of coordination and management has been that of protection of quality. Presumably this purpose is related to the preservation of diversity and the assignment of role and scope, for one of the most serious threats to quality is the undue expansion of institutions into new programs without adequate resources to support them. At the same time, quality can hardly be protected unless quality is measured, and, to this point in time, no state system (or anyone else) has developed adequate measures of program or institutional quality.

Problems

Perhaps the primary problem with state coordination is that, despite all the discussions which highlight planning, preservation of diversity, protection of quality, and other attractive phrases, the primary purposes are heavily negative—budget and program controls. These controls lead, in turn, to a great amount of paper work and frequently to great delay in processing various actions, policies, and even curricular changes. Individuals in a central office removed from a campus tend to develop, perhaps unwittingly, a dictatorial procedure in which decisions are made without fully understanding and without even being willing to take the time to find out what is involved. The apparent mission of many persons in coordinating roles is that of curbing the enterprise of campus faculty and administrators, who seem always to be promoting new ideas which ultimately, if not immediately, require more funding. There is a negativism, too, in the desire to discourage the zeal of students, alumni, and communities, which would encourage institutions to do something novel.

These negative approaches affect both the individual institutions and the central offices. In the institutions, the first effect is the introduction of another level of bureaucracy. A confusion of roles and authority arises not only between the chief executive officer at the state level and the campus chief executive, but between various subsidiary officers at the central site and the chief executive and sundry associates on the local scene. Obviously, if everything from the central office had to go through the president of the system to each local administrator, the communication system would become clogged; yet when several individuals in a state coordinating office communicate directly to their counterparts on local campuses in a manner which implies that there is a superior-inferior relationship, problems are sure to arise. Distance, time, and personalities make major issues out of minor problems. In a central office with much correspondence and many calls from the several campuses, the tendency is to respond on the basis of the priorities of the central office. Other matters are delayed even though they may seem crucial on the local campuses. And in some cases it simply is unclear whether a decision can be made on the local campus or whether it must be referred to a higher level.

The second major problem for the institutions is the enforced uniformity in procedures, rules, and regulations. Initially, these are perhaps rather limited and somewhat loosely worded, but as time goes on they become more and more tightly phrased and applied indiscriminately to all institutions. Any attempt to bypass these procedures or to make an exception is fraught with peril; yet, at the same time, the inability of local administrators to deal immediately with issues on their own campuses lowers their prestige in the eyes of the faculty and student body.

A third problem is caused by another by-product of central coordination, the central coordinating agencies and interinstitutional committees. These cause a heavy drain on the energy and time of local administrators. Repeated committee meetings on a campus are at times exhausting and inefficient, but when statewide committees must meet repeatedly to settle minor issues, the drain on human resources becomes even more serious.

A fourth major concern on the part of the local campus is the inevitable loss of autonomy, which shows up in a number of different ways. First, there is a loss of freedom to determine what to do and how to do it, for central coordination seems to take unto itself more and more decisions. Second, the local campus is likely to lose financial support. In the early days of state coordination, the argument was frequently presented (with some concrete supporting evidence) that one result of coordination was increased resources for higher education. That, however, was at a time when institutions were rapidly increasing in enrollment. Undoubtedly, revenues to the institutions would have increased under any pattern. But with decreasing enrollments and the current economic situation, the individual campus may have less dollar support. The local campus is forced toward standardization and uniformity and begins to focus on what can be done rather than what should be done. Tight budget procedures can ultimately change section sizes, patterns of instruction, faculty load assignments, size of offices and classrooms, and, indeed, almost everything involved in an institution. None of these changes has not previously been made on some campus as a result of decisions by administrators and faculty. The difference is that when the decision was made on the campus, the changes were accepted and attention could be given to other matters. But when a change, no matter how reasonable, is inflicted without an opportunity for individuals to express their unique concerns, it may generate waves and cross-currents which intrude upon and hamper other activities.

A final problem caused for individual institutions is that the flight of decision making from the campus results in an inevitable loss of imaginative, decisive leadership on campuses. Administrators and the faculty lose a sense of accomplishment. The resulting low morale grows out of the lack of outlets for energy, imagination, and innovation. Devotion to a local campus which no longer has significant autonomy is weakened.

If one turns to the problems in the central offices themselves, a number can be listed. Like those suggested for institutions, these do not all necessarily happen in any one situation and, whether any one of them happens depends upon the capabilities and sensitivities of central office personnel. Obviously, central office personnel must focus on the system. This is their job, and no one can fault them for it. At the same time, in viewing the statewide program as a single unit, they may become insensitive to the idiosyncrasies and necessary differences on local campuses. They may refuse program requests simply because that program exists elsewhere, without regard for the local scene. Since a central office is likely to be located in the capital, the orientation is likely to be to the governor and the legislature rather than to the institutions, with the result that requests from institutions are viewed more in reference to the probable reaction of the governor and the legislature than in terms of institutional and even state needs. In short, there is a tendency, when close to the offices where final allocations are made, to consider what is reasonable and possible rather than what is needed. An appropriate balance between attention to institutional and state educational needs and political exigencies is not easily achieved.

An institution (other than the one or two major institutions in any state which usually carry considerable political weight) which tries to assert its own individuality is frequently met with distrust from the central office. Such assertions may be viewed as an attempt by local leaders to curry public favor or national reputation for innovations. Thus the institution might indeed be given credit for innovation—credit which central officials would prefer to go to the system. Since innovations on any campus must be approved centrally, there is also the possibility that publicity releases come from central offices or central office administrators who thereby seize credit for the innovations. This is much easier for central administrators removed from campuses to do than it would be for an administrator on a local campus to claim credit for an idea generated by a dean or faculty member.

In most state coordinating systems, there is an extensive attempt in the early stages to visit local campuses and to demonstrate concern for and involvement in their problems. Over time, as problems develop, there is a tendency to stop these campus visits, to lose sensitivity to campus concerns. As a result, actions from the central office take on the character of edicts rather than suggestions or requests. The central office may claim maintenance of diversity, but its pressures are all in the direction of uniformity, and the longer the central office exists the greater the tendency to become rigid and to resist change in its own practices.

An additional problem is the tendency of central offices to expand. Each request or requisition encourages central office officials to engage in more and more detailed scrutiny of all funds and projects; and this scrutiny becomes so time-consuming that there are pressures for expanding staff, expanding budget, and adding new programs of control and coordination. As these develop, in turn, there is an increasing tendency to bypass the chief local administrator and to deal with individuals under him or her who are particularly concerned with certain programs. In this process particularly cordial relationships may develop between some central administration people and those on a certain campus, which suggests, and may involve, a favoritism which is particularly irritating to other institutions with innovative ideas seeking to become centers of diversity. Much of what happens in this increasing bureaucracy concerns process rather than quality. Processes become more and more elaborate, paper work increases, and administrative costs multiply. But the question of whether a more effective educational program is provided to the state (the cost-benefit problem) is left largely unanswered.

A final problem, as some evidence suggests, is that under state coordination there is, depending upon the chief administrator, a tendency to move toward the creation of new institutions or programs and new delivery systems rather than toward the strengthening of existing ones. As is pointed out in Chapter Sixteen, administrators, like everyone else, seek to enhance their own reputations. Since the chief administrative officers in large systems are very much in the public eye and are especially vulnerable to gubernatorial or legislative criticisms and pressures, only unusual people in this position can resist actions which enhance their own stature. Chief administrators who can announce publicly and repeatedly that they have developed new patterns of education have more to gain than those who can simply report somewhere in long annual reports that new programs have been added on several campuses.

Evaluation

In the evaluation of state coordination two aspects are to be considered. The first is the response to the question: Does state coordination or control attain the objectives claimed for it? The second concerns the institutions: Are they able to maintain a sense of identity and vitality under a system in which many highly significant decisions affecting them are made far from the campus by individuals unfamiliar with particular campus needs and problems?

I begin by suggesting several major factors which should be examined in evaluating the coordinating office and officers. The first and perhaps in some ways the most difficult factor to assess is whether coordination is achieving an adequate level of support for higher education and whether that support level is higher or lower than it would have been without coordination. The institutions would prefer that it be higher; almost everyone else, that it be lower. Beyond that assessment is the question of how effectively the resources are being used. This question introduces the issue of quality, which is difficult to measure and upon which there will certainly be contrasting views. If resources have not increased markedly because of the coordinative process, the process itself may have drained off from the operational level an undue proportion of funds for activities which operate to the advantage neither of the local campuses nor of the state. This is the reiterated concern of those who oppose single systems and central coordination.

A second area to be assessed is that of public confidence in higher education. And, again, it is desirable to relate such confidence to the state of confidence prior to coordination or to the confidence which might presently exist without coordination. This is a difficult task and requires sensitive evaluation procedures in which executive officers, legislators, board members, and the public are asked to state the degree of their confidence in higher education. They should base their comments on the perceived quality of education and the benefits relative to the resources expended. In addition, however, it is necessary to sort out the extent to which the actions of the coordinating or governing office are seen by people as the source of their confidence. Finally, it is necessary to determine whether the confidence expressed is extended to the individual campuses and the programs offered or whether the confidence in coordinating-board activities is artificially created by an effective publicity program. Restoration of full confidence in higher education, with the expectation that adequate resources will be allocated to it, is certainly a major justification of coordination and perhaps the only one which ultimately might endear coordination to the separate campuses. It seems unlikely that this effect will be detected in the near future.

A third aspect of coordination which requires assessment is the clarity and acceptability of the missions, roles, purposes of various institutions. Evidence for such an assessment has to be sought from the institutions themselves, the students enrolled in the institutions, the communities in which the institutions are located, as well as from the legislature, governor, and general public. Ideally, the missions, roles, and purposes should be acceptable to all groups. It would be surprising if this were true, but the purpose of the evaluation is in part to determine deviations and reasons for them. One major issue to be explored is whether the missions, roles, and purposes have been clarified to the public. Another is whether these purposes are accepted as a positive gain in that they result in educational services of high quality or as a loss because of undue limitation of the range of programs and quenching of the enthusiasm of those seeking new educational services.

A fourth major area to be examined with regard to the impact of central coordination is the extent of funding from other sources. Without any evidence, I hypothesize that under state coordination only the one, two, or three institutions that already have outstanding national reputations are readily able to get support from governmental sources and foundations; and even they may find it increasingly difficult to do so because of the involvement of the central bureaucracy in each proposal. Beyond this group of two or three prestige institutions, other institutions in the state are likely to have difficulty in raising funds from sources other than the state except through the support of central offices. And then a locally developed project may be broadened to include other campuses or may become heavily dependent upon one individual in the central office for coordination. Whether these developments, if they come to pass, would be regarded as desirable depends upon one's vantage point.

A fifth major area to evaluate is the effectiveness and the efficiency of the procedures, paper work, meetings, governance, and other practices. In addition to the effectiveness and efficiency of the procedures, the satisfaction of the institutions with them should be carefully examined. Satisfaction of the central office officers with these procedures should also be considered, although since they presumably are in a position to change such procedures, their views might well be much less significant than those of the local campuses. However, the governor and the legislature may find it easier to impose more red tape on a single office than on a group of autonomous institutions.

A sixth area for careful evaluation is the size of the central office staff, the number of activities and functions, and the extent to which these have been increasing over time. One insightful way to examine some aspects of this area is to compare at an interval of several years the campus activities or actions which require central office approval and the nature and extent of the central office deliberations in regard to them.

A seventh area to evaluate is the extent of contact of central office personnel with the various campuses. This study should include the nature of these contacts—by phone, face to face, by visit to the campus, by visit to the central office—and should look into the nature of the communication involved. Another point to be examined carefully is the extent to which lower echelons of administration in the central office and on campus have developed relationships which bypass the formal lines of communication between chief central administrator and chief campus administrator. This aspect of evaluation should also attempt to determine the amount of insight and understanding that central office personnel and local campus people have of each other's problems and the extent of collaboration in trying to ease the difficulties.

One major item not included in the seven, because it is a composite of issues involved in a number of them, is a comparison of the extent to which the identity and character of the individual institutions have been maintained and the extent to which these institutions have acquired a bland, colorless character; but this item takes us into the second phase of the evaluation.

In many respects the points already listed for the evaluation of central coordination have their campus counterparts and much the same list could be used. But a number of factors relate solely to the institutions. The most important is the extent of local enthusiasm and initiative. If these have been lost, a local operation becomes a colorless and stereotyped educational delivery system. The morale of the faculty degenerates simply because any innovative ideas are likely to be discouraged by lack of funds to support them and by the complicated steps of attaining bureaucratic approval. Even the reward system may become so prescribed by central office decisions that the extent to which individual modifications can be made on the local scene are infinitesimal. If so, local administrators are deprived of one of their major means of effecting change—that is, by rewarding those persons who are particularly effective either in carrying out their present duties or in developing innovative ways of performing them.

These developments are likely to have a direct impact on the curriculum and on the motivation of professors in their teaching activities. Any curriculum change that would seriously affect the output of the institution in credit hours and greatly modify the reporting pattern or the budget may receive careful examination at both levels in ways which have little to do with educational benefits for students. Any attempt on the part of the instructor to use methods requiring more resources or a change in the size of classes may have implications far beyond the course and the department. The possibility of significant student effect on a local program is at least as seriously impeded as is the prospect of faculty impact. Whenever decisions or recommendations have to be cleared at another level, the loss of time and the long exchange are certain to arouse resentment and dilute any enthusiasm which may originally have existed.

To the extent that faculty members and students have their attention directed beyond the local scene to various committees and central office administrators, the identity and individuality of the immediate campus are, to some extent, dimmed. If individuals in the institution must, in response to community concerns or expressed local desires for changes or services, point out that the institution no longer can make these decisions, the community may turn to its legislative representatives or to other means of exerting power on the central office. What might have been a commendable innovation yielding gratification to all becomes, then, a power play in which individuals get what they want by exerting pressure. The local campus no longer meets requests on its own volition; it does so by pressure indirectly exerted upon it. What might have been a pleasant, cooperative, interactive relationship thus can degenerate into a service relationship with unpleasant overtones on both sides.

As local institutions adapt to attempts to standardize at the central level, difficulties in purchase of equipment and in adaptation of facilities to local desires or needs may arise. Various supplies and services can no longer be purchased in the immediate area but, rather, must be ordered through a central purchasing system seeking standard items at lowest cost. In all these instances, the time spent in waiting, the development of a response rather than an active mode, and the sheer and discouraging amount of paper work moving back and forth can become deadening influences on local initiative.

As local campuses are forced into stereotyped patterns by regulations and budget procedures, the incentive for evaluation of local programs is weakened by four factors. First, innovations which call for evaluation are difficult to launch and to fund. Second, funds for educational research and evaluation are difficult to acquire. Third, the tendency is to move evaluation and educational research to a system level because of the common data base and the difficulty of acquiring local funds to support extensive data collection. Fourth, and perhaps most important, the local resistance to evaluation is likely to increase simply because local initiative and enthusiasm are curtailed. What, indeed, is to be gained by local evaluation when decisions which might be made as a result must be approved elsewhere? And evaluation with critical overtones could bring retribution. Much of this paragraph is hypothetical, but contacts on a number of campuses suggest that these effects are entirely possible and are already sensed in some measure.

Central coordination and single systems are inherently neither good nor bad. The intent is good, but practice can make them bad. A reasonable expectation is that the results will be mixed. Hence evaluation is highly desirable to discern what is effective and to correct what is found to be deleterious. Thus far, unfortunately, there is little evidence that system administrators, coordinators, or boards either accept the need for such evaluation or are engaging in it.

The lack of such evaluation has caused this chapter to be written in a critical vein and to some extent in terms of hypothetical rather than real developments. Coordination which is primarily procedural in nature (providing ways of dealing with problems or events and using consultative mechanisms) can, by hardly noticeable degrees, move to making substantive decisions enforced by the power of resource allocation and can move eventually to making constitutional changes which legally define institutional roles and missions and central agency powers. Only by sensitive and continuing evaluation can this trend and its strengths or weaknesses in providing quality educational services be determined.

Bibliographical Note

Although the literature pertaining to statewide coordination and planning is most often characterized by proselytism, the following selections highlight some of the basic issues relevant to the topic.

Glenny (1974-1975), Glenny and Dalglish (1973), and Berdahl (1975) are credited with bringing initial attention to the issue of planning for low or no growth in higher education. Glenny elaborates the implications for an institution in a steady state. As editor of a collection of articles on statewide planning, Berdahl presents a comprehensive and balanced discussion of the appropriate roles and possibilities of coordinating boards.

Leslie (1973) specifically addresses the basic assumption of many advocates of coordination. He challenges both the assumption and the planning based on it.

Perkins (1973) and Wing (1972) present varying and pertinent points of view concerning external planning and coordination.

Epilogue

Costs, Decisions, and Politics

Colleges and universities are widely regarded as powerful change agents, having marked impact upon both the cognitive and the noncognitive characteristics of their students. A more restricted and safer view would admit that colleges have great potential for promoting change, of which probably only a fraction is realized in any situation. Allowing for ability and background, it is unlikely that institutions differ significantly in their impacts on their undergraduates. The noninterest of most college faculty members in utilizing new learning techniques and in exploring seriously the assessment of learning through life experience or off-campus study reflects the widely prevalent emphasis on faculty input and traditional process rather than on output. But, on the other side, efforts to foster innovation have been limited and sporadic, and attempts to assess its impacts have had inconsequential results.

450

Reasons for Avoiding Evaluation

Most evaluation activities of faculty members have been devoted to assessing student achievement in content aspects of individual courses. When it is proposed that courses, programs, the faculty, and the institutions require continuing evaluation as a basis for providing evidence of their effectiveness, efficiency, and accountability, both lack of understanding and resistance are quickly evident. The resistance is, in part, a result of inability to comply because of lack of experience and the complications of the task. In addition, outcomes have simply not been made specific, and, in the effusive forms usually stated, they are largely meaningless. Desired or preferred outcomes are put forward despite full recognition by faculty members that what they expect and what they perceive through their own evaluation are both rather less than what they desire. Actual outcomes including unanticipated and sometimes undesirable outcomes are largely unknown, and most faculty and many administrators would seemingly prefer to leave it that way so that their voicing of the ideal is not compromised by the reality.

In such a context, the full range of alternatives to attain objectives is not considered. Faculty preferences determine instructional practices. Costs are ignored. Adjustments in the face of resource constraints are made in the most obvious ways, accompanied by assertions that quality is being endangered. But no supporting evidence is available, and no consideration is given to whether complete program restructuring might maintain or even improve quality with no increase in costs. Faculty and administrators, in the main, prefer to continue in traditional ways, feeling (with some reason) that they are not well understood and not fully appreciated. Most change or reform in higher education over the years has come about outside the existing structure—through new institutions such as the state universities, land-grant colleges, community colleges, technical institutes, and external degree programs.

This inability to adapt or change is, in great part, a result of the deficiencies of institutions in planning, policy formulation, management, and leadership. Increases in students and programs combined with new funds to support them gave to institutions an outward appearance of dynamism, of planned development, and of careful management based upon sound policy formulation. In fact, this process of accretion was not the result of sound deliberation, but rather of opportunistic (although usually commendable) response to a widely recognized need and competitive scrambling to make the most of it. With the facade of growth removed, the true character of institutional decision making is revealed to involve a large measure of drift and luck rather than conscious deliberation and choice of direction.

Responses to pressures, whether from students, government, or the public, tend to be expedients intended to quiet the criticism without seriously affecting faculty behavior or institutional structure. Thus, reduction in required courses, the hesitant and well-hedged introduction of pass-fail grading, the acceptance of remedial courses for credit all resulted from student and social pressures. These developments were desirable in many respects, but they apparently contributed to weakening of standards and to less rather than more attention to teaching. As grades have deteriorated so has the role of the faculty member in upholding standards, for there is no need to spend time grading examinations and reading and criticizing student papers when all receive passing grades. Despite this reality, the changes are publicized as indicative of more diligent students, better student services, and increased individualization. Colleges excel in seeking credit for inconsequential change, for making a virtue out of necessity, and for thereby avoiding resolution of the basic issues of costs, efficiency, and effectiveness. This reluctance to view the truth and particularly to report it is entirely understandable, though hardly commendable.

Colleges and universities (whether private or public) have become internally political in their decision making, and they are also increasingly dominated by external political maneuvering, which affects funding. When people have to make decisions through political processes, they simply cannot be counted upon to use evaluation studies with understanding. Evaluation and political decision making (whether within institutions or in the state or federal government) operate from extremely different frameworks. Evaluation assumes decision making based on concrete, objective evidence, but political decisions are made with strange compromises and manipulations. Misinterpretation of the facts at hand to justify a decision is not unknown. For this reason administrators are loath to share critical evaluations with boards and the public. It is not evident that the institutions will gain by it, and they may lose, especially if competitors and critics exploit the evidence. Meantime, faculty and administrators view with concern the increasing state and federal bureaucracy and their ever increasing agencies and staffs, which are seldom evaluated and never terminated, even when their purposes have been served or completely discounted.

Similarly, in the typical college, there is a risk in learning about deficiencies which are not readily correctable, and adequate assistance for correction of deficiencies is seldom available. Promotion or salary increments may be withheld because of negative evaluation. Even when these lead to marked improvement, the negative associations may still remain in mind. Insightful evaluations are not always rewarded. Although well-publicized recognition programs based upon evaluation undertake to identify and reward individual teachers or students, even these much publicized events bruise the egos of those who compete and fail. Others who are convinced (perhaps rightfully) of their own merit but are unrecognized because inappropriate criteria or subjective factors control the choice are frustrated. On the whole, most colleges offer little reward for examining one's own behavior or for cooperating in its appraisal by others. Of course, this is true not only in schools, but in life generally. No one wants to be evaluated by anybody at any time unless assured in advance that the culmination will be either immediate praise and recognition or suggestions as to how to attain it. Evaluation of any program or activity is in itself an indication of the worth of the activity or person, but it does not seem so to those involved unless it includes some commendation of intent and of efforts and activities to date as well as suggestions for improvement.

Under growth conditions, lack of planning and evaluation

is effectively hidden by the fact of growth, which is regarded as reflecting planning and brings credit on the administrators and faculty who cope with it, no matter how effectively. In a no-growth context, planning is difficult and distasteful because it must, in part, involve cutbacks and terminations of programs and people. Reallocations within a fixed budget to support expanding programs or launch new ones are not welcomed by those who lose, no matter how important such reallocations are for continuing institutional vitality. Those not directly affected may, nevertheless, argue against cutbacks and terminations because of their concerns about the ultimate impact on their own activities. Only if evaluation is openly conducted with specific indications of procedures, criteria, and decision-making processes can confidence and acceptance be generated. Without such confidence, policy formulation in the no-growth situation tends to be a mere updating and expansion of policies and procedures to clarify and reinforce present practice, specify faculty rights in detail, and emphasize procedural due process to consider and approve any policy, program change, or personnel action. Thereby, flexible, broad policies become rigid and narrow and procedural steps become so elaborate that, strictly followed, they void any attempt at significant change, which was precisely the intent.

Administrative leadership and management become constrained to virtually a negative role, which yields no plaudits from faculty, students, or public. Evaluation, coming entirely from administrative sources, which could document the need for a decision or a change in policy by exposing the controllable variables and values involved and possible alternative strategies, is unlikely to forward change and may only produce opposition from improbable alignments of traditionally differing groups and new schisms among formerly united ones. Thus consideration of lowering the retirement age or limiting tenured faculty produces new alignments across departments and colleges. Administrative initiative on any item of retrenchment is regarded as a violation of faculty prerogatives. At times, it appears that only external pressure can force action while preserving a sense of unity. But external pressure is also unsettling and may have little relation to institutional goals and problems.

Evaluation-Policy-Administration Trichotomy

Wildavsky (1964) persuasively argues that evaluation and organization are contradictory concepts. Effective organization requires commitment or loyalty, stability, and the establishment of well-defined routines. Evaluation is based upon a higher commitment to efficiency and effectiveness in the attainment of specified objectives, which are themselves subject to review and alteration. Thus the evaluator is continually skeptical, challenging assumptions and procedures, seeking explicit statements of goals and accomplishments, and expressing doubts of unsupported claims. Evaluators are disruptive to program developers and operators, for their views and endeavors create uncertainty, anxiety, and confusion, and may cultivate cynicism—a sense that enthusiastic commitment to any existing program is always misplaced and subject to criticism rather than reward. The objective critic or evaluator in any organization who fosters this uncertainty can well become "the traitor in our midst," as one program director commented. The traitor designation arises not solely out of the evaluator's quizzical stance, but also because confidence in a program can be undermined by the mere presence of the evaluator, who is expected to recommend changes; if an evaluator does not, administrators are unlikely to see much of worth emerging from the evaluation. Evaluation can readily become a political activity in that, as evaluators seek recognition of their efforts by advocating policies or even by insistently calling attention to their reports, they also become advocates of the values implicit in them and thereby place themselves in opposition to those holding contrasting values.

If an organization cannot be self-evaluating because of these innate contradictions, the essential nature of a university is called into question. The role of a university in the search for truth demands a continuing examination of accumulated knowledge and rejection of aspects of it as new facts are elicited. Even in the scientific disciplines, this continued culling and discarding of information creates tensions within and among researchers, but to the extent that the scholarly methods of science rise above individual subjectivity, progress is possible. This is the goal toward which higher education must direct its efforts, for a college or university which cannot objectively review its own operations in reference to its objectives and adjust or alter its policies to achieve greater impact and increased relevance to social needs does not furnish a model either to its students or to society as to how education, by improving understanding, analysis, and thought, can contribute to the improvement of the quality of life in its broadest sense. Most organizations are so committed to current operations that they do not learn by experience or observation until crises arise; and then it may be too late. Railroads degenerated because they held to one dated concept of transportation. Higher education must not only learn by experience, but also demonstrate how individuals and other organizations can do so or be helped to do so.

If higher education does not demonstrate this capability, then evaluation will be done by outside agencies, and change will be forced by political considerations and by budget control —with implications which one can only guess. However, if higher education is incapable of evaluating itself or is simply unwilling to do so, it deserves whatever fate ensues.

Continuing rejection of evaluation so constrains the quality of education that the entire system of American higher education is called into question. Such evaluation as has been evident has almost always been focused upon sorting or classifying individuals for admission, course assignment or placement, and award of credit. The purview of evaluation has thus been limited to a single course. In the future, the scope of evaluation should be broadened to include consideration of program elimination or improvement; program components including instruction; impact on learning of environment and processes; individualization of student learning experiences; time modification (acceleration and stretch-out); cumulative impact of education on a wide range of outcomes (cognitive, affective, and psychomotor); and effectiveness and efficiency. Although evidence for accountability is implicit in all these and costs should be determined, the values and associated issues of equal opportunity and of equity require a broad rather than a narrow economic approach.

The variables of costs, quality, quantity, and time should

be an explicit part of this broadened scope of evaluation. In the past, professorial preference determined educational processes, thereby fixing costs and time, leaving only quality and quantity of outputs as variables. Since quality is essentially an unknown, quantity (students, credit hours) has been the key factor in justifying increased budgets or in adjusting to decreased ones. Section size rather than faculty load is increased when constraints force it. Faculty load rather than section size is the first to decrease when resources permit, although both have been adjusted downward at times. A demonstrated increase in quality might be less likely to necessitate added resources than an increase in quantity, but no one knows, for that alternative remains unexplored. A decrease in time with maintenance of quality is quite possible, but seldom considered. The possible relations among these four variables should be investigated, for, as it is, costs always increase, largely because of increasing faculty salaries and more expensive facilities and equipment; dollar costs are attached to programs, but the comparable benefits of alternative programs (benefits forgone) are generally ignored; time required in class remains constant or is increased because of added requirements; quality is uncertain but unquestioned (except when endangered by inadequate resources); quantity (numbers, loads, credits) is the only variable available for determining program funding.

Time and quality are variables worthy of study, but until evaluation is given its rightful place as the basis for developing insight into these problems, decisions on educational issues will continue to be inconsequential agreements based on specifics emerging out of a tangled mesh of value differences or incorrect perceptions based upon incomplete or faulty data, and on emotions and ignorance or lack of recognition of the basic educational issues and social responsibilities and values involved.

In this broad conception of evaluation, there is no reason to insist that only faculty and educational processes be evaluated; all university personnel (administrators, faculty, service personnel) and processes (business, services, purchasing, residence halls, student personnel, coordinating agencies) should be evaluated. Faculty members are understandably reluctant to undergo evaluation and be subjected to possible criticism and loss of resources when they believe (and often with good reason) that administration is overexpanded and some administrators are ineffective; that the student personnel staff is needlessly large and not too productive; and that there has been an undue proliferation of special offices and services without clear indication of their worth. In addition, the faculty see state coordinating or control offices expanding in staff, in functions, and in data requirements, thereby placing additional demands upon institutions and their faculty members with no compensating benefits. Higher education has a special obligation to develop critical self-appraisal, but it should be applied to all university activities and not solely to faculty or students. State boards and their staffs should also expect to be evaluated for their efficiency and effectiveness. One might like to add the desirability of evaluating state and federal government officials and legislators, but here the evaluation comes—as it ultimately does for the institutions—from public opinion. The university does have the opportunity to mold opinion (if done tactfully) and thereby fulfill what many conceive as a major role of higher education— contributing to an improved social order.

Evaluation, as done by evaluators, will never provide definitive answers, but awareness and acceptance of the need for careful delineation of the factors and values involved in issues and problems will either enlighten those involved in decision making (which is itself evaluation) sufficiently that some agreements can be reached or demonstrate that the evidence available does not and cannot resolve basic differences. This is a pluralistic society, and there is no more reason to expect or even desire that we arrive at any single pattern of education than that we attain a single religion or one political party. But if education is a venture toward rationality, there must be a sound rationale for what we do, buttressed by more objective evidence than the preferences or subjective judgments of those who engaged in or provided the resources for it.

Democracy implies acceptance of the principle of equality in rights, in opportunity, and in treatment. The full implications of this principle do not become apparent until one thinks about human potential and the relationship of this potential to society. The relative significance of heredity and environment immediately comes to the fore. Heredity certainly plays a role, but many obvious differences in ability, motivation, and performance may be more the result of fortuitous circumstance, in where and when an individual was born, and of the educational opportunities available. If higher education recognizes these differences but ignores their sources and attends only to merit already demonstrated, the resulting meritocracy may be regarded as democratic and as the most efficient way of providing educated persons for society. If inequality of opportunity is recognized and inequality of heritage denied, insistence that education bring all to the same level becomes not only impossibly expensive, but will lead to mediocrity in all aspects of society. The extreme interpretation of this principle could lead to the view that people be accepted and recognized on the basis of their own evaluation of their own merit.

The alternative is to provide, insofar as humanly possible, equality in basic rights and in opportunity for development of potential, but to insist that placement, advancement, and recognition be based on evaluation of individual capability and performance, even though the standards for such an evaluation inevitably are based, in part, upon the judgments or the performance of others. Educational institutions have a responsibility to strive for programs which enable each individual to meet his or her fullest potential and fill some responsible role in society, although not necessarily what that person would prefer. Thus the college or university must be critical of its success with individuals as well as continually appraising the progress of individuals and directing them toward endeavors in which they contribute to, rather than endanger, others. This applies to the university faculty and staff as well as to its students. The individual, in turn, must become a reasonably objective evaluator of his or her own efforts and of the efforts of others. Evaluation by the institution should assist individuals in adapting education to their own needs, aspirations, and abilities and should serve as a model for individuals to develop their own evaluative facilities, which will be at least as important in personal satisfaction and success as any knowledge or skills acquired. Education which gives an individual an inflated sense of capabilities does an injustice to the individual and virtually assures an unhappy existence. And, equally, an experience which does not provide the individual with some insight into at least a few things that he or she can do well is not educational. Thus evaluation productive of insight and increasing capacity for self-evaluation by the individual and ultimately by society is the central responsibility of higher education. And such evaluation, properly executed, is always positive and formative.

That there are dangers and possible undesirable consequences in embarking upon a comprehensive and continuing program of evaluation is undeniable. But the present difficulties faced by higher education indicate that lack of forthright evaluation has also brought undesirable consequences. These can be mitigated only by a restoration of confidence and by improvement in the quality of educational services provided. Evaluation as a process and as a goal is essential to both. If higher education cannot emulate and be a model for "the examined life," there is little hope for democracy or for significant improvement in the quality of society by any form of government.

Bibliography

Abe, C., and Holland, J. L. *A Description of College Freshmen, 1. Students with Different Choices of Major Field.* ACT Research Report 3. Iowa City: American College Testing Program, 1965.

Adams, R. F., and Michaelson, J. B. "Assessing the Benefits of Collegiate Structure: The Case at Santa Cruz." Berkeley: Office of the Vice-President—Planning, University of California, 1971.

Ahamad, B., and Blaug, M. *The Practice of Manpower Forecasting: A Collection of Case Studies.* San Francisco: Jossey-Bass/Elsevier, 1973.

Aleamoni, L. M., and Bowers, J. E. "The Evaluation of a Special Educational Opportunities Program for Disadvantaged College Students." *Research in Higher Education,* 1974, 2 (2), 151-164.

Altbach, P. G. *Comparative Higher Education.* ERIC/Higher Education Research Report 5. Washington, D.C.: American Association for Higher Education, 1973.

American Academy of Arts and Sciences. *A First Report: The Assembly on University Goals and Governance.* Boston, 1971.

American Association of Collegiate Registrars and Admissions Officers. *AACRAO Survey of Grading Practices in Member Institutions.* Athens, Ohio, 1971.

American College Testing Program. *Assessing Students on the Way to College.* Technical report for the ACT Assessment Program. Iowa City, 1960.

American Council on Education. "National Norms for Entering College Freshmen, Fall, 1970." *ACE Research Reports,* 1970, *5* (6), 43.

American Psychological Association. *Standards for Educational and Psychological Tests.* Washington, D.C., 1974.

Anderson, J. G., and Evans, F. B. "Causal Models in Educational Research: Recursive Models." *American Educational Research Journal,* 1974, *11* (1), 29-39.

Anderson, S. B., Ball, S., Murphy, R. T. *Encyclopedia of Educational Evaluation: Concepts and Techniques for Evaluating Education and Training Programs.* San Francisco: Jossey-Bass, 1974.

Angoff, W. H. (Ed.) *The College Board Admissions Testing Program: A Technical Report on Research and Development Activities Relating to the Scholastic Aptitude Test and Achievement Tests.* New York: College Entrance Examination Board, 1971.

Archibald, R. D., and Villoria, R. L. *Network Based Management (PERT/CPM).* New York: Wiley, 1967.

Argyris, C. *Management and Organizational Development.* New York: McGraw-Hill, 1971.

Association of American Colleges. *Higher Education, Human Resources and the National Economy.* Washington, D.C., 1974.

Astin, A. W. *Who Goes Where to College?* Chicago: Science Research Associates, 1965.

Astin, A. W. *The College Environment.* Washington, D.C.: American Council on Education, 1968.

Astin, A. W. *Predicting Academic Performance in College.* New York: Free Press, 1971.

Astin, A. W. "College Dropouts: A National Profile." *ACE Research Reports,* 1972, 7 (1).

Astin, A. W., and Associates. *The American Freshman: National Norms for Fall, 1973.* Los Angeles: Cooperative Institutional Research Program of the American Council on Education and the University of California, 1973.

Astin, H., Astin, A. W., Bisconti, A. S., and Frankel, H. H. *Higher Education and the Disadvantaged Student.* Washington, D.C.: Human Service Press, 1972.

Astin, A. W., and Holland, J. L. "The Environmental Assessment Technique: A Way to Measure College Environments." *Journal of Educational Psychology,* 1961, *52,* 308-317.

Astin, A. W., and Panos, R. J. *The Educational and Vocational Development of College Students.* Washington, D.C.: American Council on Education, 1969.

Bailey, R. L. *A Report of the Sub-Committee to Survey the Acceptance of Non-Traditional Grading Patterns by Government, Industry, and Graduate Institutions.* Athens, Ohio: American Association of Collegiate Registrars and Admissions Officers, 1972.

Baird, L. L. "The Functions of College Environmental Measures." *Journal of Educational Measurement,* 1971, *8* (2), 83-86.

Baird, L. L. "The Practical Utility of Measures of College Environments." *Review of Educational Research,* 1974, *44* (3), 307-329.

Baird, L. L., and Fiester, W. J. *Grading Standards: The Relations of Changes in Average Student Ability to the Average Grades Awarded.* Research Bulletin RB-71-28. Princeton: Educational Testing Service, 1971.

Baird, L. L., and Richards, J. M., Jr. *The Effects of Selecting College Students by Various Kinds of High School Achievement.* ACT Research Report 23. Iowa City: American College Testing Program, 1968.

Baker, E. L., and Popham, W. J. *Expanding Dimensions of Instructional Objectives.* Englewood Cliffs, N.J.: Prentice-Hall, 1973.

Baldridge, J. V. *Power and Conflict in the University.* New York: Wiley, 1971.

Baldridge, J. V., Curtis, D. V., Ecker, G. P., and Riley, G. L. *Academic Politics, Morale, and Involvement: Preliminary Findings of the Stanford Project on Academic Governance.* Stanford: Center for Research and Development in Teaching, School of Education, Stanford University, 1973.

Barker, R. G. *Ecological Psychology: Concepts and Methods for Studying the Environment of Human Behavior.* Stanford: Stanford University Press, 1968.

Barton, A. H. *Organizational Measurement.* New York: College Entrance Examination Board, 1961.

Baskin, S. (Issue ed.) *Organizing Nontraditional Study: New Directions for Institutional Research.* San Francisco: Jossey-Bass, 1974.

Bayer, A. E. *The Black College Freshman: Characteristics and Recent Trends.* ACE Research Report 7. Washington, D.C.: American Council on Education, 1972.

Bayer, A., Royer, J., and Webb, R. *Four Years After College.* ACE Research Report 8. Washington, D.C.: American Council on Education, 1973.

Becker, G. S. *Human Capital: A Theoretical and Empirical Analysis, with Special Reference to Education.* New York: National Bureau of Economic Research, 1964.

Bell, D. *The Reforming of General Education: The Columbia Experience in Its National Setting.* New York: Columbia University Press, 1966.

Bem, D. J. *Beliefs, Attitudes, and Human Affairs.* Monterey, Calif.: Brooks/Cole, 1970.

Bennis, W. *Organization Development: Its Nature, Origins, and Prospects.* Reading, Mass.: Addison-Wesley, 1969.

Benson, C. S., and Hodgkinson, H. L. *Implementing the Learning Society: New Strategies for Financing Social Objectives.* San Francisco: Jossey-Bass, 1974.

Berdahl, R. O. *Statewide Coordination of Higher Education.* Washington, D.C.: American Council on Education, 1971.

Berdahl, R. O. (Issue ed.) *Evaluating Statewide Boards: New Directions for Institutional Research.* San Francisco: Jossey-Bass, 1975.

Berelson, B. "Content Analysis." In G. Lindzey (Ed.), *Hand-*

book of Social Psychology. Vol. 1. Reading, Mass.: Addison-Wesley, 1954.

Berelson, B. *Graduate Study in the United States.* New York: McGraw-Hill, 1960.

Berg, H. D. (Ed.) *Evaluation in Social Studies.* Thirty-fifth yearbook. Washington, D.C.: National Council for the Social Studies, 1965.

Berliner, D. C., and Cahen, L. S. "Trait-Treatment Interaction and Learning." In F. N. Kerlinger (Ed.), *Review of Research in Education.* Vol. 1. Itasca, Ill.: Peacock, 1973.

Bersi, R. M. *Restructuring the Baccalaureate.* Washington, D.C.: American Association of State Colleges and Universities, 1973.

Billing, D. E., and Furniss, B. S. (Eds.) *Aims, Methods and Assessment in Advanced Science Education.* London: Heyden, 1973.

Bird, C. *The Case Against College.* New York: McKay, 1975.

Blackburn, R. T., and Clark, M. J. "An Assessment of Faculty Performance: Some Correlates Between Administrator, Colleague, Student and Self-Ratings." *Sociology of Education,* 1975, *48,* 242-256.

Blalock, H. M. (Ed.) *Causal Models in the Social Sciences.* New York: Lieber-Atherton, 1971.

Block, J. H. (Ed.) *Mastery Learning: Theory and Practice.* New York: Holt, Rinehart, and Winston, 1971.

Bloom, B. S. (Ed.) *Taxonomy of Educational Objectives, the Classification of Educational Goals.* Handbook 1: *Cognitive Domain.* New York: McKay, 1956.

Bloom, B. S. "Learning for Mastery." *Evaluation Comment,* 1968, *1* (2). Reprinted by the Center for the Study of Instructional Programs, University of California, Los Angeles.

Bloom, B. S. "Recent Developments in Mastery Learning." *Educational Psychologist,* 1973, *10* (2), 53-57.

Bloom, B. S., Hastings, J. T., and Madaus, G. F. *Handbook on Formative and Summative Evaluation of Student Learning.* New York: McGraw-Hill, 1971.

Bloom, B. S., and Peters, F. R. *The Use of Academic Prediction Scales.* New York: Free Press, 1961.

Bogard, J. H. "Diversity in Arts and Sciences: Does It Exist?" *Liberal Education,* 1974, *60* (4), 531-538.

Boldt, R. F. *Comparison of a Bayesian and a Least Squares Method of Educational Prediction.* Research bulletin. Princeton: Educational Testing Service, 1975.

Bonjean, C. M., Hill, R. J., and McLemore, S. D. *Sociological Measurement: Inventory of Scales and Indices.* New York: Crowell, 1967.

Borich, G. D. (Ed.) *Evaluating Educational Programs and Products.* Englewood Cliffs, N.J.: Educational Technology Publications, 1974.

Bowen, H. R. (Issue ed.) *Evaluating Institutions for Accountability: New Directions for Institutional Research.* San Francisco: Jossey-Bass, 1974.

Bowen, H. R., and Douglass, G. K. *Efficiency in Liberal Education.* New York: McGraw-Hill, 1971.

Bowen, H. R., and Sarvelle, P. *Who Benefits from Higher Education—and Who Should Pay?* Washington, D.C.: American Association for Higher Education, 1972.

Boyd, J. L., Jr., and Shimberg, B. *Directory of Achievement Tests for Occupational Education.* Princeton: Educational Testing Service, 1971a.

Boyd, J. L., Jr., and Shimberg, B. *Handbook of Performance Testing: A Practical Guide for Test Makers.* Princeton: Educational Testing Service, 1971b.

Brawer, F. B. *New Perspectives on Personality Development in College Students.* San Francisco: Jossey-Bass, 1973.

Braybrooke, D., and Lindblom, C. E. *A Strategy for Decision.* New York: Free Press, 1963.

Breneman, D. W. *An Economic Theory of Ph.D. Production: The Case at Berkeley.* Berkeley: Office of the Vice-President—Planning and Analysis, University of California, 1970a.

Breneman, D. W. *The Ph.D. Degree at Berkeley: Interviews, Placement, and Recommendations.* Berkeley: Office of the Vice-President—Planning and Analysis, University of California, 1970b.

Breneman, D. W. *The Ph.D. Production Function: The Case at*

Berkeley. Berkeley: Office of the Vice-President—Planning, University of California, 1970c.

Breneman, D. W. *Graduate School Adjustments to the "New Depression" in Higher Education.* Washington, D.C.: National Board on Graduate Education, 1975.

Brick, M., and Bushko, A. A. *The Management of Change.* New York: Teachers College Press, 1973.

Brick, M., and McGrath, E. J. *Innovation in Liberal Arts Colleges.* New York: Teachers College Press, 1969.

Briggs, L. J. *Sequencing of Instruction in Relation to Hierarchies of Competence.* Pittsburgh: American Institutes for Research, 1968.

Browder, L. H., Jr. (Ed.) *Emerging Patterns of Administrative Accountability.* Berkeley: McCutchan, 1971.

Brown, D. G. "Criteria for Pruning Programs." *The Educational Record,* 1970, *51* (4), 405-409.

Brown, R. L. *Cooperative Education.* Washington, D.C.: American Association of Community and Junior Colleges, 1971.

Brubacher, J. S., and Rudy, W. *Higher Education in Transition: A History of American Colleges and Universities, 1636-1968.* New York: Harper and Row, 1968.

Bruner, J. S. *Toward a Theory of Instruction.* Cambridge: Harvard University Press, 1966.

Bucklin, R., and Bucklin, M. L. *The Psychological Characteristics of the College Persistor and Leaver: A Review.* Washington, D.C.: Office of Education, 1970.

Burns, G. *Trustees in Higher Education: Their Function and Coordination.* New York: Independent College Funds of America, 1966.

Buros, O. K. (Ed.) *The Seventh Mental Measurements Yearbook.* Vol. 2. Highland Park, N.J.: Gryphon Press, 1972.

Burt, S., and Striner, H. E. *The External Degree and Higher Education in the United States: An In-Depth Overview as the Basis for an Urban University.* Washington, D.C.: School of Business, American University, 1972.

Caffrey, J., and Isaacs, H. H. *Estimating the Impact of a College or University on the Local Economy.* Washington, D.C.: American Council on Education, 1971.

Campbell, P. B., and Beers, J. S. *Evaluation: The State of the Art.* Princeton: Educational Testing Service, 1972.

Carlson, D. E. *The Production and Cost Behavior of Higher Education Institutions.* Berkeley: Ford Foundation Program for Research in University Administration, University of California, 1972.

Carmody, J. F., Renske, R. H., and Scott, C. S. *Changes in Goals, Plans, and Background Characteristics of College-Bound High School Students.* ACT Research Report 52. Iowa City: American College Testing Program, 1972.

Carnegie Commission on Higher Education. *The Capitol and the Campus: State Responsibility for Postsecondary Education.* New York: McGraw-Hill, 1971a.

Carnegie Commission on Higher Education. *Less Time, More Options: Education Beyond the High School.* New York: McGraw-Hill, 1971b.

Carnegie Commission on Higher Education. *The Fourth Revolution: Instructional Technology in Higher Education.* New York: McGraw-Hill, 1972a.

Carnegie Commission on Higher Education. *Papers on Efficiency in the Management of Higher Education.* New York: McGraw-Hill, 1972b.

Carnegie Commission on Higher Education. *Continuity and Discontinuity: Higher Education and the Schools.* New York: McGraw-Hill, 1973a.

Carnegie Commission on Higher Education. *Toward a Learning Society: Alternative Channels to Life, Work and Service.* New York: McGraw-Hill, 1973b.

Caro, F. G. *Readings in Evaluation Research.* New York: Russell Sage Foundation, 1971.

Carter, N., and Wharf, B. *Evaluating Social Development Programmes.* Ottawa: Canadian Council on Social Development, 1973.

Cartter, A. M. *An Assessment of Quality in Graduate Education.* Washington, D.C.: American Council on Education, 1966.

Carver, R. P. "Special Problems in Measuring Change with Psychometric Devices." In *Evaluative Research, Strategies and Methods.* Pittsburgh: American Institutes for Research, 1970.

Centra, J. A. *Development of the Questionnaire on Student and College Characteristics.* Research Memorandum 68-11. Princeton: Educational Testing Service, 1968.

Centra, J. A. *College Freshman Attitudes Toward Cheating.* Research Bulletin RB-69-24. Princeton: Educational Testing Service, 1969.

Centra, J. A. *The College Environment Revisited: Current Descriptions and a Comparison of Three Methods of Assessment.* Research Bulletin RB-70-44. Princeton: Educational Testing Service, 1970.

Centra, J. A. *The Relationship Between Student and Alumni Ratings of Teachers.* Research Bulletin RB-73-39. Princeton: Educational Testing Service, 1973a.

Centra, J. A. *The Student as Godfather? The Impact of Student Ratings on Academia.* Research Memorandum RM-73-8. Princeton: Educational Testing Service, 1973b.

Centra, J. A. *Colleagues as Raters of Classroom Instruction.* Research Bulletin RB-74-18. Princeton: Educational Testing Service, 1974.

Centra, J. A., and Linn, R. L. *Student Points of View in Ratings of College Instruction.* Research Bulletin RB-73-60. Princeton: Educational Testing Service, 1973.

Centra, J. A., and Sobol, M. G. "Faculty and Student Views of the Interim Term." *Research in Higher Education,* 1974, *2* (3), 231-238.

Chase, C. I. "The Impact of Some Obvious Variables on Essay Test Scores." *Journal of Educational Measurement,* 1968, *5* (4), 315-318.

Chase, J. L. *Graduate Teaching Assistants in American Universities: A Review of Recent Trends and Recommendations.* Washington, D.C.: Office of Education, 1970.

Cheit, E. J. *The New Depression in Higher Education—Two Years Later.* Berkeley: Carnegie Commission on Higher Education, 1973.

Chickering, A. W. *Education and Identity.* San Francisco: Jossey-Bass, 1969.

Chickering, A. W. "Assessing Students and Programs—A New Ball Game." In S. Baskin (Issue ed.), *Organizing Nontraditional Research: New Directions for Institutional Research.* San Francisco: Jossey-Bass, 1974a.

Chickering, A. W. *Commuting Versus Resident Students: Overcoming the Educational Inequities of Living Off Campus.* San Francisco: Jossey-Bass, 1974b.

Chun, K., Cobb, S., and French, J. *Measures for Psychological Assessment: A Guide to 3,000 Original Sources and Their Application.* Ann Arbor: Institute for Social Research, University of Michigan, 1975.

Churchman, C. W. *The Systems Approach.* New York: Dell, 1968.

Clapp, M. (Ed.) *The Modern University.* Ithaca: Cornell University Press, 1959.

Clark, B. R., Heist, P., McConnell, T. R., Trow, M. A., and Yonge, G. *Students and Colleges: Interaction and Change.* Berkeley: Center for Research and Development in Higher Education, University of California, 1972.

Cleary, T. A., Humphreys, L. G., Kendrick, S. A., and Wesman, A. "Educational Uses of Tests with Disadvantaged Students." *American Psychologist,* 1975, *30* (1), 15-41.

Cohen, A. M. *Objectives for College Courses.* Beverly Hills, Calif.: Glencoe, 1970.

Cohen, M. D., and March, J. *Leadership and Ambiguity: The American College President.* New York: McGraw-Hill, 1974.

Cohen, M. R., and Nagel, E. *An Introduction to Logic and Scientific Method.* New York: Harcourt Brace Jovanovich, 1934.

Cohn, E. *The Economics of Education.* Lexington, Mass.: Heath, 1972.

Cole, N. S. *Bias in Selection.* ACT Research Report 51. Iowa City: American College Testing Program, 1972.

Coleman, J. S. "The Principle of Symmetry in College Choice." *College Board Review,* 1969, (73), 5-10.

Coleman, J. S., and others. *Equality of Educational Opportunity.* Washington, D.C.: Government Printing Office, 1966.

Columbia University, American Assembly. *Goals for Americans: The Report of the President's Commission on National Goals.* Englewood Cliffs, N.J.: Prentice-Hall, 1960.

Colwell, R. *The Evaluation of Music Teaching and Learning.* Englewood Cliffs, N.J.: Prentice-Hall, 1970.

Committee "C" on College and University Teaching, Research and Publication. "Statement on Teaching Evaluation." *American Association of University Professors Bulletin,* 1974, *60* (2), 168-170.

Cook, D. L. *Program Evaluation and Review Technique: Applications in Education.* Cooperative Research Monograph 17. Washington, D.C.: Government Printing Office, 1966.

Cook, J. M., and Neville, R. F. *The Faculty as Teachers: A Perspective on Evaluation.* Washington, D.C.: ERIC Clearinghouse on Higher Education, George Washington University, 1971.

Cook, J. M., and Walbesser, H. H. *Teaching with Behavioral Objectives: Constructing Behavioral Objectives.* College Park: University of Maryland, 1972. (Distributed by Maryland Book Exchange, 4500 College Avenue, College Park, Md. 20742.)

Cooley, W. W. "Assessment of Educational Effects." *Educational Psychologist,* 1974, *11* (1), 29-35.

Coombs, P. H., and Hallak, J. *Managing Educational Costs.* New York: Oxford University Press, 1972.

Corson, J. J. *The Governance of Colleges and Universities: Modernizing Structure and Process.* (Rev. ed.) New York: McGraw-Hill, 1975.

Cronbach, L. J., and Furby, L. "How We Should Measure 'Change'—Or Should We?" *Psychological Bulletin,* 1970, *74,* 68-80.

Cronbach, L. J., and Gleser, G. C. *Psychological Tests and Personnel Decisions.* (2nd ed.) Urbana: University of Illinois Press, 1965.

Cronbach, L. J., Gleser, G. C., Nanda, H., and Rajaratnam, J. *The Dependability of Behavioral Measurement: Theory of Generalizability for Scores and Profiles.* New York: Wiley, 1972.

Cureton, L. W. "The History of Grading Practices." *Measurement in Education,* 1971, *2* (4), 8.

Dantzig, G. B. *Linear Programming and Extensions.* Princeton: Princeton University Press, 1963.

Darlington, R. B. "Another Look at 'Cultural Fairness.' " *Journal of Educational Measurement,* 1971, *8* (2), 71-82.

Davidovicz, H. M. "Pass/Fail Grading—A Review." Hempstead, N.Y.: Center for Study of Higher Education, Hofstra University, 1972.

Davis, J. R., and Morrall, J. F., III. *Evaluating Educational Investment.* Lexington, Mass.: Heath, 1974.

Diamond, E. E. (Ed.) *Issues of Sex Bias and Sex Fairness in Career Interest Measurement.* Washington, D.C.: Government Printing Office, 1975.

DiMarco, N. "Life Style, Learning Structure, Congruence, and Student Attitudes." *American Educational Research Journal,* 1974, *11* (2), 203-209.

Doi, J. I. (Issue ed.) *Assessing Faculty Effort: New Directions for Higher Education.* San Francisco: Jossey-Bass, 1974.

Domino, G. *Interactive Effects of Achievement Orientation and Teaching Style on Academic Achievement.* ACT Research Report 39. Iowa City: American College Testing Program, 1970.

Dornbusch, S. M., and Scott, W. R. *Evaluation and the Exercise of Authority: A Theory of Control Applied to Diverse Organizations.* San Francisco: Jossey-Bass, 1975.

Doyle, K. O., Jr. *Student Evaluation of Instruction.* Lexington, Mass.: Heath, 1975.

Dresch, S. P. "A Critique of Planning Models for Postsecondary Education: Current Feasibility, Potential Relevance, and a Prospectus for Further Research." *Journal of Higher Education,* 1975, *46* (3), 245-286.

Dresch, S. P. *An Economic Perspective on the Evolution of Graduate Education.* Washington, D.C.: National Academy of Sciences, 1974.

Dressel, P. L. "Evaluation of the Environment, the Process, and the Results of Higher Education." In A. S. Knowles (Ed.), *Handbook of College and University Administration. Vol. 2: Academic.* New York: McGraw-Hill, 1970.

Dressel, P. L. *College and University Curriculum.* Berkeley: McCutchan, 1971.

Dressel, P. L., and Associates. *Evaluation in Higher Education.* Boston: Houghton Mifflin, 1961.

Dressel, P. L., and Associates. *Institutional Research in the University: A Handbook.* San Francisco: Jossey-Bass, 1972.

Dressel, P. L., and DeLisle, F. H. *Undergraduate Curriculum Trends.* Washington, D.C.: American Council on Education, 1969.

Dressel, P. L., and Thompson, M. M. *Independent Study: A New Interpretation of Concepts, Practices, and Problems.* San Francisco: Jossey-Bass, 1973.

Dressel, P. L., and Thompson, M. M. *Educating College Teachers by Degrees.* Iowa City: American College Testing Program, 1974.

Drew, D. E. *Science Development: An Evaluation Study.* Technical Report 4 presented to the National Board on Graduate Education. Washington, D.C.: National Board on Graduate Education, 1975.

Drucker, P. F. *Managing for Results.* New York: Harper and Row, 1964.

Drumheller, S. J. *Handbook of Curriculum Design for Individualized Instruction: A Systems Approach.* Englewood Cliffs, N.J.: Educational Technology Publications, 1971.

Easton, D. *A Framework for Political Analysis.* Englewood Cliffs, N.J.: Prentice-Hall, 1965.

Eble, K. E. *The Recognition and Evaluation of Teaching.* Washington, D.C.: American Association of University Professors, 1971.

Eble, K. E. *Professors as Teachers.* San Francisco: Jossey-Bass, 1972.

Educational Testing Service. *Essay Questions in Achievement Tests.* Princeton, 1961.

Educational Testing Service. *Multiple Choice Questions: A Close Look.* Princeton, 1963.

Educational Testing Service. *College Student Questionnaires.* Princeton, 1965a.

Educational Testing Service. *Studies on the Question Types in the College Board English Composition Tests as Predictors of an Essay Criterion.* Princeton, 1965b.

Educational Testing Service. *Institutional Functioning Inventory.* Princeton, 1968.

Educational Testing Service. *Institutional Goals Inventory.* Princeton, 1972.

Educational Testing Service. *Scholarship for Society.* Princeton, 1973.

Educational Testing Service. *Student Reactions to College.* Princeton, 1974.

Edwards, A. L. *The Measurement of Personality Traits by Scales and Inventories.* New York: Holt, Rinehart, and Winston, 1970.

Eisner, E. W. "Emerging Models for Educational Evaluation." *School Review,* 1972, *80* (4), 573-590.

Eiss, A. F., and Harbeck, M. B. *Behavioral Objectives in the Affective Domain.* Washington, D.C.: National Science Supervision Association, 1969.

Epstein, L. D. *Governing the University: The Campus and the Public Interest.* San Francisco: Jossey-Bass, 1974.

ERIC Clearinghouse on Higher Education. *Governance.* Compendium Series of Current Research, Programs and Proposals 1. Washington, D.C., 1970.

Ericksen, S. C., and Kulik, J. A. "Evaluation of Teaching." *Memo to the Faculty,* Feb. 1974, *53,* 1-6.

Ernst & Ernst. *Guidelines for Self-Evaluation of Administrative Management Practices in Institutions of Higher Education.* Austin: Coordinating Board, Texas College and University System, 1969.

Fear, R. A. *The Evaluation Interview.* (2nd ed.) New York: McGraw-Hill, 1973.

Feldhusen, J. F. "An Evaluation of College Students' Reactions to Open Book Examinations." *Educational and Psychological Measurement,* 1961, *21* (3), 637-646.

Feldman, K. A. *Research Strategies in Studying College Impact.* ACT Research Report 34. Iowa City: American College Testing Program, 1970.

Feldman, K. A. "Measuring College Environments: Some Uses

of Path Analysis." *American Educational Research Journal,* 1971, *8* (1), 51-70.

Feldman, K. A. "Some Theoretical Approaches to the Study of Change and Stability of College Students." *Review of Educational Research,* 1972, *42* (1), 1-26.

Feldman, K. A., and Newcomb, T. M. *The Impact of College on Students.* Vol. 1. San Francisco: Jossey-Bass, 1969.

Feldmesser, R. A. "The Positive Functions of Grades." *The Educational Record,* 1972, *53* (1), 66-72.

Fenske, R. H., and Scott, C. S. *The Changing Profile of College Students.* Report 10. Washington, D.C.: American Association for Higher Education, 1973.

Festinger, L., and Katz, D. (Eds.) *Research Methods in the Behavioral Sciences.* New York: Holt, Rinehart, and Winston, 1953.

Finn, J. D. *A General Model for Multivariate Analysis.* New York: Holt, Rinehart, and Winston, 1974.

Fishbein, M. (Ed.) *Readings in Attitude Theory and Measurement.* New York: Wiley, 1967.

Fisher, G. *Cost Considerations in Systems Analysis.* New York: American Elsevier, 1971.

Flanagan, J. C., Shanner, W. M., and Mager, R. *Behavioral Objectives: A Guide for Individualized Learning.* 4 vols. Sunnyvale, Calif.: Westinghouse Learning Press, 1971.

Flaugher, R. L. *Bias in Testing: A Review and Discussion.* TM Report 36. Princeton: Educational Testing Service, 1974.

Folk, M. J. *A Critical Look at the Cross-Impact Matrix.* Syracuse: Educational Policy Research Center, Syracuse Research Corp., 1971.

Foote, C., Mayer, H., and Associates. *The Culture of the University: Governance and Education.* San Francisco: Jossey-Bass, 1968.

Foster, W. T. *Administration of the College Curriculum.* Boston: Houghton Mifflin, 1911.

Franks, B. D., and Deutsch, H. *Evaluating Performance in Physical Education.* New York: Academic Press, 1973.

Freeberg, N. E. "The Biographical Information Blank as a Predictor of Student Achievement: A Review." *Psychological Reports,* 1967, *20,* 911-925.

Freeman, M. B. *The College Experience.* San Francisco: Jossey-Bass, 1967.

Freeman, R. B., and Breneman, D. W. *Forecasting the Ph.D. Labor Market: Pitfalls for Policy.* Technical Report 2. Washington, D.C.: National Board on Graduate Education, 1974.

Gadway, C. J. (Ed.) *National Assessment of Educational Progress.* Denver: Education Commission of the States, 1972.

Gage, N. L. (Ed.) *Handbook of Research on Teaching.* Chicago: Rand McNally, 1963.

Gage, N. L. *Teacher Effectiveness and Teacher Education.* Palo Alto: Pacific Books, 1972.

Gagné, R. M. *The Conditions of Learning.* (2nd ed.) New York: Holt, Rinehart, and Winston, 1970.

Gagné, R. M. "Task Analysis—Its Relation to Content Analysis." *Educational Psychologist,* 1974, *11* (1), 11-18.

Gerhard, D. "The Emergence of the Credit System in American Education Considered as a Problem of Social and Intellectual History." *American Association of University Professors Bulletin,* 1955, *41* (1), 647-668.

Gilman, D. A., and Ferry, P. "Increasing Test Reliability Through Self-Scoring Procedures." *Journal of Educational Measurement,* 1972, *9* (3), 205-208.

Glaser, R., and Nitko, A. J. "Measurement in Learning and Instruction." In R. L. Thorndike (Ed.), *Educational Measurement.* (2nd ed.) Washington, D.C.: American Council on Education, 1971.

Glenny, L. A. "Nine Myths, Nine Realities: The Illusions of Steady State." *Change,* 1974-1975, *6* (10), 24-28.

Glenny, L. A., and Dalglish, T. K. *Public Universities, State Agencies, and the Law: Constitutional Autonomy in Decline.* Berkeley: Center for Research and Development in Higher Education, University of California, 1973.

Godshalk, F. I., Swineford, F., and Coffman, W. E. *The Measurement of Writing Ability.* New York: College Entrance Examination Board, 1966.

Gold, R. M., Reilly, A., Silberman, R., and Lehr, R. "Academic Achievement Declines Under Pass-Fail Grading." *Journal of Experimental Education,* 1971, *39* (3), 17-29.

Goldstein, K. M., and Tilker, H. A. "Attitudes Toward A-B-C-D-F and H-P-F Grading Systems." *Journal of Education Research,* 1971, *65* (3), 99-100.

Gordon, T., Rochberg, R., and Enzer, S. *The Use of Cross-Impact Matrices for Forecasting and Planning.* Middleton, Conn.: Institute for the Future, 1970.

Goslin, D. A. *The Search for Ability.* New York: Russell Sage Foundation, 1963.

Goslin, D. A. *Criticism of Standardized Tests and Testing.* New York: College Entrance Examination Board, 1967.

Gould, S. B., and Cross, K. P. (Eds.) *Explorations in Non-Traditional Study.* San Francisco: Jossey-Bass, 1972.

Grande, P. P. "How Objective Are Measures of Campus Climate." In C. Fincher (Ed.), *The Challenge and Response of Institutional Research.* Tallahassee: Association for Institutional Research, 1970.

Green, D. R. *Racial and Ethnic Bias in Test Construction.* Final report. Monterey, Calif.: CTB/McGraw-Hill, 1971.

Greenbaum, W. "America in Search of a New Ideal: An Essay on the Rise of Pluralism." *Harvard Educational Review,* 1974, *44* (3), 411-440.

Gronlund, N. E. *Measurement and Evaluation in Teaching.* New York: Macmillan, 1965.

Gronlund, N. E. *Stating Behavioral Objectives for Classroom Instruction.* New York: Macmillan, 1970.

Gross, E. E., and Grambsch, P. V. *University Goals and Academic Power.* Washington, D.C.: American Council on Education, 1968.

Haagen, C. H. "The Origins of a Grade." *Journal of Higher Education,* 1964, *35* (2), 89-91.

Hage, J., and Aiken, M. *Social Change in Complex Organizations.* New York: Random House, 1970.

Haight, M., and Romney, L. C. *NCHEMS Overview, a Training Document.* Boulder: National Center for Higher Education Management Systems at WICHE, 1975.

Hambleton, R. K., and Novick, M. R. *Toward an Integration of Theory and Method for Criterion-Referenced Tests.* ACT Research Report 53. Iowa City: American College Testing Program, 1973.

Handlin, O., and Handlin, M. F. *The American College and American Culture: Socialization as a Function of Higher Education.* New York: McGraw-Hill, 1970.

Hansen, W. L., and Weisbrod, B. A. *Benefits, Costs and Finance of Public Higher Education.* Chicago: Rand McNally, 1969.

Harcleroad, F. F., and Dickey, F. G. *Educational Auditing and Voluntary Institutional Accrediting.* ERIC/Higher Education Research Report 1. Washington, D.C.: American Association for Higher Education, 1975.

Harris, C. W. (Ed.) *Problems in Measuring Change.* Madison: University of Wisconsin Press, 1963.

Harris, M. L., and Harris, C. W. *A Structure of Concept Attainment Abilities.* Madison: Research and Development Center for Cognitive Learning, University of Wisconsin, 1973.

Harrow, A. J. *A Taxonomy of the Psychomotor Domain.* New York: McKay, 1972.

Hartnett, R. T. *College and University Trustees: Their Backgrounds, Roles, and Educational Attitudes.* Princeton: Educational Testing Service, 1969.

Hartnett, R. T. *Accountability in Higher Education: A Consideration of Some of the Problems of Assessing College Impacts.* New York: College Entrance Examination Board, 1971.

Hartog, P. J., Rhodes, E. C., and Burt, C. *The Marks of Examiners.* London: Macmillan, 1936.

Harvard University. *General Examinations and Tutors in Harvard College.* Cambridge, 1934.

Harvey, J. *The Student in Graduate School.* Washington, D.C.: American Association for Higher Education, 1972.

Harvey, T. R. "Potential Futures and Institutional Research." *Journal of Higher Education,* 1974, *45* (7), 517-523.

Hawkridge, D. G., Campeau, P. L., and Trickett, P. K. *Preparing Evaluation Reports: A Guide for Authors.* AIR Monograph 6. Pittsburgh: American Institutes for Research, 1970.

Heath, D. H. *Growing Up in College: Liberal Education and Maturity.* San Francisco: Jossey-Bass, 1968.

Hefferlin, JB L. *Dynamics of Academic Reform.* San Francisco: Jossey-Bass, 1969.

Heffernan, J. M. "The Credibility of the Credit Hour: The History, Use, and Shortcomings of the Credit System." *Journal of Higher Education,* 1973, *44* (1), 61-72.

Heiss, A. M. *Challenges to Graduate Schools.* San Francisco: Jossey-Bass, 1970.

Heiss, A. M. *An Inventory of Academic Innovation and Reform.* Berkeley: Carnegie Commission on Higher Education, 1973.

Heist, P. (Ed.) *The Creative College Student: An Unmet Challenge.* San Francisco: Jossey-Bass, 1968.

Helmer, O. *The Application of Cost-Effectiveness of Non-Military Government Problems.* Santa Monica, Calif.: RAND, 1966.

Hemphill, J. K., Griffiths, D. E., and Frederiksen, N. *Administrative Performance and Personality.* New York: Bureau of Publications, Teachers College, Columbia University, 1962.

Hildebrand, M., Wilson, R. C., and Dienst, E. R. *Evaluating University Teaching.* Berkeley: Center for Research and Development in Higher Education, University of California, 1971.

Hilgard, E. R. *Theories of Learning.* Englewood Cliffs, N.J.: Prentice-Hall, 1974.

Hills, J. R. "Consistent College Grading Standards Through Equating." *Educational and Psychological Measurement,* 1972, *32* (1), 137-146.

Hillway, T. "Evaluating College and University Administration." *Intellect,* 1973, *101* (2349), 426-427.

Hind, R. R., Dornbusch, S. M., and Scott, W. R. "A Theory of Evaluation Applied to a University Faculty." *Sociology of Education,* 1974, *47* (1), 114-128.

Hively, W., and Associates. *Domain-Referenced Curriculum Evaluation: A Technical Handbook and a Case Study from the Minnemast Project.* Monograph Series in Evaluation 1. Los Angeles: Center for the Study of Evaluation, University of California, 1973.

Hodgkinson, H. L., Hurst, J., and Levine, H. *Improving and Assessing Performance: Evaluation in Higher Education.* Berkeley: Center for Research and Development in Higher Education, University of California, 1975.

Hodgkinson, H. L., Hurst, J., Levine, H., and Brint, S. *A Manual for the Evaluation of Innovative Programs and Practices in Higher Education.* Berkeley: Center for Research and Development in Higher Education, University of California, 1974.

Hodgkinson, H. L., and Meeth, L. R. (Eds.) *Power and Authority: Transformation of Campus Governance.* San Francisco: Jossey-Bass, 1971.

Hodgkinson, H. L., and Thelin, J. *Survey of the Applications and Uses of Unobtrusive Measures in Fields of Social Science.* Berkeley: Center for Research and Development in Higher Education, University of California, 1971.

Hoepfner, R., and Associates. *Research for Better Schools Test Evaluations: Tests of Higher-Order Cognitive, Affective, and Interpersonal Skills.* Los Angeles: Center for the Study of Evaluation, University of California, 1972.

Hoepfner, R., and Strickland, G. P. *Investigating Test Bias.* Los Angeles: Center for the Study of Evaluation, University of California, 1972.

Hofstadter, R., and Smith, W. (Eds.) *American Higher Education: A Documentary History.* Chicago: University of Chicago Press, 1961.

Hostrop, R. W. *Managing Education for Results.* Homewood, Ill.: ETC Publications, 1973.

Houle, C. O. *The External Degree.* San Francisco: Jossey-Bass, 1973.

House, E. R. *The Politics of Educational Innovation.* Berkeley: McCutchan, 1974.

Hoyt, D. P. *The Relationship Between College Grades and Adult Achievement, a Review of the Literature.* ACT Research Report 7. Iowa City: American College Testing Program, 1965.

Huckfeldt, V. E. *A Forecast of Changes in Postsecondary Education.* Boulder: National Center for Higher Education Management Systems at WICHE, 1972.

Hudspeth, D. R. *A Long-Range Planning Tool for Education. The Focus Delphi.* Albany: New York State Education Department, 1970.

Huff, R. "No Need Scholarships." *The College Board Review,* 1975, *95,* 13-15.

Humble, J. W. *Management by Objectives in Action.* New York: McGraw-Hill, 1970.

Humphreys, L. G. "The Fleeting Nature of the Prediction of College Academic Success." *Journal of Educational Psychology,* 1968, *59* (5), 375-380.

Hunt, D. E. "Person-Environment Interaction: A Challenge Found Wanting Before It Was Tried." *Review of Educational Research,* 1975, *45* (2), 209-230.

Hunt, R. A. "Student Grades as a Feedback System: The Case for a Confidential Multiple Grade." *Measurement and Evaluation in Guidance,* 1972, *5* (2), 345-359.

Ivancevich, J. M. "Longitudinal Assessment of Management by Objectives." *Administrative Science Quarterly,* 1972, *17* (1), 126-138.

Jamison, D., Suppes, P., and Wells, S. "The Effectiveness of Alternative Instructional Media: A Survey." *Review of Educational Research,* 1974, *44* (1), 1-67.

Jencks, C., and Riesman, D. *The Academic Revolution.* New York: Doubleday, 1968.

Jenkins, M. D. *Guidelines for Institutional Self-Study of Involvement in Urban Affairs.* Washington, D.C.: American Council on Education, 1971.

Johnson, A. C., and Cassell, R. D. *Appraising Personnel in the Cooperative Extension Service.* Monograph 17. Madison: National Agricultural Extension Center for Advanced Study, University of Wisconsin, 1962.

Johnson, C. B., and Katzenmeyer, W. G. (Eds.) *Management Information Systems in Higher Education: The State of the Art.* Durham: Duke University Press, 1969.

Johnson, R. A., Kast, F. E., and Rosenzweig, J. E. *The Theory and Management of Systems.* New York: McGraw-Hill, 1967.

Jones, E. S. *Comprehensive Examinations in American Colleges.* New York: Macmillan, 1933.

Judy, R. W., and Levine, J. B. *A New Tool for Educational Administrators: Educational Efficiency Through Simulation Analysis.* Toronto: University of Toronto Press, 1966.

Juola, A. E. "Illustrative Problems in College-Level Grading." *The Personnel and Guidance Journal,* 1968, *47* (1), 29-33.

Kapfer, M. B. *Behavioral Objectives in Curriculum Development.* Englewood Cliffs, N.J.: Educational Technology Publications, 1971.

Kaplowitz, R. A. *Selecting Academic Administrators: The Search Committee.* Washington, D.C.: American Council on Education, 1973.

Kauffman, J. F. *The Selection of College and University Presidents.* Washington, D.C.: Association of American Colleges, 1974.

Keller, J. E. *Higher Education Objectives: Measures of Performance and Effectiveness.* Berkeley: Office of the Vice-President—Planning and Analysis, University of California, 1970.

Kells, H. R. "Institutional Accreditation: New Forms of Self-Study." *The Educational Record,* 1972, *53* (2), 143-148.

Kerlinger, F. N. *Foundations of Behavioral Research.* New York: Holt, Rinehart, and Winston, 1964.

Kerr, D. "When Is an Educational Policy a Good Policy?" *Studies in Philosophy and Education,* 1974, *8,* 258-277.

Kibler, R. J., Barker, L. L., and Miles, D. T. *Behavioral Objectives and Instruction.* Boston: Allyn and Bacon, 1970.

Kirst, M. W. "The Rise and Fall of PPBS in California." *Phi Delta Kappan,* 1975, *56* (8), 535-538.

Klein, G. D., and Denham, C. H. "A Model for Determining the Validity of Faculty Ratings of University Administrator Effectiveness." *Educational and Psychological Measurement,* 1974, *34* (4), 899-902.

Klein, S. P., and Hart, F. M. "Chance and Systematic Factors Affecting Essay Grades." *Journal of Educational Measurement,* 1968, *5* (3), 197-210.

Klein, S. P., and Kosecoff, J. *Issues and Procedures in the Development of Criterion-Referenced Tests.* TM Report 26. Princeton: Educational Testing Service, 1973.

Klingelhofer, E., and Hollander, L. *Educational Characteristics and Needs of New Students: A Review of the Literature.* Berkeley: Center for Research and Development in Higher Education, University of California, 1973.

Knapp, J. *A Collection of Criterion-Referenced Tests.* TM Report 31. Princeton: Educational Testing Service, 1974.

Knapp, J., and Sharon, A. *A Compendium of Assessment Techniques.* Princeton: Educational Testing Service, 1974.

Knoell, D. M., and Medsker, L. L. *From Junior to Senior College. A National Study of the Transfer Student.* Washington, D.C.: American Council on Education, 1965.

Knowles, A. S. *Handbook of College and University Administration.* New York: McGraw-Hill, 1970.

Kopan, A., and Walberg, H. (Eds.) *Rethinking Educational Quality.* Berkeley: McCutchan, 1974.

Kosecoff, J. B., and Klein, S. P. *Instructional Sensitivity Statistics Appropriate for Objectives-Based Test Items.* Report 91. Los Angeles: Center for the Study of Evaluation, University of California, 1974.

Krathwohl, D. R., Bloom, B. S., and Masia, B. B. *Taxonomy of Educational Objectives: The Classification of Educational Goals.* Handbook 2. *Affective Domain.* New York: McKay, 1964.

Kreplin, H. *Credit by Examination: A Review and Analysis of the Literature.* Berkeley: Office of the Vice-President—Planning and Analysis, University of California, 1971.

Ladd, D. R. *Change in Educational Policy: Self-Studies in Selected Colleges and Universities.* New York: McGraw-Hill, 1970.

Lado, R. *Language Testing: The Construction and Use of Foreign Language Tests: A Teacher's Book.* New York: McGraw-Hill, 1964.

Lahti, R. E. *Innovative College Management.* San Francisco: Jossey-Bass, 1973.

Lake, D. G., Miles, M. B., and Earle, R. B., Jr. (Eds.) *Measuring Human Behavior.* New York: Teachers College Press, 1973.

Lansing, J. B., and Morgan, J. N. *Economic Survey Methods.*

Ann Arbor: Institute for Social Research, University of Michigan, 1971.

Lavin, D. E. *The Prediction of Academic Performance.* New York: Russell Sage Foundation, 1965.

Lawrence, B., Weathersby, G., and Patterson, V. W. (Eds.) *Outputs of Higher Education: Their Identification, Measurement, and Evaluation.* Boulder: Western Interstate Commission for Higher Education, 1970.

Lawrence, P., and Lorsch, J. *Organization and Environment.* Homewood, Ill.: Irwin, 1969.

Lenning, O. T. *The "Benefits Crisis" in Higher Education.* Report 1. Washington, D.C.: American Association for Higher Education, 1974.

Lenning, O. T., and Associates. *The Nonintellective Correlates of Grades, Persistence and Academic Learning: The Published Literature.* Iowa City: American College Testing Program, 1973.

Lenning, O. T., and Associates. *The Many Faces of College Success and Their Non-Intellective Correlates: The Published Literature.* Iowa City: American College Testing Program, 1975.

Lenning, O. T., Munday, L. A., and Mazey, E. J. "Student Educational Growth During the First Two Years of College." *College and University,* 1969, *44,* (2), 145-153.

Leslie, L. L. *The Trend Toward Government Financing of Higher Education Through Students: Can the Market Model Be Applied?* Report 19. University Park: Center for the Study of Higher Education, Pennsylvania State University, 1973.

Leslie, L. L., and Fife, J. D. "The College Student Grant Study: The Enrollment and Attendance Impacts of Student Grant and Scholarship Programs." *Journal of Higher Education,* 1974, *45* (9), 651-671.

Leslie, L. L., and Miller, H. F., Jr. *Higher Education and the Steady State.* Report 4. Washington, D.C.: American Association for Higher Education, 1974.

Leslie, L. L., and Satryb, R. P. "Due Process on Due Process?

Some Observations." *Journal of College Student Personnel,* 1974, *15,* 340-345.

Levin, H. "A Conceptual Framework for Accountability in Education." *School Review,* 1973, *82* (3), 363-391.

Levine, A. E., and Weingart, J. R. *Reform of Undergraduate Education.* San Francisco: Jossey-Bass, 1973.

Lieberman, M. *The Future of Public Education.* Chicago: University of Chicago Press, 1960.

Likert, R. *The Human Organization: Its Management and Value.* New York: McGraw-Hill, 1967.

Lindquist, E. F. "An Evaluation of a Technique for Scaling High School Grades to Improve Prediction of College Success." *Educational and Psychological Measurement,* 1963, *23,* 623-646.

Lindvall, C. M. "A Review of Selected Publications on Behavioral Objectives." *Journal of Educational Measurement,* 1972, *9* (1), 75-81.

Lindvall, S. M., and Cox, R. *Evaluation as a Tool in Curriculum Development: The IPI Evaluation Program.* Chicago: Rand McNally, 1970.

Linn, R. L. *Grade Adjustments for Prediction of Academic Performance: A Review.* College Entrance Examination Board Research and Development Reports 18. Princeton: Educational Testing Service, 1965.

Linn, R. L., Davis, J. A., and Cross, K. P. *A Guide to Research Design: Institutional Research Program for Higher Education.* Princeton: Educational Testing Service, 1965.

Lins, L. J. *Methodology of Enrollment Projections for Colleges and Universities.* Athens, Ohio: American Association of Collegiate Registrars and Admissions Officers, 1960.

Livingston, S. A. "Criterion-Referenced Applications of Classical Test Theory." *Journal of Educational Measurement,* 1972, *9* (1), 13-26.

Lockwood, G. *University Planning and Management Techniques.* Paris: Organisation for Economic Cooperation and Development, 1972.

Lopez, F. M., Jr. *Evaluating Executive Decision Making: The In-*

Basket Technique. AMA Research Study 75. New York: American Management Association, 1966.

Lunsford, T. F. (Ed.) *The Study of Academic Administration.* Boulder: Western Interstate Commission for Higher Education, 1963.

Lyden, F. J., and Miller, E. G. (Eds.) *Planning Programming Budgeting: A Systems Approach to Management.* Chicago: Rand McNally, 1968.

McAshan, H. H. *The Goals Approach to Performance Objectives.* Philadelphia: Saunders, 1974.

McCall, G. J., and Simmons, J. L. *Issues in Participant Observation.* Reading, Mass.: Addison-Wesley, 1969.

McCarthy, J. L., and Deener, D. R. *The Costs and Benefits of Graduate Education: Commentary with Recommendations.* Washington, D.C.: Council of Graduate Schools, 1972.

McConnell, T. R., and Mortimer, K. *The Faculty in University Governance.* Berkeley: Center for Research and Development in Higher Education, University of California, 1971.

McDill, E. L., McDill, M. S., and Sprehe, J. T. *Strategies for Success in Compensatory Education: An Appraisal of Evaluation Research.* Baltimore: Johns Hopkins University Press, 1969.

McGregor, D. *The Human Side of Enterprise.* New York: McGraw-Hill, 1960.

McKeachie, W. J. *Research on College Teaching: A Review.* Report 6. Washington, D.C.: ERIC Clearinghouse on Higher Education, George Washington University, 1970.

McKeachie, W. J., Lin, Y., and Mann, W. "Student Ratings of Teacher Effectiveness: Validity Studies." *American Educational Research Journal,* 1971, *8* (3), 435-445.

MacKenzie, O., Christensen, E. L., and Rigby, P. H. *Correspondence Instruction in the United States.* New York: McGraw-Hill, 1968.

McNeil, J. D., and Popham, W. J. "The Assessment of Teacher Competence." In R. M. W. Travers (Ed.), *Second Handbook of Research on Teaching.* Chicago: Rand McNally, 1973.

Mager, R. F. *Preparing Instructional Objectives.* Belmont, Calif.: Fearon, 1962.

Mali, P. *Managing by Objectives.* New York: Wiley, 1972.

Mann, R. D. *The College Classroom.* New York: Wiley, 1970.

Manning, C. W., and Romney, L. C. *Faculty Activity Analysis: Procedures Manual.* Boulder: Western Interstate Commission for Higher Education, 1973.

Marien, M. *Beyond the Carnegie Commission: Space-Free/Time-Free and Credit-Free Higher Education.* Syracuse: Educational Policy Research Center, Syracuse Research Corp., 1972.

Marshall, J. C. "Writing Neatness, Composition Errors, and Essay Grades Reexamined." *The Journal of Educational Research,* 1972, *65* (5), 213-215.

Martin, W. B. *Conformity: Standards and Change in Higher Education.* San Francisco: Jossey-Bass, 1969.

Maxwell, J., and Tovatt, A. *On Writing Behavioral Objectives for English.* Champaign: National Council of Teachers of English, 1970.

Mayhew, L. B. *Higher Education for Occupations.* Research Monograph 20. Atlanta: Southern Regional Education Board, 1974.

Mayhew, L. B., and Ford, P. J. *Changing the Curriculum.* San Francisco: Jossey-Bass, 1971.

Mayhew, L. B., and Ford, P. J. *Reform in Graduate and Professional Education.* San Francisco: Jossey-Bass, 1974.

Mehrens, W. A., and Lehmann, I. J. *Measurement and Evaluation in Education and Psychology.* New York: Holt, Rinehart, and Winston, 1973.

Meinert, C. W. *Time Shortened Degrees.* ERIC/Higher Education Research Report 8. Washington, D.C.: American Association for Higher Education, 1974.

Meyer, P. *Awarding College Credit for Non-College Learning: A Guide to Current Practices.* San Francisco: Jossey-Bass, 1975.

Micek, S. S., and Arney, W. R. *The Higher Education Outcome Measures Identification Study, a Descriptive Summary.*

Boulder: National Center for Higher Education Management Systems at WICHE, 1974.

Miller, D. C. *Handbook of Research Design and Social Measurement.* New York: McKay, 1970.

Miller, L. P., and Gordon, E. W. (Eds.) *Equality of Educational Opportunity.* New York: AMS Press, 1974.

Miller, R. I. *Evaluating Faculty Performance.* San Francisco: Jossey-Bass, 1972.

Miller, R. I. *Developing Programs for Faculty Evaluation: A Sourcebook for Higher Education.* San Francisco: Jossey-Bass, 1974.

Miller, R. W. *Schedule, Cost and Profit Control with PERT.* New York: McGraw-Hill, 1963.

Millett, J. D. *Resource Reallocation in Research Universities.* Washington, D.C.: Management Division, Academy for Educational Development, 1973.

Millett, J. D. *An Outline of Concepts of Organization, Operation, and Administration for Colleges and Universities.* Washington, D.C.: Management Division, Academy for Educational Development, 1974.

Milton, O., and Shoben, E. J., Jr. (Eds.) *Learning and the Professors.* Athens: Ohio University Press, 1968.

Mood, A. M., Bell, C., Bogard, L., Brownlee, H., and McCloskey, J. *Papers on Efficiency in the Management of Higher Education.* A technical report. Berkeley: Carnegie Commission on Higher Education, 1972.

Moore, R. S. *Consortiums in American Higher Education, 1965-66.* Washington, D.C.: Office of Education, 1968.

Morris, J. *Educational Training and Careers of Ph.D. Holders: An Exploratory Empirical Study.* Berkeley: Office of the Vice-President—Planning, University of California, 1972.

Morrisey, G. L. *Management by Objectives and Results.* Reading, Mass.: Addison-Wesley, 1970.

Morrison, D. F. *Multivariate Statistical Methods.* New York: McGraw-Hill, 1967.

Morse, P. M. *Library Effectiveness: A Systems Approach.* Cambridge: M.I.T. Press, 1968.

Mortimer, K. P. *Accountability in Higher Education.* Washington, D.C.: ERIC Clearinghouse on Higher Education and the American Association for Higher Education, 1972.

Moser, C. A., and Kalton, G. *Survey Methods in Social Investigation.* London: Heinemann Educational Books, 1971.

Mouley, G. J. *The Science of Educational Research.* (2nd ed.) New York: Van Nostrand Reinhold, 1970.

Mulaik, S. A. *The Foundations of Factor Analysis.* New York: McGraw-Hill, 1972.

Munday, L. A., and Davis, J. C. *Varieties of Accomplishment After College: Perspectives on the Meaning of Academic Talent.* ACT Research Report 62. Iowa City: American College Testing Program, 1974.

Nash, P. *The Goals of Higher Education: An Empirical Assessment.* New York: Bureau of Applied Research, Columbia University, 1968.

Nason, J. W. *The Future of Trusteeship.* Washington, D.C.: Association of Governing Boards of Universities and Colleges, 1974.

National Assessment of Education Progress. *National Assessment of Educational Progress Objectives for Career and Occupational Development.* Denver, 1971.

National Board on Graduate Education. *Doctorate Manpower Forecasts and Policy.* A Report with Recommendations 2. Washington, D.C., 1973.

Nedelsky, L. "Absolute Grading Standards for Objective Tests." *Educational and Psychological Measurement,* 1954, *14* (1), 3-4.

Nedelsky, L. *Science Teaching and Testing.* New York: Harcourt Brace Jovanovich, 1965.

Nelson, C. H. *Testing and Evaluation in the Biological Sciences.* CUEBS Publication 20. Washington, D.C.: Office of Biological Education, American Institute of Biological Sciences, 1967.

Newman, F. *Report on Higher Education.* Washington, D.C.: Department of Health, Education, and Welfare, 1971.

Nicholson, E. *Predictors of Graduation from College.* ACT Research Report 56. Iowa City: American College Testing Program, 1974.

Novick, D. *Program Budgeting: Program Analysis and the Federal Budget*. New York: Holt, Rinehart, and Winston, 1969.

Novick, M. R., Jackson, P. H., Thayer, D. T., and Cole, N. S. *Applications of Bayesian Methods to the Prediction of Educational Performance*. ACT Research Report 42. Iowa City: American College Testing Program, 1971.

Nowles, V., and Associates. *The Graduate Student Teacher*. Washington, D.C.: American Council on Education, 1968.

Odiorne, G. S. *Management by Objectives—A System of Managerial Leadership*. New York: Pitman, 1965.

Odiorne, G. S. *Personnel Administration by Objectives*. Homewood, Ill.: Irwin, 1971.

Office of Education. *Using Community Characteristics Information in Educational Decision-Making*. State Educational Records and Reports Series. Handbook 8. Washington, D.C., 1971.

Office of Institutional Research, University of Michigan. "The Credibility of the Credit Hour." Ann Arbor, 1970.

Oppenheim, A. N. *Questionnaire Design and Attitude Measurement*. New York: Basic Books, 1966.

Organization for Economic Cooperation and Development. *Methods and Statistical Needs for Educational Planning*. Washington, D.C., 1967a.

Organization for Economic Cooperation and Development. *Social Objectives in Educational Planning*. Washington, D.C., 1967b.

Orlans, H., Levin, N. J., Bauer, E. K., and Arnstein, G. E. *Private Accreditation and Public Eligibility*. Vols. 1 and 2. Washington, D.C.: Brookings Institution and the National Academy of Public Administration Foundation, 1974.

Orwig, M. D., Jones, P. K., and Lenning, O. T. *Enrollment Projection Models for Institutional Planning*. ACT Research Report 48. Iowa City: American College Testing Program, 1972.

Pace, C. R. *College and University Environment Scales*. Princeton: Educational Testing Service, 1969.

Pace, C. R. *Higher Education Measurement and Evaluation Kit*.

(Field ed.) Los Angeles: Center for the Study of Evaluation, University of California, 1972.

Pace, C. R. (Issue ed.) *Evaluating Learning and Teaching: New Directions for Higher Education.* San Francisco: Jossey-Bass, 1973.

Pace, C. R., and Stern, G. G. "An Approach to the Measurement of Psychological Characteristics of College Environments." *Journal of Educational Psychology,* 1958, *49* (5), 269-277.

Palola, E. G., Lehmann, T., and Blischke, W. R. *Higher Education by Design: The Sociology of Planning.* Berkeley: Center for Research and Development in Higher Education, University of California, 1970.

Palola, E. G., and Padgett, W. *Planning for Self-Renewal: A New Approach to Planned Organizational Change.* Berkeley: Center for Research and Development in Higher Education, University of California, 1971.

Paltridge, J. G., Hurst, J., and Morgan, A. *Boards of Trustees: Their Decision Patterns.* Berkeley: Center for Research and Development in Higher Education, University of California, 1973.

Parden, R. J. "Planning, Programming, and Budgeting Systems." In W. W. Jellema (Ed.), *Efficient College Management.* San Francisco: Jossey-Bass, 1972.

Parsons, T., and Platt, G. M. *The American University.* Cambridge: Harvard University Press, 1973.

Payne, D. A. (Ed.) *Curriculum Evaluation: Commentaries of Purpose, Process, Product.* Lexington, Mass.: Heath, 1974.

Perkins, J. A. (Ed.) *The University as an Organization.* Carnegie Commission on Higher Education. New York: McGraw-Hill, 1973.

Perlman, D. H. "New Tools and Techniques in University Administration." *The Educational Record,* 1974, *55* (1), 34-42.

Perry, W. G., Jr. *Forms of Intellectual and Ethical Development in the College Years: A Scheme.* New York: Holt, Rinehart, and Winston, 1968.

Pervin, L. A. "A Twenty-College Study of Student X College

Interaction Using TAPE (Transactional Analysis of Personality and Environment): Rationale, Reliability, and Validity." *Journal of Educational Psychology,* 1967, *58* (5), 290-302.

Peters, D. S. "The Link Is Equitability." *Research in Higher Education,* 1974, *2* (1), 57-64.

Peterson, R. E. *College Goals and the Challenge of Effectiveness.* Princeton: Educational Testing Service, 1971.

Peterson, R. E., Centra, J. A., Hartnett, R. T., and Linn, R. L. *Institutional Functioning Inventory.* Princeton: Educational Testing Service, 1970.

Peterson, W. D. "Critical Incidents for New and Experienced College and University Presidents." *Research in Higher Education,* 1975, *3* (1), 45-50.

Petrowski, W. R., Brown, E. L., and Duffy, J. A. "National Universities and the ACE Ratings." *Journal of Higher Education,* 1973, *44* (7), 495-513.

Pfeifer, C. M., Jr., and Sedlacek, W. E. "The Validity of Academic Predictors for Black and White Students at a Predominantly White University." *Journal of Educational Measurement,* 1971, *8* (4), 253-261.

Pfeiffer, J. *New Look at Education: Systems Analysis in Our Schools and Colleges.* Indianapolis: Odyssey, 1968.

Phi Delta Kappa, National Study Committee on Evaluation. *Educational Evaluation and Decision Making.* Itasca, Ill.: Peacock, 1971.

Popham, W. J. *Criterion-Referenced Measurement: An Introduction.* Englewood Cliffs, N.J.: Educational Technology Publications, 1971.

Popham, W. J. (Ed.) *Evaluation in Education.* Berkeley: McCutchan, 1974.

Posner, G., Jr. "The Extensiveness of Curriculum Structure: A Conceptual Scheme." *Review of Educational Research,* 1974, *44* (4), 401-407.

Postlethwait, S. N., Novak, J., and Murray, H. T., Jr. *The Audio-Tutorial Approach to Learning.* Minneapolis: Burgess, 1970.

Powel, J. H., Jr., and Lamson, R. D. *Elements Related to the*

Determination of Costs and Benefits of Graduate Education. Washington, D.C.: Council of Graduate Schools, 1972.

Prediger, D. J. *Converting Test Data to Counseling Information.* ACT Research Report 44. Iowa City: American College Testing Program, 1971.

President's Commission on Higher Education. *Higher Education for American Democracy.* Washington, D.C.: Office of Education, 1947.

President's Task Force on Higher Education. *Priorities in Higher Education: Report.* Washington, D.C.: Government Printing Office, 1970.

Price, J. L. *Handbook of Organizational Measurement.* Lexington, Mass.: Heath, 1972.

Princeton University. *A Study of Education for Environmental Design.* Princeton, 1967.

Provus, M. *Discrepancy Evaluation.* Berkeley: McCutchan, 1971.

Psacharopoulos, G. *Returns to Education: An International Comparison.* San Francisco: Jossey-Bass/Elsevier, 1972.

Quann, C. J. "Pass/Fail Grading—An Unsuccess Story." *College and University,* 1974, *49* (3), 230-235.

Raffel, J. A., and Shishko, R. *Systematic Analysis of University Libraries: An Application of Cost-Benefit Analysis to the M.I.T. Libraries.* Boston: M.I.T. Press, 1969.

Raia, A. *Management by Objectives.* Glenview, Ill.: Scott, Foresman, 1974.

Raths, L. E., Harmin, M., and Simon, S. B. *Values and Teaching.* Columbus, Ohio: Merrill, 1966.

Reddin, W. J. *Effective Management by Objectives: The 3-D Method of MBO.* New York: McGraw-Hill, 1971.

Reed, R. *Peer Tutoring Programs for the Academically Deficient Students in Higher Education.* Berkeley: Center for Research and Development in Higher Education, University of California, 1974.

Regents' Commission on Doctoral Education. *Meeting the Needs of Doctoral Education in New York State.* Albany, 1973.

Regional Accrediting Commissions of Postsecondary Education. *Evaluation of Institutions of Postsecondary Education, an Annotated List of Instruments.* Washington, D.C., 1975.

Remmers, H. H., and Gage, N. L. *Educational Measurement and Evaluation.* (Rev. ed.) New York: Harper and Row, 1955.

Richards, J. M., Jr., Holland, J. L., and Lutz, S. W. *The Assessment of Student Accomplishment in College.* ACT Research Report 11. Iowa City: American College Testing Program, 1966.

Richman, B. M., and Farmer, R. N. *Leadership, Goals, and Power in Higher Education: A Contingency and Open-Systems Approach to Effective Management.* San Francisco: Jossey-Bass, 1974.

Riesman, D., Gusfield, J., and Gamson, Z. *Academic Values and Mass Education, the Early Years of Oakland and Montieth.* New York: Doubleday, 1970.

Rippey, R. M. (Ed.) *Studies in Transactional Evaluation.* Berkeley: McCutchan, 1973.

Roberson, E. W. (Ed.) *Educational Accountability Through Evaluation.* Englewood Cliffs, N.J.: Educational Technology Publications, 1971.

Robinson, E. A. G., and Vaizey, J. E. (Eds.) *The Economics of Education.* New York: Macmillan, 1966.

Robinson, J. P., and Shaver, P. R. *Measures of Social Psychological Attitudes.* (Rev. ed.) Ann Arbor: Institute for Social Research, University of Michigan, 1973.

Rock, D. A., Baird, L. L., and Linn, R. L. "Interaction Between College Effects and Students' Aptitudes." *American Educational Research Journal,* 1972, *9* (1), 149-161.

Rokeach, M. *The Nature of Human Values.* New York: Free Press, 1973.

Romney, L. C. *Faculty Activity Analysis: Overview and Major Issues.* Technical Report 24. Boulder: National Center for Higher Education Management Systems at WICHE, 1971.

Roose, K. D., and Andersen, C. J. *A Rating of Graduate Programs.* Washington, D.C.: American Council on Education, 1970.

Rosenthal, R. *Experimenter Effects in Behavioral Research.* New York: Appleton-Century-Crofts, 1966.

Rossi, P., and Williams, W. (Eds.) *Evaluating Social Action Programs: Theory, Practice, and Politics.* New York: Academic Press, 1972.

Roueche, J. E., Baker, G. A., III, and Brownell, R. L. *Accountability and the Community College: Directions for the 70's.* Washington, D.C.: American Association of Community and Junior Colleges, 1971.

Roueche, J. E., and Herrscher, B. R. *Toward Instructional Accountability: A Practical Guide to Educational Change.* Sunnyvale, Calif.: Westinghouse Learning Press, 1973.

Rourke, F. E., and Brooks, G. E. (Eds.) *The Managerial Revolution in Higher Education.* Baltimore: Johns Hopkins Press, 1966.

Rubin, D. *Estimating Causal Effects of Treatments in Experimental and Observational Studies.* Princeton: Educational Testing Service, 1972.

Rudolph, F. *The American College and University: A History.* New York: Random House, 1965.

Ruml, B., and Morrison, D. H. *Memo to a College Trustee.* New York: McGraw-Hill, 1959.

Sandow, S. A. *Educational Policy Formulation: Planning with the Focus Delphi and Cross-Purpose Matrix.* Research Report 9. Syracuse: Educational Policy Research Center, Syracuse Research Corp., 1972.

Sanford, N. *The American College: A Psychological and Social Interpretation of the Higher Learning.* New York: Wiley, 1962.

Sanford, N. *Self and Society: Social Change and Individual Development.* New York: Lieber-Atherton Press, 1967a.

Sanford, N. *Where Colleges Fail: A Study of the Student as a Person.* San Francisco: Jossey-Bass, 1967b.

SASHEP Commission Report. "Basic Policies for Accreditation." *The Educational Record,* 1972, *53* (2), 149-156.

Scannell, D. P., and Marshall, J. C. "The Effect of Selected Composition Errors on Grades Assigned to Essay Examinations." *American Educational Research Journal,* 1966, *3* (2), 125-130.

Schein, E., and Bennis, W. *Personal and Organizational Change Through Group Methods.* New York: Wiley, 1967.

Schmidt, F. L., and Hunter, J. E. "Racial and Ethnic Bias in Psychological Tests." *American Psychologist,* 1974, *29,* 1-8.

Schmidtlein, F. A. *The Selection of Decision Process Paradigms in Higher Education: Can We Make the Right Decision or Must We Make the Decision Right?* Berkeley: Ford Foundation Program for Research in University Administration, University of California, 1973.

Schock, N. H. "An Analysis of the Relationship Which Exists Between Cognitive and Affective Educational Objectives." *Journal of Research in Science Teaching,* 1973, *10* (4), 299-315.

Schrader, W. B. *Test Data as Social Indicators.* Princeton: Educational Testing Service, 1968.

Schultz, T. W. *The Economic Value of Education.* New York: Columbia University Press, 1963.

Scriven, M. "Goal-Free Evaluation." In E. R. House (Ed.), *School Evaluation: The Politics and Process.* Berkeley: McCutchan, 1973.

Sedlacek, W. E., Lewis, J. A., and Brooks, G. C., Jr. "Black and Other Minority Admissions to Large Universities: A Four-Year National Survey of Policies and Outcomes." *Research in Higher Education,* 1974, *2* (3), 221-230.

Seiler, J. A. *Systems Analysis in Organizational Behavior.* Homewood, Ill.: Dorsey, 1967.

Seiler, K. *Introduction to Systems Cost-Effectiveness.* New York: Wiley, 1969.

Selden, W. *Accreditation: A Struggle over Standards in Higher Education.* New York: Harper and Row, 1960.

Sergiovanni, T. J. "Synergistic Evaluation." *Teachers College Record,* 1974, *75* (4), 540-552.

Severy, L. J. *Procedures and Issues in the Measurement of Attitudes.* TM Report 30. Princeton: ERIC Clearinghouse on Tests, Measurement, and Evaluation, Educational Testing Service, 1974.

Sgan, M. R. "Letter Grade Achievement in Pass-Fail Courses." *The Journal of Higher Education,* 1970, *41* (8), 638-644.

Sharon, A. T. *College Credit for Off-Campus Study.* Report 8.

Washington, D.C.: ERIC Clearinghouse on Higher Education, George Washington University, 1971.

Sharon, A. T. *Planning for the Development of Measurement and Evaluation Services for Use in Occupational Programs at Postsecondary Institutions.* PR-74-16. Princeton: Educational Testing Service, 1974.

Shaw, M. E., and Wright, J. M. *Scales for the Measurement of Attitudes.* New York: McGraw-Hill, 1967.

Sheleff (Shaskolsky), L. "A Credit Accumulation System: An Alternative to GPA and Pass-Fail." *The Educational Record,* 1972, *53* (3), 227-233.

Shetty, Y. K., and Carlisle, H. M. "Application of Management by Objectives in a University Setting: An Exploratory Study of Faculty Reactions." *Educational Administration Quarterly,* 1974, *10* (2), 65-81.

Shields, M. R. "The Construction and Use of Teacher-Made Tests." In *The Use of Tests in Schools of Nursing.* (2nd ed.) Pamphlet 5. New York: National League for Nursing, 1965.

Shoemaker, D. M. *Principles and Procedures of Multiple Matrix Samples.* Technical Report 34. Inglewood, Calif.: Southwest Regional Laboratory for Educational Research and Development, 1971.

Shoemaker, D. M. "Toward a Framework for Achievement Testing." *Review of Educational Research,* 1975, *45* (1), 127-147.

Shouksmith, G. *Assessment Through Interviewing: A Handbook for Individual Interviewing and Group Selection Techniques.* Elmsford, N.Y.: Pergamon, 1968.

Shulman, C. H. *Compendium Series of Current Research, Programs and Proposals.* No. 2: *Preparing College Teachers.* Washington, D.C.: ERIC Clearinghouse in Higher Education, George Washington University, 1970.

Shulman, C. H. *Employment of Nontenured Faculty: Some Implications of Roth and Sindermann.* ERIC/Higher Education Research Report 8. Washington, D.C.: American Association for Higher Education, 1973.

Simon, S. B. *Values Clarification.* New York: Hart, 1972.

Simpson, E. J. "Educational Objectives in the Psychomotor Domain." In M. B. Kapfer (Ed.), *Behavioral Objectives in Curriculum Development.* Englewood Cliffs, N.J.: Educational Technology Publications, 1971.

Singletary, O. A. (Ed.) *American Universities and Colleges.* (10th ed.) Washington, D.C.: American Council on Education, 1968.

Sirotnik, K. A. "Introduction to Matrix Sampling for the Practitioner." In W. J. Popham (Ed.), *Evaluation in Education: Current Applications.* Berkeley: McCutchan, 1974.

Skager, R., Holland, J. L., and Braskamp, L. A. *Changes in Self-Rating and Life Goals Among Students at Colleges with Different Characteristics.* ACT Research Report 14. Iowa City: American College Testing Program, 1966.

Skinner, B. F. *The Technology of Teaching.* Des Moines: Meredith, 1968.

Smail, M. M. P., DeYoung, A. J., and Moos, R. H. "The University Residence Environment Scale: A Method for Describing University Student Living Groups." *Journal of College Student Personnel,* 1974, *15,* 357-365.

Smith, J. M. *Interviewing in Market and Social Research.* London: Routledge and Kegan Paul, 1972.

Smith, P. G. "On the Logic of Behavioral Objectives." *Phi Delta Kappan,* 1972, *53* (7), 429-430.

Smith, R., and Fiedler, F. E. "The Measurement of Scholarly Work: A Critical Review of the Literature." *The Educational Record,* 1971, *52* (3), 225-232.

Smock, H. R., and Crooks, T. J. "A Plan for the Comprehensive Evaluation of College Teaching." *The Journal of Higher Education,* 1973, *44* (8), 577-586.

Smythe, W. R., and Johnson, L. A. *Introduction to Linear Programming, with Applications.* Englewood Cliffs, N.J.: Prentice-Hall, 1966.

Snider, J., and Osgood, C. *The Semantic Differential: A Sourcebook.* Chicago: Aldine, 1968.

Solomon, L. C., and Taubman, P. J. (Eds.) *Does College Matter? Some Evidence on the Impacts of Higher Education.* New York: Academic Press, 1973.

Spaeth, J. L., and Greeley, A. M. *Recent Alumni and Higher*

Education: A Survey of College Graduates. New York: McGraw-Hill, 1970.

Speizman, W. L. "Evaluation: An Evaluation from a Sociological Perspective." In C. W. Gordon (Ed.), *Uses of the Sociology of Education.* Part 2. Seventy-Third yearbook of the National Society for the Study of Education. Chicago: University of Chicago Press, 1974.

Spencer, R. E. *The Role of Measurement and Evaluation in Instructional Technology.* Urbana: University of Illinois, 1968.

Spurr, S. H. *Academic Degree Structures: Innovative Approaches.* New York: McGraw-Hill, 1970.

Stacey, C. L., and DeMartino, M. F. *Understanding Human Motivation.* New York: World, 1965.

Stake, R. E. "Objectives, Priorities, and Other Judgment Data." *Review of Educational Research,* 1970, *40* (2), 181-212.

Stallings, W. M., and Leslie, E. K. "Student Attitudes Toward Grades and Grading." *Improving College and University Teaching,* 1970, *18* (1), 66-68.

Stanley, J. C. "Predicting College Success of the Educationally Disadvantaged." *Science,* 1971, *171,* 640-647.

Stanley, J. C., and Hopkins, K. D. *Educational and Psychological Measurement.* Englewood Cliffs, N.J.: Prentice-Hall, 1972.

Starr, S. F. "A Fair Measure for Faculty Workloads." *The Educational Record,* 1973, *54* (4), 313-315.

Steible, D. J., and Sister Rose Agnes. "A College Reviews Its Policy on Comprehensives." *Catholic Education Review,* 1955, *53,* 255-261.

Stevens, E. I. "Grading Systems and Grading Mobility." *The Educational Record,* 1973, *54* (4), 308-312.

Stimart, R. P., and Taylor, A. L. "Predicting Excellence in College Teachers: A Vector Algebra Approach." *The Journal of Experimental Education,* 1973, *42* (1), 74-76.

Stufflebeam, D. I., Foley, W. J., Gephart, W. J., Guba, E. G., Hammond, R. I., Merriman, H. O., and Provus, M. M. *Educational Evaluation and Decision Making.* Itasca, Ill.: Peacock, 1971.

Sturner, W. F. "Environmental Code: Creating a Sense of Place on the College Campus." *Journal of Higher Education,* 1972, *43* (2), 97-109.

Suchman, E. A. *Evaluative Research: Principles and Practice in Public Service and Social Action Programs.* New York: Russell Sage Foundation, 1967.

Taubman, P., and Wales, T. *Higher Education and Earnings: College as an Investment and a Screening Device.* New York: McGraw-Hill, 1974.

Teachey, W. G., and Carter, J. B. "Methods of Evaluating Programmed Instruction Materials." *Learning Laboratories: A Guide to Adoption and Use.* Englewood Cliffs, N.J.: Educational Technology Publications, 1971.

Thackrey, R. I. "If You're Confused About Higher Education Statistics, Remember: So Are the People Who Produce Them." *Phi Delta Kappan,* 1975, *56* (6), 415-419.

Thorndike, R. L. "Marks and Marking Systems." In R. L. Ebel (Ed.), *Encyclopedia of Educational Research.* (4th ed.) New York: Macmillan, 1969.

Thorndike, R. L. (Ed.) *Educational Measurement.* (2nd ed.) Washington, D.C.: American Council on Education, 1971.

Thornton, R. F., and Wasdyke, R. G. *A Taxonomy for the Development of Multidimensional Test Specifications.* Princeton: Educational Testing Service, 1973.

Thurstone, L. L. *The Measurement of Values.* Chicago: University of Chicago Press, 1959.

Tinto, V. "Dropout from Higher Education: A Theoretical Synthesis of Recent Research." *Review of Educational Research,* 1975, *45* (1), 89-125.

Toombs, W. *Productivity: Burden of Success.* ERIC/Higher Education Research Report 2. Washington, D.C.: American Association for Higher Education, 1973.

Topping, J. R., and Miyataki, G. K. *Program Measures.* Boulder: Western Interstate Commission for Higher Education, 1973.

Tosi, H. L., and Carroll, S. "Management by Objectives." *Personnel Administration,* July-Aug. 1970, 44-48.

Travers, R. M. W. (Ed.) *Second Handbook of Research on Teaching.* A project of the American Educational Research Association. Chicago: Rand McNally, 1973.

Tripodi, T., Fellin, P., and Epstein, I. *Social Programme Evaluation: Guidelines for Health, Education, and Welfare Administrators.* Itasca, Ill.: Peacock, 1971.

Trites, D. G. (Issue ed.) *Planning the Future of the Undergraduate College: New Directions for Higher Education.* San Francisco: Jossey-Bass, 1975.

Trivett, D. A. *Goals for Higher Education: Definitions and Directions.* ERIC/Higher Education Research Report 6. Washington, D.C.: American Association for Higher Education, 1973.

Trivett, D. A. *Academic Credit for Prior Off-Campus Learning.* ERIC/Higher Education Research Report 2. Washington, D.C.: American Association for Higher Education, 1975.

Tucker, L. R., Damarin, F., and Messick, S. J. "A Base-Free Measure of Change." *Psychometrika,* 1966, *31,* 457-473.

Tyler, F. T. *National Merit Students in College.* Berkeley: Center for Research and Development in Higher Education, University of California, 1975.

Tyler, R. W. *Basic Principles of Curriculum and Instruction.* Chicago: University of Chicago Press, 1949.

Tyler, R. W. (Ed.) *Educational Evaluation.* Sixty-Eighth yearbook of the National Society for the Study of Education. Chicago: University of Chicago Press, 1969.

Tyler, R. W., Gagné, R. M., and Scriven, M. *Perspectives of Curriculum Evaluation.* Chicago: Rand McNally, 1967.

Tyler, R. W., and Wolf, R. M. (Eds.) *Crucial Issues in Testing.* Berkeley: McCutchan, 1974.

Uhl, N. P. *Identifying College Goals the Delphi Way.* Durham: National Laboratory for Higher Education, 1971.

Uhl, N. P. "Identifying Institutional Goals." In P. Caws, S. D. Ripley, and P. C. Ritterbush (Eds.), *The Bankruptcy of Academic Policy.* Washington, D.C.: Acropolis, 1972.

Van Dusseldorp, R. A., Richardson, D. E., and Foley, W. J. *Educational Decision-Making Through Operations Research.* Boston: Allyn and Bacon, 1971.

von Wittich, B. "The Impact of the Pass-Fail System upon Achievement of College Students." *The Journal of Higher Education,* 1972, *43* (6), 499-508.

Walcott, H. B. (Ed.) *Improving Educational Assessment and an*

Inventory of Measures of Affective Behavior. Washington, D.C.: Association for Supervision and Curriculum Development, National Education Association, 1969.

Walizer, M. H., and Herriott, R. E. *The Impact of College on Students' Competence to Function in a Learning Society.* ACT Research Report 47. Iowa City: American College Testing Program, 1971.

Wallhaus, R. A., and Micek, S. S. *Higher Education Program Assessment Profiles.* Boulder: Western Interstate Commission for Higher Education, 1975.

Walsh, W. B. *Theories of Person-Environment Interaction: Implications for the College Student.* Monograph 10. Iowa City: American College Testing Program, 1973.

Warren, J. R. *College Grading Practices: An Overview.* Research Bulletin Report 9. Washington, D.C.: ERIC Clearinghouse on Higher Education, George Washington University, 1971.

Weathersby, G. B., and Weinstein, M. C. "A Structural Comparison of Analytical Models for University Planning." Berkeley: Ford Foundation Program for Research in University Administration, University of California, 1970.

Webb, E. J., Campbell, D. T., Schwartz, R. D., and Sechrest, L. *Unobtrusive Measures: Nonreactive Research in the Social Sciences.* Chicago: Rand McNally, 1966.

Weisbrod, B. A. *External Benefits of Public Education.* Princeton: Princeton University Press, 1964.

Weiss, C. H. "The Politicization of Evaluation Research." *Journal of Social Issues,* 1970, *26* (4), 57-68.

Weiss, J., Edward, J., and Dimitri, O. *Formative Curriculum Evaluation: A Manual of Procedures.* Toronto: Ontario Institute for Studies in Education, 1972.

Wells, H. B. "Higher Education in a Day of Decision." Washington, D.C.: Education Policies Commission, National Education Association, 1957.

Werts, C. E., and Watley, D. J. *Analyzing College Effects: Correlation vs. Regression.* NMSC Research Reports 5 (2). Evanston: National Merit Scholarship Corp., 1969.

Wildavsky, A. *The Politics of the Budgetary Process.* Boston: Little, Brown, 1964.

Williams, C. "A Study of Cognitive Preferences." *The Journal of Experimental Education,* 1975, *43* (3), 61-77.

Williams, E. B. "Testing of the Disadvantaged: New Opportunities." Paper presented at the American Psychological Association convention, Washington, D.C., 1971.

Willingham, W. W. "Erroneous Assumptions in Predicting College Grades." *Journal of Counseling Psychology,* 1963, *10,* 389-394.

Willingham, W. W. *The No. 2 Access Problem: Transfer to the Upper Division.* ERIC Clearinghouse on Higher Education Research Report 4. Washington, D.C.: American Association for Higher Education, 1972.

Willingham, W. W. *College Placement and Exemption.* New York: College Entrance Examination Board, 1974a.

Willingham, W. W. "Predicting Success in Graduate Education." *Science,* 1974b, *183* (4122), 273-278.

Willingham, W. W., Begle, E., Ferrin, R. I., Gray, J., Kelemen, K., and Stam, J. C. *The Source Book for Higher Education: A Critical Guide to Literature and Information on Access to Higher Education.* New York: College Entrance Examination Board, 1972.

Willingham, W. W., Burns, R. L., and Donlon, T. F. *Current Practices in the Assessment of Experiential Learning.* Princeton: Educational Testing Service, 1974.

Wilms, W. W. *Public and Proprietary Vocational Training: A Study of Effectiveness.* Berkeley: Center for Research and Development in Higher Education, University of California, 1975.

Wilson, J. W., and Lyons, E. H. *Work-Study College Programs: Appraisal and Report of the Study of Cooperative Education.* New York: Harper and Row, 1961.

Wilson, K. M. "Increased Selectivity and Institutional Grading Standards." *College and University,* 1970, *46* (1), 46-53.

Wilson, K. M. *The Utility of a Standard Composite for Forecasting Academic Performance in Several Liberal Arts Colleges.* Research Bulletin. Princeton: Educational Testing Service, 1975.

Wilson, R. C., Gaff, J. G., Dienst, E. R., Wood, L., and Bavry,

J. L. *College Professors and Their Impact on Students.* New York: Wiley, 1975.

Wiltsey, R. G. *Doctoral Use of Foreign Languages: A Survey.* Princeton: Educational Testing Service, 1972. (Supplementary tables in Part 2.)

Windham, D. M. "The Efficiency/Equity Quandary and Higher Educational Finance." *Review of Educational Research,* 1972, *42* (4), 541-552.

Wing, C. W., Jr., and Wallach, M. A. *College Admissions and the Psychology of Talent.* New York: Holt, Rinehart, and Winston, 1971.

Wing, P. *Statewide Planning for Postsecondary Education: Conceptualization and Analysis of Relevant Information.* Boulder: National Center for Higher Education Management Systems at WICHE, 1972.

Winkler, D. R. *The Social Benefits of Higher Education: Implications for Regional Finance.* Report P-40. Berkeley: Office of the Vice-President—Planning, University of California, 1973.

Withey, S. B. (Ed.) *A Degree and What Else? Correlates and Consequences of a College Education.* New York: McGraw-Hill, 1971.

Witmer, D. R. "Economic Benefits of College Education." *Review of Educational Research,* 1970, *40* (4), 511-523.

Wittmaier, B. C. "Test Anxiety, Mood, and Performance." *Journal of Personality and Social Psychology,* 1974, *29,* 664-669.

Wittrock, M. C., and Wiley, D. E. (Eds.) *The Evaluation of Instruction: Issues and Problems.* New York: Holt, Rinehart, and Winston, 1970.

Wood, K., Linsky, A. S., and Straus, M. A. "Class Size and Student Evaluations of Faculty." *The Journal of Higher Education,* 1974, *45* (7), 524-534.

Worthen, B. R., and Sanders, J. R. (Eds.) *Educational Evaluation: Theory and Practice.* Worthington, Ohio: Jones, 1973.

Wright, J. C., and Kelly, R. "Cheating: Student/Faculty Views and Responsibilities." *Improving College and University Teaching,* 1974, *22* (1), 31, 34.

Yarber, W. L. "Retention of Knowledge: Grade Contract Method Compared to the Traditional Grading Method." *The Journal of Experimental Education,* 1974, *43* (1), 92-96.

Yuker, H. E. *Faculty Workload: Facts, Myths and Commentary.* ERIC/Higher Education Research Report 6. Washington, D.C.: American Association for Higher Education, 1974.

Yurkovitch, J. V. *A Methodology for Determining Future Physical Facilities Requirements for Institutions of Higher Education.* Madison: University of Wisconsin, 1966. ERIC ED 010850.

Zimbardo, P., and Ebbesen, E. B. *Influencing Attitudes and Changing Behavior.* Reading, Mass.: Addison-Wesley, 1970.

Zwingle, J. L., and Mayville, W. V. *College Trustees: A Question of Legitimacy.* ERIC/Higher Education Research Report 10. Washington, D.C.: American Association for Higher Education, 1974.

List of Bibliographies

Anderson, T. W., Das Gupta, S., and Styan, G. P. H. *A Bibliography of Multivariate Statistical Analysis.* New York: Wiley, 1972.

Barabas, J. *The Assessment of Minority Groups—An Annotated Bibliography.* ERIC/IRCD Urban Disadvantaged Series 34. New York: ERIC Information Retrieval Center on the Disadvantaged, 1973.

Burnett, C. W. (Ed.) *The Community Junior College: An Annotated Bibliography.* Columbus: College of Education, Ohio State University, 1968.

Burnett, C. W., and Badger, F. W. (Eds.) *The Learning Climate in the Liberal Arts College: An Annotated Bibliography.* Curriculum Series 2. Charleston, W. Va.: Morris Harvey College, 1970.

Cox, R. C., and Unks, N. J. *A Selected and Annotated Bibliography of Studies Concerning the Taxonomy of Educational Objectives: Cognitive Domain.* Pittsburgh: Learning Research and Development Center, University of Pittsburgh, 1967.

ERIC Clearinghouse on Higher Education. *Current Documents*

in Higher Education: A Bibliography. Washington, D.C.: American Association for Higher Education, 1970.

ERIC Clearinghouse on Tests, Measurement and Evaluation. *Test Bias: A Bibliography.* TM Reports 2. Princeton: Educational Testing Service, 1971.

Fink, I. S., and Cooke, J. *Campus/Community Relationships: An Annotated Bibliography.* Vol. 2. New York: Society for College and University Planning, Columbia University, 1972.

Hall, W. C. *An Annotated Bibliography on Graduate Education, 1971-1972.* Washington, D.C.: National Board on Graduate Education, 1972.

Larson, R. L. "Selected Bibliography of Research and Writing About the Teaching of Composition, 1973 and 1974." *College Composition and Communication,* 1975, *26,* 187-195.

Morishima, J. K. (Ed.) *An Annotated Bibliography of Institutional Research.* (8th ed.) Tallahassee: Association for Institutional Research, College of Education, Florida State University, 1971.

Pasanella, A. K., Manning, W., and Findikyan, N. *Bibliography of Test Criticism.* New York: College Entrance Examination Board, 1967.

Poulliotte, C. A., and Peters, M. G. *Behavioral Objectives: A Comprehensive Bibliography.* Boston: Instructional Technology Information Center, Northeastern University, 1971.

Powel, J. H., Jr., and Lamson, R. D. *An Annotated Bibliography of Literature Relating to the Costs and Benefits of Graduate Education.* Washington, D.C.: Council of Graduate Schools, 1972.

Research Corporation of the Association of School Business Officials. *Program Planning-Budgeting-Evaluation System Design: An Annotated Bibliography.* Chicago, 1969.

Solleder, M. K. *Evaluation Instruments in Health Education: An Annotated Bibliography of Knowledge, Attitude, and Behavior Tests.* (Rev. ed.) Washington, D.C.: American Association for Health, Physical Education, and Recreation, 1969.

Wilcox, L. D., Brooks, R. M., Beal, G. M., and Klonglan, G. E. *Social Indicators and Societal Monitoring: An Annotated Bibliography.* San Francisco: Jossey-Bass/Elsevier, 1972.

Index

A

Accountability: concept of, 73-74; demand for, 74-75; difficulties with, 77-80; faculty view of, 78; investment model of, 101; management related to, 80-82; motivation research model of, 101-102; policy formulation related to, 102-106; productivity model of, 85-101; requirements for, 80; and social goals, 73-109

Accreditation, self-study related to, 405-406, 410, 414

Active-passive continuum, and educational interactions, 202

Adams, R. F., 29, 185, 461

Administration: bureaucratic, 382-383; collegiality model of, 385; criteria for, 381; defined, 376-378; evaluation and policy related to, 455-460; evaluation of, 376-400; goal achievement related to, 386; human relations model of, 383-384; organizational patterns of, 382-388

Administration, evaluation of: approach to, 393-397; criteria for, 388-393; elements of, 394-395; evidence for, 395-396; problems in, 376-382

Administrators: communications of, 381-382; constituencies of, 379-380; criteria for, 388-393; power of, 378-381, 387

Admission. *See* Selection

Advanced Placement Examinations (APE), 151, 240, 248-249

Advising, evaluation of, 158-160, 358-360

Affective domain: difficulty of measurement in, 53-58; educational process related to, 204; evaluation of outcomes in, 53-72; taxonomy in, 38-39; terminology in, 61-64; writing objectives for, 49-50

Aiken, M., 26, 477

American Association of Collegiate

Registrars and Admissions Officers, 296, 462
American Chemical Society Tests, 242
American Council on Education, 250, 462
Andersen, C. J., 319, 494
Anderson, S. B., 135, 462
Answers, criteria for, 224-226
Astin, A. W., 168-169, 177, 182, 462-463
Atmosphere, 170
Audit of evaluation, criteria for, 20-22

B

Bailey, R. L., 296, 463
Baird, L. L., 178, 185, 463
Baker, E. L., 109, 463
Ball, S., 135, 462
Barker, R. G., 185, 464
Beal, G. M., 112, 507
Becker, G. S., 101, 464
Bell, D., 28, 464
Berdahl, R. O., 449, 464
Berg, H. D., 232, 465
Bersi, R. M., 248-250, 465
Blackburn, R. T., 353, 465
Bloom, B. S., 36, 52, 61-62, 141, 218, 231, 465, 483
Board. See Trustees, board of
Bogard, J. H., 51, 466
Bowen, H. R., 76, 466
Breneman, D. W., 329-330, 466-467
Brick, M., 26, 467
Brooks, G. E., 75, 495
Brooks, R. M., 112, 507
Budgeting: and credit hours, 264; decision making in, 105-106
Buros, O. K., 232, 241, 242, 255, 467
Bushko, A. A., 26, 467

C

Cambridge University, 234
Carnegie Commission on Higher Education, 408, 468
Carroll, S., 99-100, 500
Carter, J. B., 207, 500

Cartter, A. M., 4, 319, 468
Centra, J. A., 176-178, 185, 355, 374-375, 469
Challenge examinations, 248
Change: administration related to, 386-388, 392; compromise in, 387; environment for, 17-18; evaluation related to, 17-19; in higher education, 451-452; inputs for, 17-18; measures of, 113-114; outputs for, 18; processes for, 17-18; in programs, and educational process, 193-194; through self-study, 404
Cheating, grades related to, 276-277
Chicago, University of, 239
Chickering, A. W., 163, 432, 469-470
Clapp, M., 234, 470
Clark, M. J., 353, 465
Clark, P., 257
Classification, of students: clinical or individual, 148-150; prediction in, 146; probabilistic or mechanical, 145-148
Climate, 166
Coercion, and persuasion contrasted, 60-61
Cognitive domain: primacy of, 42; taxonomy of, 37-38; writing objectives for, 47-49
Cognitive styles: as idiosyncrasy, 117-118; research on, 355-356; selection related to, 141-144
Cohen, A. M., 52, 470
Cohen, M. D., 388, 470
Cohen, M. R., 34, 470
Coleman, J. S., 178, 470
College and University Environment Scales (CUES), 170-173, 182
College Entrance Examination Board, 151, 240, 248-249
College Level Examination Program (CLEP), 248-249
College Student Questionnaires, 175-176
Colwell, R., 232, 471

Combs, A., 257

Comparisons, in evaluation, 114-116

Competition, grading related to, 259-260

Comprehensive examinations: benefits of, 251-252; characteristics of, 252-255; history of, 233-236; problems with, 250-251; purposes of, 237-238; questions for, 242-245; types of, 238-241; use of results from, 245-248

Constraints, 84

Construct validity, 122

Content referencing, 115

Content validity, 121

Cooley, W. W., 207, 471

Costs: determination of, 128-131; of productivity, 89

Counseling, evaluation of, 160-161

Courses: comprehensives for sequence of, 238-239; evaluation in, 208-232; reorganization of, as individualization, 195-196

Cox, R., 317, 485

Credit hours: and budget allocations, 264; grades related to, 261-265

Credits: disadvantages of, 264-265; by examination, 248-250; functions of, 262-264; related to placement, 152

Criterion referencing, 115, 217-219, 284-285

Criterion-related validity, 121

Cronbach, L. J., 114, 125, 135-136, 471

Curriculum: basis for, 303-305; defined, 297-298; elements in, 309-311; evaluation, 313-316; goals of, 298-299; interdisciplinary structure of, 300-301, 311-313; proliferation in, 315; recommended structure for, 306-311; requirements in, 305-311; structure of, 299-305

D

Dalglish, T. K., 449, 476

Dalkey, N. C., 134

Data: comparability of, 91-92; sources and collection of, 110-113; variables in, 111-112

Dean, graduate, 322, 329

Decision making: budget reform in, 105-106; comprehensive process of, 104-105; incremental process of, 103-104; role of evaluation in, 4-5, 12-14, 23-25, 452-453

Decisions, types of, 12-14

Deener, D. R., 330, 486

Degrees: comprehensives required for, 246-247; external, and comprehensives, 247-248; requirements for, 154-155

De Lisle, F. H., 251, 473

Delphi Technique, 134-135

Democratic-authoritarian continuum, of educational interaction, 203

Departments, graduate education, role of, 318-319

Dickey, F. G., 431, 478

DiMarco, H., 185, 472

Disciplines: curriculum related to, 299-301; requirements within, 305-309

Divisions, comprehensives for, 240

Doi, J. I., 375, 472

Dornbusch, S. M., 26, 375, 472, 479

Douglass, G. K., 76, 466

Doyle, K. O., Jr., 375, 472

Dresch, S. P., 109, 472

Dressel, P. L., 207, 235, 236, 251, 255, 317, 431-432, 472-473

Drucker, P. F., 98, 473

Duration, in individualization, 197

E

Earle, R. B., Jr., 71, 483

Easton, D., 82, 473

Education: cost-benefit analysis of, 29; goal of, 9-10; humanistic view of, 257-258; off-campus,

191-192; revolution contrasted to, 61
Educational Testing Service, 151, 173-176, 238, 243, 247, 329, 473-474
Effectiveness, 79
Efficiency: concept of, 50, 73, 79; students in relation to, 162-163
Eisner, E. W., 36, 474
Emotional orientation, as learning style, 188
Environment: assessment procedures for, 167-178; defined, 166, 168-169, 182, 183-184; for learning, evaluation of, 164-185, 410-411; model of, 182-185; physical, and learning process, 189
Environmental measures: difficulties with, 180-182; utility of, 178-185
Ericksen, S. C., 352, 474
Ernst and Ernst, 431, 474
Essay tests: characteristics of, 213-215; as comprehensives, 243-244
Evaluation: and administration, 376-400; of affective outcomes, 53-72; audit of, 19-23; change measurement in, 113-114; change related to, 17-19; checklist for, 23-25; convictions about, ix-xi; cost of, 22, 128-131; in courses, 208, 232; of curriculum, 313-316; data collection in, 110-113; defined, 1, 8-9; design of, 131-133; of educational processes, 186-207; of faculty, 331-375; focuses of, 6; future scope of, 456-458; through grades, 256-296; of graduate programs, 327-329; of graduate students, 324-326; impact of, 5-6; initial questions in, 14-15; in institutions, 401-432; of instruction, 336-341; of learning environ-

ment, 164-185; models of, 3-4; norm-referenced, 217-218; objectives and, 27-52; organization related to, 455-456; orientations toward, 25-26, 451-454; policy and administration related to, 455-460; process of, 6-9; relationships or comparisons in, 114-116; reports on, distribution of, 22; role of, in decision making, 4-5, 12-14, 23-25, 452-453; sampling in, 126-128; of state systems, 433-449; and student idiosyncrasies, 116-119; technical aspects of, 110-136; types of, 15-17; value of, 9-10; values in, 4
Examinations: answers in, criteria for, 224-226; commercial, as comprehensives, 241-242; comprehensive, 233-255; credit by, 248-250; criterion-referenced, 217-219; difficulties with, 208-209, 219-220; grades related to, 285-287; in graduate education, 325-326; issues in, 216-217; as learning experiences, 210-211; purposes of, 209-211; questions in, components of, 221-224; types of, 212-219; value of, 230-231
Expressive objective, 36

F

Factor referencing, 115
Faculty: activities of, 332-333; communication skills of, 357-358; curriculum related to, 301; evaluation of, 331-375; grading advice to, 290-292; grading inequities and, 277-279; in graduate education, 321, 322, 328; in individualization, 200-201; interactions with, 201-202; nonteaching activities of, 356-358; preparation

of, in graduate education, 326-327; as professionals, 363-364, 368-369; responsibilities of, for learning, 341-345; role of, related to administration, 384-385; service activities of, 364-368

Faculty evaluation: acceptance of, 333-335; costs and benefits of, 370-372; difficulty in, 331-332; by peers, 350-351, 353, 354-355; principles of, 374; through self-evaluation, 351-352, 353; by students, 345-350, 353, 354-355

Failure, role of, in learning, 343
Farmer, R. N., 377, 399, 494
Feedback, 84
Feldmesser, R. A., 295-296, 475
Fife, J. D., 163, 484
Florida, University of, 239
Foley, W. J., 15, 132, 499
Ford, P. J., 317, 329, 487
Ford Foundation, 109, 329, 408
Formative evaluation: in affective domain, 64; and decision making, 16-17
Foster, W. T., 256, 475
Furby, L., 114, 125, 136, 471

G

Gagné, R. M., 317, 476, 501
General education, comprehensives for, 239-240
Gephart, W. J., 15, 132, 499
Glenny, L. A., 449, 476
Gleser, G. C., 135-136, 471
Goals: of curriculum, 298-299; of education, 9-10; of higher education, 30-32; instructional, 32-35; outcome and process, inventory of, 173-175; in PPBS, 95; social, and accountability, 73-109. *See also* Objectives
Grade point average, 287-290
Grades and grading: advice on, 290-292; consistency of, 279-281; criterion-referenced,

284-285; difficulties with, 295-296; distribution of, 269, 274-275, 290-291; fidelity of, 266-267; improving practices for, 279-287; inequities in, 274-279, 294; learning related to, 343; nature of, 266-270; pass-fail, 281-284; purposes of, 265-266; relative and absolute, 286-287; substance of, 270-272; test scores related to, 285-287; uses of, 295; views of, 257-261; weaknesses of, 272-274

Graduate education: courses in, 323; degree levels and types in, 320; evaluation of, 318-330; examinations in, 325-326; expansion of, 319; program characteristics in, 320-324; program evaluation in, 327-329; research role in, 323-324; teaching preparation in, 326-327

Graduate Record Examinations, 235, 236, 241
Greenbaum, W., 51, 477
Gronlund, N. E., 47, 136, 231, 477
Guba, E. G., 15, 132, 499

H

Hage, J., 26, 477
Haight, M., 83, 109, 477
Hambleton, R. K., 136, 478
Hammond, R. I., 15, 132, 499
Handlin, M. F., 72, 478
Handlin, O., 72, 478
Harcleroad, F. F., 431, 478
Harrow, A. J., 40, 478
Hartnett, R. T., 207, 478
Harvard University, 233-234, 261, 478
Hastings, J. T., 231, 465
Heath, D. H., 28, 479
Helmer, O., 134, 479
Higher education: accountability and social goals in, 73-109; change in, 451-452; convictions about, xi-xii; environment of, 106-107; environ-

mental changes in, 164-165; functions of, 107; goals of, 30-32; policy formulation in, 454; productivity in, 87-88; purposes of, 106; role of, 331, 455-456, 458-460; social benefits of, 76-77; values shifting in, 55-57
Hind, R. R., 375, 479
History, as a discipline, 305-309
Hively, W., 317, 479
Hodgkinson, H. L., 207, 399, 480
Holland, J. L., 169, 463
House, E. R., 26, 480
Huff, R., 163, 481
Hunt, R. A., 280-281, 481
Hurst, J., 207, 480

I

Idiosyncrasy, of students, 116-119
Individualization: as curricular structure, 302-303; of educational processes, 195-201; faculty role in, 200-201; parameters of, 197-199; use of, 199-200
Indoctrination, in affective domain, 54
Input evaluation, and decision making, 15-16, 19
Input-output analysis: MBO as, 98-101; PPBS as, 94-98; in productivity, 90-91
Institutional Functioning Inventory, 173
Institutional Goals Inventory, 173-175
Institutional research: increase in, 75; self-study related to, 428-430
Instruction: planning of, 356; teaching distinguished from, 337-338
Instruction, evaluation of: approaches to, 337-341; context for, 352-353; criteria for, 339-341; nonteaching aspects of, 356-358; principles of, 338-339; purposes of, 336-337

Instructional objectives, 36
Interactions, as evaluations, 212
Interval scale, of variables, 111
Inventory of College Activities, 169
Investment model, for accountability, 101
Ipsative evaluation, 115-116
Item structure, characteristics of, 221-223
Ivancevich, J. M., 100-101, 481

J

Jamison, D., 207, 481
Jenkins, M. D., 432, 481
Joint costs, 130
Jones, E. S., 234, 237, 255, 481
Juola, A. E., 274-275, 482

K

Kapfer, M. B., 40, 52, 482
Kauffman, J. F., 399, 482
Kelley, E. C., 257
Kells, H. R., 432, 482
Kerr, D., 52, 482
Kirst, M. W., 109, 482
Klonglan, G. E., 112, 507
Kopan, A., 26, 483
Krathwohl, D. R., 36, 61-62, 483
Kreplin, H., 255, 483
Kulik, J. A., 352, 474

L

Ladd, D. R., 408, 432, 483
Lado, R., 232, 483
Lake, D. G., 71, 483
Leadership, 376-377
Learning: comprehensives as evaluator of, 247; defined, 203-204; faculty responsibilities for, 341-345; impediments to, 191-192; styles of, 187-190, 198-199
Leslie, L. L., 163, 185, 449, 484-485
Levin, H., 109, 485
Levine, H., 207, 480
Likert, R., 68, 485
Lindquist, E. F., 142, 485
Lindvall, S. M., 317, 485
Linn, R. L., 114, 374-375, 469, 485
Livingston, S. A., 125, 485

London, University of, 234
Lyons, E. H., 207, 503

M

McCarthy, J. L., 330, 486
McGregor, D., 98, 486
McNeil, J. D., 353, 355, 486
Madaus, G. F., 231, 465
Majors, comprehensives for, 240
Management: concept of, 80-82, 107-108, 377; by objectives (MBO), 98-101; through state systems, 436-438
Manning, C. W., 375, 487
March, J., 388, 470
Marginal costs, 130
Martin, W. B., 51, 487
Masia, B. B., 36, 61-62, 483
Maslow, A. H., 257
Maxwell, J., 36, 52, 487
Mayhew, L. B., 317, 329, 487
MBO. *See* Management, by objectives
Meeth, L. R., 399, 480
Merriman, H. O., 15, 132, 499
Michaelson, J. B., 29, 185, 461
Michigan, 264
Michigan State University, 238-239, 269, 289, 371
Michigan, University of, 296, 490
Middle States Association of Colleges and Secondary Schools, 431
Miles, M. B., 71, 483
Miller, R. I., 375, 488
Modern Language Association Tests, 242
Motivation: concept of, 33; and educational process, 194-195; of students, 257, 341-342
Motivation research, as accountability model, 101-102
Mulaik, S. A., 133, 489
Multiple-discriminant function, in classification, 146-147, 148
Murphy, R. T., 135, 462

N

Nagel, E., 34, 470
Nanda, H., 136, 471

National Center for Higher Education Management Systems, 83, 108-109
National League for Nursing Tests, 242
National Occupational Competency Testing Institute, 242
National Science Foundation, 408
Nedelsky, L., 232, 489
Nelson, C. H., 232, 489
Nominal scale, of variables, 111
Normative evaluation, 116, 217-218
Novick, M. R., 136, 478, 490

O

Objective tests: characteristics of, 212-213; as comprehensives, 242-243
Objectives: behavioral, 44-45, 218-219; criteria for, 50; defined, 198; evaluation of, 410; in individualization, 198; management by, 98-101; in PPBS, 95; rules for writing, 46-47; of students, and individualization, 196; types of, 35-41; writing of, 46-50. *See also* Goals
Objectivity: of evaluation audit, 21; of grades, 268
Odiorne, G. S., 99, 490
Open University, 182-183
Oral examinations: characteristics of, 215; as comprehensives, 244; evaluation of, 322; in graduate education, 325
Ordinal scale, of variables, 111
Orientation, evaluation of, 155-157
Outcomes: as curricular structure, 303; measures of, in productivity, 93-94
Output evaluation, and decision making, 16, 19
Oxford University, 234

P

Pace, C. R., 71, 170, 176, 182, 490
Parden, R. J., 96, 491
Parsons, T., 82, 491
Pass-fail grading: advantages of,

281-282; reaction to, 283-294; restrictions on, 282; results of, 282-283

Payne, D. A., 317, 491

Pay-off matrix, 84

Perkins, J. A., 449, 491

Perry, W. G., Jr., 72, 491

Personal-social orientation, as learning style, 188-189

Persuasion, and coercion contrasted, 60-61

Peters, D. S., 353, 354, 492

Peters, F. R., 141, 465

Placement: credits related to, 152; of students, 150-155

Planning: evaluation of, and decision making, 15, 19; through state systems, 434-436

Planning-programming-budgeting system (PPBS): goals and objectives in, 95; as input-output analysis, 94-98; phases of, 94-95; steps in process of, 95-98

Platt, G. M., 82, 491

Popham, W. J., 26, 109, 353, 355, 463, 486, 492

Posner, G., Jr., 317, 492

PPBS. See Planning-programming-budgeting system

Precision: concept of, 120-121; types of, 125-126

Preliminary examination, in graduate education, 325

President: board evaluation of, 396-397; role of, 391-392

Problem-solving objective, 36

Process evaluation, and decision making, 16, 19

Processes, educational: components of, 193-195; defined, 186-187; evaluation of, 186-207; evaluation principles for, 203-207; factors in, 190-193; and individualization, 195-201; interactions in, 201-203; learning styles related to, 187-190

Productivity: in accountability, 85-101; categories of, 86-87; concept of, 85; cost studies in, 89; data comparability in, 91-92; in higher education, 87-88; input-output analyses in, 90-91; issues in, 85-86; outcome measures in, 93-94

Professional, faculty as, 363-364, 368-369

Program costs, 130-131

Projects, as comprehensives, 245

Provus, M., 11, 15, 132, 493, 499

Psychomotor domain, taxonomy of, 39-40

Q

Qualifying examination, in graduate education, 325

Questionnaire on Student and College Characteristics, 176-178

Questions: components of, 221-224; for comprehensives, 242-245; human elements in, 224; multiple-choice, structure of, 226-230; structure of, 221-223

R

Rajaratnam, J., 136, 471

Rate, of progress, in individualization, 197

Ratio scale, of variables, 111

Readiness, 33

Recruitment, of students, 139-140

Regents' Commission on Doctoral Education, 329, 493

Regression analysis, in classification, 145-146

Reinforcement, 33-34

Reliability: concept of, 120; of evaluation audit, 20; in examinations, 220; of grades, 268; types of, 123-125

Remediation, through comprehensives, 245-246

Requirements, specification of, 305-311

Research: attitudinal, 68-70; on cognitive styles, 355-356; criteria for, 363; evaluation based on, 1-3; evaluation of, 360-363; in graduate education, 323-324; institutional, 75, 428-430; purposes of, 360-361; satisfaction from, 333-334; on teaching, 353-356

Response set, as idiosyncrasy, 116-117

Richman, B. M., 377, 399, 494
Rippey, R. M., 11, 494
Robinson, J. P., 68, 494
Rogers, C., 32, 257
Rokeach, M., 72, 494
Romney, L. C., 83, 109, 375, 477, 487, 494
Roose, K. D., 319, 494
Rose Agnes, 235, 499
Rossi, P., 26, 495
Rourke, F. E., 75, 495

S

Sampling: in examinations, 219-220; process of, 126-128; reliability of, 123-124; types of, 127

Sanford, N., 32, 495
Satryb, R. P., 185, 484-485
Schmidtlein, F. A., 109, 496
Scholarship, continuing, evaluation of, 360
Schultz, T. W., 101, 496
Scoring, and grading, compared, 286-287
Scott, W. R., 26, 375, 472, 479
Scriven, M., 317, 496, 501
Selection: affective factors in, 143; cognitive factors in, 141-142; psychomotor factors in, 143-144; of students, 140-144
Self-studies, institutional: accreditation related to, 405-406, 410, 414; committee operation for, 423-426; committee selection for, 415-417; committee work for, 419-423; comprehensive, characteristics of, 409-411; impact of, 427-428; institutional research related to,

428-430; nature of, 401, 402-405; need for, 411-415; operation and strategy of, 415-426; patterns of, 406-409; report on, 425-426; through rolling review, 430-431; steps in, 402-403; task of, stated, 417-419

Sequential Tests of Educational Progress, 241
Service, by faculty, 364-368
Sgan, M. R., 282, 496
Shaver, P. R., 68, 494
Shields, M. R., 232, 497
Shoemaker, D. M., 136, 497
Simon, S. B., 72, 497
Simpson, E. J., 36, 40, 498
Singletary, O. A., 235, 498
Sirotnik, K. A., 128, 498
Skinner, B. F., 32, 498
Standards: as examination problem, 220; grades related to, 290-291; and individualization, 199; learning related to, 344

State systems: central offices of, 441-446; evaluation of, 433-449; institutions in, 438-441, 446-448; power of administrators in, 379; problems of, 438-443; purposes of, 434-438

Steible, D. J., 235, 499
Stern, G. G., 176, 491
Student Reactions to College, 176
Students: adults as, 144, 151-152, 153; advising, 158-160; characteristics of, and grades, 275-276; classification of, 145-150; curriculum related to, 301-302; development of, through comprehensives, 247; employment counseling for, 149-150; evaluation of, 356-357; faculty evaluation by, 345-350, 370-372; fairness to, 161-162; graduate, evaluation of, 324-326; idiosyncrasies of, 116-119; or instruc-

tor-centered continuum, of educational interaction, 202-203; motivations of, and educational processes, 33, 194-195, 257, 341-342; objectives of, and individualization, 196; orientation of, 155-157; placement of, 150-155; recruitment of, 139-140; selection of, 140-144; self evaluation of, 216

Stufflebeam, D. I., 15, 132, 499

Sturner, W. F., 185, 499-500

Suchman, E. A., 2, 11, 500

Summative evaluation, and decision making, 16-17

Sunk costs, 130

Suppes, P., 207, 481

Systems analysis: concepts in, 82-85; problem with, 83-84; steps in, 82-83; terms in, 84-85

T

Taxonomies: condensed, 37-41; critique of, 41-44

Teacher Education Examination Program, 242

Teachey, W. G., 207, 500

Teaching: evaluation of, 334-335; instruction distinguished from, 337-338; research on, 353-356; satisfaction from, 334

Technology, educational, 192-193

Thompson, M. M., 207, 473

Thorndike, R. L., 135, 231-232, 296, 500

Thurstone, L. L., 68, 500

Time, as examination problem, 220

Tinto, V., 163, 500

Tosi, H. L., 99-100, 500

Tovatt, A., 36, 52, 487

Trade-off, concept of, 84

Trait-treatment interaction, as idiosyncrasy, 118-119

Trustees, board of: criteria for, 397-398; evaluation by, 396-397; evaluation of, 397-398; responsibilities of, 397

Tyler, R. W., 27, 36, 317, 501

U

Uhl, N. P., 28, 501

Undergraduate Program Area Tests, 240, 241, 247, 250, 254

V

Validity: concept of, 120; of evaluation audit, 20; in examinations, 220; of grades, 267-268; types of, 121-123

Values: attitudes contrasted with, 63; behavior related to, 67; change of, strategies for, 60-61; commitments to, 54-55, 67; defining, 62-64; evaluation of, 64-71; kinds of, 58-60; range of, 64-66

Variables, types of, 111-112

Verbal orientation, as learning style, 188

W

Walberg, H., 26, 483

Walcott, H. B., 30, 501-502

Warren, J. R., 292-293, 296, 502

Watley, D. J., 114, 502

Wells, S., 207, 481

Werts, C. E., 114, 502

Western Interstate Commission on Higher Education, 83, 108-109

Wilcox, L. D., 112, 507

Wildavsky, A., 455, 502

Williams, W., 26, 495

Willingham, W. W., 154, 155, 163, 503

Wilson, J. W., 207, 503

Windham, D. M., 109, 504

Wing, P., 449, 504

Wisconsin, 378-379